Black Christian Republicanism

Carl Patrick Burrowes

This work is certainly a *tour de force* of Carl Patrick Burrowes amongst his many writings and research papers about Liberia. His study of Hillary Teage is the most comprehensive and captivating writing about Teage that I have seen. It offers to the reader a broad revelation of a Liberian pioneer whose thoughts and actions were about the People and Country of Liberia. Teage's life, works, and deep thoughts are revealed as never before in his writings and speeches here collected. Teage was one of the drafters and signers of the Declaration of Independence of Liberia.

This literary and historical work offers a new perspective on Liberia. The case is backed up by maps, old photos and illustrations, copious references and over 400 footnotes. This is a literary and historical work that should be required reading for all college students in Liberia. I also recommend this book to be on the shelves of both public and private libraries in Liberia and elsewhere. This book will make good reading for any person who likes history and wants to know more about Liberia and one of the men who founded this Country.

— Counsellor Henry Reed Cooper, Former Chief Justice of Liberia

For scholars looking for an alternative perspective written by someone who is the product of Teage's environment and who has immensely pursued sources of Black Nationalism not henceforth delved into, this is your book. For Pan Africanists, Africa's Sons and daughters who continuously see the need for African to assert itself to carve her own destiny this is your book. For those looking for a relevant role for the church/religion to continue to positively influence policies and politics, this is your book. For individuals blaming their environments and lack of opportunities, they will find here a man who in the midst of indomitable odds, carved opportunities for himself and others and brought forth a nation.

For African citizens and leaders, Teage will have us to dare believe that every risk towards self sufficiency and independence are risks worth taking. Some authors revived historical figures and brilliantly portrayed their significance for the age in which they lived. Carl Patrick Burrowes has literally "torn off" the buried clothing of Hilary Teage and catapulted him to speak to the current realities faced by any nation struggling with myriads of challenges.

— Rev. Andrew Momolu Diggs, Former Pastor, Providence Baptist Church

Black Christian Republicanism: The Writings of Hilary Teage is a must read. Itt is an in-depth exegesis, scholarly study, and historical research that sheds an intellectual flood beam of light on the making of the first African Republic South of the Sahara; Liberia, and the trigger to the framing of that nation, Hilary Teage. He was considered by brilliant scholars in the 1800's as a man of superior mental capacity and abilities far greater than any Black man in America.

Teage's preaching was theologically sound, Biblically based, and transformative for his hearers. His enormous contributions to nation building and international relations have been hidden by the authors of history. In this book, Carl Patrick Burrowes brings the reader face-to-face with this larger than life human being, Hilary Teage.

This book is an eye opener into the rich and vibrant tenacity and contributions of Liberian Pioneers, and their influence in the land of their repatriation, and the nation they built, choose to flee to, and call home. It is a must read for all Liberians, and students of history, especially those in government and leadership in that nation. For theologians and students of Liberation theology, The Black Church, and seminaries with Black Studies this book cannot be ignored.

— *Rev. Charles Levi Martin,* Senior Pastor, Unity Fellowship Baptist Church

Carl Patrick Burrowes

Black Christian Republicanism

The Writings of Hilary Teage (1805-1853)

Founder of Liberia

Cover art by Amane Kameko

Printed by CreateSpace

Published by Know Your Self Press, Bomi County, Republic of Liberia

ISBN 978-0-9983905-9-8

To Kassahun (number-one son),
Bendu (my flower) and Kadallah (my Hilary)

ii

MAPS

TABLE

IMAGES

CREDIT FOR ILLUSTRATIONS

Maps 1 and 2. Liberian Settlements and Indigenous Towns, 1822 to 1846, compiled from American Colonization Society. *Annual Report*. 52 (1869), p. 67; Gershoni, Y. *Black Colonialism: The Americo-Liberian Scramble for the Hinterland*. Boulder, Colo.: Westview, 122-123; Miller, R. M. (ed.). *Dear Master: Letters of a Slave Family*. Athens, Ga.: University of Georgia, 38.

Image 1. Sketch of Monrovia from riverside from New York Colonization Society Annual Report, prepared for publication by Oberlin College Library, Special Collections and Preservation Department.

Image 2. William Crane from the Baptist Convention of Maryland/Delaware. In addition to supporting the missionary efforts of Teage, his father Colin and Lott Cary, Crane was responsible for Hilary's early education and distributed the *Liberia Herald* in Baltimore.

Image 3. John Brown Russwurm from Schomburg Center for Research in Black Culture. Russwurm, a graduate of Bowdoin College and founder of the *Liberia Herald*, hired Teage to assistant him in editing the paper.

Image 4. Edward Wilmot Blyden from Library of Congress Prints & Photographs, daguerreotype by Rufus Anson between 1851 and 1860. Blyden served as Teage's assistant both at the *Herald* and during his tenure as Secretary of State.

Image 5. Providence Baptist Church, Monrovia, Liberia, from Carl Patrick Burrowes © 2008. Providence Baptist Church was founded in Richmond, Virginia, by Teage and others prior to their emigration. Its building is the oldest continuously occupied Baptist church in Africa.

Carl Patrick Burrowes

Preface

Newspaper editor, Baptist pastor, successful merchant and public servant – Hilary Teage was all these and more. While each of his achievements was significant in itself, taken together they were remarkable, especially for a man who was born a slave. Through sheer volition, he blazed across most of the boundaries of his day, whether they were defined vocationally, culturally, ideologically or geographically. An African American and native of Virginia, Teage applied his many talents and considerable energies to building a black nation—Liberia, the first republic in Africa. Despite little formal education, he displayed a mastery of several genres of writing and fields of knowledge. Moreover, Teage was one of the earliest American Baptist missionaries abroad. The Providence Baptist Church of Monrovia, Liberia, which he helped organize, is the oldest continuously operated church in Africa. Contrary to the strictures of his denomination, he often held secular and sacred offices simultaneously. An early proponent of black nationalism, he was also the embodiment of Victorian values.

As a schoolboy growing up in Liberia, I was taught about Teage's role as the drafter of the Liberian Declaration of Independence, but it was only in the course of graduate studies in the United States that I discovered the profundity of his contributions. Reading through microfilmed issues of the *Liberia Herald*, the newspaper that he edited, I quickly became enamored of his sarcasm and enthralled by his passion. Initially, my modest purpose was to transcribe his writings. As the work progressed, however, I realized that I needed to contextualize the writings by adding what biographical information could be found and by exploring the antecedents of his ideas. That required the exploration of journalism and intellectual histories, as well as religious studies and political ideology. In studying the ideas of Teage, I benefited from a profound shift in intellectual history over the last several decades toward a renewed appreciation for the role of culture in shaping ideas. This shift can be traced to the work of anthropologist Clifford Geertz, who described man as "an animal suspended in webs of significance he himself has spun." For him, the sociology of knowledge has become the sociology of meaning, "for what is socially determined is not the nature of conception but the vehicles of conceptions."[1]

Because Teage was socialized in the United States, his writings offer important but often-overlooked evidence on the political ideas and values of African Americans in the antebellum period. They fill a gap in the literature on black nationalism, which has neglected the period of 1818-47. In addition, the prominence of republicanism in his thinking calls for a reappraisal of the historic place occupied by that system of political ideas among antebellum African-Americans. This is especially imperative with regard to those like Teage who were raised in the South, where political expression was sharply circumscribed for blacks, resulting in the preservation of relatively few documentary sources for historical examination. Furthermore, Teage's writings provide important source material on African American religious thought. Although the significance of Protestant Christianity to early Liberians has been well documented, the emphasis has been mainly on the institutional aspects of religion, with little corresponding attention given to the cultural and theological contributions of African Americans to their own religious life.

More important, Teage's writings represent one of the earliest intellectual integrations of the previously disparate elements of black nationalism, Protestant Christianity, and republicanism. The result is a coherent ideology, which historian Joyce Appleby defined as "a structure of meaning expressed through a historically specific system of communication."[2] The conceptualization of ideology adopted here is rooted in the theoretical framework developed by Antonio Gramsci and those who have been influenced by him. For Gramsci, ideology (which he called "spontaneous philosophy") is embodied in language, "which is a totality of determined notions and concepts and not just of words grammatically devoid of content." It is also embodied in common sense, which consists of generally held assumptions and beliefs that are broadly accepted, and in folklore, which encompasses "ways of seeing things and acting." In this formulation, ideology does not simply describe a psychological disposition or moral stance, it embodies an epistemology.[3] The interpenetration of Teage's religious and political ideas was facilitated by the absence of a firm division between the secular and sacred in African-American cosmology. In treating the republican, Christian, and nationalist streams of Teage's thinking together, I have built upon the encounter model of anthropologists Sidney W. Mintz and Richard Price, which shifted the study of African American cultures toward the examination of "different kinds of blends and mixtures," including elements of both African and European origin.[4]

The worldview and motivations of Teage and other nineteenth-century Liberians have come to be obscured by the critical comments on the "Liberian elite" and Liberians of American descent that blanket the historical and social science literature on Liberia.[5] While commonplace, such comments are often offered gratuitously and without credible evidence. One example is the view that early Liberia was dominated by mulattoes, a claim derived mainly from the prodigious writings of Edward Wilmot Blyden. Although often uncritically quoted by modern

Carl Patrick Burrowes

scholars,[6] Blyden was a founder and ideologue of Liberia's True Whig Party. His charges against "mulatto enemies" drew upon deep-seated nineteenth-century prejudices and stereotypes of mixed-race people as particularly scheming and untrustworthy, since it was assumed that their genetic admixture rendered them incapable of loyalty to any race.[7] Blyden's view of Liberian society was often advanced to persons outside the society in an attempt to win their support in his battles for control of local institutions. This view was neither free of partisan bias nor widely shared internally.

Blyden's disparagement of mulattoes, although scattered throughout his writings, was succinctly presented in a 1895 letter to the Rev. Byron Sutherland:

> The difficulty and drawbacks in Liberia have been chiefly due, as I have pointed out ... with tiresome reiteration during the last thirty years, to the effort made to harmonize in sympathy and work two really conflicting races – the mulatto and the Negro. Such an effort might have met with greater success had Liberia remained under white rule, which by being on the spot would have forced the two classes to work together as in the days of the Colony. But as soon as Liberia was driven by circumstances into premature independence, the mixed element organized themselves into a ring to hold the Government of the country – to promote their own ascendency at all hazards and to suppress every black man who would not do their bidding. *The masses of the black people could not detect their scheme,* and of course the white friends of Liberia in America could not conceive such a thing; so plausible were the letters they wrote and so loud their protestations of devotion to the race.[8]

Several factors make it difficult to empirically assess Blyden's claims of complexional stratification as the animating factor in politics: the subtleties of complexional differences, the notorious fluidity of nineteenth-century racial categories and a paucity of portraits or daguerreotypes and other forms of photography. Nonetheless, what is know about the complexion of officeholders during this period does not support the view of fixed alliances on the basis of color: Hilary R. W. Johnson, who was of mixed ancestry and served as president of Liberia from 1884 to 1892, received his first public appointment from Stephen Allen Benson, Liberia's second president, who was dark skinned. Furthermore, light-skinned Joseph Jenkins Roberts launched the political career of dark-skinned Arthur Barclay, who eventually served as president from 1904 to 1912. Of the four presidents elected on the ticket of the Republican Party – a bastion of mulatto power, according to

Blyden – two were dark skinned: Stephen Allen Benson and Daniel Bashiel Warner. Blyden's own talent came to be recognized largely through the efforts of Joseph Jenkins Roberts, the alleged head of the mulatto cabal. It was Roberts who appointed Blyden editor of the *Liberia Herald* in 1855 and to the Liberia College faculty in 1862,[9] presumably on the basis of his merit.

As Blyden stated in his letter to Sutherland—and implied in other correspondence—the black masses could not detect the "scheme" of the mulattoes. Two published volumes of letters sent by émigrés in Liberia to their relatives, friends and former masters in the United States make no reference to the color controversy that was purportedly animating national politics. Perhaps Blyden's acculturation in the West Indies – known for its intense color rivalries – made him hypersensitive to complexional differences, unlike African-American emigrants to Liberia, most of whom were from the Upper South, where collaboration and marriages across complexional lines were more common.[10]

On which side of the complexional divide Blyden would have placed Hilary Teage is unclear. Twenty-seven years Blyden's senior, Teage had employed the younger man as his clerk while serving as secretary of state and editor of the *Liberia Herald*, positions that Blyden would eventually come to occupy. Although Teage was a lifelong political ally of Roberts, Blyden described him as having "genius" – an appellation he would not likely have applied to a mulatto nemesis. Despite a wide search, no image of Teage nor careful description of his complexion and other physical characteristics has been found. Nonetheless, anyone writing about him faces the challenge of explaining his place in Liberia's early color hierarchy, the existence of which has never been proven. According to a white Quaker colonizationist who knew Teage "well personally," the Liberian statesman was "a pure, full blooded Negro -- ... The negro race have a right to the benefit of this fact."[11]

Teage's role as a merchant makes it necessary to confront another sacred cow of Liberian studies – a consensus that trading by early Liberians was economically irrational and unprofitable. That conclusion is derived not from an examination of available evidence but from the ideological assertions of American Colonization Society officials, who viewed trading as potentially corrosive of their ideal Jeffersonian republic of yeoman farmers.[12] In contrast, the only historian known to have analyzed data on Liberian traders in the nineteenth century found evidence of considerable success. According to D. N. Syfert, "In all, fifty-eight Liberian-owned [trading] vessels are known to have existed before 1848, a considerable merchant fleet for a small, new colony." He went on to add, "Liberian merchants ... developed an extensive coastal commerce in which they attempted to wrest the function of the collection and distribution of commodities along the coast from European and American competitors. The trade which they developed provided an important source of private profit, and a major source of government revenue."[13] This was the context in which Teage enjoyed success followed by insolvency followed by success. Between 1827 and 1853, he owned at least eight vessels that were engaged in the West African coasting trade, including one vessel jointly owned by fellow Baptist pastor Abraham Cheeseman. By 1843, he owned five buildings in Monrovia, was earning an annual commission of $7,000, had five warehouses along the coast worth $30,000 with about $20,000 in trade stock.[14] In the eyes of Teage and his peers he was a financial success, especially when measured against his likely fate had he remained in his native Goochland County, Virginia.

In writing about Teage, perhaps the greatest skepticism one faces is in regards to his role as a republican theorist. This skepticism stems from two separate quarters: First, there is its contemporary identification with the conservatism of the U.S. Republican Party. During Teage's lifetime, however, republicanism was more inherently opposed to social hierarchy and forced labor than most ideologies of the day. As noted by Eric Foner, a leading scholar of American Republicans before the Civil War, support for "free labor" distinguished them from their rivals and propelled their more radical wing toward political action against slavery.[15] A second source of skepticism is a long-standing tendency in Liberian studies to view the nation's origin as inherently flawed. For example, in 1832, arguing against the efforts of the American Colonization Society to resettle free blacks in Liberia, abolitionist leader William Lloyd Garrison predicted two possible outcomes for the infant colony: either Liberians of African American descent would be subverted by the "vices, physical strength, or by the fatal amalgamation" of indigenous Africans, or they would destroy the natives through "superior knowledge and greedy avarice." Through the writings of Garrison and others of his age, this assumption of cultural incommensurability and the dualism on which it rested would come to be enshrined in Liberian studies.[16]

Such dualism is reproduced in the work of political scientist and former interim president of Liberia Amos C. Sawyer, whose book *The Emergence of Autocracy in Liberia* traces the roots of this "tragedy" to the country's origin. In the preface to a chapter summarizing his wide readings of the recent ethnographic literature, he notes,

> Incompatibility of purpose was not the only problem with the idea of Liberia. There were flaws in implementing the idea. A major flaw was the almost total lack of comprehension of the actual African situation into

which the emigrants were to be sent. ...Even though there was a paucity of literature on West Africa at the time, there is not evidence that the ACS searched out and studied such limited information as was available or contemplated undertaking a thorough and systematic study.[17]

Even if the Liberian state came to rest on the exploitation of indigenous Africans and ultimately collapsed into fratricidal war, these developments cannot be blamed on the country's founding ideology, without overlooking significant intervening factors. For example, the rise of the True Whig Party (TWP) in 1871 reflected a repudiation of the Constitution of 1847, which was infused with republican values. Two examples should suffice: upon winning the presidency, the TWP sought (1) to extend the presidential term from two years to four and (2) to secure foreign loans from private capital markets. These two policy changes – anathema to nineteenth-century republicans – opened the door to Liberian officials entrenching themselves in office and to the country's later reliance on foreign loans.

In my view, the collapse of the Liberian state in the late twentieth century resulted from a series of choices at various historical junctures long after Teage and his generation had passed away. More proximal to the collapse of the state was the fateful decision made by the administration of William R. Tolbert (under pressure from the World Bank, it should be noted) to repeal subsidies from imported rice, which led to widespread rioting and a simultaneous mutiny by soldiers in 1979, followed one year later by a military coup. In the aftermath of Liberia's disastrous war, Teage's republican values – which represent the road not taken by his country's recent leaders – should find particular resonance, as Liberians seek to repay billions of dollars in foreign loans, while simultaneously recovering from the destruction and mayhem unleashed by rulers intent on entrenching themselves in power.

Editorial Method

The writings of Hilary Teage included in this book reflect a broad range of his ideas, opinions, ethics, and passions. In selecting items for inclusion, one objective was to present a representative sample of genres, styles of expression, diction and rhetoric. Toward that end, the selections include a mix of previously unpublished letters, along with writings directed at a variety of audiences and intended for publication in various forms. Unsurprisingly, Teage's surviving letters were usually written to advance policy options to key decision makers in the United States and thus offer few revelations about his private life. On the other hand, his published writings across genres provide glimpses into his interior life, especially his frustrations with

Carl Patrick Burrowes

rivals in the leadership of church and state and anxieties brought on by financial losses.

A major objective guiding the selection of Teage's writings was to introduce readers, especially scholars with interests in ethnography, early Liberian history and Christian missionary activities, to a wide array of his intellectual preoccupations. Reflecting that principle, his writings are organized into nine sections on the basis of the following criteria: "Liberian Society" presents a mix of social commentaries and sociological analysis. "The Press" includes detailed information on the *Liberia Herald* and its inputs, circulation and management challenges, along with biting criticisms of the rival newspaper *Africa's Luminary* and one of its editors. "The Church" focuses mainly on Teage's own Baptist denomination, especially administrative challenges, leadership rivalries and demographic changes. "Local Politics and Policies" documents his seminal role in the drive for independence, as well as his various domestic policy recommendations. "Neighboring Societies" consists of ethnographic expositions on the cultures of indigenous Africans living outside the ambit of the *de facto* Liberian state. "Relations with American and Europeans" presents Teage's foreign policy perspectives. "Miscellany" includes items that highlight either his sense of humor or his penchant for empirical investigations. "Poems," which includes all of his extant poetry, shows Teage at his most passionate. Finally, "Speeches, Sermons and State Papers" highlights his expository, persuasive and rhetorical skills.

To preserve the integrity and flavor of Teage's writings, they were transcribed with the following minor exceptions: quotation marks are converted to modern usage; obvious misspelling and printer's errors are corrected; printer's brackets are converted to parentheses; and end-mark dashes have been changed to periods when this seemed to be the writer's intention. I have not completed words, added words, corrected spelling, or otherwise provided material in the text of manuscript documents except where noted in the text. Square brackets are used to enclose editorial emendations and additions. For example, I bracketed information added to the salutation and return address of letters; I bracketed material that I believe will aid the reader in comprehending the document, such as [illegible], [torn] and [rest of page missing]; and I bracketed words and phrases that I believe appeared in the original but am uncertain about because of the quality of the surviving text.

Explanatory notes are used to identify a variety of significant items within the documents, such as people, events, places, institutions, organizations, laws and legal decisions. A full note on each such item is presented at the first appropriate point in the volume. People and events that are covered in standard biographical directories, reference books, or textbooks are treated briefly in the notes, if at all.

Because this study is likely to attract readers who have little familiarity with Liberian studies, I have erred on the side of providing explanatory notes on Liberian personages and events, whenever that seemed appropriate or helpful.

In transcribing articles by Teage, the placement of the dateline, salutation, farewell, and signature has been regularized. I have used, whenever possible, the title given to the work in the original publication. Those titles appearing in square brackets were imposed because no title appeared in the original or because the original title was misleading or uninformative. In such cases, the adopted titles were usually taken from a line within the first paragraph or verse of the work. The notes indicate the newspaper, research collection or other source from which the primary document was derived. In keeping with nineteenth-century custom, Teage often used "instant" to mean the current month and "ultimo" to refer to the previous month. He also sometimes employed what are now regarded as British spellings of words, such as "labour" and "colour" instead of "labor" and "color."

A Note on Nomenclature

As used throughout this book, "Liberia" refers to a polity populated mainly by African American repatriates residing in a few scattered coastal towns that were effectively controlled by the Liberian state during Teage's lifetime (see maps 1 and 2). Such control was evident in residents' payment of taxes to the national government or the existence of institutions, such as schools and churches, for socialization into the Liberian ethos. The use of a *de facto* definition of the state seeks to prevent the projection onto the past of Liberia's current form, encompassing 43,000 square miles, sixteen ethnic groups, and four language families. Such a teleological definition of the country supports misleading conclusions whereby early Liberian officials are judged responsible for conditions in territories that rested outside their effective control. For example, recent commentators have criticized the Liberian Declaration of Independence, which was written by Teage in 1847, for having excluded indigenous Africans[18] because it reads, "We the people of the Republic of Liberia were originally the inhabitants of the United States of North America." Blinded by presentism and good intentions, these writers fail to recognize that including indigenous Africans in the declaration when they were not yet members of the polity would have been disingenuous, presumptuous, and imperialistic. It is akin to criticizing the American Declaration of Independence for not making reference to California, Hawaii, and Alaska — territories that were incorporated into the United States long after it was issued.

From 1820 to 1847, when Liberia was still under the aegis of the American Colonization Society, Teage generally referred to its residents as "colonists" or

Carl Patrick Burrowes

"Americans." After independence was declared in 1847, he applied the term "Liberians" exclusively to persons living within the *de facto* limits of the republic, the vast majority of whom were African-American immigrants and their descendants. He usually labeled residents of the region not living in Liberia "native Africans," "indigenous Africans," or "our neighbours." The application of a modifier to the term "African" was necessary because at that time North American blacks such as Teage still conceived of themselves as Africans. This can be seen, to cite just one example, in the name of the church that young Hilary and his family attended in Richmond: First African Baptist Church. Indeed, it was the establishment of Liberia that led many black leaders sometime after 1833 to begin identifying themselves as "colored" rather than "African" because they feared that a close identification with the continent of their origin might be used to support racist arguments for their deportation.

Although African-American emigrants to Liberia are often labeled "settlers," "colonists," or "expatriates," I use the term "repatriates" instead. By "repatriate," I do not intend the nonscholarly meaning of someone returning to the land of his birth. Rather, I mean someone who settles, whether by deportation or choice, in a country perceived as his or her ancestral home, a definition somewhat closer to the late Latin etymology of the term, as in re- (back) and patria (land of the father). By using "repatriate," I am attempting to interject more rationality and scholarly precision into the Liberian studies discourse, which has come to be overly polemicized. A key example of this can be seen in the work of Liebenow, who did more than any other study to characterize Liberians of African American descent as a "long-entrenched ruling group" collectively guilty of exploiting Native Africans along lines "akin to treatment of blacks in the U.S. South." In the foreword to Liebenow's book, series editor Gwendolyn M. Carter underscored the political value of his argument for domestic U.S. politics when she noted, "The progress in Africa of a black-governed state with this background has particular importance," especially at "a time when black separatism in the United States is becoming more pronounced." Other scholars have employed equally polemical analogies to frame the interethnic relations in Liberia as comparable to U.S. government treatment of Native Americans and the South African apartheid system.[19] These charged metaphors are often used by social scientists who have neither studied the two societies evoked in their comparison nor applied any of the controls that would be built into a scholarly comparative study.[20] They have served to generate more emotional heat than intellectual light.

My use of "repatriates" reflects my own commitment to a phenomenological approach to history, which involves recovering the structures of thinking and feeling of people in the past. Along those lines, it is worth noting that African Americans who emigrated to Africa enjoyed cultural and historical ties with that continent, which made the relationship different from that of, say, Britons who settled Australia or Afrikaans who colonized South Africa. As they reiterated in their letters and other records, it was perceived ties to Africa that led early Liberians to reject other possible sites for relocation, including Canada, and to brave death by malaria and other tropical diseases, as well as possible re-enslavement in the "land of their fathers." To refer to those African American as "expatriates" would be an *ex post facto* reading of the past because the United States had not yet extended citizenship to blacks. In fact, the debate over African colonization helped push the issue of black citizenship onto the national U.S. agenda. The issue of black enfranchisement would not be effectively resolved until the Reconstruction era, some forty-plus years after Liberia was founded.

Acknowledgments

This book is the culmination of a long and convoluted journey, spanning from Monrovia, Liberia, through Fullerton, California, to Huntington, West Virginia. At Temple University, Dr. John Lent pointed me toward the premier issue of the *Liberia Herald* at the Library Company of Philadelphia, which was my first encounter with a publication that was historically significant and would become central to my own research; I join a generation of international communication scholars who have benefited from both his enthusiasm for research and his vast contributions to the field. My colleagues in the Communications Department at California State University, Fullerton, especially Dr. Terry Hynes and Dr. Edgar P. Trotter, gave crucial support. At Marshall University, Dr. Alan B. Gould, executive director of the John Deaver Drinko Center for the Study of American Civic Culture and Political Institutions, provided important historical insights, witty companionship, and a stimulating intellectual environment.

This project benefited from the support of two institutions: Marshall University in summer 1996 underwrote travel to research collections in Baltimore, Richmond, and Washington, D.C., while Penn State University funded visits to the National Archives in London and the Bibliotéque Nationale in Paris. Although many librarians aided my seemingly quixotic search for obscure Liberian materials, several deserve special acknowledgment for courteous and efficient service: AnnMarie F. Price, assistant curator, Virginia Historical Society; Paul Coates and Esme Bhan, both of the Moorland-Spingarn Research Center, Howard University; and Diane Turner, assistant archivist, Lincoln University. At the Library of Congress, Beverly Gray of the African and Middle Eastern Division; Deborah Newman-Ham of the Manuscript

Division; and Charles Mwalimu of the Law Division. At Cal State Fullerton, Mona Kratzert, reference librarian, with a specialization in communication materials; Ronald Rodriguez, Senior Assistant Librarian and OPAC whiz; and Nancy Caudill, librarian assistant for interlibrary loans. At Marshall University's James E. Morrow Library, the entire staff of the Special Collections Department; Newatha Perry and Dr. Majed Khader of Government Documents; Adele Elliott of the Interlibrary Loan Service and Timothy A. Balch, head of Public Services.

Several archivists and research librarians graciously responded to written requests for information on Teage materials in their catalogues: Frederick J. Anderson, executive director, Virginia Baptist Historical Society, University of Richmond; Bill Clarke, reference coordinator, Southeastern Baptist Theological Seminary; the clerk of the Circuit Court, Southampton County, Courtland, Virginia; Pat Lynagh, reference librarian, National Portrait Gallery, Smithsonian Institution; Dana Martin, acting director of the library, American Baptist Historical Society, Samuel Colgate Historical Library; Kathleen C. McDonough, Manuscript Reference Librarian, the Library of Congress; Ellen G. Parnell, Literature and History Department, Richmond (Virginia) Public Library; Teresa Roane, supervisor of Reference Services, Valentine Museum; Martha L. Smalley, Research Services librarian, Divinity School Library, Yale University; Bill Sumner, director, Southern Baptist Historical Library and Archives; and John R. Woodard, director, North Carolina Baptist Historical Collection, Wake Forest University.

For crucial encouragement and valuable insights into Baptist theology, thanks to Dr. Alan Neely, professor emeritus, Southeastern Baptist Theological Seminary, Wake Forest, North Carolina, who graciously agreed to critique my introduction, and to the Rev. Ned N. Cary Jr., pastor of the Morningstar Baptist Church of Williamsburg, Virginia, and a relative of Lott Cary, one of the earliest Baptist missionaries to Africa, whose story is superficially covered in this study.

Although my research builds on the works of a vast community of Liberianists, I benefited from the research of three scholars in particular, who took time from their own important scholarly projects to provide helpful, critical comments: the late Dr. C. Zamba Liberty shared his knowledge of Liberian politics and nineteenth century history; and the late Dr. Mary Antoinette Brown Sherman exercised subtle but significant influence upon the overall shape of this study. In the first instance, it was her article on nineteenth-century Liberian intellectuals that first drew my attention to Hilary Teage.

Three historians, Joyce Appleby, John B. Boles and Eugene D. Genovese— none of whom had ever met me—also took time from their own important research to provide valuable critiques of my work. In so doing, they taught me a lesson in collegiality that I will not soon forget. My longtime friend and fellow mass communication professor C. William Allen saved me from many stylistic and mechanical errors, through the generous use of his editorial pen. In addition, important input was provided by Ezekiel Pajibo, along with many others who must go unmentioned. Emira Woods provided encouragement when this project was floundering. Herbert Brewer pushed me to uncover the material, moral and psychological limits that constrained Teage's actions, in order to avoid a blinding presentism. The late Willie Davis, a descendant of Hilary Teage's sister, Colinette, provided access to Teage-family lore and his extraordinary collection of primary materials on Liberian history.

I thank Adjoa J. Burrowes for preparing all of the maps used in this work and Hilary Kadallah Burrowes for altering several of them to meet the stylistic requirements of my publisher. *American Journalism* kindly gave permission to reprint some materials from my "'In Common With Colored Men, I have Certain Sentiments': Black Nationalism and Hilary Teage of the *Liberia Herald*," which appeared in volume 16, issue 3, in summer 1999. My wife, Phemie, provided support. But, above all, my three children shared a significant place in their lives with this project and to them, therefore, it is dedicated.

Carl Patrick Burrowes

Chronology of the Life of Hilary Teage

1805	Born, probably in Goochland County, Virginia, to Colin and Frances Teage, on the plantation of Joshua Nicholson, owner of his father
1806	His father was sold to Robert Bell and James Shiphard, owners of a saddlery and harness factory in Richmond
Jan. 1821	Was one of seven persons who formed the Providence Baptist Church in Richmond for transference to Africa, modeled after the Sansom Street Church of Philadelphia
Jan. 1821	Sailed with his parents and sister, Colinette, aboard the *Nautilus* to Sierra Leone
1826	Moved from Sierra Leone to Liberia
1835	Led expedition to rescue Quaker repatriates in Bassa Cove, then under attack by allies of the slaver Theophilus Conneau; Teage reportedly supplied cash, weapons, and ammunition for the expedition from his store
1835	Appointed colonial secretary
Mar. 1835	Succeeded John B. Russwurm as colonial secretary and editor of the *Liberia Herald*, the latter position he would retain until 1849
Oct. 1835	Ordained pastor of the Baptist church at Millsburg
1838	Elected secretary of committee that prepared "Monrovia Draft" constitution as an alternative to American Colonization Society laws then operating in the colony
1839	Acquired the *Liberia Herald* from the American Colonization Society

1839-1846	Operated a successful shipping and trading business
1840	Elected member of the Colonial Council and commissioner for Montserrado County
1839-1848	Served as pastor of the Providence Baptist church in Monrovia
10 Sept. 1841	Delivered the funeral sermon for Thomas Buchanan, the last white governor of the colony, during whose tenure party politics matured
1843	Published Constitution and Laws of the Commonwealth of Liberia
1844-45	Published a historical sketch of the colony in two parts in the *African Repository* (September 1844 and January 1845), which was in reality an advocacy of self-government
1845	Elected first president of the Liberia Lyceum
1845	One of a "company of gentlemen" in Liberia who acquired the *Liberia Herald*
1846	Declared an insolvent debtor
1847	Elected delegate to the Constitutional Convention, and wrote the Liberian Declaration of Independence
1848-1849	Served as senator from Montserrado County
1849	Became pastor of the Baptist church at New Georgia, composed almost entirely of native Africans
1849	Visited New York, Philadelphia, and Washington, D.C., on behalf of the Liberian government to solicit funds for the purchase of the Gallinas, then a center of slave trading
26 July 1850	Delivered the Independence Day address at Monrovia
1850-1852	Served as attorney general

Carl Patrick Burrowes

May 1852	Reelected pastor of the Providence Baptist Church
1852-1853	Served as secretary of state
27 April 1852	Signed a treaty of amity and comity with France, the second nation to recognize Liberia's independence
21 May 1853	Died
1856	His collection of statutes, titled *The Statute Laws of the Republic of Liberia*, was published posthumously, with authorship credited to G. Killian, his printer

Introduction

Born a slave in Virginia, in 1805, Hilary Teage emigrated to West Africa in 1821, where he went on — in the words of one of his contemporaries — to make the single greatest personal contribution to the "framing and establishment" of the Republic of Liberia. Upon reading a speech by Teage without knowing anything about the author, an antislavery activist concluded that it was written by "a graduate in some eastern college." That speech was published in the United States, together with speeches by radical abolitionist Henry Highland Garnet of New York and President Joseph Jenkins Roberts of Liberia, in a book intended to refute the "calumny" that blacks were incapable of higher learning. In the view of Benjamin Coates, a white Quaker colonizationist, Teage was "a very superior man" of greater ability than "any ... black man in America."[21] Teage's death in 1853 was noted in the abolitionist *Frederick Douglass' Paper*, despite the editor's life-long opposition to colonization efforts.

Teage emigrated, at age sixteen, from Richmond, Virginia, to Africa in the company of his parents and fifteen-year-old sister, all of whom were literate. The family first settled in Sierra Leone, whose capital, "Freetown," had attracted significant attention from African-Americans since 1792, when blacks who had sided with the British during the American War of Independence began settling there — including many from Virginia. The promise inherent in the town's name inspired Paul Cuffe, a wealthy free-black whaler from Rhode Island, to try colonizing African-Americans there in 1811. Press reports of Cuffe's efforts had inspired Teage's father, Colin, to sell his property in Richmond and relinquish his job as a saddler, in order to serve as a missionary in Africa.[22] After five years in Sierra Leone, however, the family moved to Liberia to join other African Americans who had already settled there.

Established in 1820, Liberia was operated as a colony for American free blacks by the American Colonization Society — an organization of influential whites — until the repatriates declared their independence in 1847 (see maps 1 and 2). From its founding through the end of the nineteenth century, it would attract some nineteen thousand blacks from the New World. From 1900 to 1930, due in part to pressures created by the European scramble for Africa, Liberia went from

Map 2. Towns in eastern Liberia, 1822 to 1846

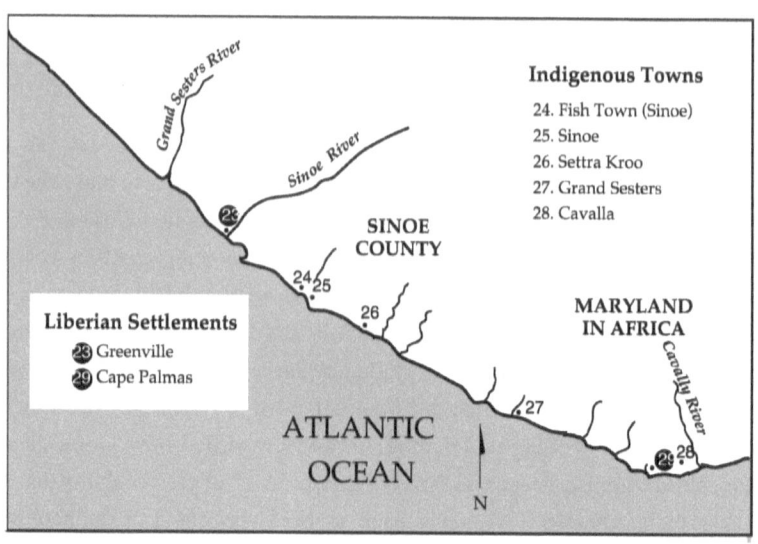

Indigenous Towns
24. Fish Town (Sinoe)
25. Sinoe
26. Settra Kroo
27. Grand Sesters
28. Cavalla

SINOE COUNTY

MARYLAND IN AFRICA

Liberian Settlements
㉓ Greenville
㉙ Cape Palmas

ATLANTIC OCEAN

N

Grand Sesters River
Sinoe River
Cavally River

Map 1. Towns in western Liberia, 1822 to 1846

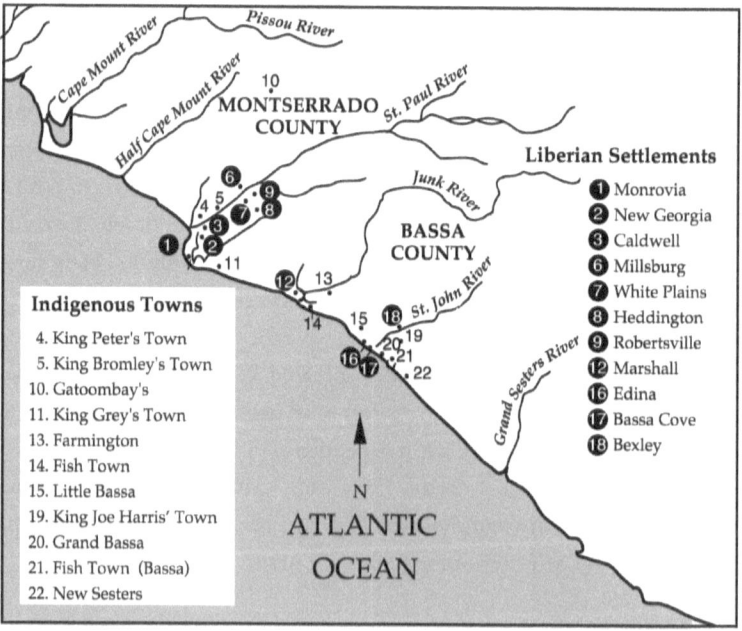

MONTSERRADO COUNTY

BASSA COUNTY

Liberian Settlements
❶ Monrovia
❷ New Georgia
❸ Caldwell
❻ Millsburg
❼ White Plains
❽ Heddington
❾ Robertsville
⑫ Marshall
⑯ Edina
⑰ Bassa Cove
⑱ Bexley

Indigenous Towns
4. King Peter's Town
5. King Bromley's Town
10. Gatoombay's
11. King Grey's Town
13. Farmington
14. Fish Town
15. Little Bassa
19. King Joe Harris' Town
20. Grand Bassa
21. Fish Town (Bassa)
22. New Sesters

N

ATLANTIC OCEAN

Cape Mount River
Pissou River
Half Cape Mount River
St. Paul River
Junk River
St. John River
Grand Sesters River

Carl Patrick Burrowes

being separated from other polities by frontier zones to having carefully delimited boundaries. As a result the population increased from about forty-five thousand mainly repatriate descendants to an estimated two million mostly indigenous Liberians.[23]

Teage spearheaded the drive for Liberia's independence through the newspaper *Liberia Herald* and then went on to write the Declaration of Independence for his adopted country. He later served the young republic as a senator from Montserrado County (1848-49), attorney general (1850-52), and secretary of state (1852 until his death in 1853). However, Teage first devoted his attention to commerce and by 1843 was earning an annual commission of $7,000; he owned five warehouses worth $30,000 with an additional $20,000 in trade stock. He began his public service career in 1835 as colonial secretary and editor of the *Liberia Herald*. After purchasing the *Herald* from the American Colonization Society in 1839, he remained its senior editor until 1849, while serving simultaneously in various public offices and as pastor of the country's leading Baptist church.

Although long ignored[24], Teage was an engaging and prodigious writer whose productions covered a wide range of forms   including poems, personality profiles, ethnographic articles and policy papers. His articles from the *Herald* — his largest surviving body of work — ranged from descriptive features on snakes, a river excursion and the social life of insects to thoughtful and often prophetic commentaries on international affairs. These articles displayed a knack for sarcasm, self-deprecating humor, and a surprisingly modern empiricism. Teage's poems, mostly on patriotic themes, were laced with allusions to Africa's past grandeur. But his speeches were especially masterful works of systematic argumentation mixed with flourishes of poetry. From these works, Teage emerges as knowledgeable, witty and modest, but devastatingly sardonic.

Through both his actions and writings, Teage tirelessly promoted Christianity, rationalism and republican government — a commitment that was derived in part from the dominant American ideology, conceived of as "a structure of meaning expressed through a historically specific system of communication." It is worth recalling that Richmond, Virginia, where he was socialized, had been a major center of political and religious ferment in the eighteenth century. Through public orations and open-air celebrations, the rhetoric and premises of the American Revolution and the Second Great Awakening of Protestant Christianity were accessible to residents, regardless of color and class. His reflexive commitment to this ideology was significantly reinforced by his father, a Baptist preacher, and by scholarly habits formed early in life. Although many details of his education are unknown, his schooling must have been highly structured and systematic, given his extensive vocabulary, precise use of language and developed reasoning skills. While several Western intellectual traditions served as the vessel for his thinking, they did not determine the content. In the process of fitting Enlightenment ideas to Liberians in particular and blacks in general, Teage altered this received tradition to accommodate the specific needs and aspirations of his oppressed race. Consequently, he became a major and early exponent of "black nationalism" several decades before "the golden age of black nationalism," which dated from 1850 to 1904.[25] His abiding obsession was achieving and sustaining black self-government, by which means the long-degraded children of Africa could be animated, regenerated and redeemed.

Teage's uncompromising stance in defense of black political interests did not extend to all African traditions. Although he took to eating local cuisine and found African hospitality and several cultural practices worthy of praise[26], he regarded slavery, the status of women and certain other pre-modern social relations as morally reprehensible and in need of change, if not excision. Writing before the emergence of cultural relativism and the anthropological traditions upon which it rested, Teage held to a nineteenth century view of "civilization," defined as a way of life characterized by monotheism, order and democratic government, and enriched by the arts and sciences. Unlike many of his contemporaries, however, he believed that all races had contributed to this higher way of life, especially Africans whom he repeatedly credited with its creation. Since all of humanity had contributed, he reasoned, all could aspire to partake of its offerings.

Teage's enormous and wide-ranging intellectual powers were not lost on his contemporaries who in 1845 elected him the first president of the Liberia Lyceum. Until about 1850, the Lyceum sponsored public speeches and debates as a means of animating and educating the larger community. Although largely self-educated, Teage occupied — by virtue of his age, activities and early arrival in the colony — pride of place among Liberian intellectuals. They included John B. Russwurm, co-founder of the African American press and one of the first black college graduates in the United States, and Edward Wilmot Blyden, who authored hundreds of essays and countless letters to a large and influential circle of correspondents in Africa, England and the United States.[27]

Sometimes called "the Jefferson of Liberia,"[28] Teage enjoyed more commonalties with the third U. S. president than just his role in penning his country's declaration of independence. The two men were born in Goochland County and shared republican commitments, although they came from opposite ends of the Virginia hierarchy. Given the denial of citizenship rights to blacks in the

Carl Patrick Burrowes

land of his birth, Teage set his sights on the creation of a black republic in Africa, convinced that the political system created in Liberia had the potential to be more democratic than that of Virginia; Liberia lacked the hereditary property that could form the basis of an "artificial aristocracy." Although the comparison of the two men must have been flattering to Teage, who considered Thomas Jefferson an "immortal,"[29] it was also diminutive because it consigned Teage to the shadow of a republican slaveholder without recognizing his own distinctive contribution to the struggle for human liberty.

Teage's writings call into question several claims about early Liberians that were widely touted by abolitionists and northern free black leaders: that their emigration was uninfluenced by a concern for liberty; that they were acquiescent toward slavery, given their willingness to be removed from the United States; and that their relationship with indigenous Liberians was characterized by unmitigated hostility and ignorance.[30] Teage's thinking was dominated by republicanism, which emphasized the attainment of virtue through hard work and the exercise of reason. Because outlets of political expression were limited for black intellectuals in the antebellum South, his is one of the few surviving examples of political theorizing by an African American from that place and period. Although republicanism, Protestantism, and black nationalism have been enduring features of African-American thought, Teage's writings represent one of the earliest intellectual integrations of these previously disparate elements, a synthesis he was able to achieve only after he was five thousand miles away from the scene of its incubation in Virginia.

That Boasted Land of Equality

Hilary Teage[31] (1805-1853) was born into slavery at a time when enslaved blacks throughout the New World were taking bold strides for freedom. One year before his birth, the people of Haiti had established a republican government at the western end of Hispaniola — the first black state in the modern world — after defeating a five-thousand-man army sent by Napoleon to crush them. This was followed by the freeing of all slaves and the killing of all whites who did not leave, forcing some former masters to seek refuge in the Chesapeake region (consisting of Virginia and Maryland), in some cases accompanied by their slaves. These former residents of Hispaniola arrived as Virginia was still quaking with anxiety over Gabriel's rebellion of 1800, which had involved thousands of blacks and was thwarted only hours before it was set to begin.

Hilary was born probably on the Goochland County plantation of the man who owned his father, Colin (1785-1839). Although a short biographical sketch of Colin (also spelled "Collin") published several years after his death did not give the first name of his owner, the "Mr. Nicholson" to which it refers was probably Joshua, the only male with that name listed in several Goochland County records from that period. Nicholson's household included his wife, Mary Kirby, whom he married in 1764, and their four children: Charles Briggs (who bore his grandmother's maiden name), Matilda, Fanny, and Lucy (the last two probably named for their paternal aunts). Mary had apparently been previously married because her will, dated 8 October 1795, named two offspring — Polly and Mary — with the last name Barsham, in addition to the Nicholson's children. [32]

It is not clear when or how Hilary's family acquired its unusual surname. Derived from Ireland, "Teage" originally meant "poet," but by the sixteenth century had become synonymous with "Irishman." Since there is no record of the Nicholsons being related to a family with that name, it is unlikely that the owners gave it to their slaves. Colin and his family could have adopted it, especially after they were manumitted, but that too is improbable since the name was uncommon in Goochland and the surrounding counties. At that time, most Virginia Teages were small-scale white farmers or yeomen who owned few, if any, slaves and lived clustered along the Eastern Shore, in Northampton and Accomack Counties. The name might have been retained in remembrance of distant relatives or a previous, more kindly slave owner, a common practice among slaves. In that case, the most plausible point of origin would be neighboring North Carolina, which, according to computerized census records from 1820, had more Teages than any other state — forty-one households to Virginia's fourteen. Furthermore, genealogical sources suggest a higher incidence of slaveholding by Carolinian Teages than by family members elsewhere. Given the economic and other ties that existed between Virginians and their neighbors to the south, it is possible that Colin or one of his ancestors was sold up from North Carolina. [33]

Like most Virginia slaves, the Teage family probably lived in a duplex shack of about sixteen by sixteen feet, with wooden chimneys and earthen floors. However, while the majority of slaves labored as field hands, Colin worked as a skilled maker of harnesses and saddles. Since slaves skilled in mechanical trade were relatively few — about 8 percent, according to one estimate — Colin must have lived on a plantation large enough to support such an unusual specialization. Within the circumscribed confines of the slave community, he was relatively privileged, as his

Carl Patrick Burrowes

artisan status would have freed him from constant supervision by whites, allowed him mobility and provided him with the chance to earn money. Colin was probably treated better than common field slaves, since artisans fetched a higher price. Equally important, artisans generally maintained higher self-esteem and "enjoyed a reputation for being the proudest and most independent of all slaves," characteristics that marked Colin and would come to mark his son. Even as a youth, Hilary reportedly had "stirring in his soul, earnest aspiration for liberty," a yearning occasioned no doubt by the divide between the conditions of servitude into which he was born and the republican rhetoric of equality that pervaded Virginia. His father was said to have been characterized by caution, shrewdness and "forcast," which earned him the nickname "Fox."[34]

Virginia, as is fairly well known, played a major if not disproportionate part in the early history of the United States. It served as an incubator for the rebellion against British rule. One of the first challenges to the authority of King George III was issued in 1758 when the Virginia Assembly voted to lower the tax obligations of state residents, in recognition of a recent agricultural failure. The king vetoed the law, in response to entreaties from the local clergy, who benefited from the higher tax. When the clergy sued for their usual payment and damages, assembly member Patrick Henry carried the day for the defense, arguing, "By this conduct the king, from being the father of his people, had degenerated into a tyrant and forfeited all his right" to his subjects' obedience. In 1765, the crown issued a Stamp Act — effectively taxing the colonists without their consent — which was rejected by the Virginia Assembly on constitutional grounds. This argument roused defiance from Massachusetts and other colonies, resulting in a riot in Boston.[35]

When the crown threatened to have the rioters taken to England for trial, a group of Virginia legislators, including Patrick Henry and Thomas Jefferson, proposed that the assembly establish a standing committee of correspondence, for the purpose of communicating on this matter with similar committees that would be established by assemblies in other colonies. The standing committee was approved, and the resulting communication among assemblies led to the formation of the First Continental Congress. As tensions mounted between the crown and colonists, Henry further stoked the flames of rebellion in 1775, calling for the formation and arming of a Virginia militia for the defense of colonists' interests. He ended that speech with his now-famous line, "I know not what course others may take, but, as for me, give me liberty or give me death."[36]

This series of legislative maneuvers culminated in the American Declaration of Independence, written by Jefferson and approved by Congress on 4

July 1776. In the subsequent Revolutionary War, Virginia was the scene of significant battles and supplied the commander of the Continental Army, Gen. George Washington. Leadership by the "Old Dominion" would continue in the new republic, with the state supplying four of the first five presidents. Equally important was Virginia's role as the locus of one of two major ideological and political tendencies in early America. In contrast to the Federalist Party based mainly in New England, which sought to expand the powers of the national government, the Republican Party, led by Thomas Jefferson of Virginia, articulated a concern with preserving state and local governance. Although the two ideologies began with an English frame of reference, liberal republicanism came to embrace the promise inherent in the French Revolution — that the past could be de-emphasized as the principal source of information about human society, "in favor of a lively connection between present and future." The Jeffersonian Republicans imbued self-interest with moral value, rooting their analysis in the works of Aristotle, John Locke and liberal English economists.[37]

The republican sentiments associated with the American Revolutionary War, together with the egalitarian promise of the French Revolution, served to intensify and quicken black demands for freedom. This was evident most spectacularly in the Haitian Revolution of 1794, which was inspired in part by its French antecedent. Unsettlingly close to the centers of Chesapeake power, the events in Haiti reverberated throughout Virginia, in the form of rumblings among blacks and fits of panic among whites. Another significant eruption of republican-inspired actions for black freedom was Gabriel's rebellion in Richmond, Virginia, in 1800. Organized by the enslaved blacksmith Gabriel, the revolt was marked by extensive planning and an attempt to ally urban artisans and rural field hands. One inducement for black action was the evidence of disunity among whites. As noted by Egerton, "Republicans wore the French tricolor, while Federalists donned black cockades. In the cities, the most vociferous Republicans were the artisans, whose egalitarian interpretation of the American and French revolutions was bound to rub off on the slaves who worked beside them." The republican cast of the rebellion was evident in the rebels' plan to spare all friends of liberty — Quakers, Methodists, French people and "poor white women who had no slaves."[38] Despite the extensiveness of the plan, it remained concealed from the whites until a few hours before the uprising was scheduled to begin. Following the arrest of Gabriel's followers, some claimed that there were hundreds of men ready to march under their banner on which would have been written "Death or Liberty," a slogan appropriated from Patrick Henry. Even after Gabriel and thirty-five co-

conspirators were hanged, further outbursts occurred— most notably the Nat Turner revolt of 1831

For African-Americans, especially those who were free, the juxtaposition of black servility with republican liberties for whites helped fuel these outbursts. Their entreaties were met with derision and repression, as was the case with an ominous provision passed by the Virginia Assembly in 1806 that required any blacks freed thereafter to leave the state within one year of their emancipation.[39] Measures such as this one served not to quench the fires of republicanism but to engender a black nationalist consciousness, a sense of racial identity and belonging that came to form one thread in the fabric of Hilary's mature thinking.

The tension between the revolutionary sentiments of America's founders and their willingness to compromise when it came to slavery was nowhere more glaring than in Virginia which was characterized by a hierarchical order. As noted by Patrick Henry, there were four classes: the "well-born" planters (drawn heavily from among English merchants who immigrated during periods of conflict at home, bringing capital and connections), the yeomen (who worked their own farms), the "lower orders" (the landless poor whites) and at the bottom the enslaved African Americans. This social structure determined the flow of religious affiliations — the well born being largely Episcopalian while the Baptist message of equality before God and wealth inhibiting entrance to heaven mainly attracted the lower-order whites and blacks. Like so many "well-born" republicans, Henry acknowledged that slavery was "repugnant to humanity," yet retained slaves throughout his life because of "the general inconveniency of living without" them.[40]

One family from the top tier of the social hierarchy was that of Joshua Nicholson's wife, Mary. However, by 1798 the members had turned on one another, perhaps as a result of having fallen upon hard economic times. Mary's grandfather, Frances Willis of Gloucester, had "conveyed" to Walter King of Bristol, England, several pieces of property in Gloucester, 60 slaves, 100 sheep and 260 cattle. Her father, Francis, who died before 4 December 1797, had nine children, including John (his eldest son), Francis, Jr., Nancy and Mary. In 1798, a lawsuit was brought against Mary on behalf of her eight-year-old niece who bore the same first name. Although the younger Mary was the daughter of Francis Jr., she was represented by her uncle John, who acted as her guardian. The suit claimed that Mary Nicholson had misappropriated some slaves left by the girl's grandfather.[41]

Joshua Nicholson was himself well born. The Nicholsons, whose name was of early Scottish origin, were the descendants of Robert Nicholson, who immigrated from Great Britain around 1654 — about forty-five years after the English colonized

Jamestown. Two years after his arrival, he patented five hundred acres of land in Charles City County, where he then settled and, with his wife, Sarah, had three sons: James (ca. 1658-ca. 1683), George (1661-1716), and Robert (ca. 1600-1720), who was the grandfather of Joshua. After the death of Robert Sr. sometime after 1667, his widow married a prominent merchant, George Lee, who moved the family across the James River to James City County and furthered his stepsons' ascent into the Virginia gentry. [42]

Like his father, Robert Jr. had three children: a daughter (whose name is unknown), John, and Joshua (ca. 1698-1764), whose similarly named son would come to own Colin Teage and his family. By the time Robert, Jr. died in 1720, the family held some slaves, for among the items willed to his son Joshua were 180 acres of land, money for the purchase of a gold ring and "some negroes." Joshua settled in Southampton County, and rapidly expanded his holdings to include 181 acres on the north side of the Meherrin River in 1728, 106 acres on the south side of the same river in 1731 and 275 acres in Isles of Wight County in 1745. He and his wife, the former Sarah Briggs, had four children: Joshua, Jr., Elizabeth Rives (or Rivers), Lucy Edmunds and Fanny. [43] Being the only son, Joshua, Jr. was probably trained to manage his father's properties and may well have inherited most of his land. It was by this circuitous route that the Nicholsons found themselves in Goochland County.

Goochland County was created on 1 May 1728, from the western section of Henrico County (map 3). Among its earliest and most prominent residents during this period was the family of Thomas Jefferson. In 1744, the western section of Goochland was given over to the creation of Albemarle County. Five years later, Goochland reached its present size, with the creation of Cumberland County. Although less developed than the Tidewater region of Virginia — and more recently settled by Europeans — Goochland was closer to the political and economic pulse of the state, being about forty miles from Richmond, the capital. As of 1790, the county held 9,053 persons, including 257 free blacks and 4,656 slaves. [44]

The elaborate edifice of Virginia society rested upon a base of tobacco cultivation, which by the seventeenth century had so penetrated that society that it displaced species as the medium for the evaluation and payment of fines, taxes, salaries and bills. Tobacco also spurred a sharp increase in the importation of Africans, from 1,700 in 1650 (or 2 percent of the population) to 190,000 in 1770 (or 40 percent) to 292,000 in 1790, by which time they formed the bulk of the labor force. In addition, between 1790 and 1810, Virginia exported an estimated 98,000 slaves to Kentucky, Tennessee, and other "slave-hungry" frontier states. With the expansion of the tobacco industry, the legal and social status of blacks shifted, as

Carl Patrick Burrowes

Map 3. Virginia, with relevant counties labeled

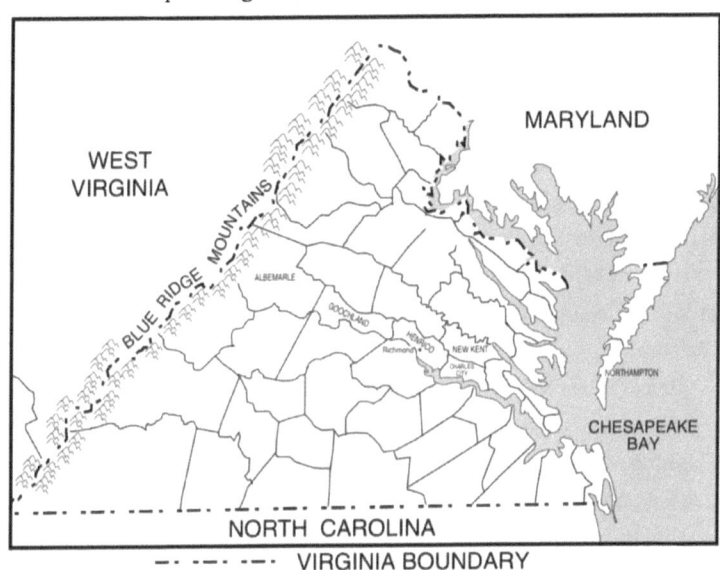

captured in a
1705 law that collated and revised all laws pertaining to slavery. Once akin to white
indentured servants, blacks became the subject of a virulent racism that sought to
assign them to a servile position beneath all whites. Nonetheless, during the
antebellum period, Virginia constituted a geographic as well as a cultural mean
between the extremes of the large, harsh plantations of the Deep South and the legal
freedoms of northern cities. By 1810, the Chesapeake region contained more than
40 percent of blacks in the United States, allowing it to set the tone and tempo of
black cultural life. The demographic weight of Virginia's black population led one
historian to call this region the "center of black life in America."[45]

Given the history of hostility, paternalism and distrust that characterized
relations between the races, it is not surprising that whites and blacks often held to
distinctly different conceptualizations of Christianity and civilization. There is
general agreement among scholars of African American cultural history that by the
end of the eighteenth century, blacks had forged their own systems of meaning and
styles of thinking, as "objectified in symbols, movement and, most crucially,
language." These cognitive and aesthetic styles were distinct from those of whites,
not owing to mistakes in the blacks' mimicking of the dominant culture or the
survival of disjointed elements of African cultures, but as a result of the fusing of
elements from both traditions into an "integrative whole" that was greater than the
sum of its parts.[46]

The thrust and tempo of this cultural creation were dictated in large measure by two impulses. On the one hand, elements of the European tradition that were reserved for free persons — such as legal marriages, decent clothes and control of institutions — came to be highly valued. On the other hand, African traditions were retained at the level of what might be regarded as "deep structure" if they were unopposed by the prevailing political and cultural orders, and especially where they were reinforced by similar European traditions. Unlike regions such as the Carolina-Georgia Lowcountry, which remained more culturally African up to the abolition of the slave trade in 1807, due to the continued infusions of blacks directly from Africa, Virginia led the way in the natural increase of population and the creation of a Creole culture.[47]

One of the few African influences retained in Virginia was the strong taboo against first-cousin marriages. Another was the social significance of "proper burials," which often featured a "slow procession to the burial site, clapping, singing, beating drums, and uttering 'shouts' that were thought to hasten the journey of the departed soul into a spirit world." In addition to providing African-Americans with rituals that were in keeping with their definitions of dignity, funerals afforded an escape, albeit momentarily, from the watchful eyes of whites. By the end of the eighteenth century, "a quasi-African body of values functioned in almost every African household in America" and came to form the basis for an autonomous black community.[48]

Although Colin Teage, being an artisan, was not routinely involved in tobacco cultivation, his wife and other kinfolk probably were, since Goochland County had emerged as a center of tobacco cultivation from the mid-1700s. A tedious and year-round process, the cultivation of tobacco engaged the labor of most Virginia slaves, including women and children over the age of twelve, who worked quarter-time. New fields had to be constantly hacked out of the surrounding forests, since on average a field was planted with tobacco only once every three years. Beginning in mid-January, the seeds were sown in specially prepared beds, while the fields were hoed and furrowed. During the spring, seedlings were transplanted to the fields. Thereafter, the plants required regular weeding, as well as repeated hoeing and plowing to keep the soil loose. Maturing plants had to be regularly inspected for worm infestations and topped to prevent growth beyond a healthy level, while saplings were removed at the base of the leaf stems. As the plants yellowed with age, the stalks were cut close to the ground, to wilt the leaves. After the leaves were harvested, they were taken to tobacco houses to be air cured for about six weeks, stripped, made into "hands," and placed in hogsheads. By this time a new crop was often ready for planting, and the routine began again.[49]

Carl Patrick Burrowes

Although Hilary was too young to have worked in the field while living on the Nicholson plantation, he would recall slavery with bitterness.[50] As early as age seven, children began working in the fields or learning a trade from their relatives or masters. From about 1730, the workload of slaves was increased, requiring them to work well into the night stripping tobacco and husking corn. The slaves were also responsible for raising subsidiary crops, mending fences, building hogsheads, and other tasks. Their free time consisted of three holidays — Christmas, Easter and Pentecost (which was celebrated on the seventh Sunday after Easter) — maybe Sundays. Plows did not universally replace hoes until the 1790s, and the increased productivity caused by this development, along with a collapse of tobacco prices in that decade, might account for why Colin Teage was sold away from Goochland County to new owners in Richmond during this period.

These developments also help explain a general increase in manumissions. Beginning in 1782, when private manumissions were legalized, the free black population increased from about 3,000 to around 30,000 in 1810, at which point Virginia accounted for a fifth of all free blacks in the United States. By the time manumissions were legalized, however, few economic opportunities were left for free blacks. The "well born" and yeomen had claimed most of the farmland, and "all the major trades and skilled occupations were occupied by newly arrived white immigrants." A shift from tobacco to grain production in the Tidewater region, led to further emancipations, as owners sought to recoup losses by allowing excess slaves to purchase their freedom or be purchased by free relatives. Also fueling this surge were the absence of children and other heirs among some manumitters, religious impulses concerning equality before God, and political ideals of equality spread by the American Revolution.[51]

For the members of the Teage family, the seed of manumission was sown by the death of their owner. In his will, dated 12 January 1781, but probated on July 12 of that year, Joshua Nicholson lent to his "loving wife Mary" all of his slaves for eight years (unless she remarried within that time) and the Goochland plantation (until the death of his mother). This will was unlikely to have been contested given the fact that the executors included Hardy Harris, Nicholson's "good friend"; John Kirby, his wife's brother; and Col. Howell Edmund, the husband of his sister Lucy, who had also served as an executor of their father's will in 1765. Following the death of Nicholson's mother in 1785 and the remarriage of his widow fourteen years later, Colin was sold in 1807 to the owners of a saddlery and harness factory in Richmond, forcing him to leave behind his nineteen-year-old wife and infant son. As the author of Colin's obituary would later note with biting sarcasm, this "transfer to other hands" was in keeping with the "custom of that land of boasted equality and republicanism."[52]

A Vague Idea of Future Freedom

In 1807, the road from Goochland to Richmond was scored by the tracks of tobacco hogsheads rolled along the ground behind oxen or horses, on the way to public inspection houses (map 4). Located at the fall line of the James River, Richmond had emerged as a cargo transfer point in the tobacco trade, as had Petersburg and other cities at the falls of other rivers. Given its inspection stations, factories for producing cigarettes, cigars, and snuff, and wharves for shipping the finished products to European and other markets, it is not surprising that the smell of tobacco hung in the air throughout the city.[53]

From a population of 3,761 in 1790, Richmond had grown steadily and was inhabited by 5,737 people in 1800, about half of whom were black. From 1790 to 1820, free blacks accounted for roughly one-tenth of the general population and one-fifth of all blacks. In the narrow confines of the black community, Colin was relatively privileged, as he was skilled and able to hire himself out for extra earnings. After all, only a third of free blacks in the greater Richmond area were skilled and no more than 10 percent of southern slaves were hired out each year. This privilege meant that blacks in the urban South often enjoyed a higher occupational status than blacks in northern cities.[54]

Although Richmond was a stronghold of the Federalist Party, Republican Thomas Jefferson carried the city in the presidential election of 1800 against Federalist John Adams. During important holidays, such as 4 July and George Washington's birthday, blacks mingled with whites in Capitol Square to hear speeches extolling republican virtues, as various militias marched by. For the city's black residents, Richmond contained some rude reminders of their servile condition, not least of which was Robert Lumkin's slave jail, known as the "Devil's Half-Acre." Just north of Fifteenth and Broad Streets was the spot where the conspirators in Gabriel's rebellion were executed (which residents avoided passing for years after the hangings).[55]

These dramatic manifestations of repression notwithstanding, a *Richmond Times* correspondent would later note that during this period "a vague idea of future freedom seemed to permeate the entire slave community." This idea was evident in the work of Christopher McPherson, a messianic black preacher. Born a slave in

Carl Patrick Burrowes

Louisa County, Virginia, he served as chief clerk of several leading commercial houses. After being terminated from one job in 1799, McPherson launched a crusade to warn the world of its eminent end. He was briefly committed to the Williamsburg Lunatic Asylum, after proclaiming himself "King of Kings and Lord of Lords." Despite his otherworldly orientation, McPherson contributed to several black community projects, including the attempted establishment of a night school for free blacks; he also supplied funds for repairing the street on which he lived.[56]

In Richmond, Colin Teage found himself in the hands of Robert Bell and James Shiphard, the owners of a saddlery located on the north side of E Street (now Main), between Twelfth and Thirteenth Streets. The building, which they initially rented from Bartholemew Trueheart, included their business, dwelling and an adjoining kitchen, all valued at about $4,000. Bell & Shiphard had been in business since at least 1793, some ten years after Bell immigrated from Scotland. In July of that year, the two saddlers acquired a legal indenture over one John McKeand, an orphan, who placed himself as their apprentice for the next six years, or until he turned twenty-one. McKeand promised not to "haunt grogshops, taverns, [or] playhouses," several of which stood temptingly near the saddlery, "but in all things [to] behave himself as a faithful apprentice."[57]

By 1807, when Teage was acquired — perhaps occasioned by the departure of McKeand — E Street was lined with taverns. Bowler's Tavern, the scene of countless slave auctions, stood two blocks east of the saddlery, just below Fifteenth Street. Directly across the street from Bell & Shiphard was the Eagle Tavern, where Chief Justice John Marshall began his examination of Aaron Burr in the celebrated treason trial of 1807. Two years later, the Eagle was visited by Thomas Jefferson, who had recently retired from the presidency. Although it ran through the heart of the city's evolving business district, E Street was still unpaved in some sections and was hence muddy.[58]

The author of Teage's obituary, with some hyperbole, would describe his new owners as mirror opposites:

> Bell was a Scotchman — and possessed more of the milk of human kindness than is usually found to flow in the moral veins of slaveholders. He regarded with paternal kindness all who were dependent upon him, and it is said he was never known to treat a slave unkindly. [Shiphard] was a Virginian — in the proper sense of the term — one whose mouth was ever filled with the cry of Liberty! Equality! while his hand was ever ready to rivet the chain upon the negro and to scourge him without mercy.[59]

Map 4. Richmond in the early nineteenth century

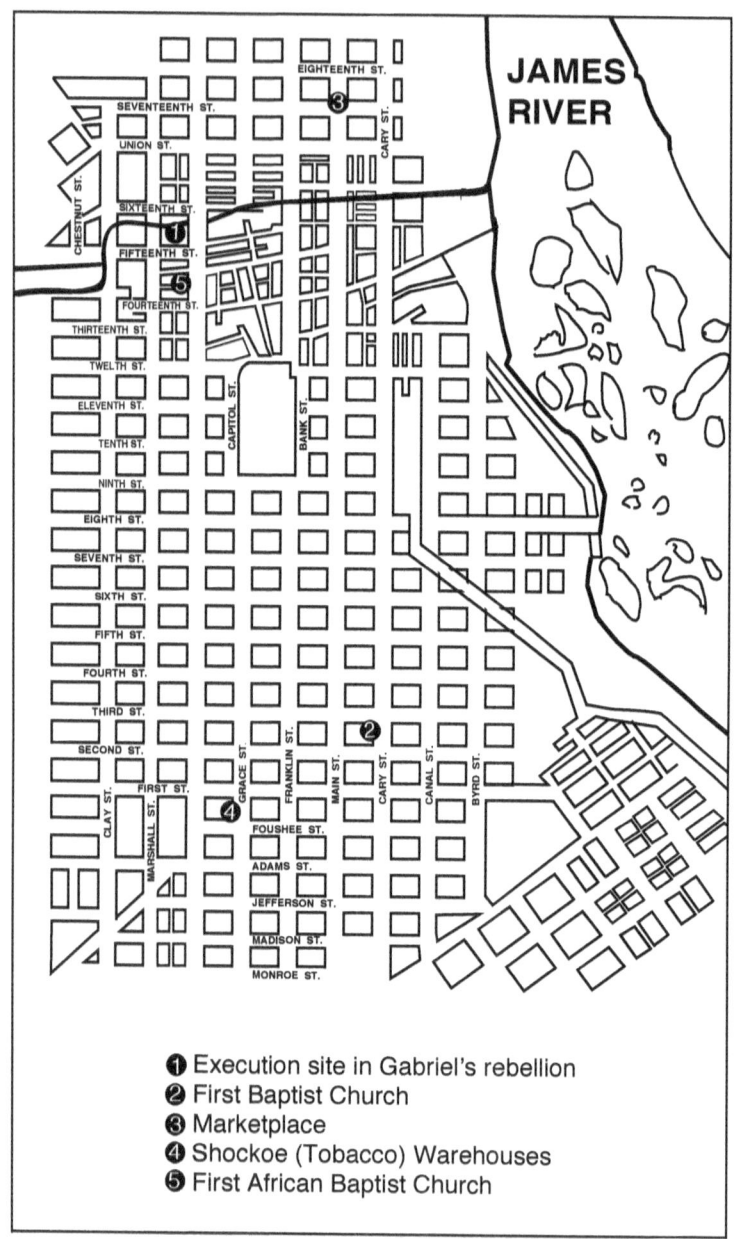

❶ Execution site in Gabriel's rebellion
❷ First Baptist Church
❸ Marketplace
❹ Shockoe (Tobacco) Warehouses
❺ First African Baptist Church

Carl Patrick Burrowes

Sometime after Teage's arrival, the two saddlers decided to dissolve their partnership. Since 1809, Shiphard had been the sole owner of a lumber store and dwelling one block away from the saddlery, near Fourteenth and E Streets, and would soon acquire several low-cost properties near the edge of the expanding city. The dissolution of their partnership — which would prove fateful for Teage — must have occurred between 1820 (the last year for which a business record can be found listing the two as partners) and 1822 (when Bell appeared on an insurance policy as the sole owner of the saddlery). Bell and Shiphard easily agreed to the disposition of all of their jointly held merchandise and slaves, except for Teage, whom both wanted, because of his superior workmanship. Allowed to choose between the two men in the presence of witnesses, Teage reportedly showed no hesitation in picking Bell, in keeping with his trajectory toward greater freedom.[60]

Given the relative freedom black Virginia Christians were accorded in choosing their own denominations, most — including Teage — gravitated toward the Baptist Church, with its message of racial equality before God and "emotional display and terror." By 1790, blacks constituted more than one-third of the Baptists and Methodists in Virginia. Writing of their church services, P. D. Morgan notes, "While trembling, quaking bodies, tears streaming down faces, and dramatic seizures were common to both white and black evangelicals, a more patterned, choreographed response on the part of blacks was noticeable."[61]

Free blacks in Virginia operated several separate black churches that attracted blacks from the large surrounding countryside, in contrast to the plantation missions in the Lower South. These churches allowed for the elaboration of an alternative theology that was less denigrating of blacks. It promised deliverance from bondage, with blacks cast as the Israelites of the Old Testament. This theme was reflected in countless black spirituals, including "Swing Low Sweet Chariot," "Oh Mary Don't You Weep," and "Steal Away." African Americans drew on this refashioned Christianity for moral and ideological support in their political struggles.[62] One such church with a majority of free black members was the Gillfield Church of Petersburg,[63] which had 715 members, several of whom would later emigrate to Liberia. Despite its large concentration of free blacks, Richmond had no separate black church until 1821, when a free black family by the name of Edwards organized the First Baptist Church in the suburb of Manchester.

Black Baptists within the city limits, including the Teage family, attended the racially mixed First Baptist Church. It was headed by the Rev. John Courtney, who published two significant Baptist hymnals. Elected to lead the Richmond congregation in 1788, he convened the first statewide assembly of Baptists within twelve months. One of the actions taken by this assembly was the presentation of an urgent request to the state legislature for the abolition of hereditary slavery. Although his father was an Episcopal clergyman, Courtney was one of three Baptist ministers who petitioned the Virginia Assembly to sell off the properties of the established church that were not in active use. These actions, coupled with the fact that Courtney owned no property and supported himself through his carpentry, made him no friend of the gentry. When he was appointed chaplain to the legislature in 1802, the *Virginia Gazette* dismissed him as "a Baptist haranguer among Negroes."[64]

After years without a meeting place, in 1794 the Baptists moved into a second-floor hall in the new brick market building at Seventeenth and Main Streets, some thirty feet away from "the Cage," which was used for detaining disorderly persons. From 1802, the congregation met in a building between Second and Third Streets at Carey Street, a boulevard lined with the residences of the upper class, including the home of Thomas Henry Prosser, owner of the slave Gabriel, who had organized the 1800 rebellion. The congregation moved to a larger building at H and Fifteenth Streets (now Broad and College) in 1804.[65] This imposing new building stood on a hillside overlooking Shockoe Valley — a district lined with tobacco warehouses and interlaced with the shacks and small businesses of free blacks, and was merely one block east and three blocks north of the saddlery where Colin worked.

It was through the First Baptist Church that Teage became close friends with Lott Cary (1780-1828), with whom he would end up immigrating to Liberia. In 1782, the New Kent County plantation of William A. Christian, where Cary was born held thirty-three slaves. This was large enough to support a separate black community with its own hierarchy, in which Cary would have occupied a prominent place by virtue of being a skilled tobacco worker. While still owned by the Christian family, he was hired out to work in a tobacco factory in Richmond in 1804.[66]

Although his father was noted to be a pious Baptist exhorter, or "plantation preacher," Cary, an only child, is said to have engaged in gambling, drinking and swearing until he was converted and baptized by the Rev. Courtney in 1807. Desiring to read the third chapter of the Gospel of John, which had been the basis for his conversion, Cary learned the alphabet with help from co-workers at the tobacco warehouse. His leisure time came to be filled with reading, and this was accompanied by increased thriftiness and industriousness. Colin Teage, too, learned to read "by chance and piecemeal," but his writing was limited to composing letters

Carl Patrick Burrowes

and his reading was rudimentary in comparison to Cary, who was "in every respect, a better scholar."[67]

The secular and sacred education of the two friends was reinforced through a tri-weekly night school organized at the First Baptist Church in 1815 for about seventeen leading black members, including Teage. This school was conducted primarily by William Crane, a prosperous businessman whose leather store, boarding house and lumber store stood at E and Fifteenth Streets, one block away from Teage's workplace. Crane had moved to Richmond just three years earlier from his native Newark, New Jersey, which was first settled by one of his ancestors. He seems to have drawn a commitment to defending liberties from his father (a soldier in the Revolutionary War), while taking his religious faith from his mother (a founding member of the First Baptist Church of Newark).[68]

Crane found such success in his leather business in Richmond that seven years after his arrival; he was followed by his younger brother James, who served first as a clerk, then as his partner. When James arrived the First Baptist Church was racked by dissension because an aging and ailing Rev. Courtney opposed an effort to organize a Sunday school, which he determined was "a secular organization." On 14 April 1820, the two brothers were among the twenty-six Baptists who organized Richmond's Second Baptist Church. According to James, the new meetinghouse, built according to the plan of their home church in Newark, cost about $6,000, a third to a half of which was contributed by the brothers. Being from New Jersey, the Cranes brought a northern perspective to their Richmond church that was reinforced in 1824 when James married Isabella Steel of Philadelphia. After opening a leather store in Baltimore, Maryland, in 1842, the brothers dissolved their partnership; James became the sole owner of the Richmond shop, with William taking over the newer but already larger operation.[69]

With a newfound literacy attained through the night school operated by William Crane, Cary soon rose to serve as a shipping clerk and supervisor of laborers in Richmond's largest tobacco factory. According to a contemporary, "Notwithstanding the hundreds of hogsheads that were committed to his charge, he could produce any one the instant it was called for, and the shipments were made with a promptness and correctness, such as no person, white or black, has equally in the same situation." In appreciation for Cary's remarkable service, the factory owner is said to have frequently rewarded him with five-dollar payments and allowed him to sell small packets of waste tobacco for his own profit. Meanwhile, Teage had risen to head Bell's saddlery, a significant accomplishment in Virginia, given the presence of white journeymen in the trade. His responsibilities included the purchasing and cutting of materials, as well as the selling of goods and collecting of money.[70]

As noted by Genovese, "The greatest contribution that the practice of allowing slaves to hire themselves out made to the black community must be sought in the strong reinforcement it gave to the thirst for freedom and economic advancement among these mechanics and craftsmen who were its primary beneficiaries." Cary, whose wife had died, was able to purchase himself and two children for $850 in 1813, as a result of his "rigid economy" and a subscription to which his employer contributed. Following manumission, he received a salary that rose to $800 per year, while permitted to trade tobacco on his own, including one transaction of twenty-four hogsheads.[71]

Around this time, a committee of white Baptists sought to buy Colin Teage's freedom so that he could devote himself to preaching, but it found its offer rebuffed by Robert Bell, who was then about seventy years old and heavily dependent on his slave. According to an anonymous eulogist with intimate knowledge of Teage's life, "A few moments afterward Bell left the room apparently much agitated. An hour from that time he returned, handed C. Teage [a deed of manumission] saying, 'do you think I would sell a man who has made me what I am? All I ask of you is to remain with me till I die and all I have shall be yours.'"[72] When Bell died in 1827, his obituary noted, "He has left no family or blood relatives among us, and the handsome competency he has acquired by his industry will go to his relations in Scotland."[73] Teage was already five thousand miles away, having abandoned the saddlery in pursuit of a higher calling.

Sometime before 1815, the First Baptist Church licensed Teage and Cary to preach to blacks in Richmond and on plantations in the surrounding countryside. While Teage was said to possess "judgment" and "keenness of penetration," Cary was described as a powerful preacher, who, "with his magnetic personality, his rugged piety and his persuasive oratory, stood easily the peer in all save the color of his skin, of the notable preachers of his day." Unpolished though Cary's preaching was, "his ideas would sometimes burst upon you in their native solemnity, and awaken deeper feelings than the most polished, but less original."[74]

By 1819, Teage had paid $1,300 to purchase his family of three, which included Colinette, born in 1809. One year later, both he and Cary held property in Henrico County, outside Richmond.[75] The purchase of their families from slavery and their leasing of property, along with their artisan roles and their leadership roles in the local church, placed them at the forefront of free blacks, among whom one could achieve renown by crusading against slavery, acquiring an education, winning his own liberation or buying the freedom of relatives. As Teage and Cary were gaining a precarious perch in black Richmond, however, increased labor competition from recent white immigrants engendered a white backlash against further manumissions and against already freed blacks, now characterized as social problems to be excised. In this context, the laws of evidence were changed so that slaves could testify against free blacks in court cases. In 1814, a poll tax of $1.50 was levied on all free black males, except those serving as apprentices; the failure to pay all taxes and levies also was made punishable by hiring out of the delinquent. As a result of new vagrancy laws, free blacks now found themselves forbidden to move from one county or town to another on penalty of being arrested and imprisoned.[76]

As the legal noose was tightening around free blacks, the idea of colonizing blacks increasingly gained acceptance among influential whites. In 1816, the Virginia House of Delegates adopted a resolution urging the colonization of free people of color. Within a year, the American Colonization Society (ACS) was organized in Washington, D.C., followed quickly by auxiliary organizations throughout eastern Virginia. It was in this context that Teage and Cary opted to become missionaries to Africa. The ACS's Richmond auxiliary formed in 1823 was supported primarily by the same white Baptist tradesmen and merchants who had helped Teage and Cary in their quest for manumission and literacy, with secondary involvement by some Presbyterians, Quakers, and Jews.[77]

The formation of the Richmond African Baptist Missionary Society in 1815 reflected a growing impulse toward missionary activities throughout the United States. Two years earlier, Richmond Baptist women had organized the Female Missionary Society, only the second such group among Baptist women in the South. The major supporters of the African initiative included the Crane brothers, with William serving as the Richmond African Baptist Missionary Society's first president and for at least fifteen years as its secretary, while James was its special delegate to the Triennial Convention in New York City in 1832. Within two years, black Baptists in neighboring Petersburg and as far away as Pennsylvania, North Carolina, and Georgia had followed the society's lead. It raised $700 in its first five years and would raise about $125 annually for many years thereafter.[78]

Cary announced his decision to leave for Africa following William Crane's reading of a report on the first exploratory mission by ACS agents in Sierra Leone, who were seeking land for a colony. Featured in the report was John Kizell, the Baptist leader of the Friendly Society, which had been established by the black entrepreneur and emigrationist Paul Cuffe. In addition, members of the First Baptist Church may have received firsthand reports on Sierra Leone from fellow congregant Jacob Gregg, an Englishman who had served there as a missionary before settling in Richmond. Furthermore, Cary and Teage may have known of black Virginians who had fled with the British following the Revolutionary War, first to Nova Scotia, and then in 1792 to Freetown, Sierra Leone.[79]

In preparation for their departure, Cary and Teage spent the year of 1820 in study, after which they were ordained in the home of William Crane. In January 1821, they organized a church, modeled after the Samson Street Church of Philadelphia, with Cary as pastor. The membership consisted of their wives, fifteen-year-old Hilary, Joseph Langford (age seventy-five), and his wife Susan (age fifty-eight). Later that month, Cary preached his farewell sermon to a packed First Baptist Church, where his transformation from slave to community leader had begun. He closed by saying:

> I feel it my duty to go; and I very much fear that many of those who preach the Gospel in this country, will blush when the Saviour calls them to give an account of their labors in His cause and tell them, "I commanded you to go into all the world, and preach the Gospel to every creature;" (and with the most forcible emphasis) the Saviour may ask where have you been? what have you been doing? have you endeavored to the utmost of your ability to fulfill the commands I gave you, or have you sought your own gratification, and your own ease, regardless of my commands?

A white Presbyterian minister in the audience characterized this sermon as "the best extemporaneous sermon I ever heard. It contained more original and impressive thoughts, some of which are distinct in my memory, and never can be forgotten."[80]

For blacks willing to repatriate in the early 1800s, the ACS provided the means and organization, despite the mixed motives and equivocating stance of its members. This improbable alliance of black repatriates and white deportationists forged a consensus around the goal of promoting Christianity, civilization and commerce in Africa — as distinct from concurrent efforts directed toward Haiti, Canada and the western United States. To describe their mission, supporters of African colonization appropriated the Old Testament phrase "Princes shall come out of Egypt; Ethiopia shall stretch out her hands unto God" (Psalm, 68: 31).

The departure of Cary's party was no doubt motivated by evangelism — as evidenced by its pastor's farewell sermon — but also by republicanism. When a minister asked him why he wanted to leave, Cary reportedly responded, "I am an African, and, in this country, however meritorious my conduct, and respectable my character, I cannot receive the credit due to either. I wish to go to a country where

I shall be estimated by my merits, not by my complexion; and I feel bound to labor for my suffering race." Given the importance of literacy to this project, the Richmond African Baptist Missionary Society appropriated $100 of the $500 it had raised for the purchase of books.[81]

Like a Motherless Child

For blacks in the New World, Africa had long been the focus of deep cultural and spiritual strivings, linked to their forced removal from that continent. One motivation behind the many suicides that occurred during the Middle Passage to the Americas — usually committed by leaping into the pounding Atlantic — was the slaves' belief that death would deliver their souls back to Africa's shores. Writing about the eighteenth-century beliefs of enslaved Africans on the island of Jamaica, one observer noted, "When a Negroe is near about to expire, his fellow-slaves kiss him, wish him a good journey, and send their hearty recommendations to their relations in Guiney. They make no lamentations, but with a great deal of joy inter his body, firmly believing he is gone home and happy."[82]

Identification with Africa further developed in reaction to both the amalgamation of African ethnic cultures in the New World and the privileging of whites in American society, as expressed in existing statutes and constitutions.[83] Blacks born in the Americas would signal their continued identification with the homeland of their ancestors by affixing the word "African" before the names of many separate black organizations, such as the African Methodist Episcopal Bethel Church. Occasionally, they expressed feelings of longings, as in the well-known words of one lamentation:

Sometimes I feel like a motherless child;
Sometimes I feel like a motherless child —
A l-o-n-g w-a-y-y-y from home.

As black culture in the New World became increasingly creolized, dreams of spiritual return were replaced, in the minds of a few, with visions of Africa as a field for Christian conversion and a land of commercial opportunity. By 1770, several young blacks were training to be missionaries to Africa. Their resolve to labor there was probably reinforced by the medical knowledge of the day which held that a racial immunity to tropical diseases made African Americans better fitted for service in the continent that had become known as "the white man's graveyard."[84]

In the nineteenth century, the emigrationist impulse of New World blacks became fixated on Freetown, a colony for the black poor of London established in 1788 on the coast of Sierra Leone in West Africa. Of the several thousand loyalist blacks who had fled to Nova Scotia and other scattered British possessions following the Revolutionary War, more than a thousand found their way to Freetown in 1792. By the end of the century, a group of blacks in Rhode Island had also requested British permission to settle in the colony.[85]

The most significant of these black emigrationist efforts was spearheaded by Paul Cuffe, a Quaker of mixed black and Native American ancestry who had acquired some wealth from trading, fishing and whaling. Combining his religious commitment to service with his penchant for business, Cuffe spent three years developing a plan that would resettle African American volunteers at Freetown to both evangelize the Africans and develop two-way trade with blacks in the United States. In 1811, he transported thirty-eight volunteers from New England to West Africa on one of his vessels and settled them at Freetown at his own expense. The outbreak of war between Britain and the United States the following year halted his plan for routine trading ventures and annual resettlements. Cuffe died in 1817 before these efforts could be resumed, but his venture had fired the imagination of many in the United States, including Colin Teage and Cary, and garnered support from important leaders of the free black community. One was the Rev. Peter Williams of New York, who would figure in the later emigration of several of his Episcopalian parishioners to Liberia, including black press pioneer John B. Russwurm, and Alexander Crummell, a Cambridge-educated African American priest. Another was the Rev. Daniel Coker whose 1810 pamphlet condemning slavery and demanding universal emancipation, *A Dialogue Between a Virginian and an African Minister*, had attracted wide attention. Coker served as informal leader of the first group of colonists sent to Freetown aboard the *Elizabeth* by the ACS in 1820.[86]

By 1820, black identification with Africa had evolved into a pan-Negro ideology that has been variously labeled Ethiopianism, pan-Africanism and black nationalism.[87] This doctrine held that blacks had a glorious past and that their common political problems would be solved through the liberation of Africa from slavery. It was present in the lead article of *Freedom's Journal*, the first African-American newspaper, which promised in 1827, "Useful knowledge of every kind, and everything that relates to Africa, shall find a ready admission into our columns; and as that vast continent becomes daily more known, we trust that many things will come to light, proving that the natives of it are neither so ignorant nor stupid as they have generally been supposed to be."[88] Along with the evangelical and other motivations that propelled the émigrés, this privileging of Africa in the worldview of blacks contributed to their selection of the area that became Liberia — over such alternative sites as Canada and Haiti.

Among whites, efforts at colonizing blacks in Africa had a long, sometimes intertwining history but were often rooted in divergent motives. One of the earliest colonization plans in Virginia emerged in 1776 from a legislative committee assigned to codify the state's laws. This body, which included Thomas Jefferson, appended to its report a set of principles that it recommended should govern future manumissions. Jefferson incorporated the committee's recommendation into his *Notes on the State of Virginia*, which gave wide circulation to what was essentially a scheme for the deportation of enslaved blacks *en masse.*[89]

Jefferson called for black children to be separated from their parents at "a certain age" to be reared by the state until the age of majority, when they would be expelled. He prefaced his scheme with the charge that black men favored white women "as uniformly as is the preference of the Oranootan for the black woman over those of his own species." Ignoring the control exercised by slave owners over the sentiments of their bondmen, he noted, "Love seems with them to be more an eager desire, than a tender delicate mixture of sentiment and sensation. Their griefs are transient."[90] Jefferson justified racial separation by noting,

Deep rooted prejudices entertained by the whites; ten thousand recollections, by the blacks, of the injuries they have sustained; new provocations; the real distinctions which nature has made; and many other circumstances, will divide us into parties, and produce convulsions which will probably never end but in the extermination of the one or the other race. To these objections, which are political, may be added others, which are physical and moral. The first difference which strikes us is that of colour. Whether the black of the negro resides in the reticular membrane between the skin and scarf-skin, or in the scarf-skin itself; whether it proceeds from the colour of the blood, the colour of the bile, or from that of some other secretion, the difference is fixed in nature, and is as real as if its seat and cause were better known to us .... Besides those of colour, figure, and hair, there are other physical distinctions proving a difference of race. They have less hair on the face and body. They secrete less by the kidnies, and more by the glands of the skin, which gives them a very strong and disagreeable odour.[91]

Although *Notes on Virginia* did not specify Africa as the point of colonization and failed to produce any immediate results, it did serve to inspire many subsequent efforts in that direction.

In 1790, fellow Virginian Ferdinando Fairfax called for the resettlement of free blacks and future manumitted slaves in an independent nation in Africa, with support and defense to be provided by Congress. Following the failure of Gabriel's rebellion in 1800, Jefferson — in his capacity as U. S. president and at the urging of the Virginia legislature — initiated secret negotiations to have those blacks deemed conspirators and criminals deported to Sierra Leone. However, the British authorities in that territory balked the prospect of receiving potentially troublesome African Americans.[92]

These scattered efforts toward black colonization would receive new and decisive impetus in early 1816 with the discovery by Virginia congressman Charles Fenton Mercer of Jefferson's previously secret correspondence. While traveling to Washington, D. C., Baltimore, Philadelphia and New York that year, Mercer is said to have canvassed members of his wide-ranging and influential political circle, seeking support for the deportation of free blacks. Upon returning to Virginia, he introduced a resolution to the legislature on 14 December requesting that the federal government obtain land in Africa for the resettlement of free blacks; it was discussed in secret and approved by a vote of 137 to 9. Another outgrowth of Mercer's visits to the North was the formation eight days later in Washington, D. C., of the ACS, which was committed to the same end.[93]

With Supreme Court Justice Bushrod Washington serving as titular president, some of the capital's most influential and powerful men soon enlisted in the ACS, such as Francis Scott Key, composer of the national anthem, and Henry Clay, Speaker of the House. Less illustrious although no less significant members included early colonizationists Ferdinando Fairfax and William Thornton, architect of the U. S. Capitol. Another member, the Rev. Robert Finley of Princeton, New Jersey, initiated a persistent correspondence that eventually won support for the ACS from the venerable Paul Cuffe.[94]

The various strains that the ACS unevenly and uneasily encompassed gave it a decidedly curious character. During the ACS's first decade, when the colonizationist cause was practically indistinguishable from abolitionism, its supporters included William Lloyd Garrison, who would later prove to be its most intractable and formidable white enemy. Some of its members, no doubt animated by a paternalistic benevolence toward those they regarded as less fortunate, also worked with the American Bible Society, the American Temperance Union, and other ameliorative organizations founded during this period. But as public debates over slavery and states rights became increasingly polarized in the 1830s, the ACS leadership's continued attempts to hold to the middle ground became as untenable as parallel congressional efforts at compromise, led notably by colonizationists such as Henry Clay.[95]

As colonization came to be championed by powerful southern whites, public support for the cause declined proportionately among free blacks, especially those in northern cities. One of the earliest and most dramatic signs that black public opinion had turned against colonization emerged at a mass meeting called in January 1817 at the A. M. E. Bethel Church in Philadelphia to consider a proposal for an African colony drafted by the newly formed ACS. Although sailmaker James Forten and the other black leaders who convened the assembly had supported Paul Cuffe's efforts and were receptive to the ACS's project, the three thousand free men in attendance unanimously rejected the proposal, precipitating a string of similar public rebuffs by free blacks in other cities.[96]

By the early 1830s, abolitionists had largely abandoned their earlier interest in colonization in favor of immediate emancipation. In the process, the ACS and its centrist course increasingly attracted those whites seeking the removal of free blacks whom they viewed with a mixture of loathing, pity and contempt. In a memorial to Congress, the Kentucky Colonization Society labeled free blacks "a mildew upon our fields, a scourge to our backs, and a stain upon our escutcheon." Henry Clay claimed that they "contaminated themselves" and spread "their vices all around them." For Charles Fenton Mercer, they were a "horde of miserable people — the objects of universal suspicion — subsisting by plunder." But, as argued persuasively by historian George M. Frederickson, colonizationists traced the "defects" of blacks, not to genetics, but to the social environment, including their own deeply held prejudices. Unlike abolitionists, however, they viewed this environment as immutable.[97]

It was under the auspices of the ACS that a group of twenty-eight repatriates — including the Teage, Cary, and Langford families — sailed for Sierra Leone aboard the *Nautilus* on 23 January 1821. This venture was an uneasy marriage of two visions of African colonization: one white, the other black. In the retelling of the colonization story, the role of men such as Teage and Cary — free, black and literate — has often been effaced, yet it was precisely these persons who would create the African colony. If powerful whites provided the material and ideological means to make colonization possible, repatriates and indigenous blacks would provide even more — their lives. If the ACS sought to set rules for the colony from its offices in Washington, D.C., it was left to individuals such as Teage and Cary to interpret them. Between 1822 and 1867, the survivors of the *Elizabeth* and *Nautilus* would be joined by fourteen thousand African Americans sponsored by the ACS,[98] along with thousands of blacks who would find their way to Liberia from the United States, the Caribbean, and various parts of Africa.

When the *Nautilus* arrived in Sierra Leone, slave ships were operating within a few miles of Freetown, despite control of that port by British authorities. Even those repatriates who returned with the hope of helping restore Africa to her "previous glory" were no less aware that the land of their fathers was now degraded by "superstitions" and their race "benighted" — conditions they blamed primarily on the nefarious slave trade. Alarmed by the high mortality rate, which quickly claimed Cary's wife, Nancy, and Joseph Langford, and hindered by failed negotiations for land near Sierra Leone, this group — joined by the remnants of the first party of emigrants — eventually moved southeast. On 28 April 1822, they settled at Cape Mesurado, the site of what would become the seaport of Monrovia.

Wanderers from Samaria

It is of symbolic significance that the *Nautilus* group was led by a man called Lott, whose name was derived from the Old Testament man of God who led his family out of Sodom. Indeed, the leadership qualities that Lott Cary and Colin Teage had displayed in Richmond would help them flourish in Africa. When tension erupted between the white ACS agent Jehudi Ashmun and repatriates at Sierra Leone in 1821, the colonists, led by Cary and Teage, renounced any control by Ashmun, whom they accused of hoarding provisions. Receiving support from the Baptist Board of Foreign Missions, as well as the Richmond African Baptist Missionary Society, the two friends were able to maintain relative autonomy from the ACS while depending on the colonial infrastructure for protection. This early manifestation of black assertion fizzled, however, when Ashmun refused to negotiate with the group. After the repatriates moved from Sierra Leone to what is now known as Liberia in 1822, the agent unilaterally reassigned land on which some repatriates had built homes. He also imposed a requirement of two days of public labor per week for each able adult and threatened to cut off supplies to those who did not work. The colonists rebelled, forcing Ashmun to abandon his post from

April to August 1824, leaving a repatriate, Elijah Johnson, in charge. In response, the ACS created an advisory council that moderated the agent's power and allowed input from the colonists.[99]

With no opportunities to earn income from their saddle-making and tobacco-curing skills (given a paucity of horses and locally grown tobacco in Liberia), Teage and Cary turned to trading to support their families. This switch was made easier by their managerial experiences and exposure to the workings of the commercial system in the businesses where they were previously employed. Cary's involvement in trading is all the more significant because shortly after learning to read he was found reading *The Wealth of Nations*, a major pillar of *laissez-faire* economic thought.[100]

In coming to Africa, the colonists, especially free blacks from the Upper South, were motivated in part by the desire to own private property. At the core of Liberian political thought was a belief in small privately owned property as source of both wealth and virtue — a belief that resulted primarily from the colonists' exposure to republicanism in America. As one repatriate would boast when explaining the liberties enjoyed in Liberia to U. S. blacks, "We are proprietors of the soil we live on, and possess the rights of freeholders." In this context, property held practical and symbolic value, serving as a measure of the worth that blacks had been denied in the United States and as a measure of good citizenship. For blacks in the American South, especially those with the dubious status of what historian Ira Berlin aptly called "slaves without masters," colonization offered longed-for freedoms. Reflecting the tortured choices many faced, one prospective emigrant noted that he would love both the United States and its liberties "if only we could share in them; but our freedom is partial, and we have no hope that it ever will be otherwise here; therefore we had rather be gone, though we should suffer hunger and nakedness for years." Writing from Virginia in 1848, Peter Butler informed the ACS that "I wish to Goy to Liberia So as I may ... ingoy the Right of man. I have tride a great meny placeis in these united state and I find that none of them is the home for the Culerd man and So I ... wish to be and Emigrant for the land of man auntsestors."[101]

In letters sent to friends, relatives and even former masters in the United States, repatriates reflected time and again on their newfound liberties.[102] Writing to his former master in 1842, Washington W. McDonogh perhaps expressed this best: "I will never consent to leave this country... for this is the only place where a colored person can enjoy his liberty, for there exists no prejudice of color in this country, but every man is free and equal."[103] That Liberia embodied blacks' quest for liberty was often muted in the propaganda of their white allies, mindful as they were of upsetting powerful slaveholding interests, and was often ignored by abolitionists, who dismissed emigrants as ignorant or selfish beings motivated by the handouts of the ACS.

Around the time of the rebellion against Ashmun, the Teage family returned to Sierra Leone. Colin's leather-working skills proved so profitable there that he reportedly was inclined to remain. However, following the death of Cary in a gunpowder explosion, he returned with his family to Liberia in 1826 to assume the leadership of the Baptist flock, which had been joined by Colston Waring and Joseph Shepherd, two of the six well-to-do trustees of the Gillfield Church of Petersburg. When the ACS decided in 1838 to revise its plan of government to accommodate the colony's expansion in population and territory, the repatriates elected a committee to draft a new constitution; it included Colin and Hilary Teage. The resulting "Monrovia Draft" limited citizenship to people of color, invested final political authority in the colonists rather than the ACS, and called for the non-involvement of the governor in the judiciary. However, by the time the "Monrovia Draft" arrived in the United States, the ACS had already issued its 1839 Revised Plan of Government. Under this plan, the governor continued as chief justice, but he now had to share legislative powers with elected representatives of the repatriates. [104]

Colin would not get to watch Hilary's spectacular social and political ascent, for he died aboard a ship while returning from Richmond in 1839. However, the man known as "Fox" had succeeded, through strenuous exertions, in securing the freedom of his family and the education of his children. From Colin's example, his son had acquired self-confidence and a commitment to self-government, reinforcing the black nationalism and republicanism that became the hallmarks of his thinking. Teage is credited with introducing in 1838 the idea of a commonwealth government to encompass the then-autonomous colonies of Montserrado, Bassa, and Sinoe. In 1843, he published the Constitution and statutes of the commonwealth in two volumes. One year later, he published a historical sketch of the Liberian colony in which he criticized European control over Sierra Leone and called for black self-government in Liberia. He would continue to argue the merits of independence for the colony as editor of the *Liberia Herald*. When a forum for public education, the Liberia Lyceum, was organized in 1845, Teage was elected its first president, confirming his peers' high regard for his intellectual abilities. He was elected colonial secretary (1835), member of the Colonial Council (1840), commissioner for Montserrado County (1840), delegate to the Constitutional Convention (1847), and senator from Montserrado County (1848). He served as attorney general (1850-52) and secretary of state (1852-1853), with a stint in May 1852 as acting chief executive, along with A. D. Williams, while President Joseph Jenkins Roberts was abroad. [105]

Carl Patrick Burrowes

In urging repatriates toward self-government, Teage reasoned, "Like the wanderers from Samaria, we shall find it certain death to remain here or to return to the city. Hope can be indulged only in going forward" (doc. 97). Speaking one year before the colony severed its ties to the ACS, he thundered:

> Raise your standard! assert your independence!! throw out your banners to the wind!! And will the descendants of the mighty Pharaohs, that awed the world — Will the sons of him who drove back the serried legions of Rome and laid siege to the "eternal city" —

> Will they, the achievements of whose fathers are yet the wonder and admiration of the world — Will they refuse the proffered boon, and basely cling to the chains of slavery and dependence? Never! never!! never!!!

Then, evoking the ancestors — a frequent theme in the speeches of early Liberian leaders — he added, "Shades of the mighty dead! — spirits of departed great ones! inspire us, animate us to the task — nerve us for the battle! Pour into our bosom a portion of that ardour and patriotism which bore you on to battle, to victory, and to conquest" (doc. 98).[106]

Teage's rapid ascent into the political class was aided by his social origins among Virginia artisans, a milieu that was geographically and sociologically central to the repatriate community. According to Ira Berlin, "Three major groups of free Negroes existed in the United States: a Northern caste, an Upper South caste, and a Lower South caste. Each had its own distinctive demographic, economic, social and even somatic characteristics. These differences bred distinctive relations with whites and slaves and, most importantly, distinctive systems of values and modes of social action."[107] Among those who had been enslaved, geographic loyalties were even more narrowly defined, for, as noted by historian John W. Blassingame, "nativity was one of the keys to status in the quarters. Every slave thought that work was lighter, masters kinder, and life better for blacks in his state than in any other." In the politics of Liberia, free blacks from the Upper South initially enjoyed distinct advantages over free blacks from other regions of the United States. Between 1820 and 1842, for example, Maryland and Virginia contributed 46 percent of the immigrants from the United States. Virginia alone accounted for 36 percent of all immigrants, far more than any other state (table 1). Of those who settled in Maryland County in Liberia, roughly 87 percent were from the State of Maryland and 10 percent from Georgia, with a smattering from Virginia and Tennessee.

Beyond the mere numbers lay the friendship and family networks that kept culture and extended families relatively intact during immigration.[108]

The political ascendancy of free blacks from the Upper South was facilitated by their previous relative political closeness to slaves. As noted by Berlin, "Poor free Negroes and slaves worked together in the same shops and factories, prayed together in the same churches, and rubbed elbows in the same back-alley retreats. Many intermarried, dissolving still further differences in status and sealing bonds of racial unity." In contrast, Berlin concluded, free blacks in the Lower South demonstrated little interest in enslaved blacks, "except perhaps as property." When allowed, they joined white Catholic or Episcopal congregations instead of the Baptist and Methodist churches where most slaves and poor free blacks worshipped.[109] Probably stemming in part from their identification with white interests, few free blacks from the Lower South emigrated to Liberia, leaving those who did — most of whom had recently been emancipated — to forge an initial alliance with free blacks from the North.

Just as white slave holders from the Chesapeake occupied a disproportional hold on high national offices in the United States, nine of the ten repatriates who acted as ACS agents in Liberia were from the Upper South. Even the tenth black agent, Elijah Johnson, might have been from the region, since he is said to have come from either New York or Maryland. Important in explaining the political dominance of people from the Chesapeake is the role played by Virginians and, to a lesser extent, Marylanders in the formative stages of the colony. This gave them a sense of self-awareness and priority, as reflected in the split noted by John B. Russwurm in 1833 between these older settlers, who were "a little lifted up with the success which has crowned their efforts," and new immigrants, with their unrealistic expectations of immediate success and acceptance. The dominance of persons from the Chesapeake would continue in the executive branch after independence was declared; the four presidents who served from 1848 to 1870 and their seven vice presidents all came from that region. With the exception of the Maryland-born Stephen A. Benson and Daniel B. Warner, all of the others were born in Virginia. As late as 1878, a visiting journalist would report that control of politics remained "in the hands of a class, consisting of the older settlers and their descendants," most of whom hailed from Virginia.[110]

Teage's ascent was also aided by the absence of an institutional basis for distinctions based on complexion and previous legal status. Of the twelve delegates to the Constitutional Convention in 1847, for example, three were former slaves,

Carl Patrick Burrowes

Table 1. *Emigrants by State of Origin, 1820 to 1885*

MAJOR STATES	1820-29	1830-39	1840-49	1850-59	1860-69	1870-79	1880-85	TOTAL
Georgia	27	179	191	664	853	250	1	2,165
Kentucky	0	99	137	422	17	3	0	678
Maryland	181	234	0	139	27	2	0	583
Mississippi	0	158	347	31	57	16	3	612
North Carolina	344	355	69	586	140	390	106	1,990
South Carolina	0	182	126	126	629	195	0	1,258
Tennessee	15	40	139	524	239	35	1	993
Virginia	432	1,112	596	1,369	219	6	1	3,735
TOTAL	999	2,359	1,605	3,861	2,181	897	112	12,014
OTHERS	163	188	288	819	352	91	296	2543
Alabama	0	2	44	59	51	0	27	183
Arkansas	0	0	0	0	0	20	125	145
Connecticut	0	6	1	39	9	2	0	57
Delaware	4	0	0	1	4	0	0	9
Florida	0	0	0	0	0	17	6	23
Illinois	2	1	23	12	27	0	7	72
Indian Territory	0	0	0	9	0	0	0	9
Indiana	0	0	5	79	2	0	0	86
Iowa	0	0	3	0	2	0	0	5
Kansas	0	0	0	0	0	0	38	38
Louisiana	0	51	119	139	0	7	0	316
Massachusetts	0	0	0	54	9	19	1	83
Michigan	0	0	1	0	0	0	0	1
Missouri	0	1	20	62	0	0	17	100
Nebraska	0	0	0	0	0	0	17	17
New Jersey	0	0	1	34	42	0	0	77
New York	54	21	18	164	49	4	2	312
Ohio	0	41	3	11	1	0	0	56
Pennsylvania	65	13	13	127	142	7	7	374
Rhode Island	32	0	0	4	0	0	0	36
Texas	0	0	0	16	1	12	49	78
Washington, D.C.	6	52	37	9	6	3	0	113
Wisconsin	0	0	0	0	7	0	0	7
BARBADOS	0	0	0	0	346	0	0	346
TOTAL	1,162	2,547	1,893	4,680	2,879	988	408	14,557

including Teage and the man selected to serve as president of the convention. Similarly, three of Liberia's first five presidents were dark-skinned in contrast to the United States, where the vast majority of African-American leaders of national stature were light skinned.[111]

Teage would follow his father into the Baptist pulpit, beginning in October 1835, when he was ordained as pastor of the newly organized church at Millsburg. Within five years, he was ministering to a congregation in Monrovia.[112] Had Teage remained in the United States, he could have aspired, at best, to become an exhorter or a saddle maker like his father, given the patrilineal transmission of artisan skills in slave communities. In Liberia, his reach would exceed Colin's wildest grasp, as he rose to serve as senator and attorney general, eventually returning as Liberia's secretary of state to the land where he had once been held in bondage.

Rising in the Scale of Being

Several features of Monrovia must have reminded Teage of Richmond. The seaport was named for James Monroe, who provided crucial support to the ACS while serving as U. S. president. He had been converted to the colonization cause by his experience as the governor of Virginia during Gabriel's rebellion of 1800. As in the city where Teage spent much of his childhood, Monrovia was divided through the center by a similarly named Broad Street (map 5). Located at the corner of Broad and Center Streets was the Providence Baptist Church, which the Teage and Cary families had founded in Richmond for transference to Africa. Erected in 1827, the church is the oldest permanent building in Liberia and the oldest Baptist church in Africa in continuous existence. From the church, it was one block to Teage's office at Broad and Gurley Streets, and another half block to his home at Gurley and Front Streets. Two blocks east of the church on Broad Street was the House of Representatives, which housed the *Liberia Herald* from 1830 to 1839, while it was owned by ACS, and to which Teage would return as Montserrado County senator from 1848 to 1849.[113]

Following Teage's purchase of the *Herald* in 1839, it was operated out of his warehouse at the landing station on the west side of Center Street near Water Street. In an editorial laced with some exaggeration, he described the office as:

a little sooty apartment of six by eight. Beneath [the editor's] dingy foolscap a portion of deal lies supinely on an empty barrel. A few odd and ends of books and newspapers lie in hopeless confusion around. At his side an inkstand — not of china — nor of bronze, but the small end of a cow's horn, on his left a quiver of quills rifled from the upper surface of a porcupine.

In one corner stands a billet of cam-wood, its opposite is occupied by what once contained four. The walls are duly chalked, not with mechanical design, nor geometrical diagrams — but with mathematical mementoes of the kroos[114] of potatoes of which he has relieved the farmer. This is his blotter[;] ledger, he keeps none. (doc. 22)

The location of his warehouse provided Teage with a direct view of the Mesurado River, which ran along the north side of the city and served as a major artery of trade with interior polities and overseas suppliers. This river was also the site of many deep-immersion baptisms preferred by immigrants from the American South. Over this town of some 912 persons, and over the larger commonwealth of 2,390 Liberians,[115] Teage would cast a long shadow, as an intellectual, merchant, Baptist pastor, and public official.

In addition to the boost provided by his father and his family's place in the social structure of black immigrants, there can be no doubt that Teage brought to his various roles intellectual powers that had been circumscribed by his previous social setting. Two years before leaving for Africa, Hilary, then age fourteen, and his sister Colinette, then twelve, were described as having "been to school considerably." During the early nineteenth century, the curriculum of private schools in Richmond purportedly included Latin, Greek, mathematics, history, geography, and natural philosophy — all of which Teage showed some familiarity with. The Teage children's education was organized in part by William Crane, the fellow Baptist who coordinated a night school for them, their father and other black adults,[116] at a time when schooling for blacks was frowned upon in Virginia. There were no public schools, even for whites, until after the Civil War.

In Liberia, Teage would undergo the same profound self-transformation noted by another Liberian leader in a surprisingly candid letter published in the United States in 1854:

Map 5. Monrovia, with significant sites labeled

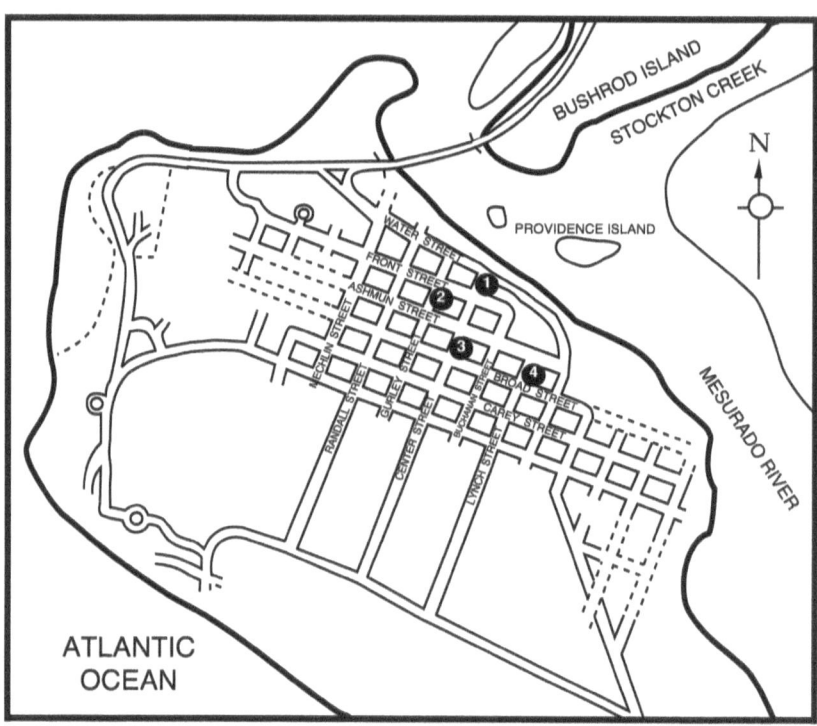

1. HILARY TEAGE'S STORE
2. COLIN TEAGE'S HOME
3. PROVIDENCE BAPTIST CHURCH
4. HOUSE OF REPRESENTATIVES

I know by experience the depressing influence of the white man. Such was its effect on me, that I failed to improve my mind as I might have done, if the slightest hope of future usefulness could have been indulged. But every high and noble aspiration appeared to me, in that country, consummate folly, and I was thus induced to be satisfied in ignorance, there being no prospect of rising in the scale of being. But how altered is my condition in this country? Here honors of which I never dreamed have been conferred on me by my fellow-citizens, and I have been treated as an equal by gentlemen from the United States.[117]

Having inherited his father's trading business in 1839, Teage served that year as a consignment agent for John Dean Lake and other traders based in Sierra Leone, where he had lived from 1821 to 1826. By 1841, he was an agent for Captain Jackson, a British trader, and one year later was representing Hatton and Cookson of Liverpool. Between 1827 and 1853, he owned at least eight vessels engaged in the West African coasting trade, including one vessel jointly owned by fellow Baptist pastor Abraham Cheeseman. By 1843, he also owned five buildings in Monrovia, was earning an annual commission of $7,000, and had five warehouses along the coast worth $30,000 with about $20,000 in trade stock. Two years later, he owned one factory at Little Bassa. With several other investors, he began a soap manufactory in November 1848, which he hoped would produce soap at a lower price, reduce the foreign currency drain and make a profit.[118]

In 1839, Teage acquired the *Herald* from the ACS, possibly in exchange for unpaid credit he had granted the Society. Shortly thereafter, the editor of the rival *Luminary* remarked, "We speak advisedly when we say that the editor, who is also publisher and proprietor [of the *Liberia Herald*], is making new and judicious effort to improve it in every respect." Stemming perhaps from his avid reading, Teage demonstrated a keen understanding of the journalistic standards of his day. In an appeal to his patrons for support, he noted differences between the news environment of Liberia and that of more industrialized countries, lamenting that his paper did not have "the privilege of arraigning and abusing public men and measures." This "privilege" was not possible in Liberia, he claimed, "not perhaps from a virtuous disposition in us, or that we write with a pen less wayward than others, that we do not make occasional drafts on this fruitful source, but rather because our men and measures are known within a circle so circumscribed that anything we could say with respect to them, would be uninteresting to our distant readers." Also absent in Liberia were those "striking events" that would serve to "vary and enliven the dull and monotonous narration of ordinary life. No mobs affording columns of matter in accounts of heads broke, — houses rifled, — magistrates resisted, — laws defied, or any other of those brilliant events which generally mark the reign of mobocracy. To this degree of "refinement," he added with no small measure of sarcasm and forecast, "the citizens of Liberia have not as yet arrived; it is left, therefore, to some more fortunate Editor to describe them, when futurity shall bring them forth."[119]

Long after the *Herald* had passed into Liberian ownership, its distribution in the United States remained intertwined with the organizational apparatus of the ACS. In a note to readers in which he acknowledged receipt of a box of type from the Rev. William McLain of Washington, D.C., for example, Teage pointed out:

> The proprietors of the *Herald*, derive but a pittance from the publication of the paper, not enough to pay one fourth of the printer's bill: — nevertheless, they have continued the paper, depending for encouragement upon the friends abroad. The office is now several hundred dollars in debt, and unless we receive help from our foreign friends, we must stop the publication of the paper. ... We are in want of paper, type, &c., &c. Tho the supply we received by the *Packet* was very opportune, it will only go a short distance towards filling our sheet.[120]

As late as 27 August 1852, the paper's printer, James C. Minor, wrote to the ACS agent in the United States, forcefully requesting paper and ink. Responding to a suggestion that lye be used to clean the type, he noted, "That is all very good, but when the hair strokes of the type are worn out, I cannot see how in the name of peace they can make a good impression. We want new type."[121]

By September 1845, business interest in the *Herald* had been acquired by "a company of gentlemen" in Monrovia, though Teage remained editor (doc. 20). One year later, a *Herald* contributor using the pseudonym "Liberia" referred to the Liberia Lyceum as the owner of the paper, but Teage immediately rebutted this claim. It is interesting to note, however, that several members of the paper staff, including Teage, Adam Anderson, John N. Lewis and Dessalines T. Harris, had served in the leadership of the Lyceum at some point.[122] In the first in a series of letters, "Liberia" urged "intelligent members" of the Liberia Lyceum — particularly farmers, mechanics, merchants, ministers, doctors and lawyers — to submit "matter in their various practical pursuits, and observations to both enlighten and engage." To ensure that these contributions would benefit many people as possible, "Liberia" suggested that subscribers read the paper aloud to those who could not read as was being done with religious tracts. Noting that Monrovia, Edina and Bassa Cove seemed to be "awake to self improvement," "Liberia" promised to enter one subscription each for six other towns, and urged nine other readers to do likewise, "for the public good."[123]

Long-standing ties between the *Herald* and the Lyceum may have prompted "D. T. H." in 1850 to ask in frustration,

> Where are those whose proud names were "Liberia Lyceum" and "Young Men's Lyceum." Are they numbered with the things that were? Have they become scraps of history or are they drowned in the sea of forgetfulness? ... "The Liberia Lyceum" has been identified with the history of the country for years; she was a wonderful auxiliary... in bringing about the change in our political affairs, by bringing the subject before the community, and discussing and deciding upon it affirmatively. Then, we ask, are you satisfied with what you have done, and determined that you will do no more?[124]

As Teage poured his energies into the campaign for Liberia's independence, his commercial fortunes declined, due in part to his debtors who didn't pay, including the ACS. An announcement dated 19 November 1846 appeared in the *Herald* on 14 December 1846, declaring Teage an insolvent debtor and urging all persons owing him money to pay it to Dixon B. Brown, listed as trustee for the creditors. The decline of Teage's fortunes may also have stemmed from his investment in ships, which were particularly profitable — and risky. By 1851, his financial situation seems to have taken a turn for the better, for he then co-owned the *Providence* with William A. Johnson, his nephew. One year later, he co-owned the *Temperance* with Johnson and George H. Shaw, his former ward, and sold a quarter acre of land in Monrovia to James S. Smith.[125]

In November 1848, Teage began a law practice in Montserrado and Bassa Counties, which he announced in the *Herald*: "He [Teage] does not set up as lawyer to plead indiscriminately in all cases, regardless of right and justice, but rather to aid in protecting innocence and in rescuing weakness from the grasp of strength. The subscriber flatters himself that from the attention his former position compelled him to give to law he is not the least prepared of all the advice-givers in the republic to manage and conduct such matters." Also during that period, Teage turned his attention to farming, reporting by way of an apology for a delay in publishing:

Here we are, at it again! We have not honored ourself with attention to the paper for the last three months. Circumstances of a most imperative character demanded that we should rusticate; and the decrees of no chancellor are so stern and irresistible as those of poverty. Hence, instead of indicting editorials and collecting extracts, we have been planting potatoes and collecting pepper. Our readers, however, need not start for we shall not treat them with an undue infusion of *capsicum* at present; and our potatoes are yet in a state of embryo. (doc. 21)[126]

Despite Teage's activist role during a time of significant social change, his was nonetheless the lonely pursuit of an intellectual, as described in his poem "Bread from Brain:"

> In that chamber lone and drear,
>   Sits a poet writing flowers
> Bringing Heaven to earth more near
>   Raining thoughts in dewy showers
> Where he sings of nectar rare,
> Only is the ink bowl there.
> Of feasts of gods he chants — high trust
> As he eats his mouldy crust.
>   Hard the labor!, small the gain,
>   Is in making bread from brain. (doc. 92)

Teage's spectacular public life notwithstanding, nineteenth-century standards of privacy and decorum served to obscure his private life. Little is known except that in the 1843 colonial census, he was listed as married to Eliza M., age 30, who had left the United States in March 1820. According to the census, their household contained seven other persons: George H. Shaw, (12), Sally Ellis (17), Walter Scott (14), Eveline Davenport (10), Eliza Demery (22), William Cary (14), and Levy D. James (17). All were born in Liberia, except Eliza Demery, who had arrived with her family in 1826. Several were orphans, relatives or children of family friends. Although William's father, Jonas, was living elsewhere in the colony, the boy was apprenticed to Teage as a printer with the *Herald*, as was Levy. Walter, Eveline, and Eliza were also listed as apprentices, but their respective fields were not given. George was the only person listed as "at school." Apparently, the man most often

Carl Patrick Burrowes

credited by his contemporaries with having fathered the republic had no offspring.[127]

Profound Knowledge: Ideas for Building a Nation

During the era under consideration, a common justification for the enslavement of Africans was that they were "uncivilized," meaning that they lacked both formal Western education and the saving balm of Christianity. Yet, in the United States at least, black access to secular education was thoroughly discouraged and conversion to Christianity did not ensure emancipation.[128] Many repatriates, reacting to the double standard of their former society, sought to make Liberia a proving ground for African humanity; here the standard of "civilization" would be unquestioningly promoted while restrictions to its fulfillment would be minimized.

A few repatriates had received formal schooling from private, segregated institutions for blacks, called African free schools, which had operated in northern cities since 1785. By 1849, it was estimated that 45 percent of free black children in the fifteen largest American cities were attending school. Most literate colonists, especially former southern slaves, probably learned what they did from individual tutors in informal settings. Some went on by their own exertions to acquire a liberal education of surprising depth while in the United States. Such persons included Harrison Ellis, who studied theology and learned Greek, Latin, and Hebrew while a slave in Alabama.[129]

For others, education would only begin after their arrival in Liberia, through various lyceums and other informal forms of schooling. This was certainly the case with one religious and political leader, who wrote,

> In America, we had nothing to incite us to proper application of mind, nothing to aspire to. We read superficially, we knew superficially many things known to our white neighbors... In Liberia we found ourselves an embryo nation, but incapable of filling many of the various important stations requiring real knowledge. Superficiality would not do. We applied ourselves to study closely and intensely and acquired in many instances, profound knowledge, that sort which gives power. Many who have thus made themselves are superior men.[130]

Given the importance assigned to literacy, Liberia would provide a fertile environment for intellectual ferment. This was evident in the number of newspapers — eighteen from 1830 to 1899[131] — and the creation in 1857 of Liberia College, one of the first institutions of higher education for blacks anywhere. However, differences over the appropriate place of blacks in civilization would affect the conceptualization of the appropriate level and form of education for repatriates, polarizing into primary and vocational schooling on the one hand and liberal higher education on the other.

Among those who claimed Liberia as their home were some of the best-known and most influential black intellectuals of that era. They included John B. Russwurm, the second black person to earn a master's degree in the United States and co-founder of the first African-American newspaper; Alexander Crummell, a Cambridge University-educated Episcopalian clergy; and Edward Wilmot Blyden, who authored hundreds of essays and countless letters to a large and influential circle of correspondents in Africa, England and the United States. After it declared independence in 1847, the country was also visited for periods of varying duration by Martin Delany, the "father of black nationalism," who was well known for his opposition to the efforts of the ACS but praised Liberian leaders while in Monrovia; Thomas M. Chester, a Civil War correspondent and Reconstruction politician; and Henry Highland Garnet, a militant abolitionist and high school classmate of Crummell who died in Liberia in 1882, while serving as U. S. resident minister.[132] The presence of so many leading black intellectuals, coupled with the centrality of Liberia and Haiti to international debates over the appropriate political course for blacks, made this community an ideological cauldron.

From 1830 to 1850 — the crucial period in which Liberia moved from colony to republic — Teage was undoubtedly the intellectual with the greatest influence over the course of local events. He was called "remarkable for his abilities, his acquisitions and his influence," "one of the ablest and best-read men in Liberia," and one of Liberia's "brightest and most cultivated intellects." Blyden, who would come to be better known, described him as having "genius." In addition to serving as an intellectual in a functional capacity by virtue of being an editor and pastor, Teage was an "organic intellectual," a phrase used to describe the thinking and organizing element of a particular social group. More than a mere eloquent mover of feelings on a momentary basis, he was the kind of intellectual sociologist Antonio Gramsci described as a "permanent persuader."[133]

True to the temper of the times, his writing reflected the impact of two dominant intellectual orientations. On the one hand, his social perspective was anchored by eighteenth-century liberal republicanism, with its emphasis on

Carl Patrick Burrowes

empirical analysis, free enterprise economics, and limited government, while on the other hand, his aesthetic was rooted in romanticism, the leading Western literary trend from about 1789 to 1839. The writers of the Romantic Period are said to have devoted their attention to "exploring every dimension of social man's earthly station" and the "dignity of the uniquely human — man's will, conscience, and yearning for order and peace — menaced as always by brutality, vanity, sloth and stupidity."[134]

In picturesque, self-mocking terms, Teage described an editor's duties in a poverty-stricken society:

The boy comes for copy. He draws on a well hacked trestle, for which he is indebted to the carelessness of the carpenter, and seats himself in front of the barrel. Seizing the fearful quill, he [the editor] thus begins —

"The press[,] the omnipotent press[,] is the most powerful engine which it has ever been the lot of mortals to possess — It is the scourge of tyrants — the pillar of religion and the Palladium of civil liberty. From it[,] as from an impregnable rampart[,] the fearless independent editor —

"There is no cassado for breakfast[,] sir.— "
"Well go, and get some and [don't] bother me."
"I have no money, sir.—"
"Don't I know that — tell Crako to let you have a kroo."
"He says he won't. We have not paid him for the other one yet, and he wants the money."
"Plague the fellow[;] what can he mean. Can't you borrow some? —"
"No, sir: I've tried, and they say we owe now more than we'll ever pay."
"Well go and collect some money."
"I have carried out the bills[,] sir. "
"Have you collected any money?"
"No, sir."
"Why?"
"Mr. __ says he has no money, and you need not be afraid of the small amount. Mr. __ says he [don't] like the paper now; you are too polite with the [__]. Mr. __ says your paper is scurrilous. Mr. __ says there is too much religion in it & too little politics. Mr. __ says there is too much politics and too little religion, and Mr.

__ says you have insulted his father's tenth cousin. They say they will not take the
paper any longer, and they will pay when they get the money."
  "That will do, go and call again in an hour for copy."

The editor resumes. — And though there is no class of men to whom the
world is under more immense obligation, yet, there is none —

"Jambo has come to get his pay for the palm oil, sir"
Be gone sir, don't you see I am engaged

— there is none we respect that is doomed to a more hopeless.

"The rats has gnawed the rollers[,] sir."
"Well[,] cast another. "
"We have no molasses[,] sir."
"Well, shut up the office, and go to dinner." (doc. 22)

Whether writing about himself, a conjurer, or the social life of termites,
Teage's reports in the *Herald* were strikingly detailed and colorful. In keeping with
his scientific cast of mind, he carefully distinguished between various types of local
termites on the basis of physical characteristics and used a powerful microscope to
scrutinize such oddities as an alleged two-headed snake and the "witch" recovered
by a traditional African healer (docs. 62 and 84). Among English-language writers,
he admired the "vigor, precision or copiousness" of John Milton, Edmund Burke, Sir
Isaac Newton, Sir James Hall, and "the almost immortals that signed the Declaration
of American Independence." Teage was modernist even in his choice of type for the
newspaper, which consisted of pica and bourgeois faces. Given his preference for
objectivity, his writing was remarkably devoid of sentimentality. Having discussed
the admirable qualities of Gov. Thomas Buchanan in a eulogy, for example, he added,
"To say he was not perfect, would be saying no more than that he was man. The sun
has his spots" (docs. 12 and 94).
    This commitment to objectivity was rooted in an empiricist theory of
knowledge — then emerging as a *sine qua non* of scientific thought. As Teage
explained in an 1845 lecture to the Lyceum, "Knowledge is derived from without.
After all that has been said about innate ideas and principles, it will, I think, be no
easy matter for anyone to show, that we have one single idea that we did not
originally receive by perception or sensation." Later he added, "The object of the

modern philosophy is to collect facts — unlike the ancient which was to explain phenomena" (doc. 97).

In keeping with journalistic standards in an era when copyright conventions were not strictly observed, Teage published samples from his diverse readings. The 7 November 1845 issue of the *Herald* alone carried a letter from a correspondent in Haiti, along with articles culled from the Republican-leaning *New York Tribune*, founded four years earlier by Horace Greeley; the Federalist *Evening Post*, founded by Alexander Hamilton; the *New York Sun*, the first successful penny press and an ally of the Democratic Party; London's iconoclastic *Punch*; the England-based *Westminster Review*, an outlet for the writings of Jeremy Bentham and James Mill; and the *New York Evening Mirror, Boston Cultivator, Boston Mail, Virginia Republican, Living Age, Presbyterian, Concordia Intelligencer, Christian Advocate, Northampton Courier,* and *Colonization Herald*. In 1846, with dramatic frequency, the *Herald* took to publishing political commentaries under pseudonyms such as "Africa," "Observer," "Theophilus," "Alpha," "Data," and "Solicitor." This resulted in some heated exchanges about controversial subjects, providing readers with a wider range of perspectives on local issues while freeing the editor from constantly soliciting contributions.[135]

Teage's poetry was mostly on nature and patriotic themes, with occasional allusions to Africa's past grandeur. For example:

Land of the mighty dead!
Here science once displayed,
And art, their charms;
Here awful Pharaohs swayed
Great nations who obeyed,
Here distant monarchs laid
Their vanquished arms.

They hold us in survey,
They cheer us on our way
They loud proclaim—
From Pyramidal hall—
From Carnac's sculptured wall—
From Thebes they loudly call—
Retake your fame! (doc. 90)

One of the poets most often cited by Teage was England's Edward Young, whose work — like some of Teage's own — was laced with tinges of melancholy and meditations on mortality. Young's "Night Thoughts" not only was "one of the most influential, praised and well known poems of the English language" during the nineteenth century but was also revered by some Christians as a "standard devotional work," second only to the Bible.[136]

Teage's best pieces were his speeches, which masterfully blended persuasive argumentation, poetic riffs and emotive passages. These speeches were often laced with poetic repetition, as when he averred, "He who would embalm his name in the grateful remembrance of coming generations — he who would secure for himself a niche in the temple of undying fame — he who would hew out for himself a monument of which his country may boast — he who would entail upon heirs a name which they may be proud to wear, must seek some other field than that of battle as the theatre of his exploits."[137] Teage's gift for vivid description was also evident in his speeches, as in this evocation of the tropical weather faced by the early immigrants to Liberia: "The rainy season that terrible ordeal of foreign constitutions, was about setting in — the lurid lightning shot its fiery bolt into the forest around them; the thunder muttered its angry tones over their head, and the frail tenements, the best which their circumstances would afford to shield them from a scorching sun by day and drenching rains at night, had not yet been completed (doc. 98). Taken as a whole, Teage's works reveal a knowledgeable and witty writer who could be self-deprecating at times yet devastatingly sardonic, if crossed.[138] However, not all of his writings have been found; among them are a journal in which he kept records of his travels, contemplated history of Liberia and copies of sermons.[139]

Teage's masterpiece was undoubtedly the Liberian Declaration of Independence, which read in part,

> We were everywhere shut out from all civil office.
> We were excluded from all participation in the government.
> We were taxed without consent.
> We were compelled to contribute to the resources of a country, which gave us no protection.
> We were made a separate and distinct class, and against us every avenue to improvement was effectually closed. Strangers from all lands of a color different from ours, were preferred before us.[140]

Carl Patrick Burrowes

The Declaration displayed Teage's poetic skills, evident in the repetition, as well as his polemical powers to describe in terms both poignant and detailed the American racism that had shaped his world view and driven him, his family, and his compatriots to Africa.

The Grand Object of a Republic on Africa's Soil

As Liberians moved to declare their independence, Teage — the man who had done more than any other to further the process — cited the planting of "a nation of colored people on the soil of Africa, adorned and dignified with the attributes of a civilized and Christian community" as the "grand object which at first brought us to Africa."[141] His commitment to Christianity and a republican government stemmed from his socialization in Richmond and was reinforced by his father, a Baptist preacher. However, he also had a critical view of "civilization," tempered by his exposure to servitude and rejection in America.

Given the significance Teage attached to this "grand object," it is not surprising that his analyses of political issues — whether local, international, or in neighboring polities — were thoughtful, detailed, and sometimes prophetic. Writing in 1850 about the independent neighboring republic of Maryland in Africa, he predicted,

> It is perhaps, well for us, that "Maryland in Liberia" has not [been absorbed by Liberia] before this. The unpracticed arm should not be subjected to a great weight at first, lest the strained muscles should contract a permanent debility. The limb attains its utmost power, by gradual developments, and by a series of exercises proportioned to the strength developed. When we are ready for them, and they are ready for us, the move will be easy. "Liberia proper" will open her arms and "Maryland in Liberia" will fall into their embraces. (doc. 53)

Within seven years, Marylanders would vote to join Liberia.

Teage and other repatriate leaders drew on American antecedents in developing their political ideas. Most were born near the turn of the century, just as partisan politics erupted in the United States. At that time American political thinking consisted of several strands, including the British common-law tradition, classical pan-European republicanism, and liberal republicanism. Some Liberian leaders went beyond contemporary debates to independently explore the same European political literature that Jefferson and other American theorists had consulted.[142] Like European and American nation-builders before them, they regarded Enlightenment ideas as applicable across cultural and national barriers.

To the extent that political opinions in the United States clustered along partisan lines, "classical or puritanical" republicanism came to be identified primarily with the Federalists, while the Republicans rooted themselves in the more "liberal or agrarian" variant. According to McDonald, "The former sought a moral solution to the problem of the mortality of republics (make better people) whereas the latter believed in a socio-economic-political solution (make better arrangements)." The Republicans had apparently made the greater impact on early Liberians, especially those from Virginia, which supplied more settlers to Liberia by 1847 (table 1) and more delegates to its Constitutional Convention than any other state in America. With Republican theorist Thomas Jefferson, many Liberians shared not only an interest in black colonization but also a belief that small property holders were the backbone of a stable, prosperous society. It is not surprising that the first formal political group in independent Liberia, the one with which Teage was identified, was called the Republican Party.[143]

The influence of John Locke and other liberal writers was evident in Teage's thinking, particularly in his empiricism and supra-historical theories of the state and human nature. But, his prescriptions for virtuous citizenship followed along classical republican lines. The link between virtue and action appeared in letters to the ACS leadership, especially in his repeated references to the need for "quality" immigration over quantity. He preferred industrious, intelligent tradesmen with "a little heap of money" (doc. 77) especially those, he added sarcastically, who would "content themselves to remain out of the presidential chair for at least one month after their arrival" (doc. 54).[144] Toward the end of his life he reiterated this point, with characteristic self-mocking humor: "Send us — if they will not come of themselves — send us for a few years to come about 500 intelligent active emigrants. Don't send us blockheads — we are blockheads enough ourselves. Send us sensible men — men with sense enough to help us think and act, not too much sense to think they are fit to be President the first year. More annually will be too much — a different sort will injure us" (doc. 69).

Even though the 1847 Liberian Constitution limited citizenship to persons of African descent, that standard was not restrictive enough for Teage, because it entitled all immigrants to the franchise "the moment they land, whether from Rice swamps of Carolina or an Oyster cellar in New York." In his scheme, blacks would become fit for the franchise only after the "atmosphere of liberty has inflated their

Carl Patrick Burrowes

lungs, and expanded and elevated their minds" (doc. 54).[145] In short, liberty was valued not only as an end but also as a means of energizing the human spirit, which had been dulled by years of servitude.

In contrast to more static theories of personalities and cultures, Teage's religious and political thought was undergirded by a view of humans as potential co-creators with God of a limitless future. He believed that virtuous works served as the criteria for determining membership in the communities of citizens and saints, for both repatriates and indigenous Africans. This emphasis on action led Teage to rail against the idleness and passion for "fashionable dress and display" of urban women (doc. 9). In a similar vein, he welcomed an upsurge in the knitting of stockings by local women in May 1843 as a decided improvement — "more profitable than the idle, but polite gossip in which ladies every where (Liberia excepted) are fond of indulging" (doc. 4).

Implicit in this denunciation was a definition of womanhood that contrasted sharply with contemporaneous European standards but was in keeping with a uniquely African American ideal. While denied voting rights, Liberian women — especially those who were connected by marriage or blood to politically prominent men — engaged in public speaking and political activism unhindered, at a time when such actions by white women were condemned and punished in America for being "unladylike." More significantly, Liberian women were guaranteed economic rights by the Constitution of 1847. This guarantee allowed some to accrue considerable economic clout — whether by birth, marriage or their own efforts, that could be translated into political power. Although among blacks valor and patriotism were associated with men, these characteristics were particularly celebrated when displayed by women.[146]

Teage's emphasis on volition extended beyond individuals to society as well. As he urged Liberians toward a declaration of independence, he framed the choice facing the colonists as one between establishing "our character as a public spirited, *enterprising* and progressing people" and tutelage to the ACS, which would "brand us as a timid, dependent and grovelling community" (doc. 43). In keeping with this voluntarist viewpoint, he regarded Liberia's subsequent declaration of independence as an "*act*" by which every Liberian "has entered upon a new career; has assumed new responsibilities and has received a new impetus and a new motive *to action*." Anyone who did not understand this declaration as a call to action was "to be pitied for his blindness, rather than envied for his indifference, and to say the least, he is not yet prepared for extensive usefulness." (doc. 47).

In this actionist scheme, the marketplace occupied a central place as a site for individuals to prove their worth through private enterprise. Despite the importance of trading, Teage warned, "no nation can be independent" — as distinct from sovereign — "which subsists wholly by commerce" (doc. 98). Since individual Liberians did not have the capital necessary for launching other potentially profitable forms of business, Teage recommended that they form corporations along lines then common in the United States and Europe. He argued, "While others unite their capital — combine their energies, mingle their counsel and concentrate all with a single heart upon a single object, we filled with dark suspicion, each of the other, separate as widely as possible apart .... This is the curse under which the colony has been withering. ...Let us abandon our jealousy and suspicions. ...Let us combine our energies, and then let each one put forth all the energy that he would if confident that upon him alone success depended." (doc. 5).

While promoting economic diversification, Teage was not uncritical of industrialization, decrying American manufacturing towns as centers of immorality and viciousness "where females of every class and character, far from the watchful eye of parental solicitude, are huddled together in one promiscuous throng, and dependent for their daily bread upon the freaks and fancies of unprincipled employers[!] Lowell in America, is, I believe, the only large manufacturing town where virtue is held in the least esteem" (doc. 98). Given the potential for such undesirable consequences, he advocated an economy that was restrained on the one hand by government, to prevent thefts and monopolization, and on the other hand by civil institutions, to ensure a virtuous citizenry.[147]

Although Teage believed that society naturally resolves itself into divisions and orders, he sought the creation of a hierarchy that would be determined by intelligence, virtue, and hard work. This was akin to the Jeffersonian notion, derived from Aristotle, of "replacing the 'pseudo aristocracy' of wealth and privilege with the 'natural aristocracy' of talent." He regarded both "high notions of natural equality, which in themselves are just[,] and ignorance of duty" as threats to democratic society (doc. 97). Teage saw this "natural aristocracy" as resting on a vigorous — and idealized — yeomanry:

Behold the farmer, as he goes forth in the morning to this daily task — how firm and elastic his step — how cheerful his sun-burnt countenance; how active his athletic arm!! Behold how cheerfully he labors — how the fat valleys around him laugh with corn — how the spacious plains teem with grain, and the ancient forests fall beneath his resounding axe!!! Follow him, when the labour of the day is over; follow him to his humble home. See him surrounded by an affectionate, industrious frugal wife, unsophisticated by the vices and dissipations of the fashionable world, and by a prattling progeny blooming in health and big with promise of future usefulness. No cankering cares gnaw his peaceful bosom — no uncertain speculation disturbs his quiet slumbers; no revolutions in foreign lands damming up the channels of trade cloud the calm serenity of his brow. Oh! if there be a spot on earth where, true happiness is to be found, here is that spot. (doc. 98)

Notwithstanding their allegiance to "civilization" and Christianity, Teage and other early Liberians often held ideas concerning the place of blacks in society that were at variance with those of ACS leaders and white republican theorists. Alluding to life in the southern United States, for example, the colony's first black governor, Virginia-native Joseph Jenkins Roberts, described Thomas Jefferson in bitterly sarcastic terms: "And still, like the persecuted Israelites, they are required to gather straw for themselves 'wherein to make brick' and yet, 'tell it not in Gath, publish it not in the streets of Askelon.' The statesman and philosopher J. — in the kind spirit of Egyptian taskmaker — would 'lay upon them a full tale of bricks.'"[148]

Roberts also attacked attempts by whites, including Jefferson, to equate blacks with apes. Displaying an independence that was not reflected in the portrayal of repatriates in abolitionist propaganda,[149] Roberts showed little deference to the man who had once held triple power over him — as former governor of Roberts' native Virginia, as a founder and the fourth president of the American republic, and as an early supporter of colonization. In a vein similarly critical of the "Old Dominion," Teage called on residents of New Virginia, a settlement in Liberia, to "copy all in the old that is good, and reject the bad — by equal laws and an equal and even-handed distribution of justice" (doc. 11).

Evident in these passages are elements of an ideology that came to be called Ethiopianism, pan-Negroism, black nationalism or pan-Africanism. It consisted of a reaction against white rejection and a belief that people of African descent share a historical mission. Both aspects of this ideology are fully articulated in the work of Teage, who regarded "the true interest" of the repatriates and indigenous Africans to be "identically the same; and it should be one among our first objects to convince them of the fact" (doc. 70). This passion stemmed from experiencing the horrors of the slave trade on both sides of the Atlantic.[150]

Based on a reading of ancient history, Teage repeatedly credited Africans with the development of monotheism and constitutional order.[151] For this reason, he regarded those indigenous societies that were engaged in the slave trade as debased, fallen from a higher state. Given his deep interest in politics and sociology, he routinely solicited information on the succession crises and ethnology of neighboring communities from African visitors to Monrovia and from repatriates living in outlying areas of Liberia. The long list of African rulers on whom he reported in the pages of the *Herald* included Doungalee, Bey, Bah Gay, Dwah Will, King Famatorah, Pah-Ko-Roo, George Cain, Gotorah, Joe Harris, Boolah , Jarah-Fingue, Jenkins, Amurah, King Shaka, Mamorah, Prince Manah, Old Mama, and King Peter Softly. Although Teage sometimes referred to "savages," this term was usually applied to military foes of Liberia and was far outweighed by his use of more neutral terms such as "neighbors," "natives," or "aboriginal inhabitants."

Since all of humanity had contributed to "civilization," Teage reasoned, all could aspire to partake of its offerings, including indigenous Africans, whose religious and cultural conversion he justified as a racial duty. Indeed, his denomination had spearheaded this work, despite meager support from abroad and an unstable financial base within the colony. While the repatriates were still living in Sierra Leone, Lott Cary converted a Vai man, John Revey, who subsequently operated a school for chiefs' sons at Big Town, Cape Mount, with material support and guidance from Cary. Although the school operated from only 1827 to 1828, one of its students went on to invent written characters for the Vai language. Following Cary's death in 1828, Baptist mission stations among indigenous Africans would be scaled back to a few towns among Bassa speakers, but the success of this denomination among Africans captured from slave ships would help ensure their complete cultural assimilation into the African-American repatriate community.[152]

Writing in 1851, Teage claimed proudly, "Now a Harriss, a Vonbrumn and a Crocker, all children of the forest, are proclaiming to their country-men the unserchble [?] riches of the gospel of Jesus Christ." He noted with satisfaction that the local wars in the area of Grand Bassa, which had divided the people "against themselves," had declined, and those whose chief employment had been the procuring of victims for the slave trade had turned to agriculture and the manufacture of palm oil. About the previous wars, he added, "nine-tenths of this excitement have been evermore the offspring of the slave trade; to which, hitherto, what has been misnamed lawful and honorable trade [in alcohol] has contributed a melancholy share."[153]

While Teage's pan-African impulse led him to welcome indigenous Africans into the polity, his commitment to Christianity and republican government made him critical of those African customs linked to servile relations. Although he ate local cuisine, sent a suit made from African cotton cloth to New York for display at an industrial fair, and praised African hospitality and several cultural practices, he found some other features of contemporaneous African societies, including the status of women and trial by ordeal, to be morally reprehensible and requiring change, if not abolishment. The involvement of several African chiefs in the slave trade notwithstanding, he was against the expropriation of land from them without just compensation. For a Baptist minister, he adopted a surprising moral indifference toward conjuring, which he was able to describe without denunciation, perhaps having been conditioned by previous exposure to similar practices in Virginia. Informed by his readings in history, he also sought to understand local standards of morality, even though he did not sanction them:

> Those who suppose that there is not in heathen minds, any connexion between virtue and happiness and vice and punishment, manifest an ignorance of their customs — or if acquainted with their customs — that they have taken but a superficial view of the subject. This will hold good at least of all the African tribes with which we have been conversant. It is true that the idea of virtue differs in different countries. The ancient Scandinavian regarded it highly virtuous and acceptable to *Thor* when he fell upon and butchered scores of helpless and unoffending victims. With the ancient Greek sensuality or wanton revelry was a virtue, accordingly so he worshipped the imaginary deities *Venus, Mars* or *Bacchus*, their presiding patrons.... Savages have *their* virtues and although they may exclude other nations from the benefit of their operations, still as it regards themselves, they connect happiness with the practice of these virtues. (doc. 60)

In Teage's view, a major failing of American society was its denial of citizenship to blacks, which sapped the all-important human will to pursue enterprise and independence:

> No hope cheered us; no noble object looming in the dim and distant future kindled our ambition. Oppression — cold cheerless oppression like the dreary region of an eternal winter, chilled every noble passion and fettered and paralysed every arm. And if among the oppressed millions there were

found here and there one in whose bosom the last glimmer of a generous passion was not yet extinguished — one, who, from the midst of the inglorious slumberers in the deep degradation around him would lift his voice, and demand those rights, which the God of nature hath bestowed in equal gift upon all His rational creatures, he was met at once by those who had at first denied and then enforced, with the stern reply, that for him and for all his race — Liberty and Expatriation are inseparable!! (doc. 98)

Contrary to the portrayal of repatriates in abolitionist literature as unconcerned with the extermination of slavery, Teage passionately and publicly denounced the "peculiar institution" on many occasions: "Every emotion of our soul — the last vestige of every principle — that shade of every idea within us, is opposed to slavery. We regard it with unmitigated and increasing hatred; we therefore hail the signs of its approaching downfall with an almost rapturous delight.[154] Writing twenty-one years before the Emancipation Proclamation, he predicted, "The accursed system is tottering to its fall. — All its aiders, abettors and apologists — all its protecting powers in the New World — intellectual and brutal, cannot long sustain it against the advance of liberal and religious principles. The day of darkness has passed. The hosts are mustering for battle. God himself is in the midst." Unlike many black leaders in the United States who viewed emigrants and abolitionists as antagonists, Teage saw the two communities as "companions in tribulation " and "co-laborers in different compartments of one structure." He regarded with anguish the "opprobrious epithets" and "contempt" meted out by northern blacks against Liberians (doc. 72).[155]

In relation to powerful whites, such as the leaders of the ACS and British officials, Teage maintained a pragmatic posture around which he, as secretary of state, helped fashion his country's foreign policy. Rather than denouncing the nations of Christendom for their involvement in the slave system, the Liberian Declaration of Independence had appealed to them for recognition. Implicit in this appeal was a desire not to follow the Haitian example of retreating into a precapitalism autarchy but rather to join the world system on the basis of commodified agriculture and trading — as graphically depicted in the Liberian national seal. Although Teage would publicly praise the British, for example, for specific acts of support for Liberia and occasionally used flattery to curry national favor,[156] his general skepticism toward them was reflected in this warning in 1847: "Better, far better will it be for us that a century find us still a weak and 'feeble folk' than to bend an ignoble neck to the Anglo-Saxon yoke — of whose unclenching tenacity, when once it has grappled, the whole history of the modern world affords most melancholy examples."[157]

Conditioned by the denial of rights to blacks in America, Teage came to view self-government as the "greatest of all blessings ... bestowed by a beneficent God upon his rational creatures." However, the creation of a state that would protect the rights of its black citizens required internal order, which he called "heaven's first law. It is this which imparts stability to human institutions." His emphasis on the need for order was occasioned in part by the tendency toward licentiousness observed in newly freed blacks, as well as by the debate on the propriety of declaring the independence of the colony from the ACS. In this context, Teage urged Liberians to restrain themselves "within the bounds of a rational and virtuous freedom." Rationality and virtue, he claimed, were at "the base and the summit of all just political theories, and which can never be separated" (doc. 98).

The maintenance of order did not require the creation of a large government with its idle "army of sycophantic officials." In fact, Teage continued, one *raison d'être* for a state was the protection of hard-earned property: "There were men, before there was a strong arm of government, and these men lived, and ate and enjoyed— and lived and ate and enjoyed by the sweat of their brow — by continual applications to our common mother earth. It was not the desire of assistance to draw treasures from the bowels of the earth, but the want of protection in the enjoyment of treasures already drawn, that first suggested the idea of Government" (doc. 5).[158] The importance Teage attached to the creation of a state led him to eulogize men who had helped establish order, including repatriate military leader Elijah Johnson and Chief Amurah. However, the requisite order was not to be imposed by a strong leader or party organization but rather by "a strict and conscientious submission to established law" (doc. 98). In a eulogy for Gov. Thomas Buchanan in 1841, Teage noted, "Salutary laws existing, but lying dormant on the statute book, demanded to be enforced, and other regulations equally required, had to be made and exerted" (docs. 59 and 94).

Going beyond a theoretical commitment to establishing a society of law, Teage played a lead role in collating and publishing the statutes of both the colony and the republic. He would also spearhead several drives to reform the judiciary, including a radical proposal to shift from the use of Latin terms to language more accessible to average citizens, which he predicted would be opposed by "the pedant and the votary of mystery":[159]

We would suggest that the expressions be simple and concise — that each idea be clearly expressed, but in the fewest possible words — that no terms be used but those to which the mass of the people has assigned a fixed and determinate meaning — that all barbarous and fatiguing repetitions be avoided, and that not one word be added to a clear and complete expression of the meaning....

What idea is there in *nisi prius*, or *Habeas Corpus*, or *non coram Judice*, or *mandamus*, that cannot be adequately expressed in English? As they now stand, none but the initiated can comprehend them. ... A poor ignorant man applies for a divorce, and after weeks of anxiety, he is told that his wife is divorced *a mensa et thora*, but not a *vinculo matrimonii*. What does he know of the matter? If instead he is told she no longer shares his bed and board, but that some of the responsibilities assumed by marriage are still attached to him, he at once knows his position. (doc. 52)

The type of order promoted by Teage was one rooted in reasoned consensus, which could be achieved only through "free and *dispassionate* discussion" (doc. 43). Enlightenment would result, he argued, from vigorous public debate, the kind sponsored by the Liberia Lyceum and conducted in the pages of the *Herald*:

Let the whole popular mind, with its "Press" and various civil institutions, be concentrated on any one subject, and truth will rise paramount. For proof; notice the progress which the subject of slavery has made. As soon as public attention is fixed itself upon the evils and dangers it is likely to entail on the American people, a great and prevailing change was evident to all, this general and popular agitation may throw up much strife and delusion. But nevertheless, error whose certain fate is inevitable must sink, and give place to truth. (doc. 42)

Notably, this discussion was to be conducted in the interest of the common good, not for the ostentatious display of oratory skill.

Based on a study of history and various societies — from the ancient Egyptian, Greek, and Roman to the contemporary African, American, and European — Teage had concluded that "the elements of national overthrow" stemmed most often from within a society. Although he showed a passing concern with luxuries as a potentially debilitating force, far greater threats were the linked evils of ignorance, idleness and passion, which he called "disease of the national heart" (doc. 98).[160] As long as the people remained ignorant of their responsibilities and the fundamental laws of society, he argued, democracy was an invitation to anarchy. Yet Teage objected not to democracy but to the "party spirit," which he associated with "croaking demagogues" and "instability" (doc. 97). Especially destructive of the social order was unbridled passion in the "public men," those who "have credit with the people and influence" and could "range their infatuated followers under their opposing banners" (doc. 98).

However, not all passions were likely to destabilize the state. Teage observed, "A common danger — a danger equally menacing all, is almost sure to sink every minor and merely personal consideration, and to be met by a combination of energy, concentration of effort, and unity of action; and in proportion as the pressure of the danger is great, will there be want of scope for those passions, which in a certain class, possess such fearful and disorganising potency (doc. 98). In this context, the major foes were to be found in racism and an attendant slave trade, enemies upon whom Teage sought to rivet the united attention and antipathy of Liberians through the pages of the *Herald*.

In the short term, respect for laws could assure order, but stability would endure in the long term only through the cultivation of reason and virtue. One means of instilling these finer qualities in the citizens was education, which Teage described in mechanical, modernist terms as "the spring that regulates the movements of society — this is at once the lever and the safety-valve of human institutions. ... Education corrects vice — cures disorder — abates jealousies — adorns virtue — commands the winds — triumphs over the waves — scales the heavens. In a word education lays all nature under tribute and forces her to administer to the comfort and happiness of man. Nor is this all that education does. It enobles and elevates the mind, and urges the soul upward and animates it to deeds of high and lasting renown." (doc. 98).

If an educated citizenry was a major guarantor of stability and of a democratic order, even more important were educated legislators:

The people therefore will do well to weigh the character, and from that infer the motive of those who solicit their suffrage. At the least they should demand of the candidates to be able to tell whether England is in Polynesia or New Zealand, or whether France is in Siberia or Lapland! These remarks have been suggested by hearing the names of some who have the modesty to offer themselves candidates for the Legislature at this most critical period of the colony's history. We trust however the good sense of the people will be manifested in the returns of the elections; and that candidates who it is obvious have no motive but the pitiful pay, will be left in that obscurity whence they should never emerge. (doc. 49)

Ultimately, however, only religion would ensure virtue — and with it the stability of a society in which blacks would be regenerated. Responsibility for the fate of Christianity rested heavily on Teage as the pastor of the leading Baptist church. Those hours of his days not given over to editorial and governmental matters were filled with such routine ministerial cares as preaching, ordaining, and meeting with his flock and other clergymen. In 1848 alone, he baptized sixty-one people — more than any other minister in Liberia. In addition to the promise of eternal salvation, Christianity offered, in Teage's view, the most advanced form of social ethics[161] and one particularly suited to a republican structure of participatory government:

> All attempts to correct the depravity of man, to stay the head-long propensity to vice — to abate the madness of ambition, will be found deplorably inefficient, unless we apply the restrictions and the tremendous sanctions of religion. A profound regard and deference for religion and a constant recognition of our dependence upon God, and of our obligation and accountability to Him — an ever-present and ever-pressing sense of his universal and all controlling providence — this, and only this, can give energy to the arm of law, cool the raging fever of the passions — and abate the lofty pretensions of mad ambition. (doc. 98)

Teage's religious faith was rooted in a covenant theory of history, as evident in his comparison of the repatriate community to "wanderers from Samaria" (doc. 97). This theory, which held that "God periodically chose certain nations to play the role of his chosen people," was evident in his poem "Wake Every Tuneful String," where he claimed that Liberia was "Favour'd of God" (doc. 93). Just as American Puritans had believed that they had inherited the covenant from the Old Testament Israelites, many African-Americans, including early Liberians, believed that the role of God's chosen people had devolved to blacks because of the involvement of white Americans in the slave system.[162]

Like the lineage-based religions of West Africa, the black Baptist tradition fostered a patrimonial transmission of sacred authority, as seen in the pattern followed by Teage and Lott Cary, whose fathers had been exhorters. In addition, church growth — in what Mechal Sobel has aptly labeled the "Afro-Baptist sacred

Carl Patrick Burrowes

cosmos" — occurred by accretions to the sacred family followed by fissions from the core lineage, rather than through the crusading impulse evident in Islam and European Christianity. This was a social Christianity from which Christ was practically effaced. Highlighted in the writings of the early Liberians was the Old Testament God, deliverer of entire peoples. Their Declaration of Independence refers to "the Great Arbiter of human events," "the God of nature," "a beneficent Creator," "the God of our fathers," "His Providence," "the living God," and "our common Judge" (doc. 99). No mention of Jesus Christ appears there or in the three hymns written locally in celebration of independence in 1847.[163]

Also important to Teage's religious vision was the Baptist view of salvation as flowing solely from God's grace, which was often manifested through outpourings of the Holy Spirit. In describing one particularly successful revival meeting, he reported:

> Christians of different denominations were present — backsliders were there and cold negligent worldly-minded professors, were there — and non-professors were there — and all felt and confessed that "The Lord is in this place." The Holy Spirit descended and by a diversity of manifestations appealed to the hearts and consciences of all classes present. The faithful consistent persevering christian was edified and cheered by the hope set before him — the frigid and worldy-minded felt shame and remorse in view of the past — backsliders repented and returned from their wanderings and the stout hearted sinners made to cry "what shall I do!" — On Sabbath night fifteen persons came forth to the altar, confessing their sins and bewailing their condition and with tears in their eyes, begged that the people of God would pray for them. (doc. 24)

Teage — ever the empiricist — routinely looked beyond these Pentecostal experiences for evidence of behavioral changes in converts. After all, he argued, the same scripture that assigned "every salutary change to the grace and power of God" also imposed a duty on individuals to serve as "instruments" of God's will. For this reason, he admonished parents to fulfill the "most solemn of all obligations ... to train up your child in the way he should go that when he is old he may not depart from it" (doc. 23). He urged the repatriate guardians of indigenous children in particular to be guided by a "spirit of philanthropy and patriotism," because their success at inculcating values would determine the "elevation of the tribes around us[,] the future well-being of the soul and the advancement of our Colony."

The importance of behavioral change as proof of real conversion among Baptists can be seen in the stories told about Lott Cary and Colin Teage, whose religious transformation were said to have precipitated greater frugality and their acquisition of literacy skills. It was also evident in the Baptist concern with

Image 1. Sketch of Monrovia from riverside

"walking the straight and narrow path to righteousness" or, as Teage put it in criticizing the immoral conduct of a Methodist pastor, maintaining the "walks of virtue" (doc. 15). Following the ritual of submersion, the convert entered a warm, embracing Baptist fellowship in which members called one another brothers and sisters. This was not unlike the polity envisioned by Teage, where the fate of each person would become the concern of all.

Poet, Prophet and Pan-African Patriot

Although an unlikely role for one who was born into slavery, Hilary Teage served as a prophet of modernity, spreading from Virginia to Africa the powerfully transforming message of a revolution that began in Europe.[164] His favorable references to Newton, Milton and Jefferson only hint at what was a deep commitment to the advances in modernism associated with each man, whether in the form of epistemological empiricism, literary romanticism or republican politics.

Carl Patrick Burrowes

His identification with this broad cause was everywhere evident, from his railing against pedantry, his fight for the creation of a black republic or his use of a powerful microscope to analyze the "magical" portions of a traditional healer (doc. 62). Although broadly concerned with redeeming the children of Africa from the grips of various forms of obscurantism and irrationality, his primary interest was the transformation of social relations along modern lines. Primarily this meant the substitution of free enterprise in place of servile dependency in economics and the displacement by republican rights of patronage relations, whether linked to "croaking demagogues" among repatriates or rooted in the "divine rights" of chiefs among indigenous Africans. To a lesser extent, this meant a break with an ideal of women as "idle" ornaments. In his view, human beings, especially blacks who had experienced the destructive effects of the centuries-old slave trade, had to be transformed from a natural state of inaction, passion and ignorance, through volition, to a more God-like state of enterprise, control and reason.

For Teage, republicanism, Christianity and black nationalism were mutually reinforcing aspects of "civilization," a way of life characterized by monotheism, the spread of literacy and democratic government, and embellished with rationalism, the arts and sciences. For example, in recommending to an ACS official the traits that ought to characterize an agent of the Society, Teage offered a description that not only fit his own traits, but also personified the qualities he idealized in a virtuous citizen; he cited "energy" as well as "knowledge" of an "African disposition," which, he argued, was characteristic of both indigenous Africans and repatriates:

> Here, Sir, is where experience is wanted in knowledge not only of human nature generally but of the peculiarities of the *African disposition*. This qualification is exceedingly desirable in a ruler here not only with regard to the natives but also in reference to the Colonists. An Agent having no physical force with which to enforce his regulations which from the nature of things will sometimes be odious and unpleasant to the people, should be sufficiently acquainted with their dispositions, habits, and manner of thinking as to be able to lead them insensibly, to what he could by no means force them. He should possess a sufficient weight of dignity and *energy* of character to obtain the esteem and respect of the people. Such a man is exceedingly desirable at present and such a one only will be of any essential service in the way of restoring and establishing habits of industry and order. (doc. 1)

When the Society's president complained in 1841 about an "offensive" article in the *Herald*, Teage presented a defense that combined republicanism and black nationalism: "In common with colored men, I have certain sentiments ... I should be altogether unworthy of your confidence and respect, if I should at any time forget for a moment that this is my indefeasible right, or so base and mean-spirited as not to claim to exercise it whenever circumstances should demand it" (doc. 14).

Teage's republicanism helped distinguish his black nationalism from the thinking of other nineteenth-century black intellectuals. For example, his concern for democratic participation by citizens led him to propose the substitution of pidgin English for Latin in the court system:

> If ... chosen exotics must adorn the borders of our beautiful English parterre, let them be the odorous and splendid productions of sunny Africa. And this is the more reasonable, as we indulge the hope that our institutions will exert a recuperative and healthful influence upon the tribes around us. Already there are certain words of equal currency amongst us and them. As for instance the word "palaver." Suppose we should name our justice court "palaver:" our oyez and terminer, "big palaver," and our supreme court, from which there is no appeal, "Great devil palaver," all would understand them, neither we who are acquainted with the African manners nor they would be at any loss. (doc. 52)[165]

Teage did not merely profess an acceptance of pidgin; he repeatedly used it in the Herald.

The absence of a firm division between the secular and sacred in African-American cosmology, which historian Donald G. Mathews characterized as one of "the most important links between African culture and African-American Christianity,"[166] facilitated the interpenetration of Teage's religious and political ideas. The conversion experience, a central component to his denomination and to black sacred cosmology, also contributed to the high level of individuation required for the exercise of civil liberties. Individual professions of conversion, rather than being the basis for automatic admission, were routinely probed by the pastor. The spectacular river baptisms preferred by Baptists further served to cut converts off from their previous worldly communities and place them under the scrutiny of church members. The process of individuation associated with conversion is captured in several black spirituals, as in the lyrics "Way down yonder all by myself,

Carl Patrick Burrowes

I couldn't hear nobody pray" and "It's me, it's me, it's me oh Lord, standing in the need of prayer. Not my father, not my mother, but it's me oh Lord, standing in the need of prayer."[167]

Concerning aesthetics, Teage was eclectic, finding value and pleasure in sources as diverse as eighteenth-century British poetry, African cuisine and American oratory. He did not uncritically embrace all that passed for modernity in his day, given his commitment to republican and Christian ethics. With regard to popular Victorian novelists, he remarked, "While the mental vigor, close observation and commanding eloquence which some of them display are worthy of all admiration, their degenerate and licentious sentiments should be an inseparable barrier to their introduction into well-ordered society" (doc. 97). This passage reveals that Teage was wrestling with a paradox of modern education: how to promote Enlightenment, which in its extreme form would question the existence of God, while preserving morality, which in previous ages was usually rooted in the fear of God or the gods.

For Teage, the solution rested in a marriage of empiricism and the deep message of religion — to manifest love in one's social relations. He claimed, "To persuade men to do justly, love mercy and walk humbly with God, should be the end of all instruction. Thus the education we recommend and advance is that which aims to prepare man for the duties of his station" (doc. 97). Elsewhere he would argue, "Education opens sources of pure[,] refined, and exquisite enjoyment — it unlocks the temple of nature and admits the awe stricken soul to behold and admire the wondrous works of God" (doc. 98). Teage believed that God — working through willing human agents — was the ultimate determinant of human liberty. Concerning the fight against slavery, for example, he noted, "Whatever nation longer resists, however it may indulge in dreams of security and of power to oppress, will be found to be warring against the God of battles" (doc. 72).

Teage's greater familiarity with Southern slaves and his immersion in an "Afro Baptist cosmos" might explain why he was less contemptuous of black cultures than other nineteenth-century intellectuals such as the editor of the *Herald* before him, John B. Russwurm, an Episcopalian who had been raised in Canada, New England and New York; Edward Wilmot Blyden, a Presbyterian raised in St. Vincent in the Dutch West Indies; and Alexander Crummell, a Cambridge-educated Episcopal priest who had been raised in New York. All these men enjoyed higher levels of formal education. However, raised by a father who had preached to urban free blacks and rural slaves, the younger Teage would prove more adept at negotiating the maelstrom of Liberian politics, given the large number of former slaves in the local population. In contrast to these intellectuals' stern, reproachful personalities, Teage laced his calls for public improvement and local production[168] with good humor, much of it directed at himself.

Regarding Hilary's personality, it was said that "he was never disposed to urge his opinions upon others, well knowing that the best and most thorough converts to the truth usually become such through the force of their own reflections and convictions." A traveling companion on a voyage from the United States to Liberia noted that, "amid trying reverses in his pecuniary affairs his vivacity and cheerfulness continued without abatement." This man described Teage as "highly accomplished in his manners, very agreeable, various, and winning in his conversations; of a kind, obliging and generous disposition, and earnestly intent upon building up the cause of civilization and Christianity in Africa."[169]

Although Teage shared with many black contemporaries a classical social ethics, which called upon churches and schools to perfect the souls of men, he viewed the nature of government through liberal Lockean lenses. In this view, government was an authority that would restrain individuals from violating the rights of others. With liberal republicans, he thought that individual enterprise could be harnessed to the advantage of the commonwealth, and he viewed political parties and other corporate identities rooted in passion as particularly dangerous to the polity. However, Teage was no mere imitator of white Republicans. Just as the American patriots had enriched Enlightenment ideas in applying them to the New World, Teage made a twofold contribution: he extended this tradition to the black race and to the continent of Africa, both of which had been viewed as outside the ambit of history. His belief that an African state would aid the freedom of blacks in the United States would come to characterize the thinking of Marcus Garvey, Kwame Nkrumah, and other twentieth-century pan-Africanists. As African countries gained their independence in the mid-twentieth century, several leaders of the nationalist movements would cite the writings and the model of self-government offered by Liberians as inspiration for their struggles against colonialism, fulfilling Teage's prediction that Liberia would "bring to the elevation of the African race a mouth and arguments which all its adversaries will not be able to withstand or gainsay."[170]

Because Teage's thinking was directed toward the establishment of a government for a society that was itself in the making, his republicanism came to emphasize the creation of an orderly government and an impulse toward enterprise, without the denunciations of tyranny found in the early writings of American patriots. Working in a society with fewer than three thousand people, he devoted his energies to enlarging the polity. This, he came to conclude, would occur through the ascension of individuals whose worthiness had been previously established through virtuous conduct. In Teage's worldview, the ideal community — of reason and religion — was open only to individuals. Individual renunciation of old habits of sin and irrationality was the price of membership in a new virtuous community. The result was a political theory that rested upon a dynamic link between individualism and communitarianism.[171]

Although Teage disapproved of group identities based on atavistic ties and partisan passions, he did not object to opposition within society if waged by individual newspaper editors or conducted by individual candidates at the polls. Nor did he object to divisions in society, since the community of God's people was already divided into denominations. What he could not abide was the institutionalization of *oppositions*. This was objectionable not only because it risked the dismemberment of a fragile community, but also because the passions engendered by such a development would inhibit deliberations on the basis of reason. Bearing continued relevance to politics particularly in Africa, was his optimism that individuals, long mired in nativism and localism, could be moved to embody a sense of nationhood through appeals to their higher qualities.[172]

Apparently, campaigns spearheaded by Teage and other early Liberian leaders through the Lyceum and the pages of the *Herald* helped establish republican values in a populace that included thousands of ex-slaves and Africans rescued en route to New World slave markets. From 1847 to 1907, the republican ideal of a small, decentralized government was preserved, along with regular elections, short tenures in public offices, checks between branches and some degree of responsiveness among the governors to pressures from the governed. During this sixty-year period, Liberia held national elections approximately sixteen times, with politicians limited to two-year terms. A similarly high, if not higher, rate of rotation seems to have existed for other elective offices at every level — from the legislators down to local sheriffs. In addition to the campaigns between parties, there were rivalries within the various alliances that yielded unexpected outcomes. The presidential contests of 1867 and 1869 were so close that they had to be decided by the House of Representatives, in keeping with the Constitution.[173]

Teage would come to be forgotten within his adopted country because of a disproportionate emphasis on the presidency in Liberian historiography, especially in the period after World War II. This forgetting was perpetuated by a general drift away from the republican principles that he did so much to promote in the first three decades of the nation's history. He also lacked sufficiently prominent descendants who might have cultivated his memory in high places. As a consequence, not a town or street or public monument in Liberia bears the name of the man who contributed more than any other to the country's "framing." In scholarly circles, the lack of attention given to Teage for over a century can be explained by two major developments occurring within two decades after his death. First, the abolition of slavery in the United States in 1865 removed many of the conditions that had made colonization an attractive option to some blacks. This gave abolitionists a *de facto* victory in their arguments against colonization. Relying heavily on abolitionist writings and perspectives, many scholars would subsequently write as if the doom of colonization had been preordained. Adding to the historical marginalization of those blacks, like Teage, who aspired to self-government in exile were the caricatures of and calumnies about blacks in government that followed Reconstruction. In writing about Liberia, many American missionaries, policy makers, and academics would draw, often inadvertently, upon Southern stereotypes concerning the inherent corruption, incompetence, and venality of black officeholders. Despite a significant revolution in black historiography the motivations and ideas of repatriates would go largely unexamined, except for those of repatriates who subsequently left Liberia.[174]

The tumultuous Liberian election in 1869 also served to erase Teage from historical memory. In this contest, the Republican Party, with which Teage had been allied, lost the presidency to the recently formed True Whig Party, led mainly by northern free blacks, most of whom had immigrated after Liberians declared their independence. The Whig victory came about a decade after immigrants from the Upper South, who had supplied most Republican leaders, lost their long-standing majority among Liberians (see table 1). The Whigs would be driven from power two years later, when — going against the grain of a cardinal republican tenet regarding the necessity of short tenures in public offices — they tried to extend the presidential term from two to four years without a clear mandate from the voters. After the collapse of the Whig regime in 1871, its major ideologues — several of whom fled into exile — blamed their failure on an entrenched mulatto hierarchy, which they claimed the Republicans represented. Their viewpoint would come to be uncritically enshrined in Liberian historiography, due in part to the True Whig Party's continuous control of the presidency from 1884 to 1980.

In a bid to recapture the presidency in the election of 1877, the True Whig Party offered a legislative seat to the Congo ethnic group, contrary to the official individualist definition of citizenship. Six years later, the Grebo ethnic group would be granted what amounted to observer status in the legislature, with limited voting rights given to its representative and none to individual members of the group. Paradoxically, the replacement of early Liberian republicanism by the chieftaincy

Carl Patrick Burrowes

and the clientelist social relations on which it is based, was furthered significantly by Edward Wilmot Blyden, a Teage protégé. Born in St. Thomas in the Virgin Islands, where he had little opportunity for exposure to Jeffersonian republicanism, Blyden (1832-1912) immigrated in 1850 to Liberia, and he was educated there. He rose quickly to serve as editor of the *Liberia Herald* (1854-56), professor at Liberia College (1862-71, 1900-01), secretary of state (1864-66), ambassador to England (1877-78, 1892, 1905), president of Liberia College (1880-84) and secretary of the interior (1880-82).[175]

Although Blyden shared Teage's commitment to "civilization," the younger man, unlike his mentor, was guided by a series of Manichean dualisms that pitted "pure" European culture against African culture and mulattos against black racial types. Rejecting creole cultures and mulattos as suspect and inferior, Blyden expended most of his intellectual energy trying to fashion an accommodation between his allegiance to Anglo-Saxon culture and his commitment to an ideal African society, which was "pure" by virtue of being Mandingo and "superior" because of its commitment to Islam. For Blyden, each racial group had a separate, genetically determined culture, written in the "manuscripts of God." By this count, Liberia was a racially "unconstitutional state in Africa." Together with Maurice Delafosse, once French consul in Monrovia, he advocated a reverse assimilation for Liberians into "African" culture.[176]

As with the differences between the Republican and Federalist Parties in the United States, the differences between Teage and Blyden and their respective political parties turned on contrasting views of human nature. One view emphasized the creation of a modern future on the basis of volition while the other stressed structuration rooted in the past.[177] Whereas Teage saw individuals and societies as malleable — capable of willing themselves into higher states of life — Blyden, perhaps influenced by the belief in predestination that underpinned his Presbyterian faith, viewed genetics as determinant of individuals, groups and cultures. Despite a central concern with willful actions, however, Teage did not view all forms of volition as equally virtuous or efficacious. He consistently advocated rational action, which required the actor to compare different means to achieving a goal, while disdaining politics that were driven by emotions.[178]

In addition to differences in their ontological assumptions, the two perspectives differed with regard to their epistemology. In contrast to the empiricism and objectivity of Teage, Blyden's scholarship and journalism were characterized by appeals to the reputation of widely accepted authorities, whether literary or political. His work also depended on the anchoring of foundational principles in the beliefs or feelings of the writer — the very subjectivism that Teage rejected as ill suited for the creation of a modern state. "Modern sophists," he noted, "have assumed for disguise a more decent and unpretending title — They adopt for their motto the fitness of things, and which fitness we will find upon examination to depend entirely upon the taste of the writer" (doc. 97). Ultimately, these contrasting approaches to knowledge and human nature seem to have rested on two different streams within the "Western" intellectual tradition: On the one hand, Blyden and Alexander Crummell exhibited an authoritarian and idealist philosophy linked to their formal education in the classics. In contrast, Teage and his republican allies had been socialized into a Jeffersonian political culture that featured an empiricism, liberalism and rationalism derived from writers such as John Locke, Adam Smith, and John Milton.[179] The fundamental difference between these two perspectives was evident to Teage, who noted in a letter to an ACS official in 1851, "You know, my dear Sir, and all who have tried it know — liberty is necessary to the perfecting of men. I do not despise education. On the contrary, I esteem & honor it, I only regret my want of it. But you may give a man Greek & Latin & Hebrew & whatever else you please[,] if he breathes the mephitic air of slavery, he is wanting — He will be like the well proportioned column — destitute of the entablature.

In his last years, Teage would increasingly express approval of life in Liberia and optimism about the future of the republic — unmindful of the drop in emigration that would be wrought by the abolition of slavery in the United States in 1865 or the shift in Liberian political culture that the election of 1869 would precipitate. He reported with pride the signs of physical improvement, but took particular pleasure in noting the liberties enjoyed by Liberians: "It is so much more pleasing to be voting for one's own representatives than to be peeking 'round the corner at those who are voting — so much more pleasing to clean one's own farm than to clean another's boot, especially when he is conscious that it is the *ne plus ultra* of his ascent" (doc. 54).

Following a long and painful illness, Hilary Teage died on 21 May 1853.[180] His career, which began in Richmond with the organization of a church for transference to Africa, ended while he was serving his adopted country as secretary of state. A letter from Liberia reporting the event read, "A great star has fallen in this Republic." A *Herald* correspondent wrote about the passing of "the chiefest luminary in our political sky" and said that through Teage "the melancholy spirit of every Liberian was raised from deep despair to hope." In January 1854, President Joseph Jenkins Roberts, in his annual address to the legislature, noted, "Superior genius and talents were [Teage's], and his mind endowed by nature with a lively imagination, and a remarkable degree of logical strength, admirably fitted him for the many responsible public stations which through the course of many years, he was called to fill." [181] However, perhaps the best epitaph was a stanza from Teage's own self-revelatory poem "Bread from Brain":

> Patriot! Poet! Prophet feed,
>   Only on the mouldy crust
> Tyrant, fool, and false priest need
>   All the crumb, and scorn the just.
> Lord! how long: how long; oh Lord!
> Bless, oh God, mind's unsheathed sword;
> Let the pen become a sabre
> Let thy children eat who labor
>   Bless the labor, bless the gain,
>   In the making bread from brain. (doc. 92)

Rising from the lowest rung of Virginia's tobacco country, the former slave some called "the Jefferson of Liberia" had seen his lifelong labor blessed by the successful creation of a republic on the shore of Africa. Through volition, he had earned the appellations of poet, prophet, and pan-African patriot.

Image 2. William Crane

Image 3. John B. Russwurm

Image 4. Providence Baptist Church

Image 5. Edward W. Blyden

Selected Writings of Hilary Teage

Liberian Society

1. Letter to Ralph R. Gurley, Monrovia, 26 September 1836

Dear Sir:

This will be forwarded by the Brig *Luna* by which conveyance Doct. Skinner[182] Colonial Agent takes his passage to the United States to recruit a constitution almost entirely worn down by the combined effects of the climate and excessive exertion. The zeal manifested by the Agent to carry into operation the views and commands of the Board, has been at all times such as to do him the highest credit as well as to entitle him to their thanks. It is therefore extremely to be regretted that his energy has not been commensurate with his zeal. This failure is attributable to many causes, but mainly to the recent unsettled state of the Colony; the fearful number of paupers which has been gradually accumulating for years past and which a misdirected charity has suffered to be thrown on the resources of the society; and firstly perhaps —I speak with the utmost deference — to inexperience. The number of paupers at present fed by the society and to which accessions are daily making and will continue to be made under the present system is such as to render it one of the most important subjects to which the Society can direct their attention. The enormous burden which it casts upon them is a small part of the evil it entails; it is in fact no evil at all compared with the demoralizing effect it exerts in the Colony at large. There are at present at least one hundred paupers daily fed from the public store, the majority of whom have been in the Colony from two to eight years. Some of them are in deed proper objects of charity, being incapacitated by disease or old age to subsist themselves. The sick and infirm should be supported[,] humanity demands it, but it is to be feared, and as such to be guarded against, that a knowledge that support will be granted to certain conditions, will become temptation to indolent and lazy persons to place themselves in that condition. That such has been the case in some instances is a fact known to many here. I know of no method by which this dreadful evil can be arrested, but by the establishment of a well regulated farm and workhouse, conducted systematically and vigorously. The Society sometime since ordered one of the Receptacles[183] in Monrovia to be converted into a workhouse, and for a time conducted a farm near Caldwell. But neither of these seemed to promise the desired effect. In addition to many other objections against locating a workhouse in Monrovia, or any other of the Settlements, a most powerful one presents itself in the impossibility there would [be], to keep the lazy and indolent at work. Situated in town there would be the most powerful temptation to idleness, in the examples that would be constantly before them; which combining with a natural or contracted aversion to labour would most probably render them not only indolent but ungovernable. The farm established and conducted by Mr. Pinney[184] was in a scale [?] too limited to be of any essential service unless in the circumstance that it proves what might be done in that way if conducted prudently and energetically. In order to render an establishment of that kind alluded to effective and convenient, I would suggest that the workhouse should be located on the farm and contrived in size and structure as to allow at once a residence for those that work on the farm and a place of labour for those whose operations should be confined to the house. To this place all the poor of the Colony[,] at least all that apply to the Agent for assistance, should be sent. If they were really sick, here they could be properly taken care of with far less expense and trouble than in any other method. Those that were able to work[,] both men and women[,] should be compelled to labour as indispensable to a participation in the Society's bounty. The impression of this establishment under the direction of an Agent should be given to some man of sturdy industrious habits, and good moral character (a man with a family would be preferably) who should keep those that were able steadily and regularly at work and at the same time pay proper attention to those who were sick and infirm. Such an establishment would have a direct tendency to reduce pauperism. It would beget and confirm in many, habits of industry, who at present manifest the utmost aversion to labour and at the same time afford an opportunity to those to labour for their subsistence whose plea for throwing themselves on the Society is the impossibility of obtaining employment. With regard to the state of the Colony, I am happy to say that among our people everything at present is peaceful and tranquil. A disposition to subordination is manifestly taking the place of turbulence, and a general quiet has succeeded that state of feverish excitement which existed during a part of last year. I am sorry to add that our relations with the natives are in rather an unpleasant predicament and I fear will result in a general rupture. In consequence of Joe Harris[185] infracting the stipulations of a treaty entered into by him and this government, the Colonial Agent threatened him with coercion if he did not with a certain period conform to his agreement. As the natives had no intention of adhering to the terms of the treaty, they considered this a formal declaration of war and have in consequence assumed an alarming and menacing attitude. Bassa Cove is thus placed in an unpleasant predicament. General treaties are of no use with natives; they invariably prove the sure ground of disputes. A

Carl Patrick Burrowes

native has no idea of conforming to an agreement any longer than it is compatible with his interest. General threats ought also be sparingly used and should never be made in the absence of an intention and sufficient power to carry them into full effect. If made and not executed, it will be regarded as evidence of weakness and lead to insolence and insult. Here, Sir, is where experience is wanted as knowledge not only of human nature generally but of the peculiarities of the African disposition.

This qualification is exceedingly desirable in a ruler here not only with regard to the natives but also in reference to the Colonist. An Agent having no physical force with which to enforce his reputations which from the nature of things will sometimes be odious and unpleasant to the people, should be sufficiently acquainted with their dispositions, habits, and manner of thinking as to be able to lead them insensibly [?], to what he could by no means force them. He should possess a sufficient weight of dignity and energy of character to obtain the esteem and respect of the people. Such a man is exceedingly desirable at present and such a one only will be of any essential service in the way of restoring and establishing habits of industry and order. You will, I am confident, Sir, excuse the freedom with which I have written when you recollect that I am established here for life, that here all my interests are centered, and of course must feel a deep concern in everything connected with the Colony. It is a fact, Sir, that the future progress of the Settlements under the exclusive direction of the parent Society depend in an important degree on the character of those that will direct affairs.

We are endeavoring to have the accounts ready to be sent by the *Luna* but from that her sailing earlier than was at first expected, will hardly give us time. The books sent out by Mr. Cresson[186] have not as yet been landed; in deed it was not know that they were on board until within a few weeks. We have not therefore commenced to keep the account according to the system sent by the Board. We are much in want of paper and type for the printing office. The paper we now use, originally of the worst description, is so much injured by the action of the atmosphere as to be unfit for use. The type also is of the worst kind, both as to size and quality; the metal of which it is made being so soft and yielding as to be almost incapable of a second impression. You will probably have heard of Mr. Russwurm's[187] appointment as Agent of Cape Palmas; he leaves in a few weeks for his station.

Your Obdt. Servant,

H. Teage

P.s. Since writing the above Doct. Skinner has favored me with the perusal of a letter from an official character in the [Mississippi Colonization Society by which he is authorized to offer me the Agency of their Settlement[188].

2. [Ladies Benevolent Society]

Liberia Herald, 26 November 1842, 8

Against some small portions of the address delivered by James Brown,[189] Esq.,before the "Ladies Benevolent Society,"[190] so we agree with it in the main we shall exercise our privilege of "censorship" to demur. Most heartily do we accord with the gentleman in all he says or can say of the ladies' omnipotent all-pervading and all-controlling influence. True, man rules this lower world, but woman, dear woman, rules man. Nor are we disposed to rebel against the stern decree that enslaved us, nor crudely to displace the "golden" yoke. Enthroned in our heart and swaying the sceptre of love meekly and willingly as all loyal subjects should we will yield to their rule. The ladies therefore will not accuse us of disaffection, if we state that for reasons which are obvious the tranquillity and permanency of their government will be best consulted [?] by a concealment of their power. The wheels of nature may as easily be arrested as woman be deprived of her power, and when arrested is easily be put in motion than power be extended. Her power is most absolute when least obvious. We therefore do not concur with friend Brown in the propriety of this public announcement of a fact, of which, assuming occasional outbreaks as an index there is already too strong a suspicion.

3. First of December

Liberia Herald, 23 December 1842, 6-7

This day destined to be memorable in the history of Liberia was observed with the usual display.

At 5 A. M., a gun from central fort announced the approach of day — at 8 another from the same place proclaimed the ascent of the flags. At 10 the military formed in front of government house whence they moved off escorting the Governor, civil officers and citizens generally to the Methodist Church.

The address on the occasion was delivered by Rev. F. Burns[191] of the M. E. Church. To say that we were delighted with the performance, would be but poor praise. Although it had rather too much at both ends that is (being less allegorical) rather prolix[192], the subject was well sustained throughout. There were some few chronological, and other minor errors, but not of sufficient importance to impair its general correctness and integrity. The matter of the address could not fail to reach the heart of every man of color, and awaken emotions at once melancholy and pleasing. The speaker briefly noticed the origin of African slavery, and correctly assigned it to European cupidity and religious fanaticism after the discovery of America, but failed as, we think, in attempting to point out any feature common to the ancient system of feudalism and vassalage in Europe and African slavery in the New World. They were based upon principles altogether different — springing from different motives and directed to different objects.[193]

The speaker's style was excellent. There was no noisy ranting, no uproarious blustering — no labouring after bombastic phrases which darken sentiment while they lengthen the sentence. There were some touches of genuine eloquence. We refer especially to his notice of the first meeting at Washington of the founders of African Colonization. Chaste, pliant and harmonious, it was the spontaneous flow of nature under deeply wrought feeling. It was decidedly the best address ever delivered on this occasion.

The address over, the procession returned to government house. At one p. m., the national salute was fired and the day closed with the usual festivities.

4. Stockings

Liberia Herald, 6 May 1843, 27

The stocking mania is raging at present in almost every home, and at every point one is met by the nimble fingers and dodging needle worrying, and winding hapless thread into all sorts of stockings, black, blue, gray, white and grizzled. This is decidedly an improvement — decidedly more profitable than the idle, but polite gossip in which ladies everywhere (Liberia excepted) are fond of indulging. What is still more remarkable, we were the other day presented by a lady with a pair of socks, the product of her own hands. Surely they are the gentlest hands — the fairest hands, and like the gifts, the softest hands in all Liberia!

5. Internal Improvement

Liberia Herald, 31 August 1843, 25

The spirit of improvement is evidently awaking in the Colony. Irresolution and idleness have had their day. Taught in the school of hunger and destitution, the colonists are rising in life and intently surveying the field around them. The fields white already to harvest, smile around and invite the hand of industry and intelligence. Among the many sources that open for private and national wealth our peculiar circumstances render it a business of no little difficulty to make a prudent choice and a wise beginning. While these sources are admitted to be as numerous here as in any other country under the sun, it will be admitted also, that our circumstances are different from those of any other people.

We have already chanted the mournful ditty of "different circumstances" and "differently situated" sufficiently long — until, indeed, we have lulled ourselves to sleep in an almost irrecoverable poverty. A stern necessity has at length swept away this inglorious refuge of lies. That our circumstances are in some particulars different from those of others is admitted – but that they are different in any very important practical degree, is denied, excepting so far so that difference is made by ourselves.

If we are awakening to industry, let us also awake to reflection and calculation. Let us ask — seriously ask ourselves — wherein does this alleged paralyzing "difference" consist. In what do we differ from others? A moment's reflection will furnish the answer. It is true, we have no strong arm of a rich government to succour us — to maintain in idleness an army of sycophantic officials — to protect us in depredations on the rich lands, and hard earning of our semi-barbarous neighbors. But, there were men, before there was a strong arm of government, and these men lived and ate and enjoyed by the sweat of their brow — by continued applications to our common mother earth. It was not the desire of resistance to draw treasures from the bowels of the earth, but the want of protection in the enjoyment of treasures already drawn, that first suggested the idea of Government.

Carl Patrick Burrowes

Admit that we are abandoned — that we stand alone — that as far as it is possible we are thrown back on the ground occupied by the primeval sons of nature. What is here for endless discouragement? Had they more faculties than we possess? They acted under the guidance of rustifief[194] and the prompting of desire, and from wild and solitary wanderers changing their habitations with the change of the seasons, they became permanent and wealthy and polished communities.

Have we not unspeakable advantages over them? Is their no influence in example? In the lessons which civilized nations of the earth every day — every where and in their every action present us? Refer a colonist to any branch of domestic industry, such for instance, as the cultivation of coffee, of the sugar cane, or the manufacture of soap — and the ready answer — with the spontaneity of instinct is — haven't means to carry on that business. This said, he turns away with perfect composure, and satisfaction at having done his duty: — in expressing his inadequacy in means to do that, on the proper means of doing what he had never given himself a thought!! Here our "different circumstances" (which in every instance should be written and spoken *character*) come into play and dig the grave of enterprise.

As individual effort is described within narrow limits, so individual means do not ordinarily reach very far. Hence the commercial, agricultural, mechanical and literary associations which are everywhere found among the wise and experienced Europeans, and their transatlantic descendants. Of a single ship how many owners? And what a number sometimes found concerned in a little cargo! We read of a certain farm — of a steamboat — a canal — a railway or a manufactory. There the man of millions has his share, and the man of twenty dollars his!! The one or two agents only are seen, but the thousand others are felt. Let the yeomanry and middle class of any country abstract their share of means from the various branches of industry, and all the capital of all the capitalists would be found inadequate to the supply.

The combination of means — this oneness of purpose and concentration of united energies, the dictate of experience, indicate a high degree of confidence and fidelity. Confidence and fidelity are correlatives, and if not inseparably united cannot long exist apart. Fidelity begets confidence, increases and sustains it. Confidence draws man to man — prompts their counsel and imparts energy to their hand. Destroy confidence by repeated recklessness of engagements and obligations, at once the right arm of enterprise is withered.

Whatever may be the cause of distrust and suspicion — whether originating in mean ignorance and selfishness, or resulting from repeated disappointment, the consequences will be the same — an isolated, and therefore enervated action of the hand of industry in all the various branches of its effort. That distrust has prevailed among us to a fearful extent, none can deny, but we leave others to determine in which of the above sources it has origin.

Here then are the "different circumstances." While others unite their capital — combine their energies, mingle their counsel and concentrate all with a single object, we filled with dark suspicion, each of the other, separate as widely as possible apart, and determine to assay only that to which we have infallible assurance beforehand, our individual feebleness is adequate. This is the curse under which the colony has been withering. Our misfortune has not sprung up from the earth, no more than it came down from the sky — it was born in our suspicious and jealous hearts and nursed in our ignorant heads. But for this, and instead of the little moscheto[195] marine that now steals its fortnight voyage along the shore and returns with its few barrels of oil, gallant and lofty ships burdened with coffee, and sugar, and cotton, the work of our hands would already be crowding into the ports of Europe and America.

It is to be hoped that the evil has at length become apparent to all; and as there are indications of a rising to honorable exertion, let us also awake to reflection and select wisely not only the most profitable field, but also the most advantageous mode of operation.

Hereafter (if some more capable will) we may attempt to point out specifically, how our alleged poverty may be made to produce all the effects of capital and our feebleness to perform feats of wonder.

Once and forever, let us abandon the theory of "differences of circumstances." Let our motto be "union is strength." Let us abandon our jealousy and suspicions. Let us come together and consult, and let our consultations be the echo of ingenuous and candid hearts. And while we will be always alive to the hand of sympathy or patronage, let us never again cast an inglorious look abroad, but with a humble and confident heart uplifted to heaven, let us direct an unwearied hand and undiverted eye to the fertile lands and smiling forest, that every where invite us. Let us combine our energies, and then let each one put forth all the energy that he would if confident that upon him alone success depended.

6. Native Children

Carl Patrick Burrowes

Some idea may be formed of the influence which the Colony is exerting upon the minds of the natives from the fact that from all the adjacent tribes native children are poured in upon the settlers by their parents until they are really becoming a burden. We have ourselves a whole yard full, and in the space of only a few days have felt compelled to refuse three or four others, sent some of them quite from Boson's.[196] The natives are beginning to "like" civilized manners and habits. *I sen you my piccanninie,* say they. *I want you for keep him, larn him white man fash; pose he no larn, flug him. I no want him go-country make fool fash all same me.*

It is hoped that those who take native children to rear, will feel the responsibility of the charge. Such have it in their power to confer a lasting blessing upon the country. One native mind imbued with the feelings and aspirations of civilized life — formed upon correct and Christian principles, going out among the aborigines, will be more efficient in good than a dozen foreigners. The complaint that "those natives that have had the advantage of civilized instruction, have only proved the greater scoundrels," may be true to a certain extent. But wherefore? Simply, because those who had them in charge felt no further interest in them than as they were serviceable or could be turned to account. It perhaps never entered their heads to impress upon them the lessons of morality and virtue, to inspire them with sentiments of self respect and an abhorrence of vice. They labored probably to make them shrewd and sharp traders, and taught them diligently to turn every man and every thing to account. This the half-tutored savage figured as the chief end of man, and returning home acted upon the principle. This should not be. He who does not look at something beyond his own immediate personal interest, is unworthy to have a native child under this care. The spirit of philanthropy and patriotism should direct the conduct of guardians. The elevation of the tribes around us — the future well-being of the soul and the advancement of our Colony, should be the governing motive. For it does not require the eye of prophecy to foresee that our population is to be swelled by the incorporation of these aborigines.

7. [Our Past Hour]

Liberia Herald, 1 January 1847, 22-23

"'Tis greatly wise to talk with our past hours."[197]

The celebrated author of the "Night Thoughts" never uttered a truth more important than the above, nor one more suitable to a maxim for the day on which we write — the first day of January in the year of Our Blessed Saviour, Eighteen Hundred and Forty Seven.

In looking back upon the period we have just left -- a period already with the --

"Years beyond the flood"[198] --

we experience sensations similar to what we conceive a man would feel who having been long entangled in a dark and dangerous waste[199], has with great difficulty emerged and gained the summit of a neighboring eminence. Thus far he is safe; and for deliverance from dangers past his bosom heaves with emotions of gratitude; but when he looks forward, the same gloom hangs over his path, the same dangers infest his course. His only comfort — which boost of but a negative sort — is in not knowing the extent and magnitude of the danger to which he is exposed.

This day should be sacred in meditation. At one and the same moment, time, ever, moving time, chants the dirge of the departed year and proclaims the birth of the rising one. He seals up another leaf of the history of humanity with all its record of crime, and perfidy, and tears and broken hearts and deposits them in the archives of eternity, to be brought forth as witnesses in that day when time himself shall be no more; and opens before the human family another, written, no doubt for many, "with mourning and lamentation and woe." It was therefore at the dictate of both philosophy and morality that the Romans called this month by the significant name "Janus[200], It is the dividing line — the solemn boundary of the past and the "shaded frontier" of the future.

Man too can look in both directions; and it is wise in him to do so. He can look however with distinctness only into the past. Human history and experience present a mirror in which may be seen as by reflection events necessary from the conditions and laws of nations — occurring somewhere, at some time and to some individuals. That men will in the future alternately rejoice and weep — that some will grow rich and others grow poor — that some will embody in outward acts all the odiousness of a vicious heart, and some shed a lustre on humanity by a virtuous and honorable life — that some will be cut off by a sudden and unlooked-for casualty and others gradually melt away by slow consuming disease, we have abundant evidence in the past history of man. The events are certain and we

Carl Patrick Burrowes

entertain no doubt that they will occur. Our ignorance of the precise time and place of their occurrence, and of the particular individuals who will be affected by them alone constitute the indistinctness we speak.

The book of the past lies open before us: and upon most of the events therein recorded we can cast a clear and a scrutinizing eye. It is no more a question whether we or our friend has been unfortunate — whether we have sighed for an absent or wept over a deceased friend — whether we have lived a vicious or a virtuous life — whether we have turned every moment to account, or let golden opportunities to do good slip by unimproved. These events are written in bold relief upon the page of the past: and on this day "whoso is wise and will observe these things even he shall understand the loving kindness of the Lord" in bringing him safely through so many and so various scenes.[201]

There is another class of events, if we may so call them, which although graven with the same indelible pen and on the same unblotted page, and preserved in the records of heaven to be produced to the inquisition of the last day, yet from the inattention of men and from their aversion to introspection is apt to be overlooked. Fortunately for man conscience here comes to his aid[,] and explores every recess of the heart — pours a flood of light upon every motive, weighs them in the scales of impartial justice and pronounces upon them her infallible decisions. How much of pure selfishness has entered into our motives to action — how often we have declined the performance of an act — not because it was really impracticable but for want of a hearty disposition to engage in it. How often we have sat in judgment on the wisdom of Divine Providence by repining at His dispensations: How we have been resigned to those dispensations when they have fallen heavily upon others and left us untouched: How when the path of day has been made known we have sought in a thousand vain and frivolous apologies a pretext to abandon it: How in a thousand instances we have sat "in the seat of the scorner" and how in instances unnumbered by thousands we have indulged in idle thoughts and idle conversation — these although deeply affecting the character which must shortly undergo the scrutiny of an omniscient Judge, are too often unnoticed by man until in the hour of calm reflection conscience lifts her voice and proclaims this in his ear. Therefore,

"Tis greatly wise to talk with our past hours,
And ask them what report they bare to heaven."

At this season which gives the idea of an accelerated speed in the whole system of nature towards its final end, how salutary it is for men to enquire what preparations they have made for that eternal state of existence which, reasons, observation, conscience tell them the present is but the embryo? And now while the events of the past year are speaking as it were from their graves, and the entombed generations from the melancholy wreck of their hopes and desires are proclaiming the vanity of pursuits whose object is limited by time, men, if they are wise, will attend to the admonition and apply their hearts to wisdom["]?

8. Christmas

Liberia Herald, 1 January 1847, 22

This has been the most lively, joyous Christmas we recollect to have seen in Liberia. Expecting to be besieged by numberless little urchins with the usual demand for "Christmas gift" we left our bed at dawn and from our piazza bid a hearty "happy Christmas" to one and all of Liberia, demanded the compliment of the season and returned to bed. This device saved us — at least from giving, which in the present confused state of our exchequer could be done only with a miserable grate. This device reminds us of an innocent and humorous trick once resorted to by one whose image is still vividly before our mind's eye. He had been usually much annoyed by hosts of children demanding "Krsmas, Krsmas giff." As Christmas drew near he collected a large number of tracts bearing the title "Happy Negro." The day arrived, and in the children poured, when as each one said "Krshmas" a tract was handed to it. Disappointed and disconcerted, the little ones turned away unhappy with the "Happy Negro" yet afraid to refuse it.

Even the natives were infested with the joyousness, and marched in scores through the streets demanding of all whom they met "Krshmas, Krshmas."

Where other people spent the fore of the day, we have no right to say. We remained quietly at home thinking particularly of nothing and generally of every thing. In the afternoon we sallied forth and directed our steps towards the beach. Hundreds had preceded us, and the *tout ensemble* was truly inspiring. There were all shades and colors, from the fair brunette to the glassy black; all ages and sizes were there, and all sexes to boot. In one place Rev. Mr. Herring was bestowing a lecture of morality and good breeding upon a collection of juveniles grouped around him. Just behind

Carl Patrick Burrowes

the lecturer stood a table bestriding a number of baskets &, which gave token of a coming demonstration in which the little disciples would probably be delighted as then as in the present. A few rods distant on one hand sat a party quietly feeding — on the other another conversing and another laughing. Here a party of ladies was jumping the rope, and there one of young gentlemen firing crackers. Some were racing, some walking, others talking and all happy; and all in so close vicinage to the lecturer as almost entirely to "drown his voice." The amusement of the day closed by exciting athletic exercises by the Kroomen.

9. Folly [The Passion for Fashionable Dress]

Liberia Herald, 1 October 1847, 87

The passion for fashionable dress and display is increasing in the colony at a most fearful pace. As soon as a vessel arrives with the faded and cast off unmentionables of other climes, a mania seizes all hands, a general chase is opened. Faded spinsters and blooming maids, mamas and little pusses, wrinkled antiquity and undentized infancy, aunts, grandaunts and driveling nieces all hobble off in a breathless race, which is to end only when one is bonneted, another gloved, the heaving bosom of another enveloped in variegated gauze and the godlike form of another shrouded and tortured in dubious silk! Until all have possessed themselves of something to show off in and be admired for, it is the all absorbing topic, and the place where the gew-gaws are offered for sale is the general resort.[202]

There are it is true some exceptions to the above, but they are few and it would be invidious to name them. Upon these few we call to set their faces against this vanity. Oppose to it the powerful influence of counter conduct. Those who shall induce our people to put less money upon their persons, and apply it to the cultivation of the soil will be true benefactors of the country.

We beseech our people to pause and reflect upon this conduct. None can be so infatuated as to think they are any better for a little would be fashionable dress or that they are more thought of by the sensible portion of humanity on account of possessing a silk shawl or Tuscan[203] bonnet or a long-tail blue coat or black satin vest. No in deed, those things only serve to procure for them contempt if their other possessions do not correspond with them. It does not require the eye of a prophet to see where this will lead, unless a timely check is laid upon it. When the passion has firmly established itself no means of recourse will be too base to gratify it. Honesty, integrity, modesty will then have no power because all virtue will be placed in showing off. Then for a lady to flaunt in silk and tuscan, and a gentleman to strut in blue cloth and high-heeledboots will be regarded as the *summum bonum* of happiness and the apex of human dignity. We will not hint about sumptuary laws, but we do say it is exceedingly desirable that people dress in proportion to their means. We are aware that we are exposing ourself to animadversion[204] and perhaps to the ogling of some gentle eyes, but as ladies are always interesting, we shall feel ourself happy in being the object of their attentions, whatever may have caused it. As to the other sex, we will bare our bosom to their shafts.

10. [Immigrants]

Liberia Herald, 30 June 1848, 84

We have lately had a large increase to our population by immigration from America;[205] and if reports are to be credited and we have no doubt they are, a still larger accession may be shortly expected. Let them come; they cannot come too fast — provided they be of the right stamp. Men, and women too, to be sure, of sense and perseverance, who have calculated on some difficulty and trial in settling a new country, who will not be dismayed by small things, who will suffer, yet go forward, these are the emmigrants we want. They may come as fast as they please, Liberia is large enough for them.

11. Virginia

Liberia Herald, 24 November 1848, 8

New Virginia is looking up. We trust we love all mankind, even our enemies (except the few whom we can't but despise), but some how we do love Virginia and Virginians. It is perhaps because we were born in Old Virginia. How strange that we should still love a place that disenfranchised and cast us out. Well let New Virginia copy all in the old that is good, and reject the bad — by equal laws and an equal and even-handed distribution of justice establish Virginia in Africa, of which Virginians everywhere may be truly proud. Such an (sic.) one we will have, if

Carl Patrick Burrowes

improvement goes on at the late[206] rapid rate. Our weekly route is along the beautiful and picturesque St. Paul's, and we cannot say whether we are more pleased at the clearings which are everywhere to be seen, than grieved to see the banks of the river despoiled of the rich mantle of foliage which nature has thrown over them.

The Press

12. Letter to Ralph R. Gurley, Monrovia, 20 March 1839

Sir,

I seize this favorable opportunity by the *Brig Franklin* Capt. Taylor to call your attention to a few circumstances, connected with the improvement of the paper which I have been entrusted to direct. It has long been and is now, more fully my desire to regenerate and improve the character of the *Herald* in both manner and matter, and to make it more worthy of the patronage of the Colonization public, and of that liberality and benevolence with which it has been regarded.[207] Many circumstances entirely beyond my control have conspired to prevent my giving that attention to the *Herald* which I have been desirous to give it. For the last 2 or 3 years the office of secretary of the Colony of Liberia has been anything but a sinecure, and the multiplicity of discordant duties which has demanded attention, has put it entirely out of my power to give that attention to the editorial department indispensable to the creditable conducting of the paper. This circumstance would have been sufficiently annoying to one who having enjoyed the benefits of early mental cultivation, could, in cases of emergency retire for resources within himself. What then must be the disadvantages in the case before us, where the circumstances are almost the opposite? When Gov. Buchanan who is hourly expected, arrives, I trust that some at least of this ground of complaint will be removed, and that I shall be able to give more attention to this matter. My object and desire are to obtain a better supply of type in both size and character, a better supply of rules and leads. Our paper also seems badly adopted to this climate. The surface is fuzzy, the texture coarse and open — from which and perhaps from other circumstances it seems almost impossible to make a decent impression. Should the Board determine to favour me with the articles desired I wish to widen the paper by about four inches by increasing the width of each column half an inch. You will please have this borne in mind in procuring the leads. The rules we can cut here if the material be sent to make them of. Any further reference to this I deem unnecessary, as you will have the paper before you. Below is, as nearly as my ignorance of the subject will permit me to describe them, the kind of type I should like to have. But after all it may be better to leave the matter entirely to you, to send such a supply in kind, quantity and quality as in your judgement you may deem necessary. Whatever may be the intrinsic worth of a publication, its reputation is always enhanced by a sprightly appearance; and though we pretend that matter and mind are all we seek, no publisher is so ignorant of modern taste as to stake the character of his production entirely on these qualities without reference to mechanical embellishment and execution. I wish to consult in some measure this principle of our nature, and to give the character of the *Herald* the benefit of a tidy appearance.

> Brevier no. 5 on long primer body, roman & italic, for editorial
> Long Primer no. 7 on small pica body for extracts & communications, roman & italic
> Pica on small pica body for extracts and communications, roman & italic.
> Pica no. 4 for hand bills and advertisements. A few pounds of Brevier or Bourgeois full face.
> Large and small capitals long primer Antique for heading.
> A small quantity of two lines double Pearl Shade for heading.
> A small quantity of two lines Pearly Italic for heading.
> Double great Primer Antique no. 2, capitals for head of the paper.
> Pica Gothic for heading.
> Flowered rules and borders for hand bills and ballads.
> Spaces, points, quotations all complete, with such other materials as you may deem necessary.

In our description we have been guided by the specimen book of Messrs. White & Hagar & Co., 45 Gold Street N. York.[208] We have on hand a large quantity of worn out type which I shall ship to America by the first direct conveyance to Philadelphia or New York. There are perhaps about 600 pounds. I trust Sir you will make the assortment of type and the needed accompaniments of lead borders as extensive as circumstances will allow. The printing office is now becoming the principal resort of all strangers who visit the Colony, and they seem to form their estimate of the Colony by the *appearances* and *performance* of the office. I am therefore anxious to make such an exhibit in fixtures and productions as will exert a favorable impression.

The idea has been recently started in the Colony that the press and the *Herald* are under the direction of the governor,[209] that he can order or forbid publications altogether independent of the editor, that he is a kind of censor of the press. This view, so erroneous in the very nature of things, I am anxious to have corrected, and

Carl Patrick Burrowes

beg that you will [make] it a subject of remark in your next communication. While I have charge of the paper I shall feel solemnly obliged to regard the interests and objects of the Society, and will assume all accustomed responsibility, provided I have the entire and independent management of it.

Your Most Obd. Servant,

H. Teage

13. Letter to Samuel Wilkeson, Monrovia, 27 January 1840

Dear Sir,

Your kind favor of 30th October came safe to hand a few days ago. The intelligence of the brightening prospects of colonization in America is truly cheering. The signs of the times in the late movements of the government at Washington, seem to indicate the approach of the period, to which the friends of the Colony have so long and so anxiously looked. Any, the least degree of attention the U. S. government may give to the Colony cannot but be of service to it. Its cruisers stationed on the coast, making this their place of rendezvous and common resort for supplies etc. while they have no political connexion with the Colony, will confer on it an importance and respectability which it cannot easily obtain of itself.[210] Another important benefit which they will confer on the Colony will be the extinction of the slave trade in our vicinity. This alone has had a greater effect in retarding the great object of colonization than all other obstacles combined, and the American flag has been of late the only, but the effectual guise under which it has been carried on. The commendable vigilance of the British cruisers has somewhat checked them for the last few months & the number of vessels lately taken by them has been so great that the slavers are unable to ship their slaves. The slaves of which the Baracoons were crammed a few months ago have been dying at a fearful rate at both the great marts of Gallinas and New Sess either from the want of food or from some disease, the consequence of their confined and uncomfortable situation. I had it from good authority a few days ago that at both the places just named, they refused to purchase slaves, assigning as a reason the want of vessels to ship them in. If the American government should establish a prise[211] Court here, and have the prise taken by its cruisers condemned and sold here, the advantages resulting to the Colony would be incalculable. It has been suggested that such a course would involve a pecuniary loss from the want of purchasers. But I think to the contrary. Commerce is a sort of self-creating business: Where there are the staples of commerce there money flows and vice versa. Should the Americans succeed in getting into their hands the whole trade of the Windward coast as they might easily do, any loss that might be sustained in the sale of prises here would amply repaid in the profits of an enlarged commerce. The supply of naval and military armament which has been granted by the navy department is truly acceptable and has come most opportunely. I trust this is but the first fruits of a large harvest of favours to be reaped from the same prolific source. The Colony is I think steadily progressing. Any movement it now makes is so much permanently gained. As I wrote you fully in regard of my wants for the printing office by the *Saluda* I need not repeat it here. I hope the articles ordered will come by her. I send in this vessel the numbers of the *Herald* up to this. As it is impossible for me to know how successful I have been in procuring subscribers I have put to your address 100 copies of each number to be distributed to suit the new arrangements. I would not ask of you a favour involving so much trouble as directing them to the subscribers must occasion[,] if I knew who the new subscribers are. I have sent none to the old subscribers. I found the list in the office 5 years ago when I took charge. I have regularly sent the paper but never heard anything about their paying. To each of the other gentlemen who I have made agents, I send in the same box 50 copies of each number. In conclusion permit me to thank you for your flattering allusion to the *Herald*.

Your Most Obdt. Servant,

H. Teage

14. Letter to S. [Samuel] Wilkeson, Monrovia, 18 December 1840

Dear Sir,

Your favors of July 21st and September 22d, respectively, arrived safely by the *Hobart*. Permit me first to thank you for the interest you have manifested to extend my subscription list, and especially for increasing the subscription of the Society one hundred copies. I trust I shall never lose the sense of the favor done me in this instance.[212]

In regard to the offensive article to which you letter of 22d September alludes, I am happy in being able to say, most truly, that, in the press and hurry of other engagements, its tone and manner, and probable effects, in America, altogether escaped my attention. The writer of the article, ever since he has been in the Colony, has been almost constantly in the Society's employment, and surely, if he is thus regarded and treated by the Society, if I had published it with its effect in America full in view, I might be supposed as merely joining my confidence to the confidence of others. As I will not regard your letter as dictatorial, but merely as advisory, in regard to the accomplishment of certain objects, and to prevent certain consequences, I beg to assure you that I shall do nothing that may operate unfavorably against my adopted country, or weaken the hands of its friends on either side of the great waters. In common with colored men, I have certain sentiments. These sentiments, however, as I do not think their being made known could possibly do any good, but would most probably do an injury, I think it proper to repress, reserving to myself, however, the right to enjoy my sentiments, and, when justice and honor require it, to speak them out. I should be altogether unworthy of your confidence and respect, if I should at any time forget for a moment that this is my indefeasible right, or so base and mean-spirited as not to claim to exercise it whenever circumstances should demand it. The scheme of Colonization enjoys my highest confidence and respect, and the circumstances are not easily anticipated that would lead me to speak or write any thing that shall compromise it. You most obedient servant,

H. Teage

15. [Fighting Alcohol and Sly Dalliance]

Liberia Herald, 26 November 1842, 3

A gentleman a few evenings ago at a party proposed the formation of a "moral reform society." We have since bestowed some thought on the subject and are at length fully convinced of the utility of doing so. Intemperance has lately made a vigorous push for triumph. Against this vice, there is but one effective weapon, and that is total abstinence by all who have hitherto indulged in the cup. As far as we are concerned, we hope hereafter by divine aid to free ourselves from our *own* and others' blood in this particular. We confess delinquency and deplore it.

There is however, another vice still more destructive of the peace of society that is said to be on the increase. It is already in high places. Yea the worthy missionary editor in this settlement has [been] publicly accused of gross licentiousness! and admonished to desist from his sly dalliances and return to the walks of virtue. The subject is of so delicate a character that were it not already public, we should take the liberty to remain silent or at most offer only a private remonstrance to the Rev. Gentleman; as it is we mention it as an additional evidence of the necessity of a vigorous effort on the part of the friends of morality.

16. [Resolutions to the Rev. Chase]

Liberia Herald, 21 January 1843, 10

In the *Luminary* of the date of Decr. 9th, there is a batch of "resolutions," presented it seems to Rev. S. Chase[213] by a committee of worthies appointed they tell us *at* - not *by* the M. E. Church Dec. 8, 1842. There is some propriety in substituting the little word *at* for *by*, because appointed *at* the Church in common parlance would be correct if the *committee* were the only persons concerned in their appointment; whereas *by* the church would have subjected them to the imputation not only of [capability], but of actual falsehood in the present instance. After considerable dragooning "to get up a meeting" they convened Nov. 20th and found to their great mortification too few to do the important business. Therefore Mr. Baxter after "some pertinent remarks" (what a pity they were not reported) moved an adjournment to 8th Dec. For this piece of devotion and service to the dispensator of eleemosynary benefactions Mr. Baxter is certainly entitled to another suit of black, or some other suitable, and substantial acknowledgement, and it is to be hoped he will not be forgotten when Mr. Chase next proceeds to reward the faithful.[214]

After another campaign of nearly a month for voters, they met on Dec. 8th, (the number all told being about 25) and after singing (to the honor and glory of Mr. Chase?) and prayer, His Honor S. Benedict, Major Hicks and Esquire McGill[215] (what a host of talent) and others "nobly defended Mr. Chase" &c., "and the article in the *Herald* are a foul aspersion" and "falsehood of the highest grade." We have looked sometime at this foolish paragraph of murdered english and can only account for such a piece of nonsense emanating from the pen of the "assistant preacher in charge" by recollecting that confusion is as ordinary attendant upon a "cause" of meanness.

Carl Patrick Burrowes

This paragraph however is made to state that after the remarks of divers gentlemen titled & untitled as aforesaid Mr. Burns presented a "preamble" with the three ["]resolutions," which by the way appears to be all they [had] done on that occasion. Here the truth is inadvertently made to appear that it come out by stealth. Mr. Burns presented the resolutions. If he could not present a large number of voters, he could present a string of resolutions. They were already cut and dried, and had no doubt been inspected by Mr. Chase and handed over to the obsequious and pliant Mr. Burns, to be passed and returned for "publication in *Africa's Luminary*." This is all right in Mr. B's code of honor. He at least knows *now* which side his bread is buttered. He has grown wise in experience. He once presumed to act and think for himself; but cut off from the missionary crib, and compelled to sneak back, make the most humiliating confessions and swear eternal allegiance to the only conditions of eating and wearing a priest's portion[,] he seems now determined to think, say and act precisely as he shall be told.

The resolutions have little to excite any feelings except those of sentiment. They contain however one new discovery — not indeed of Mr. Chase's innocence of the charge, for there was not even the shadow of investigation, but they furnish us with an excellent example how to dispose of a charge: namely, by resolving that the charge is true, *or not true* as may best suit the purpose. Resolved that all Mr. Chase has said be true, and all the *Herald* said be untrue, and nothing can be clearer. Reverse the position and still a resolve makes it as clear as moonshine. So we are not at a loss how to convict the "missionary editor" nor to clear ourselves if we should be inclined to do so. Hence these gents must of course be prepared at "any time and place" to prove all Mr. Chase would have them prove. Nor should we be astonished if they be ready whenever. Mr. C. render up his stewardship as purveyor to resolve him guilty of all the charges of which they now resolve him innocent.

Once more on this batch of resolves. They intimate that we are cognizant of the source where the charges of "sly dalliance"[216] on the part of their praise beslobbered leader emanated. This accusation is of itself (to use an African phrase) no good. And if we wait until "they give *dates and names*" connected with our cognizance of the matter, and until then shall be content with the resolve of some of our personal *friends* and *dependents* that the charge is "a groundless — a malicious, and a cowardly fabrication, and astounding to us all["]; notwithstanding their coming from the assistant preacher in charge, "capable as we believe him to be of aspersion and falsehood," we shall tread in the path the committee have marked out for us.

To conclude, we will simply remark that we are too well acquainted with these gentlemen to apprehend any evil from what they may say about us. After all, we are willing to rest the case solely on the character of the jury that tried it. Mr. Burns we have disposed of above, we now simply ask attention to the other gentlemen. Mr. Benedict's abusive tongue and pen have been so often employed that a torrent from him is rather regarded a matter of course. Neither his former pastor, Mr. Seys, nor his only sister escaped him. We appeal to all the town whether Major Hicks is not regarded as *given* to *palavering* — that is talking with two tongues, especially when his interest is concerned. We are not astonished at Mr. Gripon.[217] Human nature is human nature. We know what the mission has done for him. The gentleman's health was always feeble. Hard work did not agree with him. Four hundred dollars a year payable in good *mission* drafts is a consideration; and a man should always be grateful. And as the superintendent is the channel through which this benefaction flows, we do not wonder that he is ready to support him *through thick and thin.* It might possibly influence us if we were either dependent or lazy. Mr. McGill we wish to respect; he is generally an amiable young man, and we believe disposed to do what is right. But he is in the employment of Mr. Chase. We are disposed to touch him lightly, and shall therefore only express our conviction that differently situated, he would have spoken differently if he had spoken at all.

A few words to this scare-crow of a missionary editor and we shall have done for the present. He denies having been publicly accused of "sly dalliances." If a paper, containing a charge and posted in the street, and read by some halfdozen persons may not be called public, we know not what may. But he has made "*diligent* enquiry." It will require another batch of "resolves" to make this true. He *inquired* we have no doubt — but only of those who have *resolved* to tell him just what they know will please him. An order for a barrel of flour, or a small advance for prospective services, will have a wonderful effect in producing the disease of deafness; and to whom shall certain ones go but to Mr. C. who hath the keys of the missionary strong box. This learned editor[218] bandys the words "*assassin [in] open day*" and "*cowardly concealment*" in a most masterly manner. That he is an assassin we neither know nor care; but that he is not afraid to meet any one in "open day" the Rev. Mr. Brown's late precipitate flight is an ample illustration. We are too well acquainted with his pugnacious and pragmatical propensity to venture within reach of either his foot (which we have heard he can use both dexterously, & efficiently) or of his chair which appears to be the right hand of his power. We can very well endure the harmless effusion of his pen, which leaves its viperous gall only on the paper it defiles, but from his foot and chair it will ever be our prayer "good Lord deliver us."

It is but justice to ourself in confirmation of an opinion advanced in the preceding remarks in respect of Mr. Burns' agency in the resolutions, as well as to Major Hicks to state, that since the above has been in type, Major Hicks has explicitly stated to us in [the] presence of two or three gentlemen, that he had no share in said *resolves!* He was appointed simply as one of the committee to prepare them for "publication in the *Luminary*." The Major further states that he understood the phrase in said resolves "capable of aspersion and falsehood" not as descriptive of general character in us, but as referring exclusively to the reported allegation against the missionary editor. Indeed the Major became indignant when it was insisted that the words would bear another signification.

17. The *Luminary*

Liberia Herald, 21 February 1843, 14

In the last number of this sheet (the *Luminary*), the veracious editor has vouchsafed us a good share of abnormal attention.[219] As the value or importance of an object is usually estimated by the attention paid to it, we hereby tender our humble acknowledgement to our worthy brother for this long & flattering expression of his opinion. We however cannot consent to follow through all the little meson of baby criticisms; we commend them to the admiration of the sniveling crony who delights to follow in his wake and hold up his trail, & who has learned to weep or smile on the nice[220] calculation of dollars and cents. The sapient editor would do well to send a few copies of this his scintillation to the next exhibition of his infant school. The numberless inverted commas, dashes and italics which adorn and dignify the production, might excite their admiration and puzzle their brains, but for mature readers the flesh is rather puerile.

But why all this dodging and wincing. The editor[']s movements strongly remind us of a juvenile play called hide and seek. We stated that the editor had been charged with "sly dalliances," and somewhere in the neighborhood of a defence or acknowledgement, we expected to find him. But where is he? Like a certain fish (whose name we have forgotten,) which darkens the water by the emission of a black liquid and thus seeks to evade its pursuer; or the skunk who throws around him the impenetrable defense of his own dear *smell*, he fires his pop-gun in the face of his opponent and attempts to conceal himself in the smoke. If the editor be guilty, why not confess the fact? The guilt of such a deed is of itself bad enough; but a denial trebles it. If not guilty, why not set up a defence? Why rest the defense on the baseless resolves of individuals who reside at a distance from the supposed scene of the indignation. Is it usual in resorts to the bowers of love and criminal dalliance to open the test by a public announcement? Do men in such cases seek notoriety for their licentious deeds? If not, how were the defenders to know the fact unless indeed they possess the attribute of ubiquity. But there was a defence: was there any examination? Was the washerman or the chambermaid examined? Were the boys questioned? If so — if any examination at all were had on the case, where are the records of the testimony? Was the inquisition held at the Church or in the editor's kitchen. That no interior examination or interview was held at nor near the editor's dormitory is what we wish him to prove. But he has studiously avoided the allegation. He remembers the advice given to [S]ancho, and pitifully crouches behind a batch of resolves.[221]

If any thing were wanted to rivet the charge home upon him he has furnished it himself in his bungling and mendacious retort. If the editor, however, is lacking in honesty and ingenuousness, he is not wanting in assiduity. His attempts to escape are worthy of a better cause. Fox like he endeavored to head off on a wrong course: Now he dives into a forest of "resolves" — then he asks help of his heels in a boundless savanna of silly diatribe — anon he seeks to conceal himself in the dusty region of his own dear criticism — again he seeks refuge in accusing us of being his accuser. Verily this man must feel "monstrous" sore to resort for ease to so many postures.

But if the editor hopes to silence us by brandishing his pointless editorial rapier or firing his editorial squib[222], he has reckoned without his host. We repeat we shall reckon upon safety so long as we are beyond the reach of his foot and his chair.

The question is not who circulated the report, nor who dehorted the editor from his "sly dalliances" — but the question is[:] is the editor guilty. If so let him confess his sin. Acknowledge he was overtaken, remove the temptation far from him and be himself again. If he be innocent, let him establish his innocence by the usual method of investigation. Let him not insult the public by the mere "resolves" of any set of men whether favourable or unfavourable, but establish his innocence by the testimony of those who may be supposed to be acquainted with his domestic habits.

Carl Patrick Burrowes

The editor labors to prove that the resolutions proceeded from a "well attended meeting." Why does he not inform us of the exact number present? How many over twenty-five, and how many of the number present were in favour of the resolutions. This would be coming to one point: not certainly to the point from which he has been running during the whole controversy, namely an investigation of the charge — but the number who resolved him innocent.

He [further] labors to prove that these resolutions speak the sense of the town. Every man has a soft place is an old and common saying. The editor illustrates it. By how much he is praised by so [many] we are abused. And how this purblind[223] editor plumes himself upon the public verdict.

But is this the fact? Don't let him "holler" before he is out of the woods. If public contempt can damn a character and the editor had any to lose, it would be no difficult matter to sink him. It must be obvious to every one that the man who will so contumaciously[224] oppose a fair trial, and persist in resting his defence in so serious a matter on mere resolutions, must carry within him the conviction that a fair trial and open investigation would be altogether unfavourable. "If a good man at any time is overtaken, or surprised into a fault, by some *sudden and strong* temptation, he soon relents and acknowledges his fault. Not so with this editor." But the editor bests us. We, he says, praise beslobber ourself; but the whole town *slobbers* him all over with praise, and then that nothing may be wanted, he slobbers himself! wonderfully beslobbered he must be!! It is a pity they could not lubricate his brains, so that they might move occasionally.

But what grudge has this literary [snake ?] lately conceived against Major Hicks that he should so suddenly turn against him, and endeavor to exhibit him in so ridiculous a light? The truth is, the editor is in a dilemma, and he cares not who is left in the lurch so he but escape with whole bones. Is he so dull as not to see that if Major Hicks can be so easily changed to either side, that his quota of the resolutions is worthless? According to this editor, the Major is prepared to be all things to all men, and thus the editor by his own showing invalidates the resolutions. Mr. Hicks voted for the resolutions and has explained his meaning and now this liberal editor would kick up a quarrel with him because he is not prepared to go the whole length he wishes him, and dares to have an opinion of his own.

The editor quotes Webster. This is not the time for the niceties of grammatical and philological disquisition. Let him face the charge — let him speak out in good old-fashioned English and clear himself, so that an anxious public mind may be at rest —

and then he can buckle on his philological armor and ride forth to the death of improprieties. A good moral character is to be preferred before literary celebrity.

The editor's exceeding humility in his professed willingness to come down to the "useful and honest employment, (if need required) of [scaring crows ?]"[225] is strikingly contrasted with his imperious conduct toward Rev. Mr. Brown. No one will doubt his ability to chase a whole flock of crows when it is recollected his unbridled ferocity made the hero of Heddington take to his heels. Gotorah's[226] ghostly growl — the Kondah's[227] envenomed arrow, and the leaden death sped from the warrior's musket Mr. Brown has bravely stood; but his courage failed & he was forced to quit before the furious scowl and fiery eye of his Rev. superintendent. And what worked the editor into such a storm of passion? Ah, Mr. B. "touched him in a tender place." He wanted a little of the cash; and the editor was [cashless]. Had he asked for his blessing he would doubtless have obtained it with the second word; but he asked for cash, which with this editor is quite another thing.

But we are in debt! What a wonderful discovery: A merchant in debt. Well, we do not owe this editor any thing but goodwill. We pity his condition, and shall heartily rejoice to see him clear of the heavy charges under which he is now labouring. Let him be advised by us: If he has for a time abandoned the walks of virtue, return; if not, let him submit to a proper investigation and free himself from the odium. Let him go before an impartial tribunal. And whenever and wherever it may take place we should like to be present, as there are a few questions on some objects we would by permission introduce. It will be well when we are healing the sore to heal it thoroughly.

In reference to criticism, be it borne in mind that we are not disposed to be hypercritical, if we were we would[,] as the editor of the *Luminary* is such a critic in English, just remind him of the *excellent* grammar of that phrase *was been violated*. This however is but a minor fault compared with the general sillyness of the effusions of this self-constituted censor, and literary dictator.

A few of the grosser of the fibs in the editor's article we may probably notice in our next.

18. The *Herald* Again

Liberia Herald, 31 August 1843, 25

With a degree of diffidence by no means ordinary, and of trembling, that makes our every joint shake, and of respect singularly inexpressible, and by ourselves alone conceivable, we venture at length into the presence of our patrons and readers, and bowing with the profoundest humility at their feet — request most humbly permission to place in the same posture of humility with ourselves, our apology for our long absence and apparent reprehensible taciturnity.[228]

Shut out forever from our heart be the vanity of supposing any thing in either our presence or our voice, that is of itself entitled to regard!! In the above apology and precatory paragraph, we took the liberty to turn the eye of our inward man upon that principle in our nature, that renders us uneasy in the absence of whatever we have been accustomed to. Remove the dwarfish son of polar snows from the thundering splash of falling ice-bergs, and the awful howl of contending elements. — Shut out the idle African from his accustomed lounge on the uncouth cot, to listen to the bellowing surges as they lash the shore and die in lengthened reverberations on the ear; both will be unhappy men; in both there will be an uneasiness, and a vagrancy of mind, which all the concerts and music of Europe will be inadequate to calm and to fix. Reverse their positions — while the softer nature of the one will be overwhelmed by the terror of nature's music, the iron soul of the other will turn with uneasiness from the tameness of her accents. The instrument within both is the production of the same creating hand, but they are attuned and adjusted by the circumstances of their position.

This hitherto recondite[229] truism of philosophy, brought to the light of day partly by protracted, painful and intense thought, but partly by collecting into a locus the sickly rays of philosophic light shot by ancient and modern theories and hypothesis across the gloom of scholastic speculation, (and for which nothing but promptness on the part of our subscribers can remunerate us), may afford a clue by that feature in the character of our people, that heretofore has so completely mocked enquiry. We allude (respectfully, however, for each one has a legal right to his preference) to the penchant for lusty preaching — lusty in the sense of noisiness. It is sufficient for all the purposes of a general statement to say that sense and sentiment will be evermore inversely as the noise. As if conscious of inability to reach and fix the mind, or apprehensive of a total absence of mind as those whom they addressed, those religious stentors[230] seek to produce an effect by rousing the passions and overpowering the brain. Unlike the ancient Pythia[231] whose responses constructed with accurate ambiguity, left room to escape from any interpretation, these modern oracles first astound and overwhelm their sudatory and then leave them in a pleasing revere at the nothing they have said. Both they and their hearers seem to forget, what, if reflected upon would put them to the blush, that if strength and capability of lungs are to enter into the decision, the ass most assuredly will bear away the palm.

We trust we have thus sufficiently precluded the imputation of vanity in apologizing for our absence and silence, and in supposing we shall again be welcomed by those who have heretofore cheered us with a cordial greeting. Installed printer to the commonwealth, we have been two months engaged in printing the laws of the colony, which being at length completed we present ourselves in the presence of our readers and ask their attention.

During the past year or two, we have been frequently diverted (or perhaps more properly, have found it necessary to diverge), from our even course to administer wholesome rebuke to certain clerical officials. These meek teachers of meekness labor under a maddening itch for notoriety, and if we have met them on their own ground and kicked them into notice, while they may probably feel more from the process, they cannot with any modesty complain of the result. We are enjoying an armistice at present — how long it will last[,] events will proclaim. The enemy has gone into winter quarters. [232] He may possibly open the campaign in the spring. We have adopted the peace principles — but we [don't] go the length of non-resistance. That were downright madness [?] and suicide while these ferocious creatures are about. We remain however within our own dominion, determined at all hazards to keep out invaders, and where the sense of propriety is too noble to refrain, hearty applications of the foot shall not be wanted to repel.

19. Death of the *Liberia Herald*

Maryland Colonization Journal, December 1845, 84-85

To Our Readers: We now take up our pen to present our valediction to our readers. In concluding to discontinue the *Herald* we feel a sort of melancholy, something like what one may be supposed to feel in parting from an old companion — a companion of his joys and sorrows — one whose unobtrusive society has often diverted his melancholy and enlivened his solitude. For nine years — no inconsiderable portion of man's brief pilgrimage — the *Herald*, faithful monitor — has regularly *heralded* the flight of time. Like the living chronometer of an ancient king it has made its monthly visits to our study, and chanted in our ears the dirge of another moon. [233]

But all earthly ties are formed to be severed. Revolution and disruption are the footprints of time. For the little that this world affords of loveliness and pleasure we must look in the advance of the ruthless leveller, in his rear, nothing is to be seen but wrinkles and ghastliness. As sickening as the view is, however, "it is wise to talk with our past hours" — a maxim which we would not adopt had we not determined to alter our course. To tell of our losses would do no good, and might perhaps disturb the calm serenity of our bosom by bringing up before us the image of some scores of *quasi* gentlemen who have regularly received and read our paper yet not honest enough to pay their subscription to it. As we can have no feelings for such but contempt, we hope not to think of them while we remember our losses. After mature deliberation we have concluded that a paper which cannot sustain itself, or cannot be sustained without loss to the proprietor, can be neither useful nor interesting and should be discontinued. The *Herald* has been an annual out-of-purse affair to us. We therefore impose silence on his trumpet.

In regard to the manner in which we have discharged our obligations to our readers, we will only say in the language of an ancient writer: "If *we* have done well, and as fitting the *matter*, it is that which *we* desired; but if slenderly and meanly, it is that which *we* could attain unto."

20. [New Series of the *Herald*]

Liberia Herald, 5 September 1845, 2-3

The number of the *Liberia Herald*, for July was announced as the last, which would be published. Until that period a mortifying indifference to the paper, whether it lived or died had been manifested almost throughout the colony. When, however, it was announced that the paper was discontinued, many who had been before indifferent, became anxious that it should be maintained. The result of this awakened interest has been the transfer of a part of the paper to a company of gentlemen in this town. It is now proposed to conduct it on the join interest of the all the proprietors.

By announcing that the commencement of a New Series of the LIBERIA HERALD the course intended to be pursued, it is felt that by the possibility can any one be prejudiced but those by whom the paper is conducted, not can they, unless they fail to sustain the expectations it may attract towards us and towards our colony that attention, which, leading to an examination of our claims upon the sympathy of the world cannot fail to extort a verdict in our favor.

However despicable and unworthy of attention our colony may appear in the eyes of those, who, from prejudice or mental imbecility are incapable of tracing events from their first small beginnings until, to the eye of a sagacious foresight, they stand forth in all their full proportions and full effects: and however small and insignificant it may in itself really be, still it is certain that an enterprise altogether unique — as an experiment alone in its kind and in all the means employed to accomplish it, it is centering upon it the attention and concern of distant politicians. Nor has it awakened the concern of the mere statesman and politician only, it has also struck a chord in the generous bosom of the philanthropist and the christian.

The proof the colony has already given of its ability to sustain a well ordered government — the extent to which it has suppressed the slave trade — the wide circle through which it has shot the kindling rays of civilization — the numerous instances in which it has imbued the "dark untutored mind" with the principles of a heaven born religion, have concurred to beget the opinion now rapidly gaining ground that colonies — Christian colonies of colored men — not needy rapacious adventurers — but colonies of colored people rooted to the soil are the most efficient agents for redeeming and regenerating Africa. As such the colony is contemplated with lively interest by nearly all classes of men.

It is therefore a matter of deep importance to us that the affairs of the colony should be made known. Its difficulties and impediments, its facilities and resources, its advancement in art and science, its success in agriculture, husbandry and commerce — its possession or want of the means of social happiness, political strength, and religious improvement, should be fully and frankly stated. It will be among the objects of the *Herald* to notice those subjects from time to time, that our friends may have, when we advance, matter for rejoicing and [,] when we falter[,] monition to aid us.

It is also proposed to throw an occasional glance beyond the limits of the colony and observe on the fashions of our unreclaimed neighbors. Whatever is peculiar and interesting in the manners and customs of natives: whatever is important to be known in the geography and natural history of the country so far as we can ascertain them will be the subject of our notice.

In stating that we shall aim to give our paper a literary character we wish it to be distinctly understood now and evermore, that we use the word "literary" as it is applicable to Liberia. Our utmost vanity cannot inspire us to hope more than to keep on par with Liberia literature. Thus much however we hope to accomplish: and our hope is inspired by the known ability and industry of General J. N. Lewis, and Rev. A. W. Anderson, our co-adjustors in the Editorial department; and to enable us to sustain all these hopes, and to accomplish all these intentions we invoke the aid of our friends by their purse and their pen.

21. Here We Are

Liberia Herald, 24 November 1848, 8

Here we are, at it again! We have not honored ourself with attention to the paper for the last three months. Circumstances of a most imperative character demanded that we should rusticate; and the decrees of no chancellor are so stern and irresistible as those of poverty. Hence, instead of inditing[234] editorials and collecting extracts, we have been planting potatoes and collecting pepper. Our readers, however, need not start for we shall not treat them with an undue infusion of *capsicum* [235] at present; and our potatoes are yet in a state of embryo.

22. An African Editor

Liberia Herald, 17 March 1842, 19

To perpetrate an editorial, he seats himself — not in the cushioned [*boudoir*] of the literate idler, nor in the fashionable bower of the poet, but in a little sooty apartment of six by eight. Beneath his dingy foolscap a portion of deal, lies supinely on an empty barrel. A few odd and ends of books and newspaper lie in hopeless confusion around. At his side an inkstand, not of china, nor of bronze, but the small end of a cow's horn, on his left a quiver of quills rifled from the upper surface of a porcupine.

In one corner stands a billet of camwood, its opposite is occupied by what once contained four. The walls are duly chalked -- not with mechanical design -- nor geometrical diagrams, but with mathematical mementoes of the kroos of potatoes of which he has relieved the farmer. This is his blotter; ledger, he keeps none.

The boy comes for copy. He draws up a well hacked trestle, for which he is indebted to the carelessness of the carpenter, and seats himself in front of the barrel. Seizing the fearful quill, he [the editor] thus begins -- The press[,] the omnipotent press[,] is the most powerful engine which it has ever been the lot of mortals to possess -- It is the scourge of tyrants -- the pillar of religion and the PALLADIUM of civil liberty. From it[,] as from an impregnable rampart[,] the fearless independent editor --

There is no cassado for breakfast[,] sir. --[236]
Well go, and get some and [don't] bother me.
I have no money, sir. --
don't I know that -- tell Crako to let you have a kroo.
He says he won't. We have not paid him for the other one yet, and he wants the money.
Plague the fellow[;] what can he mean. Can't you borrow some? --
No, sir: I've tried, and they say we owe now more than we'll ever pay.
Well go and collect some money.
I have carried out the bills[,] sir.
Have you collected any money?
No, sir:
Why?
Mr. __ says he has no money, and you need not be afraid of the small amount. Mr. __ says he [don't] like the paper now; you are too polite with the [__]. Mr. __ says your paper is scurrilous. Mr. __ says there is too much religion in it and too little politics. Mr. __ says there is too much politics and too little religion, and Mr. __ says you have insulted his father's tenth cousin. They say they will not take the paper any longer, and they will pay when they get the money. --
That will do, go and call again in an hour for copy.

The editor resumes. -- And though there is no class of men to whom the world is under more immense obligation, yet, there is none --

Jambo has come to get his pay for the palm oil, sir
Be gone sir, don't you see I am engaged

-- there is none we respect that is doomed to a more hopeless.

The rats has gnawed the rollers[,] sir.
Well[,] cast another.
We have no molasses[,] sir.
Well shut up the office, and go to dinner.

Carl Patrick Burrowes

The Church

23. Sabbath School

Liberia Herald, 24 January 1844, 42

It was expected that on Sabbath, the 14th instant, an address would be delivered at the Baptist Meeting House in this place, to the scholars, teachers, and friends of the Sunday school, attached to the Church, by Colonel B. P. Yates, the president of the school.[237] Colonel Yates was unexpectedly called out of town, and Deacon F. B. James, one of the teachers[238], read an appropriate essay on the importance of the Sabbath School system — setting forth the great good it has conducted upon the world — urging the duties of the scholars and teachers — and of parents and [guardians] to lend their aid and influence in securing the attendance of the children, and by their occasional visits.

We have been pained in witnessing the apathy of Baptists in this place, in regard to the Sabbath School. If, as experience and observation appear to prove — the Sabbath School is the nursery of the Church, it would seem that no other agreement could be wanted to secure the prayers and services of every friend of the cause of Christ. It is not unnatural for Christian parents to look upon their offspring as those destined to take their place in the church; or as recruits to fill up the spiritual ranks as the ancient veterans are successively removed by death. But it is time we should abandon the visionary hope of securing an end without employing the appropriate means of attaining it. While the Scripture refers every salutary change to the grace and power of God, it also admonishes us of our duty as instruments. How many parents have been found weeping over their vagrant children? They are found either walking in the counsel of the ungodly, or setting in the seat of the scornful — or they have forsaken the house where their fathers worshipped, and gone off into strange paths! The unhappy parents are ready to regard themselves cursed with ungrateful and perverse offspring. Such should seriously ask themselves whether they performed their duty to those whom God committed to their charge — whether they sought early to instill into their minds the principles of divine truth — to impress them with reverence for the divine character — to inculcate upon them the distinction between vice and virtue — whether they took them by the hand and led them to the house of God. If not, they should at once be silent and repent of their own remissness.

We are aware that some profess to be entirely indifferent where their children go on the Sabbath, so it be to a Sabbath School or a place of worship. From this indifference to the indifference whether they be in the places above, or strolling on the beach, or at home reading some principle poisoning novel, there is but a small remove. Such recklessness of principle is [two words indistinct] unworthy of a christian. In this spirit stirring day, every soldier of the cross is called to buckle on his armour and repair to the field. He is called to a real and arduous contest, not merely to beat the air, but to "contend for the faith once delivered to the saints." This supposes clearly ascertained and firmly fixed principles on the part of the Christian — A proper conviction of their importance will incite to a vigilant use of all the means to diffuse them abroad, and implant them in the minds of others. No intelligent Christian therefore can be indifferent to the doctrines and religious sentiments imbibed by his children; under the conviction of the correctness of his own opinions, he will be anxious they should be adopted by his offspring.

We would therefore most solemnly warn the members of our denomination against this practical infidelity. Either your religious sentiments are right or they are wrong. If wrong, abandon at once your position — If right, put forth all your energies — allure, council all within the reach of your influence to form in your ranks. But remember the most solemn of all obligations rests upon you, to train up your child in the way he should go that when he is old he may not depart from it.

24. [Religious]

Liberia Herald, 1 October 1847, 87

The third Union Meeting of the Associated Baptist Churches, was held with the church at New Georgia. It commenced on the third Friday in last month. It was indeed a time of refreshing from the presence of the Lord. On Friday, the day of commencement, an unusual solemnity pervaded the assemblies, which disposed to deep and serious thought and close self-examination. This state of feeling was regarded a favorable occasion to rouse Christians to earnest and persevering prayer for the out pouring of the spirit — it was thus used and, by the blessing of the Great Head of the Church, used successfully. As the meeting progressed, the earnestness and fervour of Christians increased until on Sabbath, the Lord displayed his power in a manner that reminded us of the [Pentecostal] visitations. Christians of different denominations were present — backsliders were there and cold negligent worldly minded professors were there — and non-professors were there, and all felt and confessed that "The Lord is in this place." The Holy Spirit descended and by a diversity of manifestations appealed to the hearts and consciences of all classes present. The faithful, consistent persevering Christian was edified and cheered by the hope set before him — the frigid and worldly-minded felt shame and remorse in view of the past — backsliders repented and returned from their wanderings and the stout hearted sinners made to cry "what shall *I* do."

On Sabbath night fifteen persons came forth to the altar, confessing their sins and bewailing their condition and with tears in their eyes, begged that the people of God would pray for them. Among them was one of the captives by the "*Pons*".[239] The season was one of so much interest that having charge of the Church and being compelled to leave, we advised the church to continue divine service every evening through the week, which was done. On Thursday we received an earnest request from the deacon to go up. We went and found the interest and excitement unabated. On the following Saturday we again went up and found three of the late seekers professing to have experienced a change of heart. On Sabbath morning at six o'clock the church assembled to hear their relation. In regard to one who was to come forward, we confess we felt a little scepticism — and that was the captive by the "*Pons.*" Perhaps by this admission, we are exposing ourself to the imputation of want of faith in the power of God, or of correct understanding of the nature of that work which changes the human heart. Be it so, and be it that our want of faith and our ignorance have been reproved by the relation of this proselyte, who lately in the nakedness of sin, and infatuated by heathenisms is now clothed and in his right mind and has a place with the saints of God, at the feet of the Saviour. Still we must confess it a part of our creed that the work of conversion is wholly a work of divine power and that as soon will the Leopard change his spots, or the Ethiop his skin, as man cease from sin and turn to God.

But to the relation. Sam Clark, for this is his name, came forward. Finding he could speak tolerably good English, when he ended his relation, we thus interrogated him:

What make you pray?
Because I fear die and go for bad place.[240]
Who tell you there be a bad place?
I go meeting ebery time, I hear da palaver and I blieve him.

When you been lib for pray, how you been feel.

I feel bad too much. My heart be bad, sick too much.

You feel bad all da time you lib for pray?

All time I feel bad, I no feel good one time.

You pray all time?

I pray all time, I pray night, I pray day, I pray house, I pray bush.

What time you feel better?

One night I feel bad too much, I think I can die, I pray, den I hear something fall down all same man cut tree in bush. My heart light, I be new. I laugh, I cant cry, I say what dis? Something say dis be God. God done hear you for Jesus Christ (sake).

Do you love God?

I lub God too much.

Do you love God's people?

Too much. I lub ebery body.

Suppose church say you no converted, you must go pray again?

Spose he say I noo look God, I cant ble (believe) that no more. I go pray, because I lub pray.

These answers with others which have escaped us banished our doubt, and with indescribable feeling we gave him our hand as a candidate for baptism and admission into Christ['s] Militant Church. Three other persons received the same morning as candidates for baptism, and it gives us pleasure to state that the relations of all were marked with an artlessness, yet consistency and firm conviction of the change wrought in them, that left no doubt as to the reality of the work performed. More, perhaps six or eight[,] will soon come forward for baptism.

25. Letter to [J. B. Taylor], Monrovia, 17 November 1847

Rev. and dear sir,

In presuming to obtrude myself upon your notice I have nothing to offer in apology but the importance of the subject to which I wish to call your attention. [241]

The Southern Baptist Convention of whose foreign correspondent I perceive you are the organ, in the establishment of a mission in our midst gives us pleasing evidence of your desire for our welfare, therefore if in the following brief statement

Carl Patrick Burrowes

of facts you should find any thing to aid you in planning future operations I shall consider myself more than paid for my trouble.

There are in this country nine villages — Farmington, Marshall, Monrovia, New Georgia, Caldwell, Virginia, New Orleans and Millsburg. In each of these villages except Farmington and New Orleans there is a Baptist church and at New Orleans we expect to constitute a church the ensuing week. There are six or eight individuals there who belong to the church in this place. They have obtained their dismission, and will in a few days be erected in a separate body. There are also some there who have been baptised, but expecting a church will be shortly constituted there have not attached themselves any where. These will be incorporated with the others already referred to. There are in the country nine Baptist preachers — one at Marshall, three in this place (Monrovia), one (a native) in New Georgia, two at Virginia, and two at Millsburg. Of these nine only two, Bro. F. B. James[242] at Virginia and myself are ordained. The others are licentiates. Bro. James has charges of the church at Virginia and resides there. He has opened a school in that place which I hope the board may find it convenient to sustain. Bro. J. also gives some time in visiting destitute churches. Brother Smart, a native African but a longtime resident of Charleston, South Carolina, preaches for the church at Junk.[243] He is a good man and devoted but being wholly destitute of education his services in the way of preaching are not so effective as otherwise they might be, and not being ordained, he cannot administer the ordinances. This church is in consequence in great need of help, and as the Methodists have removed their operations from this village, a school here might be made efficient in the dissemination of truth. There are three preachers resident in this place: John T. Richardson, A. B. Anderson[244] and myself. Brethren Anderson & Richardson minister to the church here in conjunction with myself. Each of these brethren has some knowledge of the English language enough at least to teach its elements to children. But they are poor men and have families to maintain & therefore can give but a portion of their time to the churches. I have charge of the church at New Georgia. Ordinarily, I meet the church every alternate Sabbath, when I usually preach twice on that day. I also meet with them on the evening of the last Friday of every month for the purpose of holding conference. In interesting and excited seasons, like the present, I make twice weekly visits. It falls also to my lot to be called to more than an equal share of labour in the church here. The church at New Georgia numbers 63 members, all of whom are native Africans, but five; and I make bold to say that in all that concerns life and godliness, a more intelligent church is not to be found in the Colony. This church as also all our churches have six stated assemblings during the week for worship. At 6 o'clock a.m. on Sabbath for prayer[,] preaching in the fore and afternoon and every Tuesday evening prayer meeting and Thursday evening preaching. Each of the churches holds monthly conferences for the transaction of business for monthly conferences for the transaction of business for receiving members and for collecting contributions from the members for the support of the gospel. The regular contribution is different [missing: at different] churches. At New Georgia there is no fixed sum. Each member gives what he finds it in his heart to give. In Monrovia each male is required to give 2-1/2 & each female 1-1/4 cents a month. I regret that I am compelled to acknowledge we have not given the attention to Sabbath Schools which they deserve. True we have one in most of the churches, but they have not been conducted with the energy & regularity which we hope to give them in future. Bro. James & Underwood[245] labour a[t] New Virginia. (Bro. Underwood is a pious zealous man, but has no education. Bro. James is improving and bids fair to be useful.) The church at Caldwell has suffered great declension, and in fact is almost extinct, most of the members have attached themselves to the church at Virginia. There are two preachers at Millsburg. Bro. David White & Bro. Adam Lockhart both zealous & good men [but wholly uneducated.][246] The church has been in a languishing state. It has suffered much for want of the regular ministration of the word. The mode of travelling here is expensive, and our preachers being poor men & having families depending upon their daily labour for subsistence cannot travel a great deal. A little attention and under the blessing of God this church would again arise. Already there is beginning to be a better state of things there. In each church the standing rule is to celebrate the Lord's Supper once in two months. This rule is not violated unless by some untoward circumstance on the part of a qualified administrator. I have not the statistics of our churches in this country before me, but I feel safe in putting down 280 as the number of regular communicants. Thus, sir, I have given you a brief statement of facts in relation to the Baptists in this country. I intended when I took up my pen to say something about the movement of other denominations here, but this letter has grown so on my hands that I have neither time nor room. I must defer it to some future communication and I shall do it the more freely in the hope it call forth more systematic aid in support of our cause here. We are now enjoying the most extensive and I feel the most genuine renewal and reformation I have ever witnessed in the colony. The Lord is manifesting his power and grace in a most wonderful manner. On the Sabbath before the last I baptized 24 in this place and on the last Sabbath I baptised 23 at New Georgia. We have since received 8 more candidates for baptism and some 6 or more here and 4 or 5 at New Georgia will soon come forward to relate what the Lord has done for them. As we put down such large numbers of candidates & newly baptised some may fear our [scratched out: mode] terms of admission [as] more fragile than the scripture warrants. To ease such minds we can cite as a fundamental article of our creed that the church of Christ is a spiritual building, and we hold to none but believers' baptism. Further many of us came from America and were received into churches there. The rules which prevail there, when not obviously unsuited, we adopt here. Again we look not to number merely to build up our cause but to a conscientious following of the directions of the Saviour laid own in his holy word. I would like to say something here of the propriety of having a Baptist school in some of the largest villages — a school taught by one who can properly combine the business of preaching with school teaching, but this will be more obvious in our future account of the operations of our Methodist brethren. Bro. James expects on next to baptize 5 or 6 [in] Virginia.

Very respectfully,

Your Obdt. Servant

H. Teage

P.S. You will perceive by the dates of this and the papers that this letter was written subsequent to the publication of the papers, which will account for the difference in statement of the number of converts. Nov. 18th Having a spare moment I will add a few words more in respect to the revival now going on, & what I say shall be of a domestic character. I have in my house and on my farm a number of Native Africans varying in ages from 8 to 25 years, but the greater number under 20 years, and they are from several different tribes. Some of them are of the Congo by the *Pons*. The Lord is at work amongst them. Three of the Congos profess to be seeking the salvation of their souls, and from their deep seriousness and altered conduct I am led to entertain great hopes that they are "sorrowing that godly sorrow which marketh repentance unto life." Another most interesting and intelligent Vey boy about 20 is rejoicing in hope of pardoned sins & I am persuaded his rejoicings are just. Another Vey girl about 15 whom I redeemed from slavery about 3 years ago is the subject of deep conviction. So that the Lord has given me one of my household & I trust he will enable me to tell you in my next that he has given me four more. Another girl whom I redeemed about 12 years ago is now a member of Christ's visible body. She is married to L. K. Crocker[247] of the Baptist Mission at Basa. She was converted in my house and subsequently married & went with her husband to his station. An account of the number of converts to the true faith in different families, and also of their subsequent conduct would compare more than favorably with any which any mission on this coast can give.

26. Religious

Liberia Herald, 5 November 1847, 95

In our last, we put down as the fruits of the present revival and reformation, nine candidates for baptism in this town.[248] It is with unspeakable pleasure and gratitude to God that we are now enabled to report fifteen more in this place, making in all twenty four who, on the ensuing Sabbath, will put on Christ by baptism. On last Sabbath, our Methodist brethren immersed five professing believers in the Mesurado. We were privileged to be present at the scene, which afforded matter for both rejoicing and regret — rejoicing at the progress of principles which we so dearly cherish, regret that there was a manifestation of levity during a ceremony so clearly prescribed in the book of God. We trust no baptism will be guilty of such unreasonable merriment. The burial of a conscientious believer with Christ in baptism is an act too solemn, the stifled opinion and the motive of the administrator, notwithstanding, to engender mirth in the mind of an intelligent and Bible Christian. Especially should Baptists receive it with gratitude and encourage it and hail it as the dawn of the day in which there shall be one Baptism as there is but one Lord and one Faith.

On Wednesday evening last, the Church assembled in conference to hear the experience of those who made application for baptism. Three Americans had been received. The moderator by way of encouraging others, said, "We have done as Thou hast commanded and yet there is room." When, lo! to the astonishment of all in the large assemblage, "Jumbo" came pressing his way through the crowd, seated himself by the side of the moderator. "Jumbo" is one of the Africans by the "Pons;" he is an apprentice and his master was then in the house and is a member of the church. His opinion was asked of "Jumbo's" state and religious character. He stated that he was at first skeptical as to "Jumbo" that he regarded him more phenzied[249] than religiously affected, but that subsequently the man's deep seriousness, continued earnestness, humility and consistency had forced that opinion from him; that a manifest change had been wrought in Jumbo, so great a change as filled him with astonishment. Jumbo came forward not only unsolicited by anyone, but without the knowledge of his guardians. He related his experience which convinced all who heard him that the wind which "bloweth wheresoever it listeth"[250] has been working on his soul. He was received and numbered among the people of God. The extraordinary manner in which he came forward suggested the propriety of changing his name, which his friends agreed to and henceforth he will be known as *John the Baptist*. It is proper, however, to remark that he will not be the first of the company by the "Pons" that is baptized. A young woman of that company was immersed last Sabbath by Rev. Mr. Benham,[251] of the M. E. Church. It is singular and worthy of remark that when the offer was made in church to sprinkle her she resolutely refused to submit and said "I want to go to big water," pointing to the river.

The work is still going on. At New Virginia [see map 1], the station of brother F. B. James,[252] saints are enjoying a season of refreshing and sinners are enquiring the way to Zion. We received an encouraging letter from him a few days ago, giving an account of the state of things there, and requesting us to go up and help, but our time is so wholly occupied here and [in] New Georgia, we are unable to go. We regret much that we are not able to give more of our time to the work, but we are consoled when we recollect that the same authority which imposes the duty to preach the gospel, makes it a duty to provide for a family.

27. Letter to J. B. Taylor, Monrovia, 3 January 1848

Rev. & dear Sir,

In my letter a few days ago, I promised to give you in the next some particulars in regard to the operations of the Methodists here. Since then, facts have transpired which would seem to render such an account unnecessary inasmuch as we are led to believe they intend essentially to modify if not to remodel their whole system of missionary operations here. What the precise nature and extent of these modifications will be I am not able to say; nor can perhaps they tell have far goes, when they have unsettled[253] the present established order of things. Should any important changes take place tending to affect our interests here, or which may be made a data for Baptist proceedings, I shall take great pleasure in informing you thereof.[254] Nothing is clearer than that the Methodists some years back calculating upon superior men which they did not have and superior means which they did have aimed to make the colony of Liberian an entire Methodist community and consequently they rang the changes even from the pulpit upon the gold and silver and men of the M. E. Church, and God of John Wesley, was a phrase of much more frequent mention than sons of God. At one time our Zion was threatened with utter destruction; and most Baptist hearts fainted. For my part, I never yielded to such weakness. I felt confident that gold & silver can never be transmitted into religious principle, & that without religious principle no church ever stands, that the mortar was untempered and would never adhere and at the first rude concussions the building would totter to a fall. I have not been disappointed. Now that we have come not only unscathed but enlarged with a healthy increase [out] of the severe ordeal to which the Baptist cause in this place has been submitted, now that we have resisted all the allurings of fat salaries and seducings of good lumps and easy [??], it silenced these tongues of temptation to desert our past and our principles by an indignant refusal even to entertain the base proposition; and by a happy future of finding on every appropriate occasion something which if humble and forcible in favour of that cause which is every where spoken against and which by God's grace we resolved to adhere in every extremity now that these things are seen the question is not infrequently heard, [two words missing at worn edge of page] it came to pass that the Baptist in Liberia hath not only maintained their ground against such fearful odds but have continued steadily to increase? The answer is to be sought in the nature of our principle; in which there are not only the recuperative and conservative but the reserve [??] also. We have lived by the truth, and the truth has silently made its way, even to the distance of occasional triumphs over [pert] and [waggish[255]] error. Our course here is onward, & the subject of baptism is operating like leaven in the very heart of pedobaptism & threatens soon to leaven the whole man. I send you the *Herald*, from which you will learn the state of things at Caldwell. Last week, I received three candidates for baptism at New Georgia, of whom two were Methodists & more expect to come over soon.

The *Packet* arrived today from Grand Bassa. Brother A. P. Davis writes me that a reformation has commenced there — a result of our labors at the association and the first fruits which were gathered by Bro. Day[256], last Sabbath he immersed seven.

Cape Mount is an inviting field for missionary effort and so far as I can judge the people of that region are prepared for the reception of the gospel. They are the most intelligent, enterprising and generous tribe about these regions, and the Country itself is all that be desired for [???]bility and beauty; and healthy millieau. The Methodists have been looking in that region, and the conference which is now in session will I think it, probable place a teacher there. The land is however wide enough for two and far more. I called bro. Day's attention to this place, but whether his multiplied duties at stations already occupied will leave him time to give the proper attention to this I know not. But I know of no place on the coast more worthy of a missionary board's attention than this; and I sincerely trust it will be made the seat of Baptist operations. I have the assurance of the senior officer of the Sierra Leone division of H. B. M. Squadron stationed off Galenas that all needed protection will be most cheerfully extended to missionaries at that place & I have been more than once requested by him to endeavour to procure the establishment of a mission there under the conviction that it would speedily uproot the slave trade.

I have the honor to be, Rev. Sir, Your Obdt. Servant,

H. Teage

Jan. 5. I have just yesterday received a request from the members of the Baptist church at Cape Palmas to visit & administer the ordinances of baptism & the Lord's Supper; but today I learn that Mr. Day at Basa is about to ordain Bro. Underwood to go down there. It is desirable to have a minister there & I suppose this step is regarded justified by the necessity of the case. But Bro. U. has no recommendations but zeal & piety & the peculiar doctrines & practices are subject to more frequent and wide attacks there than in any other part of the whole colony.

H. Teage

28. Letter to J. B. Taylor, Monrovia, 20 March 1848

Rev. & dear Sirs,

Your very kind letter of July 2nd is before me, and I seize the opportunity presented by the accidental touching here of a vessel bound to America to make my acknowledgments. The interest manifested by you and the Board and Society, which you represent in what relates to our churches & cause in these ends of the earth is truly inspiring, and reminding, as it does that the eyes of the whole denomination in America are upon us will serve I am confident as a stimulant to exertion, and a monitor of conduct. In my letter of January by the *Liberia Packet*, I attempted to redeem the promise I made in a previous letter by the *Hollander* to inform you in respect of the operation of our Methodist brethren here. Should that letter reach you, you know how far I succeeded.

Bro. Drayton[257] is here; he has not yet determined where he will pitch his tent. This matter however need not remain long undecided, as the field is large and already white for the harvest and the laborers few; yet I cannot conjecture where he will fix himself. Bro. Day has established a school at Louisiana and has appointed my nephew W. A. Johnson teacher there. He is a youth of decided piety, good natural parts; and of studious habits & I think him fair to be useful.

Should it not be considered important I would ask that you will at some convenient time give me some definite information as to the mode in which your Board will seek to accomplish its object here. The good of the colonies and of Africa generally is, I am aware the object to which the wishes of your society are directed. But whether you intend to employ wholly or only in part the instrumentality of schools, or whether you design to combine school teaching with preaching, I have not been informed. If you intend to rely upon preaching as an instrumentality under God, will the preachers itinerate or will they be localized? These are questions upon which you will do me a favour when you have an opportunity by giving me some information.

If you have received my letter by the *Packet*, you are already in possession of my views of the importance of schools as an auxiliary in the dissemination and establishment of truth.

The vessel U. S. Brig *Boxer* not sailing at the hour first proposed, I have time to add a line or two. I have been a long time engaged in trade, and connected also for a long time with public affairs here. These two matters have so nearly engrossed my attention as to leave but little time to attend to any thing else. I have come to the conclusion that they have had their share of my brief space on this stage. Besides trade here is of all things most perplexing and deteriorating to duty. In regard to politics I reached my goal in the independence of the Republic. For this I labored hard and in the face of great opposition for many years. It having been accomplished I fell at liberty to retire from the perplexing arena of politics and have done so. I resigned my office as senator the day following the adjournment of the Legislature; and turned with renewed energy to the cultivation of my farm. This is more congenial with my feelings than with trading or political squabbling.

If it be among the objects desired by the Board to establish a school in this vicinage of a grade somewhat higher than merely elementary, I would cheerfully offer my services, provided it would be so arranged as to leave me at liberty to meet my pastoral engagements with the church at New Georgia. This is to me the most interesting church in the colony. It is composed almost wholly of Native Africans whose good order and spiritual attainments will compare favourably with those of any others in the colony. More than two-thirds of the present number 81 (some having been added since the association) has been brought into the church since I have had charge & I think I may venture to say that few announcements would be more harmful than would be the announcement that I am about to leave. Nor would it be less harmful to myself. We are going here as usual. The religious excitement has somewhat abated, & I am happy to say that nearly every one of those who joined us recently continue thus far to maintain their position.

I send you some papers. I wrote you that I would probably go to America by the *Packet.* I think I shall not do so, as I am about winding up my business.

Earnestly praying for the divine blessing upon you and the Society.

I remain dear Sir, yours in Gospel bond.

H. Teage

29. Letter to J. B. Taylor, Monrovia, 30 June 1848

Rev. & dear Sir,

I sit down to thank you for your kind letters and for the books & papers you sent me. I assure you few presents are more gratifying to us in these ends of the earth than are occasional importation of books, tracts & papers, especially if they are the productions of Baptist hands & the issue of Baptist pens. We thereby learn not merely the state of our denomination but the progress of its opinion. It is true that we should have no further revelation, or in other words cannot hope for any addition to the already completed canon of scripture, yet it is equally true that we have yet to find the man of whom it may be said, he has explored all the hidden treasures of divine truth and ascertained elucidated & fixed the precise meaning of the declarations of the sacred oracles.[258] So that while this ignorance exists and man continues an inquisitive creature there must need surely be a co-existent diversity and progressiveness of opinion. "The spirit be poured out upon the churches in those copious effusions["] which are promised to the latter days, then & not till then, the watchmen upon Zion's walls will see eye to eye or lift up the voice together.[259]

Bro. Underwood late one of the attaches of your mission goes to America by this vessel. His object is to purchase his wife & to return here. I hope that God may prosper his way & crown his journey with success. He is a good man & zealous, & although not of great attainments yet adopted to do good in some quarters.

The churches here generally are about in the same state as when I wrote you last. I regret to say the church in this place is in a rather divided state of which I will give a brief history.

Bro. Drayton had not been here but a short time before some few members (not a tithe of the church) conceived the idea of calling him to the pastorate. A meeting was called at an unusual time & an unusual place & by these few Bro. Drayton was elected. Bro. D. said nothing to any of the officiating brethren of the movement nor do I believe one of them excepting Richardson knew anything about the matter until it was over. However we concluded to rest satisfied if the church was.

Some weeks afterward Bro. Drayton in conversation with me said the church must allow him a support. I agreed with him that he should be supported & also told him that his election to the pastorate had put me in a position to do what I had long wished to do, that is to urge upon the church the duty of doing something towards the support of the gospel ministry & thus testify her love to God & her high estimate of our holy religion. I also stated that I should do so in the *Herald*. Bro. Drayton uttered not one syllable of objection. The piece came out, & just then it appears Bro. Drayton and others ascertained it would do an injury by preventing your Board from allowing him a support!! I am abused, villified and slandered on all hands — meetings have been held to take up the subject & I expect the result will be my expulsion from the church and a numerously signed letter to you contradicting my statement.

Indeed my dear Brother I did not know Bro. Drayton expected to be paid by the Board unless he rendered service at the place where Bro. Day assigned him. Bro. Drayton's conversation with me left the impression on my mind that if he remained here he would look to the church for his support. How this change came over his mind I knew not until I learned that Bro. Brander had obtained a promise from you that the Board would pay either the whole or a part of a pastor's salary. Had I known this at the time I should not have written. Yet I am fully persuaded of the truth of what I have stated in the *Herald* & can easily prove that the church here is far more able to pay a pastor than many in America which not only support their pastor but do considerable also toward missionary & other benevolent institutions. You have no idea to what extent the members of the church indulge in vain show and superfluous dress & those who indulge in it most are the most clamorous for this allowance from the Board. The fact is [indistinct word] people have no idea of sacrefices for this gospel: On the contrary as soon as a mission is formed scores are holding out unworthy & lazy hands for a gratuitous support. This in vain I tell them: Missionary societies are formed to spread the gospel to the Heathen & not to pay men to preach to well dressed and civilized communities.

When Bro. Drayton first arrived I own that selfishness prevailed & I advised him if he could consider it, do so to remain in this vicinity. A better feeling however possessed me & I referred him to Cape Palmas as an inviting but destitute field of labor. There is no Baptist minister at that place while there are six in this vicinity. I regret this state of things, but after all I hope good will grow out of it. I feel assured that the Board acted advisedly when it engaged to sustain a pastor for this church & therefore will not be influenced by anything I have written. I did not write the board but for our people. I wrote truth which I can sustain if necessary.

Yours very respectfully,

H. Teage

30. Letter to J. B. Taylor, Monrovia, 3 July 1848

Dear Brother,

I have just this moment returned from a called conference of which truth & justice concur to demand that I give you a brief account.[260]

On Monday evening last the 30th Ult.[261] a meeting was held at Bro. Brander's, (9 members being present) to take measures "to rebut the article in the *Herald*." After many speeches all loaded with vehement imputations of grossly wicked motives in the writer of the article (I the writer being present), it was resolved that a committee of three brethren be appointed to draw up a counter statement and to present it the evening the 3rd June to the conference & if approved to be sent on to the Board. General John N. Lewis, a member of the church with an estimated income of three thousand dollars a year; N. Brander, with a salary of fifteen hundred dollars a year; & J. C. Minor[262], with an income of six hundred a year, were the committee appointed.

We assembled this evening to hear the letters. There being 11 members present including myself. From the small numbers attending your will discover the indifference of the members in respect of this communication. Since the matter has been agitated they feel convenient, they are wanting in their duty & are ashamed to beg. In all the speakers in the meeting confessed, the members can do something if they had a will to do so, but they have no will & we want a pastor & the Board has agreed to give us one!! When we met this evening the letter was called for. But the committee reported that they had not completed it! One of the most eager aspirants to the mission treasury — Bro. J. T. Richardson then rose with a promptness and spontaneity, which impressed all present that it was only a maneuver to keep the communication concealed from me, and moved that the three other brethren should be associated with the former committee, making six and that they be clothed with authority to write the letter and send it on to you and the Board without going the circuitous route of bringing it before the church. This committee consists of J. T. Richardson, B. P. Yates[263] (he was not present and it was announced that he will leave tomorrow & will not return before the *Packet* leaves) and B. J. Drayton. Thus I know not what they will write. I have not written because I wish to prevent Bro. D. from getting support from you. I appeal to the searching of hearts that I only intended to urge upon our people to discharge a solemn duty. I do not envy Bro. D. I have for twenty years supported myself by my labors and in my humble manner preached the gospel, and although I am not allowed to boast, yet I am allowed in defense of myself to say that notwithstanding the abuse & calumny which from time to time is heaped. There are in heaven and in the church here at this time living witnesses that God both owned my labor and blessed them to the edification and conversion of many. My only object in writing now is to vindicate the article in the *Herald* from the charge of falsehood which I suppose they will bring against it. For the truth of what I have written I refer you to Bro. Underwood who goes to the U. S. in this vessel, to Bro. Worrell[264] of North Carolina & to Bro. F. S. James here, who if he has the moral courage to face the storm will confirm all I have said. I ought perhaps to mention that those most anxious for this dowry from the board are the most wealthy amongst us, and indulging the most largely in superfluity, excepting Bro. Richardson who is animated by an altogether different motive. Now my dear Bro. I close. Although I confess I would not have written the article had I foreseen all the objurgation[265] it has caused, yet on the whole I do not regret it. It will be provocative of good, all here, even the committee, confess much more might be done than is done, and that there is a glaring inconsistency between our eating, dressing and begging!

Very Respectfully, Your Obdt. Servant,

H. Teage

31. Letter to J. B. Taylor, Monrovia, 28 July 1848

Rev. & dear Sir,

As I wrote you very fully by the *Packet* in anticipation of events which had not taken place, I can well spare myself the labor of writing and you of reading a long epistle by this conveyance.[266]

The church, or at least a part, acted, and by a process unheard of since the [??setial] ages of the Catholic denomination, it was voted that "under the circumstances the church can't bear with brother Teage." I will not go into a detail of the particulars, especially as I do not intend to regard the decision, but shall go along in my usual way — attending to the church at New Georgia and preaching elsewhere as occasion may offer.

The church here is in a deplorable state & at the very gate of division. The pious and consecratious desire to retire from scenes of turbulence & perfidy and seek quietude in some other fold, & I think I may say without arrogating too much that they only want a word of encouragement for it from me. I however shall encourage no such procedure at least at this time.

When Drayton arrived here the church was, as a general thing, in peace & harmony, and had recently been favoured with visible tokens of the divine blessing. But alas how changed! How has the gold become dim!! The members divided and wandering like sheep without a shepherd. The shepherd squabbling for pay, the meetinghouse uncovered, exposed to the weather & going to decay!!

One acquainted with Brother Drayton's abilities or more properly his want of abilities might be tempted to ask what is there about him of so much consequence as to be risking the destruction of the church to secure him? This would evince the consequent ignorance of the following facts.

First, that as Monrovia is the Metropolis of Liberia some good folks here would have the church here regarded Metropolitan & would to have her distinguished not by superiority of praises but by a paid ministry, a parsonage house and surpassing elegance on the part of the worshippers, but determined to pay nothing themselves.

Second, Mr. Drayton arrived a pensioner of the S. B. M. averring that he had the liberty to locate where he pleased. Mr. D. fell into the hands of men far more cunning than himself, who determining to use him to accomplish their ends, studiously concealed from him every consideration of fitness of the comparative claim of different fields of labour [from ?] his attention, and silenced in his breast every murmur of a sense of duty against inclination with glaring descriptions of good society and good cheer which would be his in Monrovia. I write not this to plead my own cause. I have no cause to plead. If [I] were disposed to do so I would not because I know not what has been written against me. From the factious decisions here, I take an appeal to God and my conscience, and proceed in my course, referring "my work to the Lord & my labor to my God."

Bro. Drayton has come out as writer. He has a long article in the *Herald*. I regret the paper is not out, but will send you copy by the next. It is a production respectable for its length, singular for its novelty in the orthographic department and remarkable for its noble disdain of all the rules and the command of grammar.

I am an ill fated man. The last twenty years of my life have been devoted to Liberia in general and to the Baptist cause in particular. Neither my time nor my little talent nor my money has been withheld when either the colony or the church required it & I have all along been the object of rancorous envy and remorseless persecution. When in my opinion circumstances rendered it necessary we should be disconnected from the Am. Col. Socy. and assume an independent position, I hesitated not, but asserted the fact and boldly though alone advocated the measure. Opposition arose on every side. My motives were impugned, and I was called an Englishman at heart. Scores of letters were secretly sent to the Board against me, until at length the Society in solemn convention was about to pass a resolution expressive of the necessity that I should be banished from the colony. Mr. Pinney, who lived in my family while here & who knew me well, interposed, and assured the Board if I had acted thus I had good grounds for my conduct & further begged them to wait for explanations. In one year the Board & all the people in the colony heartily concurred in the measure. Thus it has been, thus it appears it is to be.

Your Obdt. Servant,

H. Teage

p.s. I have just recd. a letter from Bro. Day in which he says he has sent up a small box and some letters for America which he wishes me to have conveyed on board. I have not succeeded in finding them. If I should, I will attend to it.

32. Letter to J. B. Taylor, Monrovia, 15 November 1848

Rev. J. B. Taylor,

I wrote you briefly a few days ago in acknowledgement of yours of Sept. 4th, but the movements of the vessel by which the letter was dispatched are so uncertain and suspicious that I think it best briefly to recapitulate what was stated therein.[267]

I should endeavour what I can for your forthcoming memoir of Cary[268] so far at least as relates to that particular incident is concerned to which you allude — though it will be somewhat anticipating a work or book which I meditate getting out under the title of "History of Liberia." So you see Sir that vanity is still in the ascendant. I am now engaged in a memoir of my father.[269] I find great difficulty from the want of materials. My father conducted no correspondence, filled no conspicuous stations, was nothing more than Colin Teage, a humble obscure and illiterate Baptist and as such any notice of him would perhaps be inexcusable except by his son.

I have nothing to say in reference to Mr. Drayton. What I have to say will appear in the forthcoming number of the *Herald*.

The church here is in a most deplorable condition, rent in twain and the members scattered like a sheep without a shepherd. The consequence of a man being appointed at a private meeting by 25 persons a pastor over 160!! Years will not repair the injury done.

There was truth in the charge you mentioned in your letter. I confess and deplore it! I shall endeavour by God's assistance to refrain for the future and entirely and forever abandon that which so easily besets me. No one can feel and see more plainly than I do the evil to which it tends; & it shall be my constant prayer that I may [be] kept from this evil.

Bro. F. S. James died suddenly on the 9th inst.[270] Thus Virginia is without a preacher. My nephew teaches school there. Mr. Drayton seems anxious to have him dismissed by way of reprisal on me. But I suppose the whole affair will rest with Mr. Day.

I shall be always willing to contribute my share toward the support of a pastor. While I have breath, I shall not ask a foreign board to pay a pastor to watch over me. Nor would I wish such an arrangement. I wish a mutual dependence and obligation. But I shall insist in the election of officers that we shall observe the old landmarks, or to be plain, that we shall keep our eye to the principles and polity which Baptist churches in all ages have cherished. In addition, it would hardly be required of me to contribute to the support of a pastor if it were recollected that there is not a minister in Liberia of my denomination who performs so much labour as myself, and that not only without pay, but wholly at my own expense. I may hereafter make this manifest in some public manner.

Respectfully yours,

H. Teage

33. Letter to J. B. Taylor, Monrovia, 12 April 1849

Dear Sir,

I seize a moment from pressing engagements to comply with your request, that I would, if the reflection on the character of Cary in the memoir of him appeared to Gurley's *Life of Ashmun*[271] is incorrect, or unjust, set the matter right. To do this it is necessary simply to state the facts of the case.

Up to the close of 1823 owing to the almost total suspension of communication between the colonists and the natives and the presence of an unusual number of slave trading vessels, it was found absolutely necessary to allow the people rations from the government store; for which they were required to return a remuneration on labour on the public works. This the people did cheerfully. Dr. Ayers[272] before he left for America in 1822 had removed them from Perseverance Island to their allotments of land on the Cape. The lots assigned to them by him lay along the margin of the river, and it, was generally supposed they would form the most valuable part of the town as they gave a water right. In 1823 a new survey was made, the plot of the town enlarged, and other lots assigned to the people in place of those they occupied. The people remonstrated, and contended that they held a double claim on their land, first by conquest and secondly by assignment by a regular agent; and they thought it unreasonable that they should be compelled to relinquish them; or exchange them for others which were acknowledged to be less valuable. Mr. Ashmun adhered to his demand and threatened to starve them into compliance. This menace strengthened their determination to resist the demand. While things were in this state, Mr. Ashmun called upon them to cut the line for the new allotments. The call was disregarded and he at once cut them off from their rations. The people met together declared Mr. Ashmun's conduct arbitrary and inhuman, and determined to take the management of matters into their own hands until they should hear from the board. They applied to Mr. Cary in whom they had the

Carl Patrick Burrowes

highest confidence. Apprehensive that they might proceed to personal violence he prevailed over them to wait and assured them that their grievances should be redressed. A few days afterward while Mr. Johnson the commissary was engaged in serving out the rations to those who had not incurred the agent's displeasure Mr. Cary went to the already open store house [and] weighed off in the presence of the commissary the regular rations of those men who had been cut off and retired. All this was done quietly in open day and in the presence of the commissary and others.

Thus, sir, I have given you briefly the facts of the case. I will leave every one to draw his own conclusion without any remark from me, more than to say that I never heard from Cary nor from any one else nor from any quarter except from the publication at first alluded to that he ever made an acknowledgement that he had done wrong.

Baltimore, July 1, 1849

Dear Sir,

After writing the above I was solicited to come to America on public business. By the blessing of God, I have arrived. I should like to visit Richmond, but it is not certain my engagements will permit me to do so. The differences & difficulties between myself & the church were happily adjusted before I left.

Your Obdt. Servant,

H. Teage

After I concluded to come to the U. S. I had no chance of communicating with Day.

34. Letter to J. B. Taylor, Monrovia, 4 March 1850

Dear Sir,

As I presume it will be gratifying to you and to all the friends of the "mission to Central Africa" to learn the whereabouts of Rev. Messrs Bowen & Goodie and Hr. Hill, I seize the opportunity by a Bonny Trader touching here, on her way to England, to inform you that those gentlemen arrived here in the *Brig Smithfield* on the 7th Ult., landed on the 9th and concluding not to proceed to the leeward to Badagry[273] took up their quarters at my house.

On the 15th they started for Boporah, the capital of the Konah Country and late residence of the famous King Boson. I accompanied them as far [as] Vons-Wah, a native town about 14 miles from this. We hoped to get carriers there, but were disappointed. We dispatched a messenger to Lansanah the present chief of Kondah requesting him to send thirty men to carry the baggage. Business requiring my presence at home, I returned early the following morning; and as Mr. Goodale desired to spend a few days in this place while the mission would be awaiting the carriers, I left my boat for him, and he followed me in the afternoon. He remained with me until the following Wednesday, the 20, when I sent him back. On the 22nd, the carriers arrived and on the 27th they struck their camp and started for their destination. From some Mandingo traders who left Boporah ten days [ago], I learned they had reached that place and were well, though I have received no communication from them.

They left part of their stores with me, as it was not deemed prudent to take all along with them at that time. They also left some letters to be forwarded to America, but as this is a rather circuitous and not very certain route, I have retained them for the present, but will send them by the first vessel that leaves for America.

Mr. Bowen's health was rather feeble while here, so much so that I felt considerable anxiety as to the issue of an attempt at that time to go into the interior & endeavoured to shake his purpose, but all of no avail. Go he was determined. His position was marked out; and if he fell, it would be pleasing to fall harnessed in the field. He bore the walk — about half the whole distance to Vons-Wah, say seven miles — much better than I expected, indeed he seemed to improve from it.

They took four American youths with them.

Your Obdt. Servant,

H. Teage

The ink of the last sentence of the above was not dry when I was informed that Capt. Brown had arrived & would sail for New York in 24 hours. I therefore alter the route of this letter and send it direct accompanied by those left by the brethren. Mrs. Bastion[274] has just yielded up her spirit to that God, at whose bidding she left her all that was dear in her native land, not counting her life dear, so that she might spread the knowledge of Him. I formed an acquaintance with her and her excellent husband during our passage out from Baltimore in August and September; & I have seldom had the happiness to fall in with so agreeable companions or strangers who won more upon my esteem I regarded them eminently qualified for the great work to which they had devoted themselves. But He, who sees not as man sees, & who gives no account of His doings has suddenly arrested her career, & blighted our hopes. I deeply sympathize with Mr. Bastion & hopes that grace which has hitherto sustained him will in severe bereavement prove sufficient.

H. Teage

35. Letter to J. B. Taylor, Monrovia, 18 January 1853

Dear Sir,

Your letter of Oct. 10th/52 is before me, and partly in compliance with your request to write you frequently, and partly in gratification of my own feelings I sit down to pen you a line.

Knowing your heart and mind to be filled with the subject of our mission and denomination here I hasten at once to that subject. You will have learned from other sources than directly after Bro. Ball left here I was by a unanimous vote called to the pastorate of the church here.[275] Soon after that I resigned my office of attorney general. This was done no more in compliance with the wishes of the church, than with my own feelings of propriety.

The church is enjoying more harmony at present than for a long season past, although there are still some sources of uneasiness and discord not dried up. They are such however as will not give any very serious trouble.

We have a Sabbath School attached to the church but I am not allowed to draw a flattering picture of its prosperousness and efficiency. The truth is, our people have not waken up to the great importance of that element in the church's prosperity, they have not yet seen that the Sabbath School and the bible class are the nursery of the church. They admit their importance, but do not feel it. They encourage them, by voting their establishment, but discourage them by withholding the encouragement of personal influence. The people are perhaps no more to blame in this matter than the preacher. He most probably has neglected to persist in urging the matter upon them, and under the influence of the too prevalent disposition to feel no compunction for not performing a service which is not immediately and pressingly urged the felt discharges from the labour of Sabbath School and bible class. I feel the more inclined to this opinion from the fact that since I have been urging these subjects upon the people, they are obtaining a larger share of their attention; and I hope to be able at no distant day to be able to report a large and efficient Sabbath School & bible class.

We have had no revivals lately. Our regular services are kept up. I must confess that the attendance has been poor. Many professors seem systematically to absent themselves from the services of the sanctuary. The conduct otherwise is good. No other charge can be urged against them. But grace seems at a low ebb in their hearts, and any hindrance will suffice to keep them from the Lord's house. This is a sore trial to a minister who aims to do good, who after hours of [a blank space of the width of two words] for food, hours of painful labour, finds when he takes the food to the wanted place, that a morbid loathing has kept the flock away. This however will not hold good of all. There are a few on whose presence one may safely reckon. They seem to be animated by Joshua's resolution, and it is all one with them, whether there be many or few in the house of God they are sure to be there.

My labours in the church now will be hard, Bro. Richardson[276] is stationed up the river. To preach thrice on Sabbaths on the evening of every Thursday, to attend prayer meeting Sabbath morning & Tuesday evening, to attend the missionary prayer meeting, and the conference of the church, superadded to the secular business which necessity compels me to engage will be too much I fear, and cannot be long endured. I have resolved to go on with it the best I can, & when I find it too severe just drop a part of it, for while I trust I am not [a blank space of the width of two words], I do not endorse all that is usually meant by the maxim it is better to wear out than to rust out. This is written in great haste & at a late hour. Should I have another spare moment I may add something in relation to a resolution which the Board has been pleased to make in respect to myself.

Jany. 14. A delay in the vessel's departure affords me an opportunity to add a word or two more. I mentioned to Bro. Ball that a gentleman at St. Helena[277] there supplying a Baptist church in the absence of the pastor on a visit to America had written to me on the subject of missions and expressed an intention of visiting Liberia as soon as he should be released from his engagement with the church. I wrote to him on the subject, giving him as full information on all his topics of enquiries as my time would allow I have not since heard from him, but I am led to expect him shortly. Captain Foote[278] U. S. Navy who kindly handed me his letter, spoke in the highest terms of commendation of his qualifications in every respect for a preacher and teacher. His literary qualifications are of a high order, and his piety and devotedness to the missionary work are respected by all who know. I should regard him an acquisition and have accordingly invited him & offered him the hospitality of a house.

Brethren Goodman & Sherman, their wives & sister Crocker[279] are here. They have spent two days with me, and expect day after the morrow to leave for Bassa. I trust their health and their lives be spared for long and great usefulness here. I durst[280] not anticipate anything but the most harmonious co-operation between them & the employees of your Board, yet it would seem more like there was no rivalry if the contemplated high schools were at a little further distance apart — say, one upon the St. Johns & the other upon the St. Pauls. At present the two mission houses at Bexley are, so to speak, a stone's throw of each other.

I am decidedly in favor of St. Pauls. There are, it is admitted, many reasons for holding on to the Bassa, but since the Northern Board has determined on reviving efforts among them, and the Southern Board has some two or three schools there of an elemental characters. I can see no reason why the Deys & Veys should not have the benefits of your contemplated high school. I may at some future time resume this subject and attempt to show the preferences which under the present circumstances St. Pauls has over the St. Johns. It must however be recalled that the claims of the former over the latter are greatly strengthened if not wholly created by the resumption of the missionary union of its efforts & operations.

Our association is to be held next month at Sinoe. We are looking forward to it with great anxiety and many expect to attend. At that time & place we expect to ordain Mr. Harding and also Bro. Vonbrun.[281]

By the late arrivals there is a Brother Scott. He is from North Carolina, & was there attached to a church called Christian. I have no objection certainly to the name expect that [it] uses a distinctive epithet, intended to denote that its wearers adopt & hold some of the peculiarities of Mr. Campbell.[282] I have conversed frequently and at length with him on the importance of the Baptists here speaking and minding the same thing, and acting in concert. He has solemnly assured me he will use our Shibboleth –– that it was his purpose when he left home to act in concert with the Baptists here & he signified his intention of doing so to his pastor. He goes up to Virginia tomorrow & will offer to the church there three others with him. I have written to Bro. Harding on this subject & offered some suggestions as to the course proper to be pursued. Mr. Scott is an intelligent man, was ordained before he left America & has talents to be useful. Recent importations has given some 60 to 70 to the Baptist strength here. This [indistinct word] a good supply of bibles for gratuitous distribution sent out by the Am. Bible Society encourages us.

Yours in the Gospel,

H. Teage

36. Letter to [Southern Baptist Mission Board], Monrovia, 10 March 1853

Dear Sir,[283]

Knowing the interest you feel in everything that concerns the kingdom of our blessed Redeemer and you ardent desire for the more rapid and wide extension of those scriptural practices and ordinances which are peculiar to our denomination, I make bold to give you a succinct account of the state of our churches here. We have in Liberia thirteen churches: twelve in Liberia proper and one in Cape Palmas. Communicants 630. There are about eighty members having letters from their churches in America. Of these not more than twenty have attached themselves to any church, the rest having been prevented by the bustle of landing and removing up the river. It is expected they will all shortly attach themselves to some church in the vicinity of their location. We may safely treble this number as the stated hearers of our preachers. Here then are nearly two thousand souls in this small community constantly looking up to us for instruction and receiving from our mouth the law of Christ. I say two thousand, but our occasional hearers greatly exceed that number. So sir you can see our responsibility and sympathize with us in our arduous toil. Our churches have indeed passed through a fiery ordeal. At one time their glimmering, flickering light seemed at the point of extinction. But God in his infinite mercy came to our relief: verifying the poetic adage

> "The mount of danger is the place,
> Where God displays delivering grace."[284]

The heretofore barren and sterile waste where nought was seen but the melancholy forms of withered herbage is again blossoming and budding as the rose and clothing itself with eternal beauty. Our members are again returning to their posts and their duty, and as a consequence our churches are assuming a more respectable and commanding attitude. They are now looked upon by others with an altogether different set of feelings from those with which they were regarded some three or four years ago. The late exhilaration of our strength and capabilities during the session of the association at Sinoe has operated to the conviction that God is in the midst of our Zion. Great good, I am confident, will result from that meeting. We propose to establish a kind of domestic mission in each county, to have at least one station in some eligible country village where some one or two of our preachers would attend such Sabbath as catechists and preachers.

I am not able to report any very large number of converts. On the third Friday of this month we hold our first quarterly reunion meeting at Caldwell. Some two or three will be baptised there. There is also one here to be baptised. I think our views of baptising are commanding more attention now than at any previous time, and I am encouraged to look and hope for great results. But we have great opposition to contend with. The Methodists are a numerous, vigilant zealous body well supplied with necessary means. Their preachers are enabled to give their whole time to the work & thus they have a great advantage over the most of ours. Their numerous schools are also a powerful auxiliary. The settlement at New York near Millsburg is rapidly filling up. There are already a number of Baptists there. I shall recommend the constitution of a church there. A school would be of great service there. I have not heard, but judging from the past venture the affirmation that the Methodist Conference now in session will before they close determine on a church and school at New York, and station a preacher there.

This field of labor is becoming more & more interesting. It is widening on every side, whitening to the harvest and inviting the entry of laborers. "A little leaven leavens the whole lump." The intercourse between American settlers and the aborigines is daily increasing. There will be an assimilation of the one to the other insensible 'tis true, but still an assimilation. The latter must take an upward tendency to the former, or the former will gradually descend in the direction of the latter. The American has many advantages. His superiority, his possessions of the conveniences and comforts of life excite the inquiry, why is this? and incline him to make 'Merican fash'. Let him now be directed to the religion of the bible, and impressed with it as the cause of all this difference and you fix his mind upon a theme from which it will reluctant to turn. While at Cape Palmas the other day, I asked the old king if he did not see that 'Merican man pass him & his people. He said yes. I asked the cause, he said he did not know. I told him it was God Jahovah make 'Merican man pass him. He said, "True. I look dat. All the old men go die. Den dem chick (children) go make God Jahovah den 'Merican man no pass him again." Hence the importance of instructing our own people properly. As I have no time to write Bro. Taylor a long letter, I ask for him a perusal of this.

Respectfully yours,

H. Teage

Carl Patrick Burrowes

Local Politics and Policies

37. Letter to Samuel Wilkeson, Monrovia, 12 April 1829

Dear Sir,[285]

The corn which you were so kind to send for the benefit of the Colony has been distributed according to your request & I trust it will prove a valuable acquisition. I have been careful to give it to such as I am confident will give its adaptation to our soil and climate a full & fair test. With regard to agriculture, though I am not even a novice in the art, I am of the opinion, that in producing articles for commercial exchange we shall find it to our advantage for the present at least, to confine our cultivation to the culture and manufacture of such species are indigenous as or long since naturalized to the country. The introduction of new and untried species might require more time and skill than we can give them & thus years of labour might be unprofitably consumed. Your scheme of regular packets between this place and America is a most excellent one, if it can be carried into full operation. If backed by our agricultural and commercial association, it cannot fail to realize the highest hopes of the most ardent friends of the Colony. I hope this scheme will take; it is of all that have occurred to my mind the most big with hope. The Colony has certainly passed the crisis, and is looking up. She is again making steps — slow, but steady — and every step is so much gained, not again to be lost. And now is the time of all times in its history when help may be most precariously and beneficially afforded. I am preparing a suit of clothes manufactured in the Colony from African cotton which I shall forward to you I hope in time for the fair of the American Institute. I send you by this conveyance some fur articles[286] as mentioned below. They are all African. I shall embrace every leisure moment to advance your views in regard to a collection of African curiosities. By the Brig *Franklin*, which sailed a month ago, I made a requisition to the Board at Washington for an assortment and apparatus for our printing establishment here. As they are very much needed, and as the character of the paper to a considerable degree depends upon their being forwarded, you will confer a lasting favor, by having them sent on by the first conveyance. The letter in which the request was made was directed to Mr. Gurley, and you will probably find it in the Office at Washington. In that letter you will perceive the reasons more at length why I have requested them, and the greater the supply of the articles the greater the favour you will confer upon us. Seeds adopted to flower and culinary gardens are always acceptable. Any little you can conveniently send will be gratefully received and duly appreciated.

Your Obdt. Servant,

H. Teage

P.S. This letter will be handed you by my father who after a sojourn in Africa returns on a visit to America. I beg leave to commend him to your regards. [287]

38. Letter to Samuel Wilkeson, Monrovia, 24 October 1840

Dear Sir,

By the *Atlanta*, which leaves in a few days for Baltimore or Philadelphia, I seize the opportunity of sending you a few lines. Though you have been apprised of some circumstances of excitement in the Colony, you are not prepared to hear what you will hear by this vessel. The lawsuit is over but Mr. Seys[288] is yet [at] work maturing his plans and preparing I fear to resist yet further the mandates of the Col. Soc. I know not nor will I attempt to conjecture what course they will pursue with regard to this ambitious man. But one thing is no longer a subject of doubt and that is, if they do not recall him and break up this hierarchy, they may prepare to resign the authority of government to Mr. S. and his chosen few.

No concession or palliation will answer[;] this man will be all or nothing. I wait with anxiety to know what the Society will do for certainly if the Society knuckles[,] the Colony will no longer form a home for me. I heard today that Mr. S.'s friends are getting up new meetings. I very much fear the result will be serious ere[289] they are done.

Since this affair has come up, the following queries have started up in my mind. Was it originally intended that the money given by the pious poor in America for mission purposes should be expended upon the Colonists? This Mr. Seys says he has been doing with the large sums committed to him (See the report of the trial in the *Luminary*). Are we Colonists so debased that we need so many missionaries in our midst and so extensive an apparatus to recover and civilize us? Were these missionaries intended to sit here in town simply to write and make fine representations of sufferings and self denial never endured and of conversions which never occurred while they themselves are in reality feasting on the fat of the land? Is this the object of African missions? I trust not and hope we shall speedily be convinced that the people at home have been duped, and that as soon as they ascertain that charities not been applied to their appropriate object they alter the channel.

In this remark, I would be understood as pointing exclusively at the Mission whose party colored head is in Monrovia. The missions in Bassa and Cape Palmas as far as I am acquainted have adhered to their proper course. For particulars I refer you to the *Herald* and my ambitions would impel me to sustain it even at a pecuniary sacrifice until (this) affair is over. I learn today that Mr. Seys will come out bitterly against the *Herald* when the *Luminary* next irradiates the earth. He has thrown down the gauntlet. I accept the challenge and shall yield the contest only after a desperate resistance.

I trust Gov. Buchanan will be sustained. He is doing more for the Colony than any man that ever came here. The Missionaries are his greatest impediments, and unless they are checked will effectually retard him. An effort is making to put in a missionary council who will, it is expected, alter the whole code of law.

I have the honor to be your ob. servant

H. Teage

39. The Colonial Council

Liberia Herald, 29 February 1844, 46

The Colonial Council assembles on the first Monday in the ensuing month. It has been said there is little to be done; and already it has been determined by some how long the session should continue. While we think no time should be needlessly consumed — as time in this case is truly money — we are fixed in the opinion that hasty legislation, will nine times in ten be found useless if not pernicious legislation. Hitherto we have drifted along in the wake of some of the American legislatures. — Each succeeding session going might and main into a repealing of all the preceding one had done, with as much zeal and eagerness as if the existence of the country depended on a clearing of the statute book when perhaps only a cursory thought had been given as to what was to be substituted in the place. Human laws in the nature of things will ever be found imperfect. Human sagacity can never contrive to meet critically all the various shades and the endlessly varying complexity of cases that will arise. The most that can be done is to lie down general rules upon the broad basis of equity. The incapability of human laws to apply to specific cases was long ago discerned and gave rise — to the maxim *summum jus summa injuria.*[290.]

Unmindful of this fact, men finding the imperfection of existing provisions, have, as though a positive benefit necessarily results from change, hastened with a greater eagerness to repeal, then with solicitude to remedy the defective regulation. Although we (the colonial legislature from its first institution will be understood) — have just commenced our apprenticeship in the art of making laws, we have advanced rapidly — at least in that branch of the business that wind up with *"shall be and the same is hereby repealed."*

We would not, however, in these admonitory hints be understood as expressing an opinion that no change can be advantageously made in the laws of the colony. That would be indulging too much complacency. The growing condition of the colony — our rapidly extending commerce — the enlargement of our territorial borders will soon imperiously demand provisions and regulations to the wants of which we are only just now beginning to awake.

One subject, however, demands the immediate attention of the colonial legislature. And that is the wretchedly contrived judiciary system.

40. Our Affairs [1]

Liberia Herald, 15 March 1845, 46

Our last letters from America present us with encouraging prospect[s] in regard to African colonization.[291] Colonization appears to be attracting somewhat more of attention than was given to it the three or four years last past; and the attention now paid to it is of a more favourable character. Connected with this, however, is a fact of which the people of these colonies should ever be observed in placing reliance upon a cause which depends for its onward movement upon a foreign popular favour. Such are the fickleness and variability of the multitude — such their anxiety and burning for something new and striking that many regard them unworthy and unsafe arbiters of even their own destinies. The object of ardent pursuit today will likely be among the forgotten of the morrow. Colonization should not take these irregular and spasmodic impulses as the preclusive movements of a regular and abiding force, but should regard them as indicating for the time the direction of the public mind, whose most striking characteristic is ceaseless change. Whilst we should ever close our minds against the entrance of the conceit which would affect to disdain the sympathy and aid of others, let us remember that to expect to be made "a people" solely by the efforts of others, or even to desire it would prove *de facto* that we are unworthy of the boon we desire. A name and place are among heaven's brightest gifts, and heaven rarely bestow[s] its benisons upon the enervate[292] and irresolute. While therefore we should never be implacable to the efforts of our friends abroad, nor to any indication of a favourable public regard of our cause and condition, but receive with grateful hearts every emotion of sympathy, let us yet recollect the heat and burden of the day are to be borne by us.

The lesson fraught with the greatest blessing to us we have yet to learn. The bone and sinew are ours — others can only advise the direction of their movement. The eager anxiety and the numerous enquiries on the arrival of letters from America to know what the society is doing indicates too truly, we fear, an unworthy and unmanning reliance on the efforts of others; while the great objects to which our friends abroad direct our attention is the certain highway to independence, because they involve in their accomplishment difficulty and labour, are too systematically neglected.

That we have recently made some improvements and that there have been some development of capacity among us, there can be no doubt, but these have not been commensurate with our opportunities. The present position of the colony is one exceedingly perplexing and anomalous; and, as if past annoyances to which the colored man has been every where subjected are not sufficient, foreigners are now welding this anomaly greatly to our disadvantage. We have long seen the probability of this difficulty but would not allow ourselves to believe we should be soon plunged into it. Professing as the English do, so much philanthropy and so extended and high-toned benevolence, we hoped every thing from them: but Commodore Jones' last letter[293] to the Governor has dispelled the illusion, and warns us that we have most to fear where once we had indulged the most pleasing expectations. This diplomatic communication contains one sentence which we presume would find a place in a correspondence with no people on earth except Liberians. It is a kind of genical braggardism — or diplomatic gasconade[294] over a prostrate victim from whom nothing is to be apprehended. We have compared the style and spirit of this communication with the commodore's correspondence with American commanders on this station, and we can find no escape from the conviction that when passing this letter he kept distinctly before his eye the resources of the people he was addressing.

It is clear we cannot exist if the British maintain the position assumed by the commodore, as we shall be exposed to incursion by every British trader that comes to coast — to which if we dare oppose resistance, we shall feel the full vengeance of all powerful England.

But until it be denied that we are men, it will not be denied that we have certain rights — among these the right to breathe God's free air, to purchase land from its rightful owners, to dig that land and eat its fruits, to govern ourselves on that land, and to adjust the conditions on which others shall come among us. These are altogether distinct, in our opinion at least, from international rights. The former are founded on the unavoidable wants of our common nature, that is they are the gift of God and therefore cannot be conferred by any people on another; the latter is founded on conventional agreement, the former is necessary to our existence, the latter not.

It behooves us therefore to prove ourselves worthy of these rights, by our industry, perseverance, good order and virtue. By clearing away these primitive forces and developing the rich resources of the unreclaimed country — by recovering these semi-savage tribes around us from their barbarism and tutoring them in the arts and manners of civilized and Christian life, we will exhibit a claim to be let alone which no people who have any respect for justice will dare to disregard.

We are aware that we are exposing ourself by attempting to awaken the people to a perception of their condition, and by calling on them to prepare against a premature end. Our well meant endeavours in this as in other things have been traduced and our sincerest motives impugned. We heed it not. We [felt] strong in the rectitude of purpose. Already we are stigmatized in America as having attempted a revolution in the colony and to get a recognition of the independence of the colony by England without consulting the society. The charge is too ridiculous for vindication, but if it needs any we leave it to be made by the people of Liberia. When the proper time arrives to speak out we trust we shall not be wanting in courage to do so.

Carl Patrick Burrowes

41. [The Present Condition of Our Colony]

Liberia Herald, 31 May 1845, 11

The present condition of our colony, and the [aspect] of everything connected with it irresistibly impel the mind of every thinking colonist forward, and agitate it with a painful anxiety to pierce the future unknown. The most meagre acquaintance with the science of political economy, or more plainly, with those circumstances which constitute the elements of national prosperity must apprize every one that we are not now on the highway to glory. The permanent and substantial prosperity of a country consists in a happy and increasing population. We say increasing because where the people are contented and happy their number will increase. The happiness of a population in the sense we are speaking depends upon the supply of the means of subsistence. Universally the supply of the means of subsistence regulates population. It follows that where the supply of conveniences of life (not to say of natural wants, as men will not be contented with that, but of such a supply as will render them contented) is inadequate to the demand, there can be no permanent prosperity. In order to render the supply certain the means of obtaining it must exist in the country. The people must raise their food or they must procure it from abroad. Of course when it is obtained from others something must be given in exchange for it. The methods by which the articles for exchange are obtained are various; but the most ruinous of them all is that, in which the price of the articles given in exchange for provisions bears the least proportion to the original cost, or has given employment to the least number of persons. Let us now illustrate this everlasting truth by an example, and let that example be ourselves.

What have *we* to give in return for our provisions. Nothing absolutely nothing! What do we give in exchange for beef, pork, hams, butter, sugar, tea, coffee, soap, hats, shoes and cotton and woolen clothing? The answer is at hand. We procure by barter with the natives camwood, palm oil and ivory, and these articles we give in exchange for our provisions. We send them off in the same state in which they are procured excepting a small drawback in the shape of leakage, dryage & etc., so that the employment which the mode of paying for our foreign commodities gives to the people is not to be mentioned. The proportion which the annual purchase of provision bears to the whole annual importation may we think be safely put down at two fifths. Assuming for the mere purpose of estimation $100,000 as the amount of our annual importation, we have an annual expenditure of $40,000 for which we have no earthly return, literally and absolutely none. If we paid it in articles of whose value only a portion was of our own production — say for instance in soap made from the oil — in coloring matter extracted from the wood or in articles of use made of the ivory, there would be some deduction from the loss; if we gave in exchange coffee, cotton, sugar, dyes, arrowroot, ginger or any thing else of our own raising, by raising as much in the colony as we send out the account would balance itself and thus far there would be no loss. And if we raised our own food and paid these articles for other things the whole amount would be so much clear gain. But being consumed by a people, who, while they are consuming are producing nothing, the whole amount paid, over and above its cost from the natives, is a total loss to the colony. Nor may it be supposed the people are otherwise engaged in profitable employment. The first object of men is the supply of their immediate and pressing wants; until this is done, they will find neither time nor inclination to engage in other pursuits.

Nor is this the only evil. We do not export our own commerce in our own bottoms[295] and thus save the benefit of freight and give employment to our own people. This advantage is engrossed by others, as is also that of the advanced price of produce in foreign markets and of the freight and advanced price of articles imported.

What is the result of the mode of supplying our wants? Surely we need not tell our readers what they already know by bitter experience, that the end of every three months during which we have had no supply from abroad has invariably found our stock deplorably short.

Now let us test what we have assumed as an unalterable principle. Are our people contented and happy? does our population increase? For an answer to the first question, enquire at the upper settlements, and in regard to the second consult the census.

He who should throw a cursory glance over this settlement and then resolutely close his eyes and his ears, might perhaps draw an inference adverse to our position. A house going up here and there might be to some indicative of prosperity; and it might be true of those individual builders. But if he could be prevailed upon to open his eyes and estimate the proportion these builders bear to the whole population, he would accordingly form a different conclusion.

Turn away tho' we will the ghostly question stares us in the face. What is to be done? Let us face it. The people must have employment, such employment as in its returns will not only supply their immediate and pressing wants, but such as will awaken in them hope, excite their ambition of a comfortable and easy condition of life, and, thus, by engendering self-respect, nerve [t]hem with the energy to persevere. The vast resources of our own country must be explored and drawn forth and in this employment the people must be engaged. But *labour* such as we can employ unaided by capital cannot be made the basis of a commerce with foreign nations. And capital we have not. The question then returns. What is to be done? Why[,] we must obtain capital from those who have it. But to impute all our difficulties to the want of capital and in the next breath to say, we must get it, without pointing out the means by which it may be done seems worse than begging the question. There are three modes by which men ordinarily obtain money. The first is by rendering personal service; the second is by giving the production of labor; and the third and the last is by loan on a guaranty mutually agreed on. As the first and second modes are in our case out of the question, we have no alternative. It becomes then an interesting question: Is the last mode practicable, and if so would it be safe to resort to it.

42. Public Discussion [of Liberia's Independence]

Liberia Herald, 7 November 1845, 15

There is an old maxim, but never too old to be reiterated (viz): When public sentiment is agitated, truth spontaneously springs up. Let the whole populace mind, with its "Press" and various civil institutions, concentrated on any one subject, and truth will rise prescient. For proof, notice the progress which the subject of slavery has made. As soon as public attention is fixed itself upon the evils and dangers it is likely to entail on the American people, a great and prevailing change was evident to all, this general and popular agitation may throw up much strife and delusion. Yet nevertheless, error whose certain fate is inevitable will sink, and give place to truth.

The subject of Liberia's independence, is much discussed by all classes — by the learned and the unlearned, — by the mechanic[s] at their work — by men on ship board, — by the farmer in his farm, — by the way side, and public halls.

Who does not see the probable result, — the inevitable conclusion of these inquiries? How much of that spirit which is wrong will be detected? How rapidly is our present advance to that point of light where the truth of this great subject can be seen!! A happy circumstance for the human race when an enlightened people consents to elicit truth from the smallest political or moral question. Man is sure to gain something. Could the people of these colonies for one year concentrate their reasoning powers upon the great question: "How shall the whole people of these colonies better their condition by severing the connection that subsists between them and the American Colonization Society[?]" Could this subject become a general topic[?] Scrupulously view[ed] from its origin to its end, or from its cause to its effect as general as other matters are now, how much might be hoped. Until this is so or something near it, in vain may we hope to see any thing permanently done about the independence of Liberia.

If the people desire freedom and all that follows in its train, they will better insure it by this method than by any other, they too will better elicit the sympathies of all classes of citizens in this matter, but as long as some men prefer to be the sole actors in this affair, regardless of the opinions and counsels of the whole colony, nothing can, or will be done. This we predict.

The people must be enlightened on all subjects touching their interest, either by public meetings or by other proper and laudable mediums, which we believe is the uniform course taken in every other country, and which in time past was practiced in these colonies.

43. Our Affairs [2]

Liberia Herald, 18 December 1846, 19

The colonial Legislature meets on the first Monday in the ensuing month — January. Matters of the greatest element to us — matters which cannot fail to affect us deeply for good or evil — to establish our character as a public spirited, enterprising and progressing people or brand us as a timid, dependent and grovelling community will come up for discussion and determination. Hence the ensuing session is looked forward to with the most intense anxiety by all classes of people. Considerable anxiety is felt by many in regard to the course which rumor says the members from the lower counties will pursue.[296] Rumor says they intend to maintain the position which they took and so strongly and strenuously defended in the session of last July. We know nothing of the views of these gentlemen except through the uncertain channel of rumor, as we are not honored with a place among their correspondents, yet we are unwilling to believe that no change has come "over their dreams," that they still refuse to vote for a new and distinct organization — that they will still hold out their leading strings and endeavour to hang an unwelcome load on the hands of the Colonization Society, when that Society has given indications as unequivocal of a desire to be relieved of them. We are unwilling to believe that those gentlemen, in all the time which has elapsed since the last session have not been able to separate the question, now every where mooted from all that is extraneous and foreign from it, and to look at "Sovereignty" naked and alone, wholly distinct and discovered from those circumstances, which, although usually found to attend it in established and full-grown communities, enter nevertheless not in the least degree into its character and integrity.

In the discussion of practical questions which may be supposed to affect the interest of more parties than one, great deference is undoubtedly due to established maxims and usages. These are indispensable to the peace and repose of nations. They regulate their intercourse, define their privileges and, in litigated cases, form a standard of appeal: but in determining cases of a purely abstract character, there is danger, by an exclusive regard to them, of being conducted to an erroneous conclusion. Into this error, our highly respected opponents in our humble opinion have been betrayed, and it is with us an earnest hope that their mind may be freed from its influence which they shall meet in legislative capacity in January.[297]

Indeed there is no alternative. "The Rubicon is crossed." To falter and hesitate now can serve only to display a child-like imbecility on the part of the colony, while at the same time that it must greatly embarrass the Colonization Society. That Society has dissolved the connection — re-organized itself to meet expected re-organization on our part and invited us to take up a position to which, from our previous boasting and swaggering it was supposed we would rush with all the ardor of a proud and enthusiastic patriotism. Although we are aware that opposition by the members from the lower counties cannot arrest the progress of things, or defeat the consummation of the measure, yet we are not willing to close our eyes against the evils and inconveniences which will assuredly attend opposition. A transition state is always a critical state, and demands more than all other states unanimity and concord. In addition to the dangers which evermore attend that state, there is one, which threaten, the disintegration of the members of the community, that difficulty cannot be looked upon by the most careless but with the deepest solicitude. But we feel confident that these dangers so threatening in the distance will vanish before the face of free and dispassionate discussion — that if those who are called to determine the question will but open their minds to truth and their ears to reason, and not suffer the pride of opinion to usurp the throne of judgement, it will be determined in a way honorable to Liberia and satisfactory to its friends abroad. Let our Legislators therefore look well to this matter. The fate of the colony — awful responsibility! depends upon their decision; the record of their vote will be the bright register of an honorable name or the gloomy imprint of a melancholy epitaph; and let them further remember that their action in this case will for mental ability and political sagacity decide their character in the estimation of the present and the coming generations.

44. Legislation in Liberia

Liberia Herald, 15 January 1847, 26

The colonial legislature assembled pursuant to law on Monday the 4th inst. The first business in the order of proceeding was the swearing of the members to do faithfully and conscientiously the work of legislators and to discharge such other duties as the time and circumstances might demand. It occurs to us that it will not be out of place to ask, while on this subject, whether by becoming a representative a man disfranchises himself and assumes *de facto* the obligation to pocket his conscience, to close his eyes against evidence and his mind against argument, and to vote only as bidden by those who honored him with their suffrage. If this be the duty which the honor imposes, Heaven save us from both. If *we* can serve a people only on the condition that we resign the dignity and the privileges of a man, we shall never aspire to the high honor of serving them. To demand such a surrender is an insolent in the *sovereign people* as it is absurd in the *people's servant* to submit to it. It is in effect to say, there is a better way to arrive at truth than argument and discussions and that he who has heard only one side of a question is as well prepared to decide upon it as he who has weighed carefully the arguments on both.[298] These thoughts have been suggested by the very frequent use by members of our legislature of such phrases as "the people at ___ think that, and your constituents wish the other, and therefore, we must oppose this measure and support its opposite."

Directly after the members were qualified by swearing to do their duty, the governor's message was read. This document we have spread before our readers in this number of our paper. It is an interesting paper and contains a correct and succinct statement of the state of the question of Liberia Independence. The legislature then adjourned to meet the following day.

Carl Patrick Burrowes

The question of independence was the all absorbing theme. The members of the lower counties at once threw themselves to their old position[299] supported by an auxiliary from Sinoe[,] and in their maneuvers to keep the enemy without their intrenchment[,] displayed considerable skill in parliamentary tactics. They were, however, opposed by formidable battalions of truth and reason.

On the fourth day of the session the house went into a committee of the whole, Mr. Weaver[300] in the chair. After a little half in earnest and half in play skirmishing, in which the parties were evidently rousing their energies for a desperate struggle, Governor Roberts advanced to close quarters, in the introduction of a resolution to determine whether the wishes of the people as expressed in the late vote should be complied with. This more than Corsican maneuver brought opponents of a new organization to a dead stand. A more effectual and better timed resolution could not possibly have been brought forward. It was better than whole tomes of argument, inasmuch as a vote in the negative would have arrayed the voter in direct opposition to the wishes of a majority of the whole people solemnly and decidedly expressed, upon a question long and anxiously agitated from one end to another of the colony. Having mentioned this our readers will not require to be told that the matter is settled. A resolution was passed ordering an election on the 17th proximo,[301] for delegates to meet in convention in July next for the purpose of framing a constitution. These resolutions, or rather this act, we insert below.

There was very little other business done. The independence question had absorbed all attention and kept the minds of all within and without the house wound up to their highest tension. So, that matter accomplished, all other affairs appeared unimportant. In our humble opinion, there were other matters growing out of the independence act which were eminently entitled to the immediate attention of the legislature, but which they, for some reason which has not transpired, omitted to attend to. These may be the subject of future remark.

45. [That Great Object Which Loomed in All Its Grandeur]

African Repository, January 1847, 15-19

The extra session of the Legislature closed its deliberations on the evening of the 15th ult. It was convened for the purpose of receiving the despatches sent out by the American Colonization Society. These despatches contain resolutions announcing a most important movement on the part of the Society — a movement involving nothing less than a total severance of the Society from all political connexion with the colony and an entire withdrawal of control from all its affairs, both internal and external.

A movement so solemn — an act so pregnant in its consequences with weal or woe to the people — opening up before them, as it does, scenes never discovered before — launching them upon an ocean never before explored — calling them to the exercise of functions and to the discharge of duties they had scarcely ever contemplated, and committed to their unpracticed hands that destiny which hitherto they had suffered to lodge elsewhere, may be well supposed to have created throughout the colony the most intense sensation. And accordingly we have never witnessed a session of the legislature where the members seemed more firmly fixed in the position which they had marked out for themselves — never one in which there was more uncompromising argument, more inflexibility argument, more inflexibility of opinion, nor one in whose deliberations the inhabitants appeared to take so deep an interest.

Numerous circumstances concur to create and to sustain this sensation. The mass of the people have been accustomed to regard the society as not only the parent and nurse of their political existence — not only the source of their power and authority, but also a shield, which, thrown around them, has warded off blows which but for this defense would long since have laid their little political fabric in the dust. There can be no questioning that the society, including as it does in the number of its members men who are not only high in the confidence and influential in the councils of the American people: men the fame of whose wisdom and talent and varied accomplishment has circled the globe — there can be no questioning that the society thus composed has exerted a salutary influence on behalf of the colony, that, if it has not attracted toward it the kind and sympathetic regard of foreigners, it has in some instances withheld the blow which would have fallen with fatal energy upon its head.

This is most freely admitted. But while this is admitted, the peculiar circumstances which gave birth to this influence and which imparted to it force, should be kept steadily in view. Two of these circumstances, and the two most efficient, at once present themselves — misconception in respect of the political alliance of the colony, and its non-interference with the interests and pursuits of others. The first of these no longer has place — the character and position of the colony having been accurately stated and defined, and the second (if we may so speak) is rapidly following the fate of the first — the growth of the colony and its necessary territorial extention bringing it into collision with the supposed or at least claimed rights and interests of others. This being the case, it were idle to suppose that the colony will not henceforth attract attention and awaken feelings altogether different in kind from those with which it was wont to be regarded. The great bulk of our people, however, unmindful of these great and important changes, still look up to the society as to a guardian angel, a tutelary genius — still regard it as able to bear them up on its wings of power, and as strong to deliver them safely and triumphantly out of every difficulty. We say that this opinion, the fallacy of which we shall not here combat, exerts a powerful influence on the minds of many of the people and agitates them with painful apprehensions. But other considerations determine others to halt in their course and to withhold from any action at the present time. It should not be concealed that there is entertained on the part of some the opinion, that the time has not yet arrived for the colony to take so important a step — that matters and things connected with the colony are not yet ripe for a change so vast and radical as must be effected by a dissolving of the bonds which have hitherto united us to the society. This opinion, however, although entertained with all the seriousness and conscientiousness of conviction, will not be suffered to arrest action and concurrence in the resolutions, any longer than the moment arrives when those who hold this opinion shall receive that information to which they hold themselves entitled. The information received from the society is in the form of bare, naked resolutions; setting forth the expediency of declaring Liberia independent, but unaccompanied by a single syllable of explanation or a single word of stipulation. In the opinion of this class — and the whole people met on this common ground — some other relinquishment on the part of the society besides that of mere political authority is absolutely — yea, indispensably necessary; and they hold that this other relinquishment should be a preliminary, or at least an accompaniment of the relinquishment of political authority: and they hold further, that without such relinquishment a declaration of independence would be altogether inconsistent, an empty sound, a mere mirage, a baseless, unsubstantial fabric.

We are not allowed to suppose for a moment that the society contemplates a cessation of its operations here. The continued deportation of colored people to this colony is a cherished and avowed purpose; and we have no doubt that this people will stand with open arms to receive them and to greet them with a hearty welcome to their fatherland as fast as circumstances render it prudent for them to come. The question then presents itself, under what circumstances will they come? To whose authority will they be subjected? What authority will determine their location? To whom will they look for land? From whom will they derive a title to it? The question which covers the whole ground is, to whom, in the event of a declaration of independence, will the territory belong which is now styled Liberia? Will the American Colonization Society continue to hold an exclusive claim upon the land so as to parcel it out or transfer it when, how, and to whom it pleases? Or will such a transfer be made to the people as will give them an exclusive, independent and irresponsible right to it? Or will the society retain only such a claim upon it as will enable them to secure to those whom they may hereafter deport from America a title allotments independently of the concurrence of the government, and should opposition at any time be manifested in the face of its wishes? These are questions which were eagerly asked in the house and out of the house; but no one was prepared by documentary information from the society to give a satisfactory answer.

Although these considerations presented themselves to the mind, without perhaps an exception of a single man in the colony: although they are regarded by all of a very grave character, and necessary to be definitively settled and understood, yet it should be mentioned for the satisfaction of the society, and for all who have recommended the measures, that there are those in the colony, both in the legislature and out of it, whose confidence in the wisdom and integrity of the members of the society, in their wisdom to perceive and their integrity to do all that is proper to be done, to effect fully and completely the object in view, as leaves them free and untrammeled to move forward with unfaltering step in the course marked out by the resolutions.

Perhaps we would not be very wide of the mark should we conjecture, that considerations not very dissimilar from those we have mentioned as embarrassing the people, pressed with no light weight upon the mind of the society whilst contemplating a separation from the colony. It were not unnatural for the members to ask themselves what assurance have we, that the people of Liberia will not, when sovereign power be lodged in their own hand, seek some other alliance as a means of strength and of security against insult and aggression. And when it is recollected how much American philanthropy has done for the colony, how great sacrifices, colonizationists have made of time, of ease, of money and of life, to conduct it to its present condition; how lightly they prize it as a practical illustration of the efficiency, and with what intense interest they cannot but regard it as an extension to the eastern hemisphere of those principles of republican liberty and popular institutions, which, among the moderns, their fathers were the first who had the sagacity to discover, the independence to proclaim and the courage to defend —

when these circumstances are present to the mind, not only does the question not appear unnatural, but rather one which would arise with prompt and ready spontaneity; and thus arising, become the subject of deep and anxious thought.

This, however, is one of those cases, which in the progress of human affairs are continually arising, and against which no infallible provision can be made. The mind is as fruitful in ingenious devices as the heart is strong in its unnumbered desires. In this respect they are linked in an indissoluble co-partnership, and working into each other's hands, each derives and imparts support and countenance. We cannot be at a loss for instances in which the most solemn compacts have been shamelessly violated: and guarantees the most solemnly pledged have often failed to bind the hand and the heart of faithlessness and perfidy. But what wretch has yet proclaimed his treachery; and what usurper has not sought to justify his usurpation. But we think we do but speak the fixed sentiment of the whole people of these colonies, without the exception of a single individual capable of thought, when we say, the great object which at first brought us to Africa is still kindly and tenderly cherished. That great object which loomed in all its grandeur of outline before our eye — which dazzled in our imagination, and roused lofty aspirations, and lured us on from home, and kindred and social endearments — which induced us with patience to suffer, and with fortitude to endure — which gathered motive from danger and strength from defeat: that grand object, to plant a nation of colored people on the soil of Africa, adorned and dignified with the attributes of a civilized and Christian community, is still the object dearer than all others to every Liberian. Indeed, so thoroughly are we penetrated with the conviction of the necessity, that in order to the consummation of this purpose we should stand alone and unembarrassed with any foreign allegiance, we should regard the document which conveyed away our independence nothing less than the record of an abject fate to last through all coming time. Better, far better will it be for us that a century find us still a weak and "feeble folk" than to bend an ignoble neck to the Anglo-Saxon — of whose unclenching tenacity, when once it has grappled, the whole history of the modern world affords most melancholy examples.

On this score the society need entertain no apprehension. Here motives the most powerful — fear and hope and burning desire, all concur to forbid treachery and to sustain honor and integrity.

Having said the above, it is not necessary we should add, there were very opposite views entertained by the counsellors as to the course proper to be pursued. And although the members in favor of immediate action formed the majority of the council, yet as immediate action did not appear to be demanded by an imperative necessity, the earnest remonstrance of the minority against what they called precipitancy united with the considerations above alluded to, determined the legislature to the course mentioned by our co-adjutors [sic.] in our last number. And thus for the present the matter rests. But the die is cast, the Rubicon is passed. The society has acted, nor will the people be long in following their example.

46. [Articles of Trade]

Liberia Herald, 19 February 1847, 35

We have often invoked the people of these colonies to give some attention to the growing of such kinds of produce, as foreign merchants will take from them in exchange for their goods. Again and again, have we endeavored to convince them, that unless we possess within ourselves the resources to keep up a commercial intercourse with other countries, — our hope of obtaining a respectable standing, rests upon a very precarious foundation. We have up to this time, looked to the native for the means to carry on a small commerce, and tho' it is sufficiently known that there is no stability in their operations — yet we continue to linger out a servile dependence upon them, for those articles of trade, we are accustomed to barter with to foreigners; and by which we support ourselves.

At the present time, our trade is lamentably deficient. There is scarcely a trading spot between Grand Bassa and Cape Palmas that is not inhabited by foreign traders; and it is impossible for us to compete with them. Their vessels must be loaded, and palm oil they are determined to have, whatever its cost may be. Cam wood is becoming quite scarce, and its price, in the United States, is less now than it has been for a number of years back. We have already informed our readers, that there is a duty of ten per cent on cam wood in the United States, which will, unless it takes a rise operate materially against us. We can see but one safe and profitable course to pursue. Our soil is rich and capable of yielding with very little labor, a variety of productions that will readily command a market in commercial countries — let us lay it under contribution. We have no time *now* to spare, in considering, whether we will take this course or search out for some other, that may present to our misguided minds, less difficulties.

The cultivation of ginger, arrow root, pepper, ground-peas, and coffee ought to claim our immediate attention, the latter article will require some three or four

Carl Patrick Burrowes

years growth, before the cultivator will be repaid for his trouble — but after that time he will be richly rewarded — the older the tree grows, the more abundantly it yields. The other articles, if planted in March will, in a year's time produce plentifully.

47. The Constitution

Liberia Herald, 31 July 1847, 67

On the first page of the present number, our readers will find the Constitution of the Republic of Liberia.

Pursuant to the Act of the Legislature, the delegates met in Convention in the Council Chamber, in this place on the 5th, instant, set heartily to work, and concluded their labors on the 26th. The result of their labors we present in the constitution, which is now submitted to the consideration of the people, and which it is hoped will be acceptable to them. Should they adopt it, our government will, by the act of acceptance, be re-organized and go fairly to work a complete and entire system.

This act upon which the people of these Colonies have been forced by stern necessity, is pregnant with weal[302] or woe; and should be regarded as the first in a series which conducts infallibly to credit or disgrace.

Apart from the solemnity that must ever attend the act by which a young community throws off the yoke of its tutelage, and asserts its character of political manhood, these are circumstances attendant upon our case of a most impressive character. These circumstances stand out with a striking prominence, upon every page of the history of the colony so obviously as renders it unnecessary that we should mention them. This fact will in some measure account for the deep and undefinable sensation which ran through the hall and almost stilled every bosom, when on the 26th, inst., the members in presence of a numerous assembly composed of males and females, advanced one by one to the Secretary's desk to put their names to the Declaration of Independence and appeal to the nations of Christendom. It seemed like entering upon a new era, the commencement of a new existence — the launching up on an ocean vast in its extent, and unexplored by any whom we can call to the helm.

That man among us who does not feel, that by this act, he has entered upon a new career; has assumed new responsibilities and has received a new impetus and a new motive to action, is to be pitied for his blindness, rather than envied for his indifference, and to say the least, he is not yet prepared for extensive usefulness.

We would warn our people against the infatuation of supposing that because we have declared ourselves sovereign and independent, therefore [we] have fulfilled our destiny, and attained the summit of political perfection; and we would also warn them against despondency, in view of any difficulties we may be called to encounter. Our condition affords no scope for idle enthusiasm, nor for unmanly timidity. All great undertakings are attended with difficulties, and usually demand an effort proportioned to their magnitude. It is of the last importance for us to know where, and by whom this effort is to be made. We need, and, if we are wise, we will seek the sympathy and friendly countenance of foreign nations. It will be encouraging to be recognized as forming one in the great community of nations, and to receive the usual comities[303] of that relation; still we must learn to call off all unreasonable expectation from every foreign quarter, and be penetrated with the conviction that the proper scene of this extraordinary effort is the Republic of Liberia, and the effort itself to be made by us.

On another page will be seen the declaration of independence, followed by a brief statement of the causes which led to that act. The peculiarities of our condition seemed to require some little explanation which is there attempted to be given. Thus we have fairly launched upon the ocean, expanded our sails to the breeze, trusting to the merits of our cause — to the genius of justice and humanity, and to the guidance of a benignant[304] Providence.

[Left out are six paragraphs concerning a resolution of thanks from the people of Liberia to the ACS.]

48. [The Prospect of Our Domestic Affairs]

Liberia Herald, 24 September 1847, 83

The prospect of our domestic affairs, though not presenting a very flattering appearance to the indifferent observer, is, nevertheless, very cheering to those who have taken the care to examine them. The people seem to be alive to the importance of exerting themselves to improve their circumstances. On every side we notice the march of industry, and a willingness among the people to cultivate the soil. The banks of the beautiful St. Paul's interspersed comfortable cottages and well cultivated farms, represent truly, that the inhabitants are comfortably situated. Less cannot be said of the industry of the inhabitants on the Stockton Creek. New Georgia continues to be foremost as an agricultural settlement, and though the "Virginia settlement" may in a year or two take the lead of her, it must not be supposed that there is any diminution of labor on the part of the New Georgians, but that her competitor gets the advantage by having a larger working population (see map 1). Monrovia presents a thriving appearance, the wharves are well lined with crafts varying in size from seven tons to thirty tons. Warehouses are undergoing repairs and speculators are busily traversing the wharves. Dwelling houses are being erected; workmen of every grade are employed, and contentment appears to be the order of the day. Marshall, with *a very small* population, in comparison with the other villages, is, notwithstanding, well entitled to consideration. It is supposed that its inhabitants excel all others in the growing of rice. Its trade is very small, excepting in that of cane, which can be had in large quantities. If an addition of one hundred enterprising colonists could be added to its population, the trade and importance of the place would increase considerably.

The county of Grand Bassa is not behind Montserrado County in industry. Bexley, an agricultural settlement on the St. John's is in a prosperous condition. The inhabitants give their whole attention to the cultivation of their farms. Edina has considerable trade; very few of the inhabitants are engaged in agriculture. It has some half dozen encouraging coffee farms. Foreign soap will find no market here, as the people make more soap than is necessary for their consumption, which is not the case elsewhere in Liberia. Bassa Cove is certainly the most important village in the colony. The people are industrious and enterprising. Several crafts of respectable sizes, have been built by them in the last year; and the trade is rapidly increasing. The majority of the inhabitants are engaged in the cultivation of the soil, and some very pretty coffee farms may be seen here.

The county of Sinoe is the smallest county. The people are very industrious, the greater part of them are living on their farms from which they derive their principal support. Considerable trade is carried on at Greenville. Population only is wanted to make this county equal in importance to her sister counties.

We have attempted a brief statement of the condition of Liberia, and in doing so, we see much to encourage and very little to discourage us. We fell assured that the present state of Liberia is decidedly a favourable one; for the last six months the people have supported themselves mainly from what they raised on their farms. We are now ready and willing to welcome to our land a large number of industrious and enterprising families; they will find every inducement to labor — a soil capable of yielding the richest inducement to labor, a soil capable of yielding the richest productions with very little exertion — a permanent home, free from oppression, for themselves and their children.

What more is required?

49. Constitution of the Republic — Legislature

Liberia Herald, 1 October 1847, 86

It is with feelings of mingled pleasure and pride that we announce to our readers the adoption of the Constitution by a large majority of the votes polled. The government is therefore fairly constituted and waits only the election and appointment of officers to be completely organized.

Candidates for office under the Republic, should endeavour to rise to a perception of the great responsibilities and arduous duties that will be theirs should the people honor them with their confidence. Now, less than at any former time this government can have no sinecures. The man who accepts office with the expectation that he will receive anything like an adequate pecuniary compensation for his services gives proof of one of two things — either that he intends to do little else than receive the stipend, or that he is conscious of the poorness of his ability. In either case he proves himself unworthy of the people's confidence. The people therefore will do well to weigh the character and from that infer the motive of those who solicit their suffrage. At the least they should demand of the candidates to be able to tell whether England is in Polynesia or New Zealand, or whether France is in Siberia or Lapland. These remarks have been suggested by hearing the names of some who have the modesty to offer themselves candidates for the Legislature at this most critical period of the colony's history. We trust however the good sense of the people will be manifested in the returns of the elections; and that candidates who, it is obvious have no motive but the pitiful pay, will be left in that obscurity whence they should never emerge.

But the successful candidates will have a Herculean task to perform — that is provided they be so simple as to undertake all that some of our good and considerate people expect them to do. We have recently been somewhat attentive to the signs of the times; we have listened with some attention to the people's expression of their wants and wishes — and we venture to affirm that Sir Robert Peel backed by Lord John Russell and he helped by Webster and Calhoun of America could not meet these wants and wishes by the exertion of all their immense abilities.[305] In the first place they wish provision made for the employment of the poor. Very good and very natural wish, and we wish with them. In the second place they want a *circulating medium*, which will answer as *an exchange* with *foreigners*. There is truly no crime in the mere wish, but it is certainly very idle in us at present. Government can only be furnished with the means of employment by a revenue drawn from the people, but the people who have nothing cannot pay anything. Foreigners cannot be expected to give their commodities in return for nothing. When we go to work upon our farms and raise something besides cassado and potatoes, when we raise groundnuts and ginger, and arrowroot and pepper — for export, when we collect the valuable timbers and gums abounding in our forests, then we may talk of these things and not till then. Nor will we deserve these blessings until we have gone fairly to work. That we can do these things, no sensible colonist will deny, for what is above the reach of individual effort can be imminently effected by combined exertion.

We therefore can see but little for the Legislature to do more than meet present exigencies. We have enough law, in all conscience, and if the legislature embark boldly into the vast ocean of law making, there is danger that they will never again see the land. Let them simplify our judicial system; abolish useless courts –– reduce the number of officers — civil and military, provide a revenue to meet current expenditures, set a good example of low pay, by voting themselves a *fair* sum for services rendered in the legislature and returning to their homes. Thus they will do the people a service.

50. Letter to Samuel Wilkeson, Monrovia, 29 June 1848

Dear Sir,

Your letter by the *Packet* came safely to hand and the deep interest which you take in our affairs as well as the importance to us of the matter of which it treats induced me to publish it in the *Herald* of which I send you a few copies.[306]

For those who take only a cursory glance at things and only estimate appearances there is no doubt somewhat[307] exceedingly strange or even farcical in the declaration of independence by Liberians. To such, the idea of independence and sovereignty on the part of a few ignorant blacks is a ridiculous novelty. This however would be the language of ignorance or prejudice. And strange to say, language similar to this was held by some here when the subject was first brought up.

We were beset with difficulties on every hand which were constantly increasing and which our friends in America could not, from our anomalous character and peculiar position, at all remove. I saw them & felt them first, and I hesitated not to point them out and to advocate the only course which could relieve them — the declaration of independence and the assumption of sovereign powers. The result to me at first was obloquy, calumny and misrepresentation at home and abroad. But thank God I have lived to see my counsel adopted and many of the bitterest opponents scramblers for office.

We are moving on as well as can be expected. The people are giving more attention to agriculture and seem at length to be impressed with a conviction of the necessity of supplying themselves with provisions. There is however some reason to fear we shall be embarrassed in our fiscal affairs. The expenditures will greatly exceed the revenues, and, to meet this exigency, those at the head of affairs seem disposed to resort to a regular system of trading. Nothing I venture to predict will be more disastrous. The monopoly of a few articles of commerce authorized by the last legislature, although a scheme of my own devising, I consider altogether problematic, especially as the territory of New Cess continues to be the seat of an extensive slave dealer. While this place is a port for the introduction of merchandize free of duty of course there can be no monopoly on the part of the government. If the government gets goods — say tobacco and powder, it having no money must get things on credit and of course at a greatly advanced price. The slaver and others who choose to avail themselves of the facility which his establishment affords for introducing these articles into the Country will be able to undersell the government, and I need not say that purchases will invariably go where they will be most cheaply furnished. On these accounts I rather regret the monopoly act and am induced to hope it may not be carried into effect until the coast is locked up or cleared of these establishments otherwise we may heap up on our heads a debt which we will not get rid of for years to come.

Your mention of the name of Buchanan[308] awakened melancholy feelings in my mind. I esteemed him while he lived and I cherish the tenderest regard for his memory. Traces of his judicious and energetic measures are yet to be seen, and I can truly say I never saw a man more critically adopted to mould the character of an infant people to call forth and direct their energies and excite their ardour than Thomas Buchanan. I am generally withdrawing myself from mercantile pursuits and giving my attention to agriculture. I have about 20 acres of land under cultivation in rice, cassava, potatoes, corn, pepper and ginger. Next year it is my purpose to extend my operations and attend a little to coffee. If you could send us out a supply of ground seed, it would be a great favour. If some seedsman or gardener would send me a supply of seeds put up airtight (in sealed bottles or they will soon spoil in this climate) such as cabbage, turnip, carrot, radish, mustard, melons, pumpkins, sweet potatoes of different kinds and flower seeds, I would sell them on his account and remit the amount either in pepper (cayenne), ginger or cash.

Your Obdt. Servant,

H. Teage

51. Currency

Liberia Herald, 24 November 1848, 8

The Act of the last Legislature establishing a currency has in one respect succeeded admirably.[309] When it was first proposed to make the duties payable in species or in government note, based upon species, many thought the scheme visionary and declared the consequences would be sorely embarrassing to all concerned in trade. We thought differently, adhered to our plan and got the bill through the Legislature.[310] The plan went into operation, and we believe there is no one in the colony who is not now in favor of it.

It should be stated, however, that great praise is due to the Officers who manage our financial affairs, in systematically restraining the issue of these notes within the ability of the treasury promptly to redeem them, and so far as we know, no application has been made at the treasury which has not met a ready and satisfactory response. Consequently the bills retain their full value and circulate readily from hand to hand. This is well and we hope it may continue so.

The whole object of the bill, however, is not met and it cannot be met but by another arrangement, an arrangement which will keep money — hard money — in the Republic. We think so too; but we are very far from concurring in any of the plans which have as yet been proposed. There is one plan to effect this desired object, which will infallibly effect it, which is so obvious that to hold it up or recommend it would be a reflection upon the good sense of the community.

It should not be disguised, however, that no little inconvenience is felt by the poorer class of people in consequence of specie being drained off by foreign vessels. Many persons are forced off in the country with the natives. There is but one remedy for this evil and we will do well to look to it.

52. Republican Legislature

Liberia Herald, 29 December 1849, 10

The legislature is in session, and at the time we write is drawing its deliberation to a close. The multitude of affairs which has demanded our attention, added to feeble health, has deprived us of the pleasure which we no doubt would have received from a constant personal attendance at the deliberations of this important branch of our government. For, although not at present a member of the government, our interest is unabated in its vigorous and healthy sustentation. The subjects taken up at this session are not numerous. The most important is the judiciary.

The system of judiciary established by the last legislature has been from the first moment of its operation up to the present, the subject of loud and almost general complaint and although we will not say how just these complaints are, yet it is but fair to confess that the system was *perfected* and *thrown* through on almost the last day of the session, when the minds of the senate were wholly absorbed and greatly agitated by angry discussions which had taken place on other subjects. No alteration has yet been made, though modifications and amendments have been submitted and we are in doubt whether if an alteration should be made, it will be for the better, unless as is rarely the case in Liberia, it has been the subject of previous prolonged attention. It is perhaps better to let it alone for the present, and give the subject the benefit of another year's consideration.

A new code of criminal law is talked of, and it has been suggested to appoint an individual or a committee to draw up a code and present it at the next legislature.[311]

We confess the necessity and we are confident every one who has anything to do with the law, will respond a hearty amen. Nothing can be conceived more perplexing than our present code; the enactments of one session have invariably been the subjects of repeal the next. And if there had been as invariably a wholesale repeal of the entire act or an entire section of an act, there would not be so much confusion. But when "so much of the act as relates to ___ is hereby repealed" this year, "and so much of" this same repealing act is next year "hereby repealed," and this killing and making alive process has been moving steadily forward for years, it requires a "Philadelphia lawyer"[312] to say which of all that cover the statutory pages is the living conservator of manners today and which the antiquated regulator of the day which has passed. And who is to blame for all this? No one. It is the necessary consequence of rapidly enacting without previous thought.

We fall in with equal readiness with the suggestion as to the mode by which the code should be prepared.

It may seem in the eyes of some a presumption to talk of preparing a criminal code *in* Liberia. Law, we are told, has become a science, and a science so abstruse that deep and profound learning is required to understand it, to explore what is dark — trace analogies and discriminate differences. If so, it is not the law adapted to man; for of the people who inhabit our globe, not two in ten have the requisite ability to determine whether they are in the road that conducts to the degradation of the scaffold or to the pinnacle of honorable ambition; and were we not afraid of being written a clown, we would declare it as our settled conviction that, where to an honest man of common sense mystery in law begins, at that point its utility and efficacy for general good are deplorably enfeebled; and the facts that we are not a learned people and cannot fathom the depths of scientific law are amongst the strongest arguments why we shall have a code prepared in Liberia. But that we are competent to form a system of law efficient for all practical purposes is demonstrated by the well known fact that up to the present moment, we have been regulated by laws made by ourselves; and if anarchy, disorder and irregularity arising from hasty legislation have rioted here, we have felt their inconvenience not more than is confessedly experienced in those communities where law is a science of which the governed herd can never attain one clear idea.

We therefore strongly advocate the measure — extending the work beyond what is usually understood by the phrase criminal law to the whole intercourse of man with man in his domestic circle and relations, to all that relates to his reputation, person and property.

Nor need the matter end here; it might embrace a system of judiciary. The present system, as we have already stated, is a subject of general complaint. Some improvements can doubtless be made, but we are far from the opinion that the reasons for disturbing the present judiciary are as urgent as for an enlarged, settled and well defined code of law.

It should be borne in mind that in the remarks made above, we have reference to laws which effect ourselves and those only who come amongst us. In our intercourse abroad, we must expect to conform to the maxims of the world and prepare to be lost in that labyrinth of scientific law, out of which no man not scientific can hope ever to find his way.

We would suggest that the expressions be simple and concise — that each idea be clearly expressed, but in the fewest possible words –– that no terms be used but those to which the mass of the people has assigned a fixed and determinate meaning, that all barbarous and fatiguing repetitions be avoided, and that not one word be added to a clear and complete expression of the meaning.

It occurs to us that another great improvement might be made: and although the pedant and the votary of mystery might frown with indignity upon the attempt, yet the genius of the English language would applaud, and if we succeed, crown us as reformers. The improvement we suggest is the banishment in every possible case of every word which is not purely English or a well known denizen of the language, by long and familiar intercourse among the people. There would be nothing unreasonable in this: On the contrary, it would be a redeeming of our language from the odium of incapability, for all the purposes of communicating thought and expressing action. The language which gave expression to the lofty conceptions of Milton and Burke, and Newton and Hall, and Chalmers,[313] and of the almost immortals who signed the Declaration of American Independence, cannot be wanting in vigor, precision or copiousness, for all the purposes of life. What idea is there in *nisi prius*, or *Habeas Corpus*, or *non coram Judice*, or *mandamus*, that cannot be adequately expressed in English? As they now stand, none but the initiated can comprehend them: whereas were they expressed in English even [periphrastically], the learned and the unlearned would at once understand them. A poor ignorant man applies for a divorce and after weeks of anxiety, he is told that his wife is divorced a *mensa et thora*, but not a *vinculo matrimonii*. What does he know of the matter? If instead he is told she no longer shares his bed and board, but that some of the responsibilities assumed by marriage are still attached to him, he at once knows his position, and how easily can anyone possessing an English tongue express the sentiment, or English brains, understand it.

Carl Patrick Burrowes

If, however, chosen exotics must adorn the borders of our beautiful english parterre, let them be the odorous and splendid productions of sunny Africa. And this is the more reasonable, as we indulge the hope that our institutions will exert a recuperative and healthful influence upon the tribes around us. Already there are certain words of equal currency amongst us and them. As for instance the word "palaver." Suppose we should name our justice court "palaver," our oyer and terminer, "big palaver;" and our supreme court, from which there is no appeal, "Great devil palaver," all would understand them, neither we who are acquainted with the African manners, nor they would be at any loss. Everything would be plain. In that court chief justice would be "grand devil" and the subordinate officers of that court "devil's mates."[314]

53. [Expansion Along the Coast]

Liberia Herald, 15 September 1850, 14

It seems difficult to cut an old acquaintance. Our connection was of so long standing — formed in 1835 and severed only in 1849,[315] that I cannot maintain an entire silence. During that whole period you were the faithful *Herald*, which was given you in charge to announce; and never in any one instance did you expose yourself to the imputation of adding one word to, or of subtracting one word from any communication you were desired to make. And, although now that our connection is dissolved, and you are transferred to be the response of a far abler and more profound oracle, I cannot speak to you in [the] tone of command which our connection authorised to assume, yet I can speak through you in that language of frankness and candor which uniformly marked your past proclaiming.

In common with many amongst us, who are termed thinking men, I deem it of great importance that we shall secure a long line of coast — that we shall extend our boundary line in the direction of the North, as far as will be agreeable to our neighbors at Sierra Leone, and of the South — not simply to Grand Cestos, because 'Maryland in Liberia' is just on the other side, but as far beyond Cape Palmas as we can conveniently get. The fact that in the event of the advocated extension, the coast line of territory of "Liberia Proper," would be dismembered or disjointed by the intervening and indenting territory of "Maryland in Liberia," and the more plausible fact that, under the two difference and distinct constitutions, there would be something approaching to an *Imperium in imperio* would furnish no solid argument against the propriety of the proposed expansion. He is not only simple and shortsighted — but something worse; who does not see that what is now only in name "Maryland in Liberia," must at no distant day be integrity, "Maryland in Liberia." It is perhaps well for us that "Maryland in Liberia" has not come in before this. The unpracticed arm should not be subjected to a great weight at first, lest the strained muscles should contract a permanent debility. The limb attains its utmost power, by gradual developments, and by a series of exercises proportioned to the strength developed. When we are ready for them, and they are ready for us, the move will be easy. "Liberia proper" will open her arms and "Maryland in Liberia" will fall into their embraces. There will be a mutual drawing together, and the coalition will be easy, quiet, and mutual — and become natural — permanent.[316] Other objections have been urged against the proposed extension, the most grave of which are: — first, that we are not able to protect a long line of coast; — and secondly, that we cannot afford its native inhabitants an adequate supply of suitable merchandize, and thus by a deficient stimulant to industry and enterprise retard the development of the country's resources.

Aside from the light in which a regard to those principles which regulate the great community of nations, would place these objections, and in the lowest possible view which can be taken of them; it may be affirmed that nothing can exceed their futility.

When it is said we are unable to protect a long line of coast, the meaning must be that we are unable to protect the present aboriginal occupants of the soil, or that we are unable to protect it from the aggression of foreigners. If the first — it is a sufficient answer simply to say, the coast cannot possibly have less protection in future than it has been in the past. What power has ever interposed to protect them against the depredations and impositions of unscrupulous traders? What peace maker has ever come in and employed a soothing voice to allay the ferment and excitements which foreign influences excited? What friendly arbetrator has stepped between combatting tribes, when paid to cut each others throats and steal each others' children: — whole villages have been reduced to a heap of ruins, burying and charring the bones of its aged and infirm inhabitants? If the inhabitants of the coast were visited at all by a power superior to theirs, it was to lay upon them the hand of a double chastisements for imaginary or real wrongs committed in the way of retaliation. In fact, it is well known, that the coast of Africa, except at the few inconsiderable sites of European settlements, is considered beyond the territory of law and justice, and decency: a domain where all the passions and propensities, avarice, cruelty, lust — may throw off all restraint and go forth to boundless indulgence. This fact is notorious. These spectacles, so frequent a few years ago, are now of rare occurrence on any part of the coast under our jurisdiction; and these desolating feuds among the natives are nearly at an end.

It should be recollected, that the natives, if left alone to pursue their own avocations, in their own way, require no protection. Each tribe has its separate laws, regulating its own affairs; and, the tribes collectively have a few simple, general laws — something like the public laws of Europe — regulating their intercourse.[317.] Experience has taught them the sufficiency of these; and it is only when they are suspended, or violated by lawless cupidity; that any great inconvenience is felt, and it were but a tiresome repetition to state that nine-tenths of this excitement have been evermore the offspring of the slave trade; to which, hitherto, what has been misnamed lawful and honorable trade, had contributed a melancholy share. If by 'to protect' it is intended to alleged an inability on our part to enforce a system of judicious and equitable maritime laws on so long a line of coast, it is conceded if the force we may be called to protect against, is superior to ours.

But that is true of every nation — of Britain, France [and] the United States. If France be so much more powerful and populous than England, that a large number only of its citizens would go forth as freebooters, and successfully resist or elude the maritime laws of England, it might be contended upon the same principle that Queen Victoria should not claim and possess the coast of Ireland and England! If this doctrine should prevail very many nations that have been long in undisturbed and undisputed possession of their domain would have to contract their lines and throw open part of their governed and regulated dominion to the operations of lawless and unrestrained passion. For where is the nation whose force and vigilance are such as to keep its territory free from the pollution of piratical entry! Over all the coast which we may acquire, we shall, I trust exercise a salutary authority. It will I doubt not, be the aim of our legislators to establish such a system of law, and enforce such regulations, as the nature of the case demands. They have the past and present laws of other nations before them. They have also the past and present condition of those nations before them. Let them take the experience of others for their torch and keeping the peculiarities of our position steadily and distinctly in view let them avoid a Procrustean legislation avoiding alike the bigotry that would chain them to the formula of antiquity, and the novelty that would wholly disregard all the lessons of experience. Having thus spun out my remarks on the first objection, I must defer what I may find to say to the second, to some future communication. In the interim, Mr. *Herald*, believe me to be ever

Yours &c.

H. Teage

54. Letter to William McLain, Monrovia, 2 January 1851

Dear Sir,

As the *Edgar* sails tomorrow, I sit down to drop you a line. From a letter I received by the *Edgar*, I learn that the steamship enterprise is likely to go into operation. The prospect fills me with a commingled emotion of hope and fear.[318] We need help in the shape of an increased population. The country asks it. There is room for all the sons & daughters of Africa. But Liberia is not yet prepared for them, or, more to the point, they are not all prepared for Liberia. You cannot give us too many working men — men of the hoe, plane, axe, etc. — men who will content themselves to remain out of the presidential chair for at least one month after their arrival here. Men of such habits and moderate pretentions will be of some service; if you have plenty such in America, send them. We will receive them with open arms; when the atmosphere of liberty — perfect liberty, which is inhaled by the colored man no where but in Liberia — when the atmosphere of liberty has inflated their lungs, and expanded and elevated their minds, and they have thus become prepared for the discharge of public functions, we will then hold them morally & personally entitled to franchises, to which, from the defect of our present constitution, they are now legally entitled the moment they land, whether from rice swamps of Carolina or an oyster cellar in New York.

This is no disparagement to the colored man — I am of that race, & I hold it second to none in natural endowment — 'tis no disparagement to that race that they are not all prepared for Africa. You know, my dear sir, and all who have tried it know — liberty is necessary to the perfecting of men. I do not despise education. On the contrary, I esteem & honor it. I only regret my want of it. But you may give a man Greek & Latin & Hebrew & whatever else you please if he breathes the mephitic air of slavery, he is wanting –– He will be like the well proportioned column — destitute of the entablature.

I have tried England & America and Africa –– but I am free to confirm I breathed freely and saw clearly no where but in Africa. Send us modest men, not boasters — working men, not office seekers — sensible men, not stupid pedants. We have one

Doctor of Divinity out here now in the person of A. J. Woods.[319] He is enough for all Africa. May I take the liberty to ask, what it is in Mr. Woods that Mr. Pinney should distinguish him with a cabin passage?

The colony is moving slowly. Much improvements are going on in this town — more than ever before at one town. The people as a generality are about as happy, content and fat as I ever saw them. We have plenty to eat; and are able to say to a Captain when he asks an unreasonable price, keep your pork & flour, we have plenty rice, cassava, fish, fowls, sheep & beef. We intend to be quite independent in the respect of eating. We have found out that your food is too heavy for the Torrid Zone. Rice & palm oil — if a man wishes to live long, let him eat rice & palm oil & whatever else this country produces. Did not he who made us know best? If heavy wheat & pork had been best would he not have put it here? He put here rice & cassava, oil, and sheep & goats & leaves. We shall soon tell you to keep these things away or to send them in small quantities, just enough to meet the cravings of the unregenerate stomachs of new comers.

To conclude — I am here better pleased with Liberia every morning when I awake and find myself in it. I do not say everything is just what it should be. I do not say Liberia is an Elysium — by no means. There is room for improvements. But it is so much more pleasing to be voting for one's own representatives than to be peeking 'round the corner at those who are voting — so much more pleasing to clean one's own farm than to clean another's boot, especially when he is conscious that it is the *ne plus ultra* of his ascent. On these, and on some other accounts, Liberia is now & ever will be preferred to all other places by

Your obdt. Servant

H. Teage

Neighboring Societies

55. Native Salutations

African Repository, July 1837, 193

We know of no people who evince more cordiality and ardent feeling on meeting old friends and acquaintances, than the natives of Africa. Their mode of salutation, though strikingly different from that in use among civilized people, is certainly not less affecting, and by far more expressive.[320]

When two old acquaintances meet, as soon as they perceive each other, they reciprocally address each other by name, and apply the left hand to the breast and quicken their pace, until they come in contact. The chin of the one is then laid over the shoulder of the other, reiterating a dozen times, while in this position, their terms of salutation. This done, they mutually recede, eyeing one another as closely as though each was apprehensive he had been mistaken. They again address each other by name, as rapidly approach as before, and go through the former ceremony.

We once witnessed the meeting of two venerable hoary headed sires, in the Sherbro country, which we shall never forget. After approaching each other, as described above, they receded to a distance of ten or fifteen feet, seated themselves and during an interval of eight or ten minutes, eyed each other with a significance that is altogether indescribable. They then mutually addressed, approached, embraced, and gave vent to their joy in a half stifled tone, as though their feelings had paralyzed the power of utterance. Let those who deny to the man of colour the possession of acute sensibility, witness such a scene, and say if they have ever been conscious of emotions so deep.

56. Excursion

Liberia Herald, 29 April 1842, 22

We treated ourselves a few days ago, with an excursion to Mama's Town [see map 1]. Our good folks here have not agreed to the full perception of the benefit of an occasional aquatic excursion. After weeks of dull rounds of ordinary cam wood and similar deadening avocations an excursion in the country is truly exhilarating and refreshing.

Old Mama, was as usual ceremonious and formal. We saw her as we approached the landing, cautiously eyeing the boat from the angle of a house. We no sooner struck the landing than she precipitately retired, and when we next saw her, she was gravely seated in her hall of reception. To rise on the approach of Ladies is no part of African dignity, she therefore stolidly kept her seat although the ladies were in near approach of her. As soon, however, as we approached, being a favorite of old "Mama's," she arose[,] came forward, and gave the cordial African welcome, by pressing our right hand between both of hers. Then followed the snap of the finger with all the party. This concluded, the old woman conducted us to a house which she had allotted for our occupation. Notwithstanding our approach to the town was rapid, this house[,] the best in the town[,] was ready cleared and prepared before we were ready to enter upon its occupancy.

This house, we are inclined to believe, was erected for the express purpose of accommodating strangers. It is furnished in the best style of native workmanship. It contains two apartments. In both there are ottomans — that is banks of earth thrown up in [the] form of sofas, which are intended for an occasional lounge, or for sleeping at night. The ceilings are in the finest style of taste and fashion, arched and fluted with bamboo. The walls and floor like the couches, are of a greenish colored clay, rubbed hard and smooth.

In this imperfectly described apartment, we deposited ourselves and our stores;[321] and after refreshing ourselves with a few moments rest, we farther refreshed ourselves with the contents of our baskets. The natives as usual stood around, extremely surprised at our burdening ourselves with the encumbrances of knives and forks, when each of us was blest with nature's own production of two hands and ten fingers.

Old Mama was summoned to join our repast, but refused to eat in our presence, she was therefore supplied separately with a portion which she took away, and served out in small portions to her dependents, leaving only a meagre share for herself.

The situation of Mama's town is one of the handsomest that we have seen. It stands on the extreme point of the island, about a half mile from the bar. The noble St. Paulsweeps gracefully around it. The water is clear and deep, and encumbered by nimble trees which dip their green foliage in the refreshing scene. There is almost always a pleasant breeze from the sea, which sweeping over the waters is sufficiently cool for any who has been twenty years in the climate.

We rowed down to the bar, back again up the stream and landed on the opposite side. On approaching the landing the boys espied a tree burdened with fruit (monkey apple) bending down to the surface of the water, as if to keep it cool and ready for use. As soon as we struck the shore, a general race commenced, and soon like monkeys each one returned with a modicum of the spoil. The ladies made an excursion some distance up the "path," gathering flowers, while we contented ourselves with joining the boys in devouring the fruit.

We arrived home about 7 o-clock in the evening after a day of pleasant and refreshing recreation.

57. [The Condition of Women]

Liberia Herald, 30 September 1843, 31

There is a striking similarity in the domestic and social customs and habits of all uncivilized nations. This is especially the case in the condition of woman. [W]herever a people is little advanced in civilization, the lot of the female is hard. In Africa they are regarded as servants, instruments of pleasure and profit. Not only are they subjected to domestic drudgery, but at regular seasons compelled to the severe tasks of the field, exposed to the full blaze of the sun while their ungallant lords are enjoying the three fold luxury of the shade, a hammock and a pipe. Their tasks however are not always unpleasant to themselves nor without interest to those who witness them.

When the fountain, as is often the case, is situated at a distance from the hamlet, the business of conveying water is made an occasion of gossip and recreation. The usual task [??] of watering is in the cool of the morning or afternoon. They usually go in companies — threading their narrow and tortuous paths in Indian file — enlivening the solitariness of the way by sprightly conversation or inspiring song. Occasionally they form their party about noon and start for the brook. They first fill their vessels and deposit them nearby. Afterward they descend a small distance below the place where the water is taken, and bury their bodies in the refreshing stream. They carry the water in vessels on their head, poised with an accuracy that leaves their arms and hands at perfect liberty, while a green branch immersed in the water prevents it from splashing.

Women are sometimes made instruments of the most disgusting and revolting avarice. An unprincipled husband will prompt an illicit intercourse between his wife and some man upon whose purse he designs. When the affair is ripe for explosion, a pretended suspicion will demand a trial by ordeal, when the woman pretending fear will *break the palaver*, and thus subject the ensnared [wretch][322] to a heavy fine if not to perpetual slavery. Of course the guilty husband to save appearances must vent his indignation against his incontinent partner. She will probably be condemned to a shaved head and rustication for a month in some half town, whence she will return pleased at having contributed to the wishes of her lord.

58. Tender Mercies of Heathenism

Liberia Herald, 30 September 1843, 31

A friend recently from the Gallinas related to us the following fact which not long ago occurred there. Following out the acknowledged truth that great men can't die, but by foul or rash means — directly after the demise of King '[323] whose death we noticed at the time, a secret inquisition was set on foot to ferret out the *witch-man*. For a long time the search was fruitless; at length a gregree man by continued incantation, and daring diabolic communications succeeded, and the hapless regicide was brought to light. Confronted with his accuser, he protested he was innocent — the *dotter* protested he was guilty, and the all discovering ordeal was resorted to, to decide the question. Of course the man was condemned to die, and as King Shakah was *big king too much* — the severity of the punishment was proportioned to the dignity of the deceased. Sentence was pronounced and thus executed — the man was taken to the mouth of the river — his tongue cut out, and he thrown alive to the sharks that infest the place.

This ordeal is a most powerful engine of state policy in Africa. It is the right arm of an African monarch. He has only to keep on terms with the doctors or gregree men who are the constituted inquisitors, and nothing is easier than to rid himself at any time of a dangerous or aspiring subject. Whether the ordeal be the saucy water, the boiling oil, or the heated iron, they are never at a loss for means to produce any result they wish.[324] If it be the first process, they weaken or strengthen the concoction

Carl Patrick Burrowes

and increase or lessen the quantity so as to render it innocent or fatal just as interest or inclination may lead. If the second or third they can by previous application of some preparation to the part to be operated upon, enable it for a short time to resist the effect of heat; and then by burying the ordeal, the accused escapes unscathed. If they conclude to murder the victim,[325] they reverse the operation and guilt is as clear as noonday. Thus this constitution puts the life of the whole community in the hands of this tribe, and renders it a formidable fraternity of conjurors.

59. Last Days of Amurah

Liberia Herald, 23 December 1842, 6-7

This celebrated African chieftain whose capture we noticed directly after it occurred perished by the basest of perfidy.

For years his prowess and activity maintained a successful contest against the whole of Shakah's forces and more than once he drove them back upon the very gates of Kendamah. The whole Vey country at length took the alarm and combined against him. Being closely pressed by an over whelming force, Amurah retired to a fastness which he had prepared against reverses. The walls of this town instead of being the rude fragile stockade of which the enclosures of African "war towns" are usually made to consist, were of earth, of great thickness and solidity. They were constructed of successive strata of well digested clay.[326] The material after having been sufficiently moistened with water, and thoroughly masticated by innumerable thumps of innumerable lusty feet, was conveyed to the site of the superstructure. Early in the morning a layer of a certain depth and the proper thickness was laid on, and left during the day exposed to the full force of the sun. By next morning it was sufficiently hard, when another was laid on. Every morning the process was repeated until the walls attained the intended height. A covering was then thrown over them projecting on each side so as to protect them from the attack of rain. He farther strengthened his position by a deep ditch around the whole fortification.

Here Amurah retired, and whenever his assailants would venture "too close" his barricade his "big guns" and musketry from the portholes and embrasures would chide their rashness, and teach them that Amurah "be man" and was not to be played with "all same he be boy."

This fortification was the walls of Babylon to his cowardly assailants, and they regarded scaling the moon and carrying the place by storm fetes of equal practicability.

But what they wanted courage to do manfully, they achieved by expedient. Beyond the reach of Amurah's big guns, they erected a sufficient number of "small towns" at convenient distances to encircle the whole enclosure, determined to prevent his egress and starve him into submission. Having finished their "towns," they sent off and bought a "war" — that is procured a large number of mercenaries, stipulating that each one should pay himself in the event of a breaking up with whatever he should be able to steal. Although the "town" was completely hemmed in, he was able to hold out a long time. His foresight had provided a large store of provisions, and his walls enclosed on the falling spring of excellent water.

After some months of delay, the enemy sent a flag of truce, and requested a parley. Amurah consented, and appearing upon the walls held a conference. Conditions were submitted by "Prince Manah" the commander-in-chief which the haughty spirit of Amurah rejected indignantly, and the conference was about coming to an abrupt close, when the latter discovered among his enemies the son of his ancient friend King "Kiamo." Amurah immediately called him, and the following conversation ensued—

> Amurah — Kiamo, is your father dead?[327]
> Kiamo — *Yes.*
> Amurah — Who be king to him place?
> Kiamo — *Me be king.*
> Amurah — What you come do here?
> Kiamo — *I come for make dis war set. All country spoil for dis war palaver.*
> Amurah — How dis war go set?
> Kiamo — *You must stop fight.*
> Amurah — Me one fight? You no see all dem people dem gun? Me one fight?
> Kiamo — *You one no fight — no more spose you stop fight — war can done.*
> Amurah — Me stay fight for dem kill me all same. I no fear? — no I can stop fight.
> Kiamo — *Spose you stop, dem stop too.*
> Amurah — Who say so,
> Amurah — Spose I stop, wheat dem can do wid me?

Here Manah and all the headmen united in assuring him protection and honorable treatment if he would lie down his arms. He requested a day to consider the matter, when, he retired from the wall and they to their "towns."

The next day Amurah called them to the walls and after obtaining from them solemn assurance of protection of his property, his followers and himself, he opened the gates and they marched in. As soon as they had entered Manah dispatched a messenger to his royal Father, King Shakah, informing him they had possession of the town and requesting to known if he should carry the "lion" to Kendemah. The King sent this laconic answer — If you think it would be safe. Manah saw at once the pleasure of this father, and his own feelings, were strictly accordant with his father's, as he had long regarded Amurah a dangerous rival, who might one day prove an insuperable obstacle in his way to the "horsetail."[328]

Having pledged to Amurah the most solemn assurance of protection and safety, it required some days of anxious and solicitous planning to furnish a pretext for his treacherous and bloody purpose. This he at length found in the haughty and indomitable spirit of his intended victim. They had not been long in possession before Amurah penetrated their design and in the sullenness of his character had resolved to meet his fate with calmness. As he was one morning relaxing in his hammock, one of Manah's slaves (tutored for the business) approached and stood near him. Indignant at the unusual familiarity of such a character, he demanded what he wanted — bid him begone and emptied the vial of his wrath, by adding "you stink," the harshest degree of indignity in the estimation of an African. The insolent varlet maintaining his position, Amurah said, I know what you want — your master sent you — he wants to kill me. The slave went off. In a few moments, a rush was made upon him where he lay. He now saw his hour had come. He offered no resistance, but said he had only one request to make — that being a Muslim, he wanted time for devotion. For once the savages delayed for a few moments to murder a fallen enemy. As soon as the last word of his prayer fell from his lips, they threw him to the ground, tied him and cut his throat.

Amurah's mother, hearing an unusual bustle enquired for her son. Some of the fiends took her by the hand and said they would lead her where he was. A moment & she beheld him withering in his blood. They threw her upon the body yet quivering with life and cut her throat.

Thus perished one of the noblest of the Vey.

Amurah was a noble fellow. Powerful and influential in the country, he was dreaded by all the chiefs and headmen. He was also very rich and possessed among other valuables, a large amount of silver plates. In the days of his prosperity he has given us many a "dash" of silver basins of unwonted massiveness, each of the capacity of a peck. It was of him we purchased a thousand dollars contained in a bag marked with the name of a vessel subsequently captured with slaves and of which our friend, John Dean Lake made such a flourish before a committee of the British House of Commons: which money, a part at least, we paid to John Dean Lake for goods purchased of him, at the same time giving him the bag at his request to keep the money in. [329]

60. African Belief

Liberia Herald, 30 March 1844, 2

Those who suppose that there is not in heathen minds, any connexion between virtue and happiness and vice and punishment, manifest an ignorance of their customs — or if acquainted with their customs — that they have taken but a superficial view of the subject. This will hold good at least of all the African tribes with which we have been conversant. It is true that the idea of virtue differs in different countries. The ancient Scandinavian regarded it highly virtuous and acceptable to *Thor* when he fell upon and butchered scores of helpless and unoffending victims. With the ancient Greek sensuality or war or revelry was a virtue, accordingly as he worshipped the imaginary deities *Venus, Mars,* or *Bacchus,* their presiding patrons. We have not to conjecture what the Mohammedan or the Papist or the Protestant Christian would reply, was the question, what is virtue, put to him. Savages have their virtues and although they may exclude other nations from the benefit of their operations, still as it regards themselves, they connect happiness with the practice of these virtues.

These reflections were forced upon our mind by a conversation recently had with an intelligent Vey man who was once under the tutelage of the celebrated King *Peter Softly* of Big town. [330] The conversation related to Jenkins [331] of whom we gave some account in a former number of our paper. He said: —

"King Peter was a great man — and Jenkins was his boy. — The King made Jenkins head man to land the cargoes from vessels coming for slaves and ivory. Jenkins became rich, and the King was very fond of him. At length King Peter died and was buried, and a great quantity of silver in cups, spoons and basins was put in the grave with him. Soon after the King died, Jenkins went off and built a town for himself and became a great man. Afterwards a dispute between Jenkins and Jarah Fingee[332], the son and successor of King Peter, over portion appeared to arise. After years of combat, Jenkins' arms succeeded. He took Big town, Jarah Fingee's capital, where the late King was buried. The conqueror made an indiscriminate butchery of all the captives and prepared to level the town to the earth. Before, however, he burned the place, he sacrilegiously exhumed the mouldered remains of the King — consumed the body under the smoldering ruins of the town, and bore away the head, and the silver of which he robbed the grave as the trophies of his arms. The whole country was smitten with consternation by this act of impiety. Jarah Fingue retired sickened in heart to invoke the aid of that power, which, ignorant as he is, he believes will punish vice and impiety.

"Jarah Fingue took a mug of water and poured forth before it the following lamentation — 'Jenkins was my Father's boy. My father gave him water to drink — rice to eat and cloth to wear. He made him man. My father died — we buried him and put money in the grave with him. Jenkins and I quarreled, my father did not quarrel with him — we fought — my father did not fight him. He took my town. — That was nothing. — If he beat me, that was no palaver. But why did he trouble my father? Why did he dig him up and burn him? Why did he carry away the silver we put in the ground?"

Then follows the imprecation — thus: After breathing violently on the mug he exclaimed:

"Whatever he attempts let him not be successful in — if he plant, let it not grow; if he make war, let him be killed; if he remains at home, let him die soon."

The ceremony seems simple to us — but it is their ceremony; fixed in their minds as an acceptable recognition of an almighty power not inattentive to the concerns of mortals. We have ventured to put it down.

Twelve months afterward Jenkins died. I asked my informant who was one of Jarah Fingee's subjects if he supposed that the gregree killed Jenkins -- he replied at once "no, but that thing Jenkins do, God no like em."

It has been supposed here that Jenkins was carried off by poison.

61. [Journey to Bah-Gay]

Liberia Herald, 15 March 1845, 46

Having been joined with friend James Brown in a commission to settle some matters with the kings and chiefs of Little Bassa, from which place we returned on the 17th ult., we give below an extract from our journal:[333]

"Wednesday 13th, made arrangements with Mr. Jonas Carey for his canoe and six boys to accompany us to Bah Gay's, and having furnished ourselves with supplies as far as Messrs. Jones and Carey's stores would enable us to do, so we left at 8 a. m. for the king's residence.[334] Our route was along a beautiful river studded near the coast by numerous islets mantled in the deepest green. The river here is exceedingly beautiful and expands itself almost into a bay. Bah Gay lives about seven miles from the embouchure[335] [see map 1]. [We] reached there about 10 o'clock. "He appeared much pleased to see us and granted us a gracious reception with "eh, how due my friend!" and a loud and sonorous snap of the finger. After mutual enquiries about *old friends* his majesty retired, rather unceremoniously *we* thought. He returned soon after, and we discovered why he had gone. He went to adjust his wardrobe. We found him in his undress — that is, with only a part of his haunches covered. He now had his whole person wrapped in blue cotton from his shoulders to his heel.

"We announced to him at once the object of our visit, and enquired where we should hold the palaver. He said the chiefs would not come to his town and he would not go to theirs. We must (continued he) have 'de palaver for beach a you (Teage's) factory.' We saw at once there was jealousy and suspicion among them. In fact Bah Gay showed symptoms of apprehension unworthy of a personage of so high standing. He has for two or three years suffered with some mesenteric disorder which no gregree has been able to correct, and as usual in such cases the *dottor* has concealed his ignorance by assuring his majesty that he is *witched*. This important fact having transpired it was sustained by evidence in the Harem. Two of his majesty's wives voluntarily came forward and assured their lord that they had witched him by putting the gregree into his chop; and moreover that they had been induced to do so by one Bey[,] a chief in the country. Bey's name having been mentioned in connection with the king's sickness, he avoided his majesty's vengeance by flight. The chiefs of the country, who have been long jealous of Bah Gay and desirous of an opportunity to reduce him, took up the fugitive. Bey is a convenient tool for their purpose and persuaded him to call a devil palaver. His satanic majesty[,] always to be found by those who seek him[,] granted a ready audience and took up the case. The time for the ghostly consistory[336] was fixed and the intended victim summoned to attend. Bah Gay saw at once the snare spread for him and knew that once in the toils[337] his fate would be inevitable. He therefore returned for answer — 'I no go.' Again the women of his town were made to tremble by a ghostly voice sounding in the bushy suburbs the fatal summons. Again Bah Gay refused, and knowing the next notification would be the ring of the musket and the whoop of savage war, he dispatched with all speed a letter to Governor Roberts imploring his interposition. We arrived just in time to arrest the blow.

"Dwah Will, one of the chiefs, is the head devil of the country. We have not seen his excellency, but if he be more a devil than some we have seen in that country, then he is truly all sorts of a devil. This devil palaver seems to be a politico-religious institution, and is the highest tribunal known amongst them. When any one under accusation desires the decision of the devil, he goes to Dwah Will, the 'devil's mouth.' He then confers with his superior and fixes the time and place of the audience. They usually select for the purpose a dark and gloomy forest suited to the genius of the infernal arbiter. When preliminaries are arranged, a messenger is dispatched to notify the appellee to attend. The messenger disguised by a hideous visor[,] rudely carved and painted to caricature the human face divine, wends his way through the woods, avoiding roads[,] lest he should be seen, and so regulates his speed so as to reach the residence of his victim at night. Then when sleep has buried all the inhabitants in soft oblivion, he raises his awful voice and startles them with the dreaded notice. The messenger is always a ventriloquist, and the sound comes as from the bottomless pit. The women wrap their children up and cover their faces. The men turn out and signify by significant noises their audience of Diabolar's legate.[338] Should the individual summoned to attend fail to appear at the proper time, the message is repeated with threatenings of vengeance. No other indulgence can ever be granted. If he continues disobedient, the messenger is sent the third time; but he now carries with him three or four masks similar to those he wears on his face — called by the natives Devils, and creeping up to the town at night, he throws these visors or masks into it and retires. All the inhabitants are de facto placed under the ban of the country. They can be captured[,] sold or slain and their property confiscated by any and every one. Indeed they are then lawful prey, and seeing they "be" under the malediction[339] of the devil in whose good graces all those people are fond of securing a place, the whole country will eagerly combine against them. Under any circumstances it is death for a woman to see the devil, and the man who should show a woman any of these devils would surely have to give the devil the satisfaction for exposing him to the curious gaze of a female. African devils are like devils everywhere else. However they may simper and smile and flatter when they have no power, they are terrible when once they have infixed their claws. We once witnessed a devil palaver from which the victim escaped only by the payment of twenty slaves; and although the amount was paid by Bah Gay, the man to release whom he paid it, is now leagued against him. We resolved at once to go on the beach and made a requisition on our baskets for strength for the task. Bah Gay promised to follow us, tomorrow. Having dashed the king a few bars of tobacco and piled our baggage on the boys' heads[,] we commenced to trace a path which we had been told was "'good too much and have no more one water to cross.'"This latter we soon found to be nearly literally true. The path a great part of the way is neither more nor less than a gutter which the water has made for herself, in which it lay in filthy alliance with its own depth of high sand, threatening indelible darkness to whatsoever may come in contact with it. We enquired whether there was any way to avoid the water, when being assured there was not, we trudged on affecting no little fun in wading. The path lay along a ravine which was in days of yore an extensive marsh but now partly filled up by decayed vegetation and debris from the adjunct elevations. These lowlands offer excellent site for plantations of rice and all kinds of succulent vegetables. Emerging from this gloomy and filthy canal we found a firmer dry path furnishing all sorts of angles through a forest of ancient trees, whose abundant drapery completely canopied us, and concealed the sun from our view. About two miles brought us to a grave field, where we were exposed to the full force of a fiery sun. Such was the fury with which he shot his breaths upon us, that it seemed as if he was paying us for the shelter we had just enjoyed. Perhaps it was the sudden charge from the invigorating shade of embowering[340] trees to exposure to the direct rays of the sun that rendered the heat so oppressive.

"We could now distinctly hear the surf beating its everlasting symphony upon the beach, and knew there from that 'we close ketch em', and a walk of sixteen kilometers brought us in full view of the old Atlantic.

> Roll on, thou deep and dark blue ocean — roll!
> Ten thousand fleets sweep over thee in vain;
> Man marks the earth with ruin — his control
> stops with the shore; — upon the watery plain
> The wrecks are all thy deed, nor doth remain
> A shadow of man's ravage, save his own,
> When, for a moment, like a drop of rain,
> He sinks into thy depths with bubbling groan,
> Without a grave, unknell'd, uncoffin'd, & unknown.[341]

Carl Patrick Burrowes

"We turned our eyes in the direction of the factories, sad that they were, basking in the sun as a distance of about two miles. Inspirited by the sound of the surf and refreshed by the spray which was continually thrown upon us, we soon measured the distance, and reached the factories about 5 o'clock p. m. Anxious to exercise our mission, we dispatched a messenger to each head-man — and to each we send a little tobacco and a fathom[342] of white cloth, charging each one to say Messrs. Teage and Messrs. Brown give you sarvice, Dey come for bring Gobnor word — dey want for see you beach tomorrow.

"Having done Mr. Ferguson,[343] whose factory was our hotel, all the harm we could by eating one half of its fowls for supper and threatened him with eating the remainder 'tomorrow,' we then betook ourselves to mat. ["][344]

62. Conjurer and Conjuration

Liberia Herald, 3 July 1846, 70

A few days ago a deputation of mentally [diseased] individuals leading a physically diseased individual besieged Governor Roberts humbly beseeching him to help them. They were all from New Georgia. The boy [,] for that is the sex of him who was impotent, had been sick a long time "sick too much." At length disease reached a crisis and "every body been think he go die one time." His friends were in paroxysms of grief. Just then a Congo, one of Captain Bell['s] protégés came along.[345] Prompted by benevolence, "no cry mammo" he said, "your child be witch; pose you pay me I go make da witch come up." He commenced operations and the result was an extraction from the boy's belly of a leopard's claw and a handful of strange and odious larvae. These were all carefully preserved and brought down to the Governor. He, however, was skeptical and endeavoured to bring them over to his belief that it was all a delusion. All argument however was lost upon them and they returned home either mortified at his stolidity or chagrined at his obstinacy in resisting the conclusive evidence of the claw and the grubs which they had presented to him.

The affair was not to stop here. Truth cannot be suppressed. It was soon ascertained that another boy was similarly affected. The "dottor" was sent for who at once declared that "witch ketch em." A fine opportunity was now presented to convince the incredulous Governor or to expose his stupidity. At once he who was witched[,] his friend and the dottor presented themselves at government house and solicited audience. "Nother boy" said they "be witch all same da other one and we fetch em and the dotter for let you see him take dem ting him belly." A crowd assembles and ourself in the sunlight. The possessed with a most woe-begone and witched aspect of countenance was planted in a sartorious posture upon the floor; directly in front of whom and almost in contact, the "dottor" planted himself in a similar posture. Assuming a look of imperturbable gravity and importance he prepared to operate. First he produced from a satchel a medley of herbs and roots; part of them he placed in a shell, the others he [chafed] in his hand. This done he produced a razor. He then fixed his eyes with a stern and intense gaze on those of the boy; the "dottor's" hands at the same time moving alternately in a saltatory[346] and rotatory motion. Soon he commenced his exorcisms using some caballistic phrases which no one understood but himself. Soon "he look da devil," and his hand now stationary pointed directly at that part of the boy's body where diabolus had taken. Although found[,] the devil was not yet captured; a more powerful charm was necessary to dislodge him. Having scarified a small space directly over the midrif he applied his mouth there to and exerted his utmost power of suction. Whatever or whoever else could stand this charm[,] it was soon evident the devil could not. That the conflict between the exorcist and the devil was fierce and severe was soon announced by a quivering of his muscles and an apparent involuntary movement of his arms. Victory however was decided in favour of the "dottor" who looking around upon the spectators with an air of satisfaction and triumph held the devil firmly in more than "durance vile" between his teeth. The believers in the operation signified their satisfaction by furtive glances at the unbelievers and by half suppressed smiles; which brought strongly to our mind Gay's ["F]able of the [J]ugglers["]

> But, when from thence the hem he draws,
> Amazed spectators hum applause.[347]

We however were not to be thus discomfitted, but determined to submit this devil to a close and searching scrutiny. For this purpose we brought his satanic majesty under the focus of a powerful microscope and found him to be no more nor less than a piece of blue cloth wrapped with the fine fibres of the palm leaf in the form and size of an ordinary larva. This which the fellow had before he commenced operations concealed either in his mouth[,] nose or throat was coated with clotted or coagulated blood, and to the naked eye very closely resembled a grub. Nothing abashed by this exposure he renewed his manipulation in order to extract another devil, but disgusted with the mummery and vexed at our want of authority to administer to the exorcist the moral and mental sanative[348] prescribed by Moses, we left the scene.

63. Scarcity

Liberia Herald, 4 June 1847, 62

We have heard with much sorrow that the natives in the interior will suffer and indeed are at present suffering from an unprecedented scarcity of provisions. This is owing to the fickleness of the weather. Last season in the month in which there is usually very dry weather, there was so much rain as to prevent them from burning their farms. We are pleased however to be able to say, we can help them in the way of African bread stuff: such as cassado, potatoes, rice, &c., &c. Of these articles, we have an abundant supply — enough for ourselves and some to spare to our neighbors.

64. The Bunglers Besieged and Taken

Liberia Herald, 28 July 1848, 38

About four months ago a large and populous native town in the vicinity of Bo Porah,[349] [see map 1] and directly on the great road which leads to that formerly celebrated emporium of slaves and merchandize, was furiously assaulted by a large force, which suddenly presented itself before the walls of the town. As no known provocation has been given for the war, there was no expectation of it and no preparation had been made for defence.

Boolah-Jah (Boolah's town), for such was the name of the city, had been newly rebuilt — greatly enlarged and surrounded by a wall about twenty feet high, pierced with numerous gates for facility of egress and ingress. The wall had just been completed and the scaffolding around the outside had not been taken down. After a short resistance, the besiegers by means of the scaffold scaled the walls and carried the town. Having secured the victory, they at once commenced the work of destruction, and a venerable Mohamedan priest fell first under the blow of the battle axe. They proceeded in their butcheries until the blood of fifty victims drenched the earth, when their avarice of blood a little glutted, they passed for a while in their sanguinary[350] career.

Very fortunately for the whole country, Boolah, the King or chief of this town, with his principal men were absent at another town on business of state or of pleasure. Had this formidable chief been involved in the common destruction, the whole country would have been ravaged by these foreign marauders. The news of the capture of the town soon reached the king, and with characteristic energy, he commences to consort means for resistance and revenge. It required no long argument nor much persuasion to kindle the rage of the whole Kondah and Mandingo population, as the attempt on this town was considered by those trafficking tribes, a general injury. Boolah-Jah was formerly an inconsiderate hamlet. It is situated on the interior boundary of the Golah country. It has long been a kind of caravanserai[351] and object to constant attacks by predatory bands of Golahs roving in quest of plunder. Boolah anxious to preserve the peace of the country and to keep open a safe and constant communication between the Atlantic and interior tribes, made war upon a bevy of petty Golah chiefs, compelled them to sue for peace, which he granted, on condition that they would remain quiet and throw no obstruction in the way of trade and in order to keep them to the terms of their stipulation, as well as to be able to keep open communication[,] enlarged and fortified his town. He had just completed it when the Mendians[352] made their attack. The Mendians come from a considerable distance. Their country, we are told[,] lies to the northeast of Gallenas and the force which attacked Boolah-Jah, is one of three divisions sent out to different quarters on similar errands of robbery and murder.

While the Mendians were rolling the midst of fancied security and triumph and exulting over the easily conquered and defenseless captives and displaying to themselves that skill and prowess in uncouth gestures and fiendish grimaces and anticipating the gratulations with which they would be received on their return to their homes, they were suddenly appalled by the appearance of a powerful force, advancing on all sides upon the town.

They made no attempt at a parley — they had known that was altogether out of the question; they were the aggressors and now they had nothing to hope from the humanity or lenity of their enraged enemy. They remained quiet for some time meditating plans for escape; and they connived to convey a message to their country for a reinforcement. The detachment came, but was met by the Kondays, and after a hard and bloody fight, the Mendians were driven back. The siege was vigorously kept up, and the small stock of provisions which the Mendians had in the town, was nearly exhausted. They determined to abandon that town — to commit themselves to the issue of a desperate struggle, and[,] if possible, cut their way through the enemy's line and thus regain their liberty. This was a noble resolution, and they attempted to carry it into effect. It appears, however, their counsels or rather determinations were anticipated, for when the gates were thrown open, and the Mendians rushed forth with a hideous yell and furious onset, the Kondays, with a firmness and bravery which unprovoked injury always inspires, met them and instantly drove them back. The Mendians made two subsequent attempts to evacuate the town and cut their way through, but with similar results -- on both occasions they were driven back, and the lines of circumvallation[353] were drawn closer.

After some weeks their stock of provisions entirely failed, and famine — gaunt and spectre-like [—] made its appearance. Still they held out -- and with a sullen obstinacy would neither open the gates nor submit to capitulate. Death followed in the train of famine and when the town became an extended burying ground, with this difference, that the dead bodies either through the carelessness or weakness of the survivors, were rather *sprinkled with earth* than *buried* in it. The town at this time presented a most sickening aspect. Huge carcasses of bones — held together only by a skinny integument through which they threatened to cut their way — and thus streaked and smoked and caked with the accumulated filth of weeks and pierced by a bristly beard, the growth of months, the whole moving along in a teetering and wavering gate, gave some indication of the misery to which these wretches were reduced.

Close upon the footsteps of famine its sure attendant, black and deathful pestilence made its appearance. Relaxed and debilitated by starvation, these walking carcasses presented an easy prey for the first approach of disease and as the fetid exhalations arose from the putrid, half-buried bodies, they fell to the earth and the dying and the dead mingled in one promiscuous and melancholy heap!!

The town where this nefarious affair took place occupied an important position. It stood in the great thoroughfare of the country, on a confluence of many *paths*, which diverge thence to all parts of the interior. Consequently there was a total cessation of trade from all the regions interior to that. The effects were severely felt even here; and the answer of the natives to every inquiry "why no trade come," was "*war done stop all dem parfs;*" and it was constantly affirmed that the country would continue unsettled and trade depressed until a decisive victory should declare in favor of one or the other party. Of course, the traders of this place became not only anxious for this event, but willing to aid in accelerating its arrival. In aid of the Kondahs messengers — instructed in the management of rockets — were despatched with a supply with instructions to throw them into the town among the thatched huts. The messengers arrived a few days before the pestilence broke out, and strange to say, when they arrived the houses were uncovered and divested of everything which could be easily ignited. Such an opportunity, however, for the display of military genius was not to be lost; and the rockets were thrown, but fell harmlessly to the earth. A few days afterwards the pestilence broke out and by scores. "Dis fire be debil," said they, and opened the gates and yielded themselves to their fate.

It is a singular fact and worthy to be noted that wherever a Mandingoman establishes himself among pagans, he invariably attracts respect and defference –– gains influence in the country of the people among whom he sojourns –– becomes the pride of the place and not infrequently gathers the realm of power in his hands, and governs whole regions with an absolute and uncontroled sway. He prescribes in all matters pertaining to religion — presides in all religious exercises — directs in all matters of the healing and decides in political deliberations and leads the army in battle. Indeed a well educated Mandingo, which is but another term for Mohammedan, is regarded with a degree of respect, bordering upon idolatry and a town is regarded fortunate in which one of them *bookmen* takes up his residence and all are readily to *do him savice,* from the owner of the *horsetail* to the meanest of his slaves. We will not undertake any say whether this sentiment is inspired by the fact that he *sabby-book*[354] or that *he be God man,* we only know the fact and leave others to assign the cause. Perhaps we would not be far from the truth were we to attribute it to the latter. The natives have some secret police religious system among themselves, to which the devil is allowed to have an important influence, and in the unsophisticated minds of these heathen, religion and diabolical agency are synonymous terms.

65. A Beautiful Custom

Liberia Herald, 28 July 1848, 38

A very simple custom prevails among the natives of these parts, which we do not remember to have seen adverted to. It is this. When a native is traveling in the territory of another tribe or through the territory of a different clan of his own tribe, approaches a town, he invariably provides himself with a leafy branch from some tree or bush. We have seen them go some distance from the road to provide themselves with this emblem of peace. This they hold in the hand, or if they carry a kinjah or other wallet[355], they attach thereto and hold it so as that it shall be conspicuous. If there be fifty in a company, each one provides himself with an "olive branch" and it seems to be the very first object to which the people of the town direct their attention as soon as they enter. Especially if there has been recently a war or rumor of war, they deposit all their baggage and trading [apparatus] in some conspicuous place, surmounted by the friendship-declaring twig.

66. Slavers at New Cesters

Liberia Herald, 18 May 1849, 26

In our last number, we stated in a few words that success had attended the expedition against New Cesters and that the slavers had been routed and their factories destroyed. Not only were the establishments at that far, but ill-famed place broken-up, but the factory at Trade Town was involved in the same fate. The slaver at New Cesters had raised the whole country in his defense: -- had supplied the natives liberally with munitions of war, and when our men attempted to land, led on in person the natives by thousands to oppose the landing. A few bombs from the French steamer[356] kept them at bay, and under cover of her fire our men pushed boldly ashore and formed on the beach. The Spaniard did not show himself afterwards, but the natives concealing themselves behind rocks, trees and bushes kept up a continual and annoying fire for two days. It was very soon ascertained that they did not intend to come to an open combat; indeed such a number of men — 400 and such courage displayed in rushing to the charge whenever a body of the enemy showed themselves, was something altogether different from what they expected. As soon as the line of march was taken up for the barracoon, the slaver, who had all the time been concealed in the vicinity of our army, mounted his horse, hastened to his factory and applied a torch. When our people arrived there, nothing was seen of the house but a heap of ashes. The wall which enclosed it was standing. It was built of mud — so thick and well dried that it would have resisted a six pound shot. It was three feet thick, twelve feet high and beautifully whitewashed and enclosing a perfectly level and well cleaned area of about two and a half acres of land; presented a beautiful sight in the deep green wilderness, in the bosom of which it was situated. The wall was demolished and a cow and a horse, which the hero left in his flight, were all the booty which fell to the men. No resistance was offered at Trade Town. The slaver there had heard of the fate of his compatriot below and as the men marched up to his factory, he advanced to meet them, offering his property and suing for mercy in the humblest attitude. Property he had none. As our men advanced on one side, his friends the natives, advanced on the other: and racing their speed with the time, they had borne everything away before the Americans arrived. And truly the Spaniard was an object of pity. The most violent were touched with commiseration. Imagine a man standing something over six feet high, with sunken eyes, hollow cheeks, blanched skin, swollen feet, the rest of his frame a skeleton, sans hat, sans shoes, covered only with a pair of cotton drawers and a cotton shirt. This was all the natives had left him and for these he was indebted to the rapid movement of the Americans. So far is well. But this expedition, although we were ably and honorably assisted by the French, has involved us in a heavy expense. This was not a propitious time for such an expedition. We were not prepared to encounter the outlay of money it demanded. But unwilling to decline the aid which the French government so generously offered the President, [we] determined to proceed and trust to the liberality of the friends, of humanity abroad, to enable us to sustain it.

67. The Delightful Consequences of War

Liberia Herald, 18 May 1849, 26

We are already tasting the delightful consequences of war and it is to be feared the present scarcity and high prices of provisions, especially of bread stuffs, are but a forerunner of what will be experienced ere the season has passed over. The expedition from causes which could not be controlled took place just at the time when we should have been burning off and preparing our lands for planting. The natives had been some time kept in excitement awaiting the war, and neglected their farms. They are already beginning to pour in upon us, to divide by theft or otherwise the little stock of provisions which we have. Already Bacon, middling is up to 25 cents; Flour, 13 to 14 dollars the barrel; and rice, $2[.]00 to $2[.]50 a bushel. When all these things are taken into account, we will find that breaking up those slavers has cost us from seven to ten thousand dollars — an enormous sum for young Liberia. We do not repine. We had rather suffer those inconveniences multiplied ten fold, than permit so gross violation of our laws, so great an outrage upon humanity within our territory. It is to be feared we shall have again to take up the

Carl Patrick Burrowes

cudgel and use it vigorously both to the windward and leeward. If the state of things demand the movement, it is well to get at it at once! We cannot expect peace and quietness while the slave trade is going on near us. Nor can we hope to exert our full influence upon the surrounding tribes until the accursed traffic is wholly destroyed. When that most desirable object is accomplished, we shall then breathe freely. We may stretch freely and safely to the north, south and to the interior. The natives then instead of viewing our approach with distrust as calculated to destroy their trade, will court us, will receive us hospitably, and be anxious to learn our arts, our mode of agriculture, and vigorously apply themselves to produce from their fat soil and teeming forests, the rich and valuable articles of commerce. Then indeed, instead of dotting little settlements along the sea board, contiguous to each other, we would strike out boldly into the interior, form settlements where the feet of civilization has never yet penetrated, and feel abundant security in the natives' eagerness to learn.

One of the original objects of the American Colonization Society — an object for the entertainment of which they were ridiculed as enthusiasts, namely, the practicability of establishing a colony, has been fully and triumphantly accomplished. Here Liberia stands, a proud monument of American philanthropy; a fact as stubborn as that the three angles of a triangle are equal to two right angles. But another object of equal, if not greater magnitude, was proposed, which was: through the colony as a channel, to regenerate this continent. What a noble ideal. We can hardly conceive of one more grand. The first step in that regenerating process is taken: namely the establishment of the colony. The second is now to be made -- but preparatory to this, the slave trade must be crushed to rise no more. Then the work of christianity and civilization will go forth as with the "morning step" — the earth will open her bowels and reveal its treasures; peace will go forth, and, with her magic wand dissolve to the ground the frowning barricade -- highways will open through the desert -- visits of lawful trade and friendship will be paid & received -- the man of God will go forth preaching his master's message of love and peace to a people thus made ready for God -- the now besetted African will come, and say, we will go with you, for we have heard that God is with you; and America although Liberia may not prove a cure for American slavery, will be able when for different causes, the voice of boasting and rejoicing, shall ascend from many nations to point to Africa, the once spoiled of all and now the song of praise and salvation shall be thrown in echos back from her mountains to her valleys, regard with an elevated pride this noble triumph of American genius.

68. [Civilization of the Bassa]

Liberia Herald, 4 June 1851, 32

Mr. Herald --

My attention has been directed, for some time, to the progress of civilization, and the very important and gratifying changes that have taken place in the manners, customs, and religion of the aboriginal inhabitants of the Grand Bassa Country, since my first acquaintance with them in 1835: and it occurred to me, that a short statement of the progress these people have made in civilization, as observed by me, might be of some interest to your readers. I shall not attempt, in the course of my remarks, to give a precise and accurate account of the manners, customs, and religion of the Bassas — but I design merely to notice briefly those things in which there have been manifest improvements. [357]

While I readily admit that the Bassas are not yet civilized; all who know them will admit that they are in a transition state and rapidly approaching to civilization[358] — though it may still require years to consummate the good work now going on, especially unless, a more general interest be enlisted in their Christian welfare. I shall speak first, Mr. *Herald*, of their —

Religion — When I first knew them in 1835, the "devil" worship was universally venerated; now the "devil bushes," in almost every part of the country, are demolished, and in many cases there remain not even a vestige of them, to remind the inhabitant of the superstition and folly of his fathers. The stranger can now pass fearlessly through those once sacred forests, and females enter and trample them now with impunity. Then it was "holy ground," upon which no stranger or female could stand and live. Now at or near some of these places, once dedicated to Diabolus — temples, dedicated to the "living and true God" have been created. In these, Bassa men by the side of their brethren from across the mighty deep, bow before the shrine of the great Jahova, confessing their sins, and asking forgiveness in the name of Him who gave himself a ransom for them.

Gre-gre — Less than a score years ago, these people indulged implicit faith in the efficiency of the Gre-gre to preserve and protect them from all the evils of life — and to prosper in their undertakings — consequently the Gre-gre house was the glory of every village. No native ventured to engage in any pursuit or sallied forth to battle, without consulting these oracles through the priest or "doctor," and receiving from him the earnest of the *Divine will* in a "rams horn" which he attached to his person and pressed on ward in full assurance of success; now their faith is not only shaken, but they are ashamed to bear about them, these badges of ignorance and superstition. They are therefore laid aside, seen only occasionally, and Gre-gre houses are comparatively rare and the "Doctors" have fallen into disrepute.

Sassy-wood — Their judiciary was established upon their mythology and as they relied upon their oracles they were induced to regard sassywood[359] as an impartial ordeal of any crime, and that it would let the innocent go free, but destroy the guilty with unerring judgement. Anyone who refused there to attest his innocence was considered a [heretic]; a profligate wretch who was unworthy of life.

But this ordeal too is now almost nugatory, as very few men will submit to it.

If a charge is brought against one, he demands a regular trial before the tribunals of, and according to the laws of the Republic.

Employments — The employments of the Bassas have undergone a material change since the years of my acquaintance with them. War was their chief pursuit, which was carried on for the express purpose of procuring victims for the slave trade, which was their main source of affluence and self-aggrandizement. These wars spread devastation all over the country, and threatened to exterminate the people who were thus divided against themselves. Now that the slave trade has been abolished, by the influence of colonization and the strong arm of the law; wars have ceased and they have directed their attention wholly to agriculture and the manufacture of palm oil.

Education — They regarded it as an imperative paternal duty to send their sons to the Devil Bush, where they were taught the duties that [indistinct] to them as members of community, and the rites and [ceremonies] of their religion; now the greatest privilege they can enjoy is to "learn 'Merica man fash," they say, "country man be fool, he no sabby sense."

Burial — In this respect also there is a marked difference; in former times they laid the dead body away in a small house set apart for that purpose, in which a slow fire was kept up until desiccation was perfected.

During this process all manner of charges were brought against the deceased and his estate must be settled before his interment. Sometimes old Kings were kept in this way form three to ten years.

At the appointed time there would be a hold convocation from all the regions ranged about, bearing with them presents, sometimes of considerable value — The fatlings were killed and a solemn feast ordained[,] the grave dug, and over it a small house erected — then commenced the funeral rites with singing, dancing, feastings and wailings, some gashed their breast, and if the tears forbade to flow, charged their eyes with pepper. The body was then let down into the grave, and loaded with presents from the mourners, consisting of crockery, hard ware, dry goods, &, which are entombed with it for the use of the deceased. And I have heard, I can not vouch for the truth of the assertion, that long ago slaves were sacrificed to attend their masters in the world of spirits. Be this as it may, they believe strongly in the immortality of the soul, and in future punishments and rewards; they also entertain the doctrine of transmigration, and often name the first born of the town after the deceased, believing that his spirit has returned in the person of the infant. But now if a great man dies, they procure for him a coffin (before they used a mat)[,] shroud him, and lay him away as soon as possible, in all respects according to civilised customs.

The causes that have led to these happy reformations in this tribe, may be attributed to the combined influence of colonization and missionary efforts: —

The minds of the natives, for miles and miles around the civilised settlements, have been imbued with the principles of our holy Christianity, by the preaching of missionaries among them, and the influence of Christian colonists; among the Missionaries, Crocker, Barton, Clarke, Mylne and Day,[360] stand conspicuous. By means of the native boarding schools kept by these gentlemen, and others in the settlements and country, under the auspices of different benevolent American institutions.

There are but few if any within 20 or 30 miles of us, who have not heard of the creation of the world, the fall of man, and the plan of redemption, who have not heard of the goodness, omniscience, omnipresence, justice and love of God — colonization has strengthened the arms of the missionary, by affording him protection. The colonists have cooperated with him by raising up, in their families, native youths in the nurture and admonition of the Lord, and training them up in civilized habits. Indeed by the intimate intercours[e] of the surrounding tribes with the colonists, they too have been led to admire the supremacy of civilized institutions and are beginning to imitate them.

Many, we are led to believe, "have heard the voice of the Son of God and live," as they bring forth fruits meet for repentance.

Now a Harriss, a Vonbrun and a Crocker,[361] all children of the forest, are proclaiming to their country-men the unmatchable riches of the gospel of Jesus Christ.

Should we not be encouraged, Mr. *Herald*, in this noble enterprise of evangelizing and christianising Africa, after so much has been achieved in so short a time? Look upon the fields, they are now white to harvest, and the laborers are few, — pray therefore [to] the Lord of the vineyard that he send more laborers into the field.

Let us see to it, both missionary and colonist, that we improve our talents, least we be found unprofitable servants and the vineyard be given to others who are more worthy.

Much has been done, but the work is not yet accomplished. The Bassas are not yet fully civilized, they are not all christians yet, the strong holds of their superstition and prejudices have been broken but they require more knowledge of the Bible, and greater acquaintance with the arts and sciences before they can be profited much thereby —

In my opinion, one of their Kings had arrived at a just conclusion of the matter when he said that "We no be Bassa-man, we be 'Merica man. What we do first time, we no do dis time, no more. Me now sabby 'Merica fash' proper."

69. Letter to William McLain, Monrovia, 9 March 1853

Dear Sir,

As we have just returned from Little Cape Mount where we had gone with about two-hundred armed to quell if it be possible a spirit of reckless spirit of insubordination, I take pen to give you the results.[362] Thus far, you have doubtless heard that a war has been for some time raging between the Veys & Gorahs. Some year or more ago the chiefs were convened here and induced to promise to abandon hostilities and live in peace. They pretended to make friends and bound themselves to keep this under penalty that he who should violate the agreements should feel the combined force of the Americans, or rather Liberians and the unoffending party. They however had returned home only a few days when the whole country was alarmed by a blow struck by none of us know whom. Boombo at Little Cape Mount[363] stands forth the leader and representative with matters of the Veys. Dorah-eh-boy is the chief of the Gorahs. These personages are long in mutual recriminations, and as they are supported in their charges by their adherents it is no easy matter to determine who is the aggressor. At present Boombo stands in the most doubtful position perhaps only because he has been more successful, has burned more towns and slain more captives than his rival. I estimate that at least six hundred people have been killed and six towns laid in ruins by these feuds during the last eight months.

We have Boombo now under arrest, and about fifty of his followers in custody. We brought him down with us; he was unwilling to come and even endeavoured to escape. We were however too soon for him. Had he got away from us, we would no doubt have had some hard fighting for it. The other chiefs have promised to be here this week. If they come we will enter upon the Palava on Monday. It is now hard to tell how the matter will be settled. It is of the utmost importance to us that the country be quieted, but it seems almost an impossible matter to keep things in peace. Boyer of Trade Town celebrity is at length melting down. The interdict has brought him to his senses, by cutting off his [indistinct] suppliers & thus placing him at the mercy of his neighbors. Messengers from Trade Town report him collecting bullocks to beg the palava with.

I think we are moving onward. In every department improvement is clearly manifested. Industry and enterprise are making up. Never before has there been so much activity and energy. The forests are falling, houses are rising, & boats are in building — every thing is going ahead. The English line of steamers has supplied or wakened unwonted [?] energy. I think the day is dawning, or not far distant, to which I have long and earnestly looked forward, when intelligent, enterprising colored men will not ask the Colonization Society to send them to a land of liberty but will come on their own hook, and live and die in ungiven freedom. There is room enough, work enough and liberty enough for them all and we wait to receive them and greet them with a hearty welcome. Send us — if they will not come of themselves — send us for a few years to come about 500 intelligent active emigrants. Don't send us blockheads — we are blockheads enough ourselves. Send us sensible men — men with sense enough to help us think and act, not too much sense to think they are fit to be president the first year. More annually will be too much — a different sort will injure us.

Respectfully yours,

H. Teage

Relations with Americans & Europeans

70. [Gurley's Mission to England]

Liberia Herald, 21 September 1842, 42

We received and read with much pleasure "Gurley's Mission to England."[364] It contains much valuable information, and shows what we have long known, and recently explicitly stated, to wit, a deplorable ignorance on the part of English philanthropists of our true character and position. The good people of England regard these settlements American colonies; and they required Mr. Gurley to apprize them of the "fact that with the government the Colonization Society" and of course the colonies, "had no direct connection."

We stated in an article not long since, that any application by the Society to foreign government to concede to us territorial or national rights would be nugatory — rendered so — first by the position of the Society, and secondly by the frigid neutrality which the United States government has maintained towards us. The result of Mr. G's. interview with that eminent statesman and philanthropist Lord John Russell, fully justifies our assertion. We quote Mr. Gurley's words. "He" lord John Russell "indicated that in regard to the limits of territory it would be desirable that some proposition should come from the United States Government, although I fully explained to him the fact, that with that government the Colonization Society had no direct connection."

The British Government does not, that we have ever heard, claim any territory nearer us on the north than Sierra Leone, nor on the south to the windward of Cape Palmas. It could scarcely be required to concede to us that, to which it never laid claim, and therefore we are at liberty to regard the requisition as looking to stipulations not to purchase within certain limits, and to a guaranty from disturbance by British traders and adventurers. Such an arrangement is not only desirable, but absolutely indispensable to our future peace and extension.

We however, entertain no fears from the *English people* on this score. Our confidence in their magnanimity and philanthropy is too strong to allow us to indulge for a single moment the idea, that they would for the sake of a few acres of land, or for the commerce which the possession of them would afford, adopt any course that would injure a few miserable outcasts, seeking an asylum from oppression on these distant shores. In the stipulations and guaranty alluded to, there are no important principles involved which they would be required to abandon. It might however involve a small sacrifice; but it would be such a sacrifice as a lofty humanity. Our condition is one of no ordinary character. We are a foundling upon the great common[365] of the world. Our past history and present condition, and our last hope should be every where proclaimed, and we are in favour of pouring the tale of our woe in the ears of all who will listen to us; and so sure as commiseration and sympathy yet linger in the human breast, will we obtain all we can reasonably expect. But who is to make known our wants? This is a subject on which there is a diversity of opinion, but with all due deference to those who differ from us; we think none can be so eloquent as those who are personally concerned.

But while we entertain no apprehension of being immoderately compressed in our territorial limits, by the action of the British government, we are not free from feat of annoyance and vexatious disputes on account of the conduct of some of its subjects. Nor from British subjects alone may disputes hereafter arise unless measures are taken by their respective governments to prevent them. Some American traders and recently we believe the French are adopting a course, which must at no distant day become the source of serious misunderstanding between then and us. We allude to their pretended purchase of land in our vicinity for the purpose of trading. In some instances the land thus claimed are parts of tracts ceded to the colony by the Kings and Chiefs in solemn palaver, & in every instance to which we refer, in the intermediate distance between the settlements. They set up the same kind of claim to these tracts which a regularly organized community would. They claim the privilege not only of controlling all who come within their "dominion" but of excluding all who in their opinion would prejudice their interest. What is their object? Not to raise the debased character of the natives — not to teach them the arts and habits of civilized life[,] preparatory to their absorption in a civilized and Christian community — not to enlighten their minds, and gradually draw them away from their vices and degrading superstitions. This in their opinion would defeat the only object that brought them to the coast — and that is the collection of the greatest possible quantity of produce, in the shortest possible time and at the lowest possible rate; and in accordance with this, the motto generally is — *the more ignorant the natives the better for us.* Hence as a general thing (for there are honorable exceptions), there is no class of men to whom they are more averse than missionaries and teachers.

It must be evident at the very first glance that with neighbors whose opinions and object are so widely different from ours — opinions and object which cannot fail to lead to the adoption of conflicting measures, we cannot long remain on terms of friendship. On this subject however we are not left to the uncertainly of conjecture or inference. We know from what has past that the meanest and basest arts have been resorted in, to force us into an unfriendly collision with the savages. Attempts have been made to cut off our trade by reducing the price of imports, and raising that of exports, & by pouncing upon the most prominent places of traffic. Attempts have also been made to exasperate the natives against us by representing us as the destroyers of their idol, the slave trade, and by assuring them that our ultimate object is to subvert by force all their customs and usages — to cut down all their devil bushes and to bring them *nolens volens*[366] under such laws as we may choose to make for them. These however are evils of minor importance which it would require no great effort to remedy. There are still greater evils which cannot fail to grow out of this system, that demand attention. Our stay here is not intended to be merely temporary — nor is commerce our chief object at the present time. In the absence of any other place where we may rest the sole[s] of our weary feet, we have adopted this as our home — the home of our posterity and the asylum of such of our persecuted race as shall be so fortunate as to escape from the land of degradation. Our object is to form a regular community to be gradually matured into a nation. It is manifest that the most ready way of effecting the object is, by elevating the character, and enlightening the minds of the natives preparatory to incorporation in the body politic, to swell our number and augment our strength. Immeasurable tracts of fertile land densely covered with primitive forests, require to be cleared and brought into cultivation & other exhausted sources of national wealth and greatness require to be developed, and the greater the number of intelligent minds and brawny hands that are brought to bear upon them, the sooner will they be explored and brought into service. Hence it follows that the true interest of the colonies and natives are identically the same; and it should be one among our first objects to convince them of the fact — which if it should in all future similar instances be kept in view, and suffered to exert its proper influence, will forever embrace the sad complaint so often heard, that the artless unsophisticated lords of the soil are doomed to melt away before the face of their civilized visitor like the forest under the strokes of his axe. It is important then, to the interests of both ourselves and the natives that we should, in order to effect our object which is their happiness, no less than our own, bring them as far as possible under our immediate influence. This is utterly impossible, while there are around us and almost within our doors, those who with perfect impunity foster their prejudices, pander to their vicious appetites, encourage their superstitions & inflame their jealousy of us & our design. It should not be concealled that they look[367] with suspicion upon the colony, and a word from a "white man" (a generic term for all classes[,] colors and conditions enveloped in clothing) justificative of their unfounded jealousy, is to them "confirmation strong as proof holy writ." Their can be no doubt the debased character of the native is a great auxiliary to the transient trader, and there can be no more doubt that the residence of an unprincipled irresponsible trader in our vicinity goes far to neutralize effort to tame and civilize the savages.

If the pretensions of these claimants are valid, we shall have the singular spectacle, not of an *Imperium in imperio* but of *Imperia in imperio*,[368] for there are some half a dozen claimants to as many different portions of sea coast between this and Sinoe!! They claim the right to admit and expel whom they please — to order you off peremptorily should you by any accident find yourself within their domain, and to fire on you before they have given you time to obey the order. In deed they are perfect autocrats — *mimick*

> — Monarchs of all they survey,
> Whose right there's none to dispute,
> From their centre all round to the sea,
> They are lords of the fowl and the brute.[369]

They demand perfect exemption from control and responsibility within their purchased territory, which they say is part and parcel of the empire to which they belong, and the right not only to excite and foster the jealousy of the natives, but to arm them against us whenever they think proper.

By the jealous and selfish interference of these persons we have been in more than one instance defeated in our attempts to form friendly relations with the natives. By secretly misrepresenting our designs they have effectually closed the natives' ear, and caused them to decline all negotiation. Themselves they represent as the "proper friend of country man," and in proof of the same not only applaud and encourage his habits and superstitions, but, in some instances descend to adopt them. They find it no difficult task to persuade them that those who would have them lay aside their heathenish customs and adopt the manners and habits of civilized life are their enemies, and that the destruction of the slave trade is attributable to the colony.

These irresponsible trading establishments must render our maritime and commercial regulations a perfect nullity; and by the facility they offer for the introduction of merchandize free of duty, effectually defeat all our attempts to raise a revenue.

It has been argued that one individual has as much right to purchase land as another — that these traders having purchased of the natives must be allowed to establish any system or pursue any course necessary to the accomplishment of their object. The question however is not one between individuals, but between an individual and *communities* — summarily, whether the pecuniary interest of one individual is to be put in the balance against the temporal and spiritual well-being of numerous communities and of their rising progeny. Whether a few puncheons of oil or tons of cam wood are to weigh against the civilization of these benighted heathen, and whether for the sake of enriching one or a dozen, the last hope of the outcasts is to be extinguished in despair. He who takes any lower view of the question falls short of its full perception. It is an important subject, involving, as we said before, our present peace and future prosperity. It is not however an intricate question — it involves no nice distinctions — no important principles the abandonment of which would leave stain upon the fame of any nation. Important principles it certainly does involve — the eternal principles of justice and humanity in their broadest and most extended sense. We are therefore willing to leave the question to be decided by those to whom we may appeal, confident that wherever all the circumstances of the case are made known, they will awaken the emotions of sympathy, and call forth the decision of justice.

We repose too firmly on the benevolence of those hearts in America and Europe that thrilled at the death cry of the expiring Poles, that leaped for joy at the emancipation of the long oppressed Greeks, that interposed the arm of protection for the descendants of Israel in Syria, and raised the beseeching voice for the Baptists in Germany, to doubt for a moment that our appeal will be in vain.

71. [Mr. Kennedy's Report]
Liberia Herald, 31 August 1843, 27

We have read with much pleasure the report presented by Mr. Kennedy of the committee on commerce, to the House of Representatives.[370] It is an able document, and embraces many important topics, deserving the attention of the United States, or of any other government.

However busy the affairs of the different nations of Europe may keep their respective rulers; and however extensive their foreign possessions may be, recent events on this coast and late developments in the Islands of the Pacific too plainly declare they are still avaricious of territory.[371]

The commerce of Africa is increasing, and her vast resources rapidly opening. Superabundance of capital in the commercial world will assuredly seek employment in this new and unexplored field. The effect will be to develop and bring to light the hidden treasures of the vast peninsula. Once manifest and there will be a general rush upon all the most prominent and advantageous parts.[372] Nothing in the past affords grounds for hope that our appeal will be heard, or our rights respected amid the din and war for commercial ascendancy, which will then take place. It behooves us now while the primitive forests sleep undisturbed upon the soil and the hidden treasures lie concealed in the earth — while there is nothing apparent in our position, nor in our possession to provoke jealousy, nor excite cupidity — while whatever may be granted, would seem simply a response to the beseechings of helplessness, to obtain a recognition of a right to undisturbed possession of and sovereign and independent jurisdiction over whatever territory we may by fair and honorable treaty obtain from the natives.

Two methods for accomplishing this end present themselves. We shall not undertake to say now which is entitled to the earliest adoption. The first is, by direct application to Christian powers — the second by such an alliance with some friendly power that would secure us its influence and support. At the last mentioned of these, it is but justice to ourselves to say, we have more than once hinted in the *Herald*, and explicitly stated it in a letter not long since, to an eminent and tried friend of African Colonization in America. It is with heartfelt pleasure, therefore[,] we find the measure recommended in the report. It may not be immediately acted upon, but the mere agitation of the question, its simple presence before the public mind heralds a movement of immense and abiding moment to our colonies.

72. The Weekly Elevator

Liberia Herald, 30 March 1844, 2

This (the *Weekly Elevator*) is the title of a hebdomadal[373] published in Philadelphia, the first number of which has been sent us by some one, requesting us *to use our influence*. Its object is, as its name imports — the elevation of the colored people to that position, and to secure for themselves those rights to which the common parent of mankind hath given them a title. We are not able to determine to what object specially the *Elevator* desires to direct our attention — whether to the extension of the subscription list, or to the great object it has in view; most cheerfully will we attend to both as far as it is in the power of our hands. To the latter object — namely to evince that colored people are human beings — that with proper opportunities of acquiring information, they can, after a while learn when they are and when they are not treated with justice, our whole residence of 23 years in Africa has been devoted. We have therefore seen with pain the opprobrious epithets which have been unsparingly measured out to us — and the contempt with which our labor has been regarded by our colored "companions in tribulation," in the northern section of the United States. Knowing that we are doomed by the same damning law of proscription, and that we profess to aim at the same object, we have thought we might charitably accord to each other the virtue of sincerity, though differing as to the *modus operandi*, and cordially hail each other as co-laborers in different compartments of one structure.

Every emotion of our soul — the last vestige of every principle — the shade of every idea within us, is opposed to slavery. We regard it with unmitigated and increasing hatred; we therefore hail the signs of its approaching downfall with an almost rapturous delight. The accursed system is tottering to its fall. — All its aiders, abettors and apologists — all its protecting powers in the New World — intellectual and brutal cannot long sustain it against the advance of liberal and religious principles. The day of darkness has passed. The hosts are mustering for battle. God himself is in the midst. Whatever nation longer resists, however it may indulge in dreams of security and of power to oppress, will be found to be warring against the God of battles. It remains then that the colored people be true to themselves — show themselves worthy of the boon;[374] that they be orderly, industrious, pious; that while they pertniciously demand the concession of their rights, they cautiously and conscientiously avoid the use of unhallowed and irritative weapons of vituperation and scurrility: that they shut out forever, the idea of violence in either word or deed. Theirs is the cause of life, liberty, religion and God. They may safely therefore trust the cause with Him who, although "He tarry will surely come."[375]

73. [England and France Send Naval Forces]

Liberia Herald, 5 September 1845, 3

From late papers we learn that the two great powers of Europe, France and England, are about to invest this coast with a gigantic naval force.[376] The joint armament is to consist of forty sail, and over and above this England has engaged to keep an additional force sufficient to suppress the slave trade. It is certainly within the range of physical possibility to prevent by a naval force the exportation of slaves from Africa, but the present state of the market for human cattle in the Christian republics of the west will render it a most difficult experiment.

These movements of France and England are big with interest to us and to Africa generally. They are most likely the last link in a series of fruitless experiments, made only to fail and to disappoint the projectors; and it is on this account we think they will be important to us.

We are not allowed to doubt that political motives prompt much that is done for Africa, and give strength and tone to the proclamings of philanthropy. In the good of Africa[,] nations find their own account. Her interminable forests in the woodman's axe is reverberating, her soil of unequaled powers in producing valuable staples of commerce, and her unopened mines of metalic wealth offer a tempting field for the operations of commerce, which the slave trade alone, by debasing the people and diverting their attention from legitimate pursuits, prevents European capital from entering. In seeking to suppress the slave trade the powers of Europe are seeking an outlet for the production of their overstocked artisans and employment for their immense commercial marine.

We feel assured that a guaranty of our right to the exclusive trade of the coast could not be obtained by any one nation from the others, even on the condition that the favored nation should effectually suppress the slave trade. A spirit of captious jealousy is now on the alert, and manifests itself too clearly in the treaty between the high contracting powers. The stipulation that neither shall land and break up a slaving establishment without the consent or concurrence of the other looks so much like a reserved check in the hands of each over the other's power to appropriate territory that we can hardly regard it in any other light. This stipulation grows out of the opinion now pretty generally entertained and before the term of this treaty shall have expired will have ripened into conviction, that colonies planted along the coast, will more speedily and effectually than any other means suppress the detestable traffic in slaves, and thus unlock the vast resources of the country. When this conviction shall have been formed and nations desirous to participate in the benefits of the African trade shall prepare to act upon it, the most anxious question which will then present itself will regard the materials with which to form these colonies. Tropical Africa seems to have declared eternal war with the constitution of the white man. If he live here at all, it is by such nice circumspection, such systematic abstinence from all service involving fatigue and muscular exertion, and such precise measure and kind of food and raiment that except in a few situations such as those of a professional and official character he can be but of little service to a colony. Nature seems to have decreed that none but the African constitution shall bear up under the pressure of the African climate and so powerful is its influence upon foreign constitutions that even persons of African descent, born and reared in other climates, however long their residence here rarely if ever become fully acclimated.

The material for these colonies must be procured from America or any other place where civilized and intelligent colored people are to be found. These will impart the lessons of order, industry and civilization to the nations immediately around them, and they in turn will instruct others more remote until the circle of civilization shall bound the whole of Africa.

We do not think it would be extravagant to affirm that one half of the amount which it has cost Britain in the five years last past to maintain the Squadron stationed between Sierra Leone and New Cesters, judiciously expended in planting and maintaining colonies, would have effectually rooted out the nefarious traffic within those limits, whereas after all that has been done the trade has still a vigorous existence. Such indeed is our conviction of the efficiency of colonies to root out the slave trade that we think this colony might engage — with safety engage to suppress the trade in five years from Gallinas on the north to New Cesterson the south with the direct assistance of only the amount of the cost of the frigate *Penelope.*[377]

74. [It is rumored that the British]

Liberia Herald, 16 October 1846, 2

It is rumored that, the British government have, sent out instructions to their Naval commanders, to take immediate possession of Grand Cape Mount;[378] — and that troops are now being embarked at Sierra Leone or at some other British port for that purpose. The reason assigned for this determination of Her Majesty's Government, is, that the Chiefs of Cape Mount, in violation of their treaty stipulations, permit the slave trade still, to be carried on in their dominions.

Although we are as anxious as any people can possibly be, for the abolition of the accursed traffick in slaves, and would willingly tax ourselves, to assist in putting it down, — nevertheless, we cannot give our hearty concurrence to the plan now contemplated, for its suppression at that place. If the British Government take possession there, we need no longer hope, to have it form a part of the territory of Liberia — we have been sanguine, that at no distant day, we would be enabled, by fair negotiation with the chiefs of the country, to have it under the authority of our laws; — and the fact is too well known, that at whatever place we have the right to exercise our authority, the traffick in slaves *cannot* exist. The acquisition of the territory of Cape Mount to the British Crown, cannot in our opinion be an object of much importance to that power, as the resources of the country, are the same as those of any of the countries lying between Sierra Leone and Liberia. But the adoption of any plan, that will place this territory beyond our reach will materially cripple our operations, and confine the limits of Liberia to a space too limited in extent, for the exercise of that salutary influence which we fondly hoped to introduce among the tribes surrounding us. If the British Government have the right to take possession of Cape Mount or any other country adjoining to Liberia, for a violation of treaty stipulations in regard to the slave trade — will not that Government, if the Government of Liberia pledges itself that the slave trade shall no longer be continued in such place or places, act with that benevolence and magnanimity which ought always to characterize a great and powerful nation, make the violators of the treaties accountable to the Government of Liberia, instead of taking forcible possession of their countries, at the hazard of shedding blood? We are supposing, that the main object of the British Government is, to destroy the slave trade, and not for the acquisition of territory, — and we further suppose, that the violation of the treaties gives the complaining party a right to the territories of those, who refuse to comply with their treaty obligations.

We are opposed to the Africans being deprived of their lands, without a fair equivalent is paid to them, for it, and in no instance, after purchasing their lands have we ordered them to remove from them, on the contrary, they have invariably been urged to remain and adopt civilized customs.

We are particularly interested about the territory of Grand Cape Mount. Twenty years ago we sent missionaries there to instruct the natives in the truths of the Gospel — they were well received and hospitably entertained — a piece of land was granted to them; — a friendly intercourse was kept up between them and the colonists, and many of their children are now living in the colony, understanding and following our customs. For more than ten years, scores of our enterprising citizens lived among them, and carried on an extensive commerce, which benefitted both parties — and but for the savage war that has raged there for more than ten years and which has nearly depopulated the country, large numbers of our citizens, would now be residing there.

75. [Gratitude to the British]

Liberia Herald, 28 February 1849, 18

The gratitude of the people of the republic is eminently due to the British nation for the deep sympathy and prompt, and we may say, spontaneous kindness which they have manifested for us.

It is known by all that we have ever been sanguine,[379] and from the first movement of the independence question, when some were opposing, others halting, we went steadily along and ventured to predict success — complete and entire — if once the people could be induced to act.

In the English, we always expect a friendly feeling. Their well known magnanimity — the deep interest they evince in the welfare of the African race — their inflexible adherence to principles of justice, and their ready response to the calls of humanity left no room to doubt that they would eventually accord to us all we could reasonably desire. Thus, we confess with satisfaction that in kindness and courtesy in promptness of responses to our appeals, they have very far exceeded our most sanguine expectations.

Every attention was paid to our President while in England,[380] which is usually paid to public functionaries from foreign countries and the government listened with attention to every representation he had to make.

In our last number, our co-adjuster, who is a member of the government,[381] informed our readers, that England and France have recognized us, and that assurances have been obtained that Prussia will shortly follow their example. This is indeed a great point gained. To be acknowledged and recognized by the leading powers of Europe, as composing one of the families of nations, is a matter of no small consequence. It will enable us to give vigor and energy to our laws throughout the republic, while at the same time it will silence all that bickering and complaint at their enforcement, in which some foreigners have delighted to indulge.

Perhaps we would not be very wide of the mark were we to say that more considerations than one induced this prompt action on the part of the European powers. The British people regard themselves pledged to put down the slave trade. To attain this object they are annually expending thousands of pounds and frequently sacrificing valuable lives. Nor are the French people far, if at all, behind them in zeal to destroy this abominable traffic. The cruisers of both nations are continually hovering over the coast watching these pirates, but their vigilance is frequently eluded, and the slaver escapes with his cargo. It is now universally admitted that settlements such as Liberia present the most effectual barrier against the operations of the slave trade, that so far as their influence extends, the trade is wholly destroyed. In proportion therefore, as the Republic of Liberia increases in strength and influence — in proportion as it extends its territory and acquires strength to protect it and suppress illicit traffic in the same proportion will their object be attained, and the necessity of keeping cruisers in the vicinity of the settlement be decreased.

This is a correct view of the matter. From observation, we have been long convinced that the slave trade cannot be put down by cruisers. The profit of the business is so great, that it will allow the slaver to resort to expedients to procure goods and ship slaves which none but a slaver would ever devise, and in spite of the utmost vigilance of the cruiser watering the pirate, he would carry on his operations and escape with two cargoes out of three. The slave trade will be more easily put down by the combined energies of colonies and naval force acting in concert. It would be eventually [be] destroyed at a given place by a colony alone without the aid of a naval force; but the process would be tedious. A long time would be required to effect it. The natives are so wedded to the traffic — it having descended to them as an heirloom from their fathers, that they are easily roused into hostility against any and every thing they are taught to believe is arrayed against it, and they are every ready to protect the slaver. The cunning slave dealer takes advantage of this propensity of the natives excites their suspicions and at length converts them into inveterate enemies of the colony. Hence a colony would act rashly to come out boldly against a slaving establishment before it had become sufficiently strong to sustain itself against both the natives and the slaver, unless it were aided by a naval force. Well do we recollect what indignities our little crafts had to suffer in the early years of this colony. Well do we recollect how they were frequently fired into with the most wanton cruelty by the slavers; –– well do we recollect what anxiety possessed the bosoms of our sailors when at sea, they espied a vessel in the distance. And this was at a time when the colony was not engaged in any active operations against the trade. But the sagacity of the slaver foresaw the destruction of his trade in the growth and permanent establishment if the colony and this awakened his hostility. At that time there were but few cruisers on the coast, and their station was principally on the southern [part]. Of late years, a division of the English squadron has made this a cruising station, and we have not been annoyed.

It is perhaps with a view to accomplish this great object as well as from motives of sympathy that the British government and people have given us some more substantial proof of their regard than mere recognition on parchment.

We have heard that it is in contemplation to treat[382] for the Gallenas and to extend our borders to the Sherbro. It was stated in our last, that as the Gallinas is now in a state of blockade, this [is] a favorable time to open a negotiation. We think so. I[t] is desirable perhaps that we should possess those places. But would it not be well to consider whether, if the cruisers should return, we are able to protect them and keep out slavers. This seems to us an important question. Should we succeed in getting these points, it will in all probability, be expected that we will suppress all illicit traffic there — that we will at once and forever destroy the slave trade. Should we fail to do this, many generously affected for us may be disappointed and sympathy for the republic become greatly weakened. We are persuaded of nothing more firmly than we are, that no soon as the present investing force of the Gallinas is withdrawn, the slavers will recommence their spoliations[383] — unless they are repressed by some other force. Is it not worthy of inquiry whether we have such a force? The place has been often destroyed, and as often resettled. If we do not mistake, Captain Hagan of H. B. M. brig *Thistle*[384] routed the slavers there more than twenty years ago. Since then thousands of slavers have been sent off. But admitting that we can go up there and destroy the place, are we prepared for annual expeditions of that character? These appear to us grave questions, and eminently entitled to serious consideration.

When we drew up the bill of our present boundary, making "Grand Cape Mount" river our northwestern frontier, many regarded it extravagant and we ourself believed we were assuming a responsibility fully equal to our resources.

We have thrown out these hints and suggestions to call public attention to the subject, and to bring it before minds more capable than ours of determining correctly. We would by no means be unscathed as being opposed to the purchase of these places. We only question the propriety of acquisition, if it is to be burdened with stipulations which we might find difficult if not impossible to perform.

76. West Indian Immigrants

Liberia Herald, 26 October 1849, 46

Now that the colony has thrown off the yoke of tutellage, and assumed the character of manhood, [i]t should endeavor to take a comprehensive view of matters which is proper to its assumed condition. It has no longer the Colonization Society to think for it. It should think for itself.

Men and means are now wanted for the onward march. Not men who from past habits are unable to think or act for themselves, who will be of no service to themselves and a burden to us, but active industrious, intelligent men, who can aid in all the departments of government, in arts and manufactures and commerce and science, are wanted. But where are such men to be obtained? There are many in America of the right kind. But will they come? This is the question. It is not unlikely that the intelligent colored community in America is at this time looking with a kindlier regard to Liberia, than at any former period. But when they will start and come, cannot be told. They have been for so long a time prejudiced against the scheme of colonization with which Africa, in their minds, has been always identified, that evidence as clear as noonday will be required to expel it. It has been not the bad repute of the climate alone which has kept them back, but chiefly their hatred of the scheme which founded the colony. The evidence necessary to dispel the illusion will eventually be given and they will come, like doves to their windows, but in the mean time we suffer for want of a vigorous and thrifty population, what then is to be done?

There are many colored people in the British West India Islands who possess all the desirable qualities for good citizens here. They are well educated, are well acquainted with the culture and preparation of coffee, of the sugar cane, and many other articles which can be produced abundantly here, which are valuable as staples of commerce. They are also men of considerable property and they would have but little to fear from change of climate. From a memorial which some of them addressed to Queen Victoria, it appears they are now looking to the coast of Africa with a view of forming settlements under the auspices of the British Government. Let a correspondence be opened with these people setting forth the present condition of this republic — its resources[,] capabilities, its present wants and future prospects. A more tempting field for the profitable investment of their capital and for the operation of their skill and industry, and let them be further assured there is nothing in our constitution, nor in the disposition of the people to withhold from them, more than from any colored people from the United States of America, the full privileges of citizenship, and that equal facilities and advantages will be extended to all colored persons from any and every quarter of the globe, coming here to settle themselves.

We are not certain what feeling is in the West Indies in respect of Liberia. But whatever it might have been, when the colony was under the direction of the Colonization Society, we can hardly think it is one of hostility now. The colored race has been for ages suffering one general decree of oppression. The chord of sympathy has been struck in some bosoms, and it finds a ready response in every other. A generous ardor is kindled by every [argument?] to vindicate the race and to demonstrate its capabilities. These sentiments are universal among intelligent colored people and as Liberia presents a favorable field for the exploit, it is of great importance it shall be essayed. Let the educated and monied men of the West Indies be invited. [385]

77. Letter to J. B. Pinney, Monrovia, 17 May 1851

Dear Sir,

Our little republic is decidedly advancing. Our people are improving in all the different branches of industry to which they have attained, and they are entering new and wider fields of labor. To sum up the whole in a few words, our course is onward. Give us two or three industrious, intelligent immigrations; let them have a little money — for you know, however combustible the fuel, a little heat is necessary to create combustion, or raise to incandescence — let them have a little heap of money, and we will soon astonish you. I now close, by soliciting an interest in your prayers. [386]

Yours, in affliction,

H. Teage

78. Letter to J. B. Pinney, Monrovia, 27 August 1851

Dear Sir,

This goes by way of England, and must serve in default of a much longer one that I intended to send by the *Ralph Cross*. That ill-fated vessel was wrecked some weeks since at Cape Palmas.[387]

It is a matter of deep regret and disappointment to the government in being thus deprived of the liberal subsidy of the society sent out by that vessel. Our only consolation is that the society will receive the amount of its insurance, and will speedily make good the present loss to us.

Among ourselves things are quiet, and a spirit of industry and enterprise is evidently on the increase. Were you, who are so well acquainted with our town and country, here at the present time, you would not call it, as you used to do, *urbus in rure*, and the banks of the St. Paul's an unawakened wilderness.

Thatched huts have given place to commodious brick or stone buildings, both in Monrovia and on the banks of the St. Paul. The tenants live happy under their own vine and fig tree, or, literally true, under their banana and plantain, and wondering why our friends in the United States think us foolish for fleeing from contempt in America to respectability in Africa.

There is not a man in the United States who wishes more ardently the elevation of the colored people there than I do; nor is there one who feels more keenly the injustice of the laws and the sentiment that depress them, than myself; and if talking and writing would avail to correct the injustice, I would not be wanting in the use of these instruments; but on taking a retrospect, what have they availed.

It seems to me that going up by land is a more practicable method of gaining the head of Niagara, than ascending the stream. Let those who think best stay in America, and talk, and we, who are otherwise minded, stay out here and act and at the close of the nineteenth century, it will be seen who have operated to the greater advantage in putting down prejudice.

Able statesmen, orators, philosophers, divines, artists and mechanics, &, of Liberian growth, will bring to the elevation of the African race a mouth and arguments which all its adversaries will not be able to withstand or gainsay.

Long ere that period arrives I shall be numbered with the dead; but it is my most cherished hope that then, on some favored eminence, where the noise of human passions and the collision of opposing theories cannot reach, I shall be able to survey

Carl Patrick Burrowes

the mortal progress; rightly estimating every action, and carrying out infallibly, and at a glance, every cause to its ultimate results.

79. Letter to J. B. Pinney, Monrovia, 18 October 1851

Dear Rev. J. B. Pinney:

… Our little Republic is steadily progressing. Like a little ship on the ocean, she is receiving an occasional thump from a passing wave; this does not alarm me, but, on the contrary, I regard it as evidence she is making headway. Our government is receiving, by almost every mail from England, official documents, in the shape of complaints and remonstances against our laws regulating commerce. — What else ought we to have expected? Some of these complaints, I must say, are just, and demand immediate attention. It is not allowed to talk of abstract rights, when they have been modified or yielded by treaty stipulations. I saw the surrender when I first saw the treaty; and I saw in the acts of the first Legislature subsequent to the ratification of the treaty, an infringement on its provisions. I spoke of it, but I was alone in my opinion.[388]

H. Teage

Carl Patrick Burrowes

Miscellany

80. Letter to the *Philadelphia Herald*, 4 August 1835

Sir,

Agreeable to your request, I now sit down to give you a correct and circumstantial statement of an affair which the lovers of the coloured man have trumpeted far and wide, as evidence that Colonies are auxiliaries to the slave trade, and, as such, ought in all Christian charity to be broken up. In the year 1829, I was sent by Dr. Randall, to Sierra Leone, to purchase a load of rice and other articles which he wanted. I went up in the Agency schooner *Mesurado*. While there, I bought from a merchant a schooner of 130 tons; and as soon as I had obtained the articles for Dr. Randall, sent the *Mesurado* home. I remained in Sierra Leone two or three weeks fitting out the vessel, and making preparations for a trading voyage to leeward. These being completed, I left Sierra Leone, and on my way down the coast, called at the Gallinas. As soon as I arrived in the harbor, many natives came on board; and among the number, one very rich, and well known by every person that has traded there, named Amurah — a native of the Gallinas. He inquired for tobacco and powder; I replied I had none. — He said he had one thousand dollars, and if I would get him one hogshead of tobacco and some powder, he would purchase them. I remained there three or four days, and then proceeded down the coast. At Mesurado, I purchased tobacco and powder, and returned to the Gallinas, where, on my arrival, I found an English brig from Liverpool. As soon as I anchored, I ordered the boat, intending to go on board the brig. Before I started, however, I discovered a canoe leaving the brig and proceeding towards me. I waited her arrival, and found it was Amurrah. He had gone on board the Englishman with a view of purchasing, but knowing my vessel, and conceiving I had tobacco, for which his demand at that time was greater than for any thing else, he left him. As soon as he reached the vessel, and before he came on board, he handed up a bag of money. He then came on board himself. — He asked for tobacco. I sold him one hogshead, together with other articles, to the amount of $1,000. The bag was then opened — money counted. The money was again put in the bag and Amurrah went ashore. I staid there some days trading, and then proceeded down the coast. Having completed my voyage, I returned to Sierra

Leone. Previously to going down the coast, I purchased goods from different merchants, to be paid on my return. John Dean Lake I owed sixty pounds. — The several sums I put in the bag I got from Amurrah, and proceeded to pay them. — Lake, who was the last I paid, observed the mark on the bag, and intimated that it was dangerous to be in possession of a bag thus marked; or at least might create surmise and obloquy. I replied I apprehended nothing: I knew I had traded with no one but native Africans, and I doubted that a man would be condemned for that of which he was not guilty. I paid him his money, and he pretending to have nothing to put it in, asked me for the bag, to which I readily acceded, having no further use for it.[389] These, sir, are the circumstances of the "startling" fact that has been exhibited to the world with so much parade, as proof incontestable that colonies are subsidiary to the slave trade. But, sir, if circumstances like these are to be considered slaving, and as such condemned, the same principle which urges it, condemns with equal force every fabricator of cottons, beads, tobacco, or whatever else finds its way to the coast of Africa. I have the testimony of an approving conscience, when I say I have never been concerned in the slave trade. And however I may be repudiated and slandered, I shall, regardless of the calumny, continue to pursue that course which a conscientious sense of duty to God and man may point out. Such miserable subterfuges cannot serve the purpose long. From the progressive order of things facts will ere long develope themselves that will condemn to oblivion all such slander, and publish the weakness of those, who, while they call themselves enlightened and philanthropic men, draw conclusions from exparte evidence on a contested question, and then, in the plentitude of *charity*, abuse, villify, insult, and misrepresent a distant and ignorant people, who have no means of defending themselves.

I conclude by subscribing myself, your very humble servant

Hilary Teage

81. Not Quite

Liberia Herald, 17 March 1842, 19

In an American paper of late date, we find "Mr. Teage died at Sierra Leone, on the 13th of August last." We admit that we are sometimes loud of notoriety; but we are not dead yet, although much exhausted from *depletion*. It rests with our subscribers to revive us by timely application of their *arrearages*.[390]

82. Misguided Philanthropy

Maryland Colonization Journal, 1 August 1839, 127[391]

We have heard that our friends, the anti-colonizationists in America, are talking of sending out a ship to carry the colonists back to *Egypt*, that they may wallow a little longer among the pots, and again browse on gourds and melons. Success to them. We shall hail the arrival of the ship with pleasure: there are some here whose going would cause but little regret, and who would answer as an excellent shuttlecock for the different parties in America. So much pure benevolence as is manifested in such a step, will, surely, provide the expedition with every thing conducive to comfort; and, therefore, we are not certain we will not avail ourselves of a gratuitous trip, reserving, however, the privilege of returning when we think proper. As the object of the expedition will be to benefit the man of colour, it would greatly conduce to this object if they were to send by the vessel, for those who might not choose to return, a few pairs of cards, spinning wheels, looms, hoes, ploughs, &c; and they might also instruct the captain, as 't would not be much out of the way, to call at Cape de Verd, and bring along a few jackasses, horses, &c. This would be a most acceptable service, and would confer a double benefit to carry away those who are anxious to go, and effectually serve us, who are so simple as to wish to be free.

83. [Bug-a-Bugs]

Liberia Herald, 26 November 1842, 3

As it is not our fault, but simply our misfortune that we are not acquainted with entomology, ichthyology,[392] geology or any other *logy*, we hope for a tolerance of the following plain unscientific account of a treak and battle of —

Ants. The ants to which we now refer are of the species we call *Bug-a-Bug*; but not those that make food of our houses and apparel; though a few of this kind are occasionally seen in the *Bug-a-Bug* house.

A few days ago our attention was arrested by a countless number of these spreading themselves in every direction around our dwelling. On close examination they were found to emerge from the earth in the vicinity of the house but principally from the foundation. They speedily filled every crack and fissure in the wall of which there are many near the ground. Here they halted for a short time as if in consultation, while the larger ones with wings were to be seen running in every direction — now losing themselves in the fissures and anon mingling with the crowd without, as though they were delivering orders or disclosing the plan of future action. Suddenly the whole body was seen in motion, moving in an almost solid & unbroken mass up the wall, headed by some of their winged numbers, while others as before were moving in every direction through the serried[393] host, as if to notice and regulate the march. It soon became evident that the number at first seen was not the advanced guard of the army. As the foremast ranks moved in, their places were continually supplied by others that emerged from their subterranean abode, until the wall presented a black and animated surface. Excepting the winged commanders, each soldier carried a young one in his mouth, from which circumstance we inferred they were moving in search of another habitation or bringing out their progeny for the benefit of light and heat. Having completely covered the wall they bivouacked[394], without depositing their young. Apprehensive that they might make too long an encampment, and having but little desire for the society of this class of our fellow animals, we determined on an effort to dislodge them. Scalding water occured to our mind as the most effective method of conveying to them our wish for their removal; and we at once acted upon the idea. Hundreds fell at every application until the ground was literally covered with the slain; but true to their character the broken ranks were speedily filled by recruits from below. Wearied with the vain effort to remove them we determined to await their pleasure. They continued to ascend until they reached a hive which a swarm of bees had formed between the outer and innerboards of the upper story of the house. These bees had been for some time a source of sore annoyance, compelling us frequently to abdicate in their favour, and we had more than once mediated their death *en masse*. It soon became evident from an unusual stir among them — from their rapid rush from their honied dwelling and hovering around the apertures of entrance that the bug-a-bugs had infested the city and were vigorously pressing the siege. But the bees did not tamely yield. A vigorous fight was maintained during the day. The bees however had the worst of it. On every side the victorious bug-a-bug was seen dragging away the lifeless body of his antagonist and bearing it off into this subterranean dwelling. Whether the action was continued through the night we will not undertake to say; but if not, it was renewed early on the following morning, and continued to the great loss of the bees for three days, when they fairly beaten, retreated and formed in a shrub about twenty rods from the house. The Victorious *bug-a-bugs* continued in the vicinity of the arena of conflict until they had disposed of their booty and then

Carl Patrick Burrowes

suddenly disappeared. The mortified bees did not remain long in their last encampment, but took to wing and cheered us with the hope that we would see them no more. But we were mistaken. In three days they returned and entered their old habitation. They had scarcely settled — certainly had not time to repair any of their prostrated fortifications when the *bug-a-bugs* again emerged from their ambuscade,[395] moved up in order of battle and renewed the engagement. Lifeless carcasses born off in triumph to the place of deposit again proclaimed the success of the Ant. The battle was kept up for two or three hours when the beast were again forced to take to wing. As soon as the work of carrying off the booty was completed, the Ants again disappeared. On both sides the battle was obstinate. The bees fought to defend their habitation, the ants to dislodge and destroy them. In some single or personal encounters there were displays of determination and courage that would not disgrace animals of a far higher order. An ant would grapple a bee with those hard and curved protuberances from his head, and immediately drop with him to the ground, the bee exerting himself to use his lance. But in vain: the [smooth] scaly mail of the ant prevented effectual resistance, while the bee as if conscious of the unequal contest would struggle to free him of his adversary. The ant would make use of his feet to secure his antagonist while he would continue to move his hold in the direction of the head, where having arrived he infixed his horns in the eyes of the bee, when the battle would soon be over, and the enemy born off in triumph to form a meal for the conqueror.

These ants were much larger than those that are so destructive to houses and in fact to every thing that has not the imperviousness of stone or iron, and that employ themselves in erecting those earthy conical structures called *bug-a-bug houses.* They are also of a different color, the latter being of a grayish color, while that of the former is a dark brown. They are however usually to be found in small numbers running up and down the streets of these commonwealths; and when their habitations have been disturbed, we have seen them suddenly present themselves at the gates, course rapidly around on the outside of the habitation as if reconnoitering and then suddenly disappear. We regret to add that on this sixth day after their last glorious retreat the bees have returned. For their sakes, we invoke the return of the *bug-a-bug.*

84. [Two-headed snake]

Liberia Herald, 26 November 1842, 3

A friend from Marshall has sent us a snake for our cabinet. It was supposed to be of the double-headed kind. It is admitted now by naturalists that no such animal has been discovered. The close similarity of both ends of this species of snake, and the extreme minuteness of its eyes have probably produced the illusion: but the improvements which modern art has made in optics have discovered a head and a tail. The snake sent us is about eight inches long, and a dark color, both ends truncated, eyes extremely small, scarcely discernible by the unaided vision, and placed near together on the top of the head. We brought it under the focus of a microscope and feel bold to pronounce it a *one*-headed *two* eyed animal.

85. Magnanimity

Liberia Herald, 31 May 1845, 11

A boat belonging to H. E. M. ship *Waterwitch*[396] with a crew of nine men became by some means separated from the ship. Near night a heavy squall came on and they made the best of their way to one of our little colonial crafts lying at Teembo[397] [see map 1]. They reached her half drowned with rain and solicited a supper and lodging. The latter was readily granted as also this former would have been if the rain would have permitted them to cook. Early, next morning breakfast was provided for the guests of the best there was on board. The guests remained to dinner.

Afterward espying a vessel which supposing to be one of their squadron they put off for. A heavy squall came on and drove them back. They again lodged on board the colonial craft. Next morning they were provided with another breakfast, of which when they had partaken they then prepared to take their leave. Before doing so, however, they expressed very much thanks for the kind hospitality they had been treated with, and advised the commander of the colonial craft to run into Trade Town [see map 1] should he be in want of provisions and assured him he should be abundantly supplied from the *Waterwitch*.

A few days afterward, the craft was on her way home when she espied the *Waterwitch* bearing down for her. A shot which very nearly struck him, brought him to. They compelled the little craft to dodge about after them until she was nearly ashore on a reef of rocks. As they could not tell how long they would be detained they sent a canoe to ask for a little provisions. The canoe returned with the message go to H___ and the Water witch was making her way out to sea.

86. Hard Times, Hard Times!

Liberia Herald, 30 June 1848, 84

This is the general cry throughout the town. The reply prompt and invariable is — hard times! As an evidence of the hardness and dullness of times, let it be borne in mind that there has been created this season a greater number of houses than in any previous season, since the settlement was formed, and of these the fine stone store of Messrs. Payne and Yates, stands conspicuous.[398] This is a fine building and has a more commanding appearance than any in the business part of town. Until our neighbors stop building they ought in modesty to stop complaining.

87. A Novel Fisherman

Liberia Herald, 24 November 1848, [6][399]

Coming down the river a few day ago, we espied a huge alligator lying with his body on the sloping margin of the river, his lower jaw submerged in the water, while the upper was extended in the air, showing his formidable array of teeth. We stopped to gaze at him. Anon, a hapless mullet ventured within the dread hiatus when the treacherous jaws suddenly closed and severed the fish asunder.[400] The native boys, who were with us, took the opportunity to assign the rationale to some of the alligator's movements. They say he lies with his mouth open to attract a certain insect which floats upon the surface of the water. These collect in large numbers around his mouth. Fishes feed upon then, and when lured by the desired prey within the vortex, they become a prey themselves.

88. The Harmattans

Liberia Herald, 29 December 1849, 10

The Harmattans[401] are blowing. They have commenced earlier than usual and they have brought with them their usual accompaniments of colds, chills and fevers. Mr. Ashmun was correct when he said the period when these winds blow are very irregular. They sometimes commence as late as the middle of January. This year they blew a strong breeze as early as the middle of the present month.

Poems

89. Him, Who Rides Upon the Sky

We sing the wondrous deeds of Him,
Who rides upon the sky;
His name is God: The glorious theme
Is sung by saints on high. [402]

His days are one eternal now; --
His kingdom has no bound:
Before his feet Archangels bow
In reverence profound.

He guides revolving years; -- He sits
High on the circling skies,
In glory, majesty and might,
O'erpowering angels' eyes.

We were by those beset around,
Who craved to drink our blood,
Whose malice, hatred, knew no bound,
Whose hearts of love were void.

Hark from afar the trumpets' send
The dreadful notes of war,
And tinkling bells, and drums, portend
A bloody conflict near.

The savage yells, the dreadful cry,
Fell on our frighted ear,
The gleaming spear, the barbarous throng,
With terror did appear.

Their gods of wood and stone they trust,
To give success in fight;
The warrior and the stupid Priest
To murder here unite.

To God we cried, Lord, hear our prayer
In this our deep distress,
We have no hope but Thee: His ear
Attended to our case.

He spake, the savage host retired,
He look'd: and deep dismay
Seized those who were with courage fired,
Like smoke they fled away.

Be still, he said; for I am He,
That's powerful to save,
For all that put their trust in me
Shall full deliv'rance have.

Why do the foolish heathen rage?
Why do they thus unite?
Why in these hellish leagues engage,
Against our land to fight?

Nor might, nor wisdom of our own,
To speak we now unite,
All praise we give to Him alone
Who taught our hands to fight.

91. Land of the Mighty Dead

Liberia Herald, 23 December 1842, 8

Land of the mighty dead!
Here science once displayed,

And art, their charms;
Here awful Pharaohs swayed
Great nations who obeyed,
Here distant monarchs laid
Their vanquished arms.[403]

They hold us in survey,
They cheer us on our way
They loud proclaim—
From Pyramidal hall—
From Carnac's sculptured wall—
From Thebes they loudly call—
"Retake your fame!["]

"All hail Liberia! hail!
Arise and now prevail
O'er all thy foes;
In truth and righteousness—
In all the arts of peace—
Advance, and still increase
Though hosts oppose."

At the loud call we rise
And press toward the prize,
In glory's race:
All redolent of fame,
The land to which we came,
We'll breathe the inspiring flame—
And onward press.

Here Liberty shall dwell.
Here Justice shall prevail;
Religion—here:
To this, fair virtue's dome
Meek innocence may come,
And find a peaceful home,
And know no fear.

Oppression's cursed yoke
By freemen shall be broke,
In dust be laid;
The soul erect and free,
Here evermore shall be
To none we'll bend the knee
But nature's God.

Proud science here shall rear,
Her monuments, to bear
With deathless tongue:
By nations yet unborn
Her glories shall be known,
And art her tribute join,
The praise prolong.

Commerce shall lift her head,
To auspicious gales shall spread
Expanded wing;
From India's spicy land,
From Europe's rock bound strand,
From Peru's golden sand
Her tribute bring.

Oh Lord, we look to Thee—
To Thee for help we flee,
Lord hear our prayer:
In righteousness arise,
Scatter our enemies,
Their hellish plots surprize
And drive them far.

O happy people they,
Who Israel's God obey,
Whose Lord is God
They shall be blest indeed,
From anxious cares be freed,

And for them is decreed
A large reward.

91. Catch the Proud Spirit

Liberia Herald, 28 November 1845, 20

Bound like bright fetters of the pole
An abject slave to man's control?
No, give me liberty, Natur's boon,
To raise the soul and cheer the gloom.[404]

Tell not of brilliant halls of state,
In Columbo's boasted land of great,
With calamus[405] lots on freedom based
Luxuries sweet and luscious taste.

Of skies serene as "classic Italy's" pride,[406]
Whom men beneath it soon can rise--
Posterity's boasts -- unsullied names
Stimulating sons with brightest flames.

"Catch the proud spirit" and debark,
Leave the shores of Flummery[407] Art
All, tho friends may wail and others rail,
Bend thy canvas to the pleasing gale.

For prejudice unruled is law,
I, a man? kept to hew and draw,
Luxuries such, have no sweet taste,
For one who will not manhood waste.

No, Afric's coast is here my home,
And, I, a freeman now can roam,
Beneath a sky whose solar rays,
Speaks better things in after days.

92. Bread from Brain

Liberia Herald, 15 January 1847, 28

Where the iron of our lives
Is wrought out of fire and smoke;
There the mighty Vulcan[408] strives:
  Hot the furnace, hard the stroke,
There the windy bellows blow,
There the sparks in millions glow,
There on anvil of the world,
Is the clanging hammer hurled.
  Hard the labor! small the gain,
  In the making bread from brain

Where that nameless stone is raised
  Where the patriot's bones were placed,
Lived he — once loved and praised;
  Dies he little mourned and graced:
There he sleeps who knew *no* rest,
There unblest by those he blessed;
There he starved while sowing seed,
Where he starved, the worms now feed.
  Hard the labor, small the gain,
  Is in making bread from brain.

In that chamber lone and dreary
  Sits a poet writing flowers,
Bringing Heaven to earth more near.
  Raining thoughts in dewy showers.
While he sings of nectar rare,
Only is the ink bowl there;
Of feasts of gods he chants — high trust,
As he eats the mouldy crust.
  Hard the labor! small the gain,

Is in making bread from brain.

When the prophet's warning voice
  Shouts the burthen of the world,
Sackcloth robes must be his choice,
  Ashes on his head be hurled.
Where tyrants live at ease,
Where false priests do as they please,
He is scorned and pierced inside,
He is stoned and crucified.
  Hard the labor! Small the gain,
  Is in making bread from brain.

Patriot! Poet! Prophet feed,
  Only on the mouldy crust
Tyrant, fool, and false priest need
  All the crumb, and scorn the just.
Lord! how long: how long; oh Lord!
Bless, oh God, mind's unsheathed sword;
Let the pen become a sabre,
Let thy children eat who labor;
  Bless the labor! bless the gain,
  In the making bread from brain.

93. Wake Every Tuneful String

Liberia Herald, 26 August 1847, 76

Wake every tuneful string,[409]
To God loud praises bring;
  Wake heart and tongue!
In strains of melody,
and choral harmony,
Sing for the oppress'd are free!
  Wake cheerful song.

See Mesurado's height!
Illumed with new-born light.
 Lo the lone star:
Now it ascends the skies,
Lo the deep darkness flies!
While new born glories rise
 And shine afar.

Shine life-creating ray!
Proclaim approaching day,
 Throw wide thy blaze;
Lo savage Hottentot—
Bosjasman from his cot—
And nations long forgot
 Astonish'd gaze.

Shout the loud Jubilee'
Afric once more is free
 Break forth with joy;
Let Nilus' fettered tongue,
Let Niger's join the song,
And Congo's loud and long
 Glad strains employ.

Star in the east shine forth!
Proclaim a nation's birth:
 Ye nation's hear!
This is our natal day;
And we our homage pay
To Thee O Lord we pray —
 Lord hear our prayer.

All hail Liberia! hail!
Favour'd of God all hail!
 Hail happy Land!
From virtue ne'er remove:
By peace, and truth, and love—
and wisdom from above

Carl Patrick Burrowes

So shall thou stand.

Carl Patrick Burrowes

Speeches, Sermons and State Papers

94. Sermon on the Death of Gov. Thomas Buchanan

In conclusion, we must be permitted to say something more particularly relating to our late beloved Chief Magistrate. Governor Thomas Buchanan arrived here in 1839 and directly assumed the administration of the government of the colony. His policy, and the character of his administration are known to you all. The condition of the colony when he arrive was such as rendered the duties of his office trying and arduous and demanded no small degree of firmness and moral courage, to perform faithfully. Many ancient land-marks removed from their position had to be replaced. Salutary laws existing, but lying dormant on the statute book, demanded to be enforced, and other regulations, equally required, had to be made and exerted. These and other circumstances, which the time will not permit us even to enumerate, brought him frequently in contact with some one or another party. But his duty was plain, and he was not the man to shrink from it. In order that we may properly appreciate his character and rightly estimate our loss in his death, I crave your indulgence, while I descend to particulars. [410]

I instance first his influence over the natives, our savage and restless neighbors.

Not unfrequently to be met with in the history of nations is the fact of some individual's name, from a fortuitous concurrence of circumstances, carrying terror wherever it was heard among his or his country's foes. The brilliant and continuous chain of success, which crowned the campaigns of Napoleon, is to be accounted for as much from this fact, as from their universally admitted skill in their science and courage on the field of combat. Victory was supposed to hover over their march, and in the field, to perch upon their sword. Thus their enemies palsied with terror were prepared at the very first onset to yield an easy victory to seek safety in an ignominious flight or unconditional surrender. From similar coincidence, united with the strict integrity and good faith, which marked all Governor Buchanan's intercourse with the natives — readily conceding to them all their rights and inflexibly demanding his — the like impressions pervaded their minds. The brave encounter of him in the hall of palaver or in the field of fight, was regarded by them as an earnest of defeat. Never was man more feared or respected by the natives than

Governor's Buchanan, nor is there a man in all the colonies, the influence of whose presence can so effectually check and hold in abeyance their blustering passions, as did the presence of our lamented Governor. And to relieve my judgment from the imputation of being warped by the partiality of friendship, I am happy that I address many who are witnesses for my assertion, that by many of the natives, he was regarded somewhat more than human.

Many acquainted with the state of feeling among the natives are already the subjects of anxious forebodings, as to our relations with these people. Freed from the restraint in which fear encharmed them, it is apprehended their restless spirit will not be long in finding a pretext for renewing hostilities. Their ideas of policy, as well as desire to follow the time-hallowed pursuits of their fathers, will long render this colony an object of their implacable hatred. At the slave trade, their idol, and their source of supplies, we not long since aimed a deadly blow. This they regarded not only a serious affront, but also a serious injury, as their conduct proved at the time. And can any one, acquainted with them be duped into the belief, that they will speedly cease to regard it so, and become inclined to regard us as friends? No, they secretly cherish sentiments of deep revenge.

The circumstances to which I have thus briefly adverted will serve in part as an answer to any who may inquire, why, if this be the state of feeling, they have not before manifested it. The remaining part of the answer is found in the fact that Governor Buchanan had obtained the occasional presence of American naval vessels and had kept up a friendly communication with the commanders of the British squadron. The natives in ignorance how far in the way of assistance their friendship would extend, if assistance should at any time be demanded, regarded it as utter madness to array themselves against one so terrible in himself and backed by such powerful auxiliaries.

But while I believe the remarks in respect of the opinion which the natives entertained of our late governor to be strictly correct, I am far from supposing we do not possess in ourselves the ability to assert our rights, at any time to teach these savages the folly of the encroachment. Our affliction on this score does not arise so much from the belief that the death of the Governor has left us unable to combat them, as from the loss of his personal influence, to render a combat unnecessary. The same courage, courage which heretofore animated the bosoms of Liberians, will again animate them when a proper occasion shall call it into play. In the hour of danger they will recollect themselves and recollect a Buchanan, and advance to their object.

Nor will the benefits of his administration appear less conspicuous if we direct our attention to the military department of the colony: In what state did Governor Buchanan find this department when he landed here in 1839? There was scarcely a show of military defence. The martial spirit so necessary not only to our peace, but also our existence, had sunk into a slumber from which nothing but his uncommon energy and activity could arouse it. Where were our ordnance and other motions of defence? Our guns dismounted and scattered, the carriages rotten and decayed, proclaimed to the visitor both native and foreign, our weakness and poverty! Soon however under his vigorous administration, our military preparations assumed a new and formidable aspect. Our guns were remounted or new and efficient ones took the place of the old and worthless. Arms were placed within the reach of all, and although at the time some dissatisfaction was expressed, with the regulations by which these arms were issued to the people (and what regulation was ever adopted here that did not at first encounter opposition), I leave it to any reasonable man, whether these arms were not a public benefit. It was entirely owing to Governor Buchanan's influence at home, that we obtained them; for to an application by Lieut. Governor Williams to the Board for defenses for the Colony, he received as answer: "the Board, as punishment for our prodigality with those that had been before sent, would send no further supply." To our departed governor, we owe the respectable and martial show which this house at this time presents; to him we owe the soul-subduing music to which he so much delighted to listen and whose solemn-measured melody has already today and will presently again restore him from the darkness of the grave and present him with the ownness of real personality before us.

The chief complaint urged against the Governor by the citizens of the commonwealth was a rigid parsimony in the fiscal concerns of the government. This, however, instead of depressing should rather exalt his character, when all the circumstances of the case are taken into consideration. A solemn trust had been committed to his hands. To his management had been entrusted the affairs of a society burdened with an enormous debt and so far sunk into disrepute as to be able to make scarcely any annual collections. To him the society looked more than to any other man, to retrieve by his prudence and management, their waning character; to restore to him public confidence, to summon patronage to their aid; and thus enable them to maintain a share of operations and to silence the clamors of creditors by small annual instalments. This was his duty and he did lay down his rules, and no consideration of friendship could induce him to depart therefrom. Friends and foes were all meted the same measure, for he was a stranger to favoritism. I can, however, believe that the stern necessity which drove him to adopt this odious rule was altogether repugnant to the native goodness of his heart and that it was as much deplored by him as by any one whom I have now the honor to address.

But it is not to the forum of violence nor to the frozen regions of ceremonial convocation, that you should go to study the character of man. If you would know it, you must repair to the domestic circle, to the parlor assemblage of private friendships. There he unbends from the stiffness of character assumed to meet the public eye, displays the genuine sentiments of the soul, which itself beams forth without disguise. Governor Buchanan in the administration of public affairs was an altogether different person from Mr. Buchanan in the social meeting. There he was firm and inflexible, here he was courteous and affable. In the one he had not friends, in the other with open arms he received all. And while a rigid parsimony marked his management of the public funds, a profuse and genteel liberality was displayed in every thing when only his private interest was concerned.

From the charge of selfishness, I feel bold to exempt the lamented subject of our present remarks. If ever a man was free from sinister view, was actuated by pure motives of philanthropy, Thomas Buchanan was[;] and if ever a man sincerely desired the happiness and prosperity of a people, he was desirous for the happiness and prosperity of this people, and was anxious for their character. In his intercourse with foreigners, in his letters abroad, in his published communications, his constant aim was to represent them in the most favorable light that honesty would admit. And objections sometimes urged with much plausibility and apparent justice against our habits, our institutions, and our tardy improvement, he promptly and cheerfully met with every extenuating circumstance the case would admit. This inflexibility and firmness in enforcing our laws as well upon citizens as foreigners who affected to despise and who wished to disregard them are known to you all. He advanced steadily along the line of his duty, regardless alike of odium here, and consequences abroad; and to this feature in his administration more than to anything else is to attributed that attention which the colony is attracting abroad.

"Woe unto you," says the Oracle of Truth, "when all men speak well of you," and it seems, therefore, fortunate for the good, that virtue will always have a persecuting enemy in bad men. The tongue of calumny, the malignant spirit of envy, will always seek to detract from the good man's character; and in proportion to the distance there is between him and those to whom he is an object of envy will be their endeavor to reduce him from an elevation to which from their moral and mental imbecility they can never hope to rise. Our Governor experienced, in its full force, the truth of these remarks. But as the sly arts of feigned friendship for selfish purposes failed to seduce, so the more obvious weapons of slander and calumny were powerless to deter him from the apprehended path of his duty.

To say he was not perfect, would be saying no more than that he was man. The sun has his spots. His failings, however, were of the most innocent kind! Such as are triable by all the good with lenity and forbearance. I am not attempting a delineation of his character: that demands an order of talent far above mine. I will only add that his soul was formed for friendship. Frank and open, he was a stranger to duplicity; and, therefore, weighing the character of others by his own, he sometimes became the victim of design and intrigue. He possessed largely that charity that thinkest no evil, and acknowledged readily whatever was commendable, even in the character of his enemies. He was long in taking offence, invariably placing the most favorable construction upon the saying and doing of others; nor would he unnecessarily offend the meanest or the poorest with whom he might be thrown in contact. He presented a harmonious union of dignity and gentleness. To sum up his character, he was a Christian and a gentleman.

95. [Eulogy for Elijah Johnson]

We have been recently, frequently and forcibly reminded of the solemn truth, that in the "midst of life we are in death." The awful messenger has read his lesson in tones calculated to startle the dullest ear and thrill the most insensate heart. Scarcely has the sound of the bell, proclaiming the departure of one pilgrim, died upon the ear, when its solemn voice was gain heard announcing the departure of another. Happy indeed is he, who in the sound of the solemn knell hears the admonition of the Son of Man, "What I say unto one I say unto all — watch!" Thrice happy he, who not only hears, but is also incited to stand, with "his lamp trimmed and his loins girt about," ready to "meet the bridegroom at his coming."[411]

These thoughts have been suggested by the fearfully rapid strokes which death has been recently commissioned to deal out in our midst. For a moment the archer seemed to suspend his work, and we were fondly hugging our remaining friends to our bosoms, when suddenly an arrow flew, and Johnson fell!

Rev. Elijah Johnson departed this life at White Plains, a station of the [Methodist Episcopal] Mission, on Friday, 23d March.

In announcing the death of Mr. Johnson, and referring to his manner of life, I am at a loss how to express adequately, in the brief space to which I must confine myself, either his intrinsic worth as a Christian citizen or the high sense entertained of him by one, and all, of this community.

Mr. Johnson was one of the pioneers in the enterprise of Americo-African Colonization. He came out in 1820 in the ship *Elizabeth* — the May-Flower of Liberia — and was among the ill-fated ones who were thrown out upon the deadly swamps of Sherbro. It was in the order of Divine Providence that he should survive and enjoy comparatively good health, to animate by his habitually lively disposition and irrepressible activity, the languid few, who were spared from the pestilential influence of the place. And perhaps it was to his sagacity and constancy more than to any thing else, or to any other man, that a vestige of the colony remained, when in 1821 the *Nautilus* arrived at Sierra Leone.

Mr. Johnson removed to this place in 1821 with the shattered remains of the two expeditions. The agents of the Society in charge of affairs were not long in discovering his worth, and he was soon appointed to offices of responsibility in the colony. He was almost wholly destitute of education; but he possessed good natural abilities; to which, by careful observation and close attention, he added more than an ordinary acquaintance with human character. In illustration of this I will mention an incident which occurred a few days before the battle of the 11th of November. A palaver was held on Cary's Island between the chiefs of the country, and the colony — Messrs. J. Ashmun, F. James, and E. Johnson acting in behalf of the colony. The chiefs were unappeasable by any talk or professions of amity and friendship. Anxious to prevent an open rupture, for which the settlement at that time was very poorly prepared, Messrs Ashmun and James proposed to *buy a peace* — to win back the lost friendship of the natives with a bonus of some two or three hundred bars. The perfidious chiefs accepted the proposal, and professed, when they received the amount, to be perfectly satisfied. Mr. Johnson wholly dissented from his colleagues, and could not be prevailed upon to give his assent, constantly affirming the amount would be thrown away, as they would assuredly have to fight. The amount however was paid, and a few days after intelligence was received that the combined forces of the country were rapidly advancing upon the settlement. Mr. Johnson had paid attention to the natives' character, and his intercourse with them in the ordinary transactions of life, had taught him that no reliance can be placed on any offering made to their friendship, if an opportunity to increase their acquisitions by violence, combines with a chance to escape with impunity — a fact which, however some may be slow to learn, has been made painfully known to many.

His services in the conflicts in which the colony has been engaged with the natives, in most of which he bore a conspicuous part, were invaluable. His bosom was the seat of a spirit that never quailed. The energies of his mind rose with the exigencies of the occasion; and the furious shock of conflicting hosts, like the collision of flint with steel, only struck out the fire which had lain concealed within. That he was skillful in planning attack or defence I will not undertake to say, but all will admit, that when the enemy presented himself, Johnson met him — and met him with sure discomfiture.

Mr. Johnson was at one time entrusted with the administration of the affairs of the colony during the temporary absence of the society's agent. His conduct in that affair evinced his fidelity as an agent, and his firmness and impartiality as a presiding officer. He was also at different times charged with commissions, to treat with the chiefs of the country on both general and special subjects. In every instance he so discharged his trust as not only to prove his qualification for the business, but also to evince his firm attachment to the best interests of the colony; while at the same time he impressed the natives with a deep sense of his impartiality and justice. There has never been in the colony, a man who exerted a more extensive influence over the native mind than he; there has never been one of whom the natives stood more in awe. They regarded him with superstitious dread. In peace, his word was law — In war, his name was a tower of strength.

One grand peculiarity in the character of Mr. Johnson was this, he was always on the side of the government. Not that he was blind to errors, or to peccancies in men or measures; but he deemed that the government had never been so distinctly marked by either, as to demand that he should put himself in hostile array against it. The colony was his nursling, and he preferred to trust to the modifying hand of time before a resort to violent correctives. In this particular at least, he has left an example which many would do well to ponder.

To give an adequate idea of Mr. Johnson's character — of his disinterestedness — of his benevolence — leading him at times in the fullness of his heart into extravagant bestowment — of his patriotism — of his unyielding regard for order and subordination — of his profound respect for law, and of his ardent attachment to the best interests of the colony, would require that its whole history from its first settlement to the present time should be written, and that the exigencies which arose, and the conduct they called forth, be also minutely put down.

Having already extended my remarks beyond the founds within which I at first limited myself, I must close my paper by a brief reference to Mr. Johnson's character as a Christian.

However much he was esteemed as a good neighbor, a faithful friend and a patriotic public spirited citizen, it was as a Christian, and a Christian minister, that he shone most conspicuously. Let not the pedantic and the idolaters of worldly wisdom, smile at the application of the word shine, to one confessedly destitute of literary acquirements and high mental culture. Manly sense, shining parts, and brilliant wit, serve well as hand-maids to religion — they may set it off to advantage, just as a gilded cornice imparts an additional beauty to an elegant apartment, or the tasteful carving on the capital adorn the well proportioned column, while they afford neither strength nor durability. Religion can subsist, and subsist in all its purity, and its beautiful simplicity, and its sustaining influence, can animate to a holy and useful life — sustain in death, and introduce into all the joys of heaven without them; while dissociated from religion, the sparkling corruscations of the proudest intellect, and the widest excursions of genius, like the transient meteor, flame for a moment, and are extinguished forever. The portals of the temple of science had never opened to admit Mr. Johnson; but into the inner temple of his own heart he had been introduced by the spirit of God. There he made discoveries altogether above the reach of science — discoveries which induced him to "flee for refuge to lay hold on the hope set before him." This hope he soon found, and found it to be an "anchor sure and steadfast," and possessing it he "rejoiced with joy unspeakable and full of glory."

Mr. Johnson attached himself to the M. E. Church, and in the fullness of a grateful and benevolent heart, soon asked and obtained permission from the church to recommend to others that Saviour whom he had found so precious to his own soul. From that time until his death he remained a consistent member, and an active, indefatigable minister of the church with which he first united. To Mr. Johnson the Methodist Church in Liberia owes more than to any other man; not indeed that he has done more than other men during the time they have been in the field. But he was with the church in her destitution, in the infancy of the colony, when there were but few to help. His time, his talent, his money, his bodily strength were all freely and cheerfully given to the church. Indeed it may be truly said that he was, under God, the father of Methodism in Liberia.

Although ardently attached to his church, and ready to defend her on all proper occasions, he was of an enlarged and liberal spirit. He delighted to associate with those who love God of whatever denomination they might be, and he sought opportunities to do so. In short, in all the relations of life, as a father, a husband, a friend, a citizen and a Christian, his conduct bore testimony to his profession.

Mr. Johnson has left a wife and eight children to mourn his loss. Five of these, together with their mother were wholly dependent upon his daily exertions for their support. Recently his affairs have not been in a prosperous condition; but it is to be hoped that as his whole life was devoted to the good of others, the blessing of the righteous will be bestowed upon his family.

96. [Treatise on Self Government]

An examination into the history of this colony — its rise, progress thus far, its influence upon the moral and intellectual character of the colonists, and its practical effects upon the natives and upon the slave-trade, would well repay in the gratifying facts it would evolve all the pains and trouble it might occasion. Although the objects which the American Colonization Society in its most incipient stage had in view to accomplish, as well as the inducements which moved the colonists to act upon it plan, have been long before the Christian and civilized world, it may not be amiss briefly to state them here. [412]

A few benevolent and christian men, looking over the fact of society in the United States, beheld two millions of members of that society laboring under hopeless bondage, and sunk in the lowest degradation. Against their improvement and elevation, law and prejudice had erected an insuperable barrier. What was to be done? The almost universal cry was — they must be removed. The question at once presented itself — where shall they be sent? The whole map of America was inspected, and first one point and then another was selected and rejected, until at length the continent of Africa, their father land was by almost universal acclaim pronounced the best adapted home for the trodden down colored population of the United States.

The millions whom this arrangement was intended so deeply to affect not only in themselves personally, but in their descendants to the remotest generations, were admitted to no share in the discussions, selections, or plans. They were sealed up in a silence as mute and as passive as the land to which they were to be sent; but under a conviction that no possible change could make their condition worse, they eagerly embraced Africa with all its proverbial horrors, as an anchor of hope. This is a brief history of the beginnings, both of the society and of those who availed themselves of its offers. That the whole scheme was at first contrived by Providence, and that it has been thus far conducted by the same unfaltering hand — however it may in itself and in its results be derided by those who overlook the order of nature, and despised by others who are ignorant of its details, there will not remain a shadow of doubt on the mind of any who will be at the pains to examine it.

The plan of the American Colonization Society was something altogether new in the history of human society, and human operations. It was indeed a bold and daring enterprise. We have histories of colonies successfully planted at periods which date far back towards the infancy of the world; and we have accounts of colonies planted at various place, and at intervals that reach down to the present time; but in all the means employed to plant them, and in all the machinery relied upon to conduct them to maturity, they were wholly different from the American Colony of Liberia.

This is the secret of the success which has attended the operations of the American Society. This difference is the lever, hitherto overlooked in the eager search after something grand and imposing, the ordinary attendant upon a nation's movements, that has urged the colony of Liberia on far in advance of all the colonies on the coast of Africa.

The bare idea that this colony has outstripped any other — that it has in fact done any thing, will, we are assured, be every where scouted and ridiculed. Nothing is more fashionable than to ridicule the colony and every thing connected with it, because it is so much less laborious to ridicule than to investigate. But we shrink not from comparison with any colony on the coast. Let us single out for an example the colony of Sierra Leone, which we presume is admitted to be as prosperous a colony as any on the coast. It will be necessary first to consider the advantages which Sierra Leone has enjoyed over the colony of Liberia.

Sierra Leone was settled by the English in 1792. A powerful colony of eleven hundred and thirty-one souls was planted at one time, with every convenience and comfort, and with all the means to insure success, which kindness and sagacity could suggest. For fifteen years the colony was nurtured by the fostering hand of a powerful voluntary organization. In 1808 it was turned over to the British crown — made a naval depot, a garrison, and a home for the slaves taken under the different treaties. All the machinery necessary to conduct the operations of government was set in motion — numerous offices were created and filled by well salaried incumbents. Government was lavish with money. Every man, woman and child who would work, obtained it, and was liberally paid for it. Indeed it appeared that the only object in view, was to furnish all with the means of living, without regard to the utility or the value of the returns made for it. A church which now stands in Freetown — a fifth rate structure in an American or European city, was some ten or fifteen years in building, and cost upwards of eighty thousand pounds. Millions have been expended upon this colony, and hundreds of lives have been sacrificed there. It is the offspring and the pet of a lofty philanthropy. It was designed to bless the colored emigrant, and to regenerate Africa.

How has it succeeded? We speak with the most profound respect. But while we yield to the authorities in England the fullest credit for good intentions, we will, we trust, be pardoned for putting down Sierra Leone as signally unfortunate as an experiment.

Where are the once numerous settlers and their descendants? Where the Maroons? Of the remnant that remains, what is their position? Have they grown wealthy? Do they conduct the commercial operations of the colony? Do they cultivate the soil? Do they fill important offices of trust under government? What is the intellectual character of the place? We suppress the humiliating answers.

If the examination should be extended to the influence which the colony at Sierra Leone has exerted upon the slave-trade, the same deplorable inefficiency will be apparent. The natives, so far as all considerations of a moral character are concerned, remain the same that they were fifty years ago; and the slave-trade, despite the vigilance of the police, is secretly but extensively carried on, in and around the peninsula. It would be proper also to ascertain the exports of the colony, and the proportion of its productions to the consumption. The chief exports from that place, are timber, hides, cam wood, palm oil, gold, and ground nuts. But these are almost exclusively obtained from the natives. Correct answers to these questions will indicate infallibly the progress of the colony.

What has been the cause of this failure — this death of so many high hopes and cherished expectations? Without taking upon us to assign every cause, we do not hesitate to assert that the inefficiency of the colony for the purposes designed by its founders and patrons is, up to this time, owing in part, to the method and constitution of former local governments.

Until recently, throughout every department of the government, the offices were almost exclusively filled by those who had no permanent interest in the colony. The permanent residents, settlers, Maroons and liberated Africans, were almost systematically excluded from any share in the government. They were thrown quite in the background. All laudable ambition suppressed, every noble and manly aspiration smothered. There was no scope for that self confidence and self-respect, the off-spring of a feeling of equality, and which is so necessary to an honorable course.

Inferior in every thing, in intellect, in pecuniary resources, and in official power, to another class amongst them, they gradually settled down to the position of obsequious attendants, until the grades of society founded upon color, became as marked and distinct as in the northern States of America. It is exhilarating, however, to find that a change is taking place in this respect, in Sierra Leone. There appears to be a growing disposition on the part of the Europeans now resident in that colony, to admit the colonists to a share in the management of affairs, and to meet them on terms of civil equality. The different missions there are prosecuting their heaven-born enterprise with a laudable energy; and the efforts and plans of the Wesleyan Mission especially, are entitled to the highest praise, and henceforth the movement of the colony must be onward towards the point first aimed at by its patrons. We trust the revolution thus set on foot will be completed.

The American Colonization Society commenced active operations in 1820, with only eighty-eight emigrants. In 1821, forty-five more arrived at Sierra Leone. In 1822, the remnant of these two companies removed to Cape Mesurado. They had one white agent amongst them as chief superintendent of the colony. Small annual immigrations continued to arrive, but such in the first years of the colony was the fatality of the climate and the number of casualties, these importations served rather to keep up the original number than to increase it. The colonists were early warned against the delusive expectation of governmental patronage; they were constantly exhorted to rely upon their own resources, and their own unaided energies. A plan of government was formed and committed in all its details, almost entirely to the hands of the colonists. The agent amongst them was rather an adviser than a controller. Every thing in the history of the past taught them the folly of looking back to the land whence they had come out. The assistance afforded them by the Society, extended no further than to the purchase of land, and a meagre supply of articles of necessity.

The colonists, thus thrown upon their own resources, felt their responsibility. They saw at once that their destinies were in their own hands — that to falter or to hesitate, was to sink. It was in the nature of their peculiar circumstances to inspire with ardor and to call forth into active exercise all their ingenuity and judgment. In all their regulations, civil and political — in all their relations with the natives, they looked not merely at temporary advantages, but chiefly at permanent results. In

Carl Patrick Burrowes

fact, they saw that in order to rear a solid and durable edifice, they must dig a broad and deep foundation. Having all their hopes staked upon the success of the experiment — chained to the place by circumstances entirely beyond their control, they cheerfully resigned present advantages, when, temporary and limited in themselves, they exerted an unfavorable influence upon future prosperity. Hence they became at an early period of the colony most uncompromising enemies of the slave-trade; and although we will not assert that this traffic has never found an advocate amongst us, nor that some few has not criminally abetted it; yet we do not hesitate to challenge the instance of another colony, in the vicinity of which it is so completely crippled. They saw that this trade, the scourge of the natives, would prove a curse to the colony, and effectually prevent its improvement; they therefore determined to put it down at all hazard. Wherever they obtained a right todo so, they beat down the baracoon, knocked the chain from the slave, and proclaimed liberty to the captive. The natives began to understand the nature of the colonial institutions, and regarding the colony as an asylum, thousands of helpless and oppressed sought refuge within its borders. The colonists gladly hailed them as important accessions to their strength, and encouraged them in all the pursuits of an honorable life.

The stale prediction of those who oppose our elevation has been — that we would be found incapable of self-government. Pausing here only to remark that Africa with its hundred millions, (every where possessing a government and laws) has ever been a standing refutation of this malignant vaticination;[413] as if guided by Heaven, the American Colonization Society at once hit upon an expedient that will, we trust, effectually wrest this weapon from the hands of our enemies. The government was at once lodged in the hands of the people. The idea of government in Liberia will be ridiculed by those in whose minds pompous titles and fat salaries are inseparably connected with good government. We will not argue to so obvious an error, nor cite instances to show that anarchy and misrule have generally been in proportion to the elevation of the governing above the governed. We will only invite an examination of our social, civil, and political order, our legislature and our halls of justice. This state of things is the result of early habits of self-government — of laws made and executed by men whose last hope was involved in the experiment. Society here has never been (and God grant it may never be) split into two orders — one to govern, the other to be governed; the one dominant, the other suppliant. Political equality elevates and expands the mind and nerves the arm, servility enervates both. That people will be most incapable of self government that is longest debarred from it.

The colony has now been settled twenty-two years. In December of 1822, when the whole country was combined against it, thirty-five souls, including six native youths, was the sum total of its available force. Under the guidance of a beneficent Providence, it rode out the gale of that stormy year, and by its own energy year, seconded by the timely British mediation, it composed the elements of a decorative discord, and arranged stipulations which have prevented the recurrence of those violent scenes.

The colony was then limited to the heights on which Monrovia now stands; but freed from the anxiety always attendant upon apprehension of war, and receiving continually assurances of firm friendship on the part of the natives, the colonists begun to extend their acquaintance with the country. As their numbers gradually increased by fresh importations, they found no difficulty in obtaining land, but having no ambition of territorial aggrandizement, they limited their purchases to actual necessities.

The first line of extension ran up the St. Pauls river. Here they formed agricultural settlements. Negotiations were shortly afterwards opened for Cape Mount, where a school for native youths, taught by a colonist, had been some time in successful operation. The high road to the interior, the nursery of victims for the slave market at Gallinas, winds its way through this region. It was also the theatre of continual war, excited by the demand for slaves which at that time was very great. Apprehensive that an American settlement amongst them might prejudice this traffic, and most probably assured that it would do so, by the slavers scattered through the country collecting their cargoes, the natives refused to sell at that time, but guarantied to colony a small plat of land for a school, agreed to furnish the necessary buildings for the purpose, and pledged the power of the country to its protection. The extremely unsettled state of the country rendering the object impracticable, it was for the time abandoned.

The colonists now felt, in its deadliest force, the blighting influence of the slave trade. It raged on every side. Heralded by conflagration and murder, the whole country was in a state of consternation; and, as if safety consisted only in absolute solitude, each one appeared anxious to kidnap all others! While clouds of murky smoke ascended from smouldering ruins, while the heavens rang with the shrieks of mangled victims, the slave ship might be seen hovering near the land ready to barter for those who should fall alive into the hands of the conqueror, or to receive them in payment for debts already contracted. All lawful trade was suspended, and agriculture entirely neglected, and the whole attention of the natives was absorbed in pursuing and eluding pursuit. It appeared that the utter extinction of the tribes involved was at hand. The colonial authorities resolved upon an effort to arrest the progress of this disorder and to compose the natives to peace. While the land was in possession of the natives, the idea of force could not be entertained. Mediation was proffered, and treaties formed, in which, by mutual consent, a prominent article always appeared condemnatory of the slave trade. The most effectual method was to get possession of the land and by this means the right to put down the trade by force. This method was adopted, and the colonial territory was extended by purchase exactly in proportion to its increased in means to exercise over it a salutary control. Never for a moment was it intended nor even wished, that the natives should remove from the land they thus conveyed away. Invariably they were earnestly solicited to remain, to enroll themselves as citizens of the colony, and urged to adopt the manners and customs of colonists. It has been the steady policy of the Society at home and of the colonial authorities here, as a means of rapidly advancing the colony and of improving the natives, to incorporate them with the Americans. The measure has had a most gratifying effect. Thousands of natives are now residing in the territory of the colony. Many have come from distant tribes induced by the security enjoyed here, which they in vain sought beyond the jurisdiction of the colony. Others, although they have conveyed away the sovereignty over the land, yet remain near the graves of their fathers, content to conform to the mild regulations imposed, while they enjoy all the privileges they could wish. The slave trade has ceased, and they are in peace.

The territory claimed by the colony extends from Cape Mount on the north to Cape Palmas on the south. Actual purchase has not been made of the whole extent of this line, but of many of the intermediate points; while of others, grants of lease have been obtained, and of others still, the natives have engaged to make no conveyance except to the colony. It is exceedingly desirable that this territory should be under the control and jurisdiction of the colony, and it would long ago have been purchased but for the petty jealousy and low intrigue of foreign traders. While the territory is thus cut up and divided by intermediate hordes of sovereign savages, indulging, unrestrained, in all the excess of barbarian liberty, the moral energies of the colony must be deplorably crippled, and at no distant period its growth permanently arrested. The moral influence of the colony over the natives in its own territory will be enervated, while in these independent communities within its bosom, no system or enterprise could be suppressed, however disastrous, that the cupidity and avarice of others might encourage.

Should the colony be permitted to obtain the control of this territory, a measure demanded by every consideration of humanity and philanthropy — and which nothing but foreign interference will prevent — no interest will be prejudiced by it except such as is stigmatised by all civilized nations. The ports of the colony are, and it is to its interest to keep them, open to the vessels of all nations on an equal footing. It excludes only such as are known to be engaged in trade for slaves. Past experience shows that the amount of legal trade in any given territory is inversely as the slave trade. Wherever the demand for slaves is great, there the supply of all other articles of commerce is meagre. It is the direst of curses — it steels the heart of man and clenches the hand of nature. Slaves are procured more by predatory incursions than by purchase, and the demand is met only by a state of alarm and ambuscade that leaves no room for attention to any other pursuit.

By closing the line of coast referred to, against this traffic, which can only be done by actual possession, the great incentive to continual hostility would be precluded, friendly relations would be entered into and maintained, agriculture would flourish — the arts of civilized life could be introduced — the articles of commerce would rapidly increase, and the native ear now closed by an infatuating traffic, would be open to the instructions of civilization. That this is not merely a picture of what is rather wished than can be rationally predicted, is, we think, susceptible of moral proof. We judge of the future by the past. These results have followed wherever the influence of the colony has been exerted. Voluntary native residents amongst us parade in our military ranks, vote at our elections, and bow with us in our temples before the feet of our common Parent. This is the last aim of the colony, the high elevation to which it aspires. Not to dispossess the natives of their land and drive them to die barbarians in the forest, but to guide them by a salutary control, and instruct them in the arts of peace — to pour into their ear the lessons of civilization and christianity, to incorporate them into our political and social body that they may be one with us. But should the colony be astricted, should the barriers which law and order would erect against the operations of lawless traders on the one hand, and of the constant feuds and heathenish practices of the natives on the other, this most desirable consummation for which so many lives have been sacrificed and so much treasure expended in vain, will be pushed back to an indefinite period our colony will languish and our hopes expire.

It is worthy of remark that the gigantic scheme proposed by Mr. Buxton, is precisely the scheme of this colony with only inconsiderable modifications. It is not ours to say why it sustained a defeat when commenced on the Niger, under such imposing auspices. It is sufficient that all the elements of good to Africa which philanthropy

Carl Patrick Burrowes

beheld in that scheme, are found in this, arranged and combined and ready for enlarged and efficient operation. Never was there a better occasion for the display of disinterested benevolence and philanthropy than this colony presents. It is emphatically the cause of mankind, and to the sympathies of human kind it appeals. It can never be sufficiently regretted that the agricultural interests of the colony have been suffered to languish — in fact to be almost totally neglected. Although the soil offers to the cultivator the richest reward for his industry, yet the productions have never equalled the consumption. The attention of those who have pretended to cultivate, has been directed almost exclusively to the commonest articles of tropical produce; while coffee, cotton and sugar, have been neglected as demanding too large a share of time and money. These article are pointed out to us by nature as the great staples of commerce. Coffee and cotton, although growing spontaneously in the forests, require a larger amount of capital to make them important as articles of commerce than the colonists have possessed. The land is in the primitive wildness of nature. The forests of ages rest upon it. These are to be cleared away — the soil prepared, and the seed to be sown. This demands an amount of labor and money which none have been able to command. Enough however has been accomplished to cherish the hope, that, at no distant day, the colony will be able to offer these productions in return for productions of other countries, and the earlier the attention of the natives be drawn to this subject, the sooner this hope will be realized. Sugar making is now in successful operation at the Society's farm on the Stockton. The article produced this year is of a superior quality, equal to any of the West Indies, that we have seen. Admitting, however, that we have exported no coffee, nor cotton, nor sugar, we shall hardly be branded as peculiarly worthless, seeing the same may be written of so many other colonies on the coast settled long anterior to this, and favored with advantages which we have never possessed.

Great efforts we learn are being made by traders at the leeward, to prejudice the natives against the colonists; in some instances, they have so far succeeded, that the natives have declared they wish no communication with us. Should they incite them to aggression on the persons and property of the colonists, which is evidently their aim, the consequence may be disastrous to the property of the movers of the mischief. It should be borne in mind that the natives know no friends in a time of war. The property of all is alike booty.

In the present number, our readers will find the diplomatic correspondence between the government of Great Britain and the United States, relative to the character and jurisdiction of this colony. Although the colony is deeply interested in this discussion, and will be immensely affected for good or evil in which ever way the question shall be decided, yet we are happy that it is now brought before the world, as not time can be more proper for it, than the present. In discussing this matter, it would seem important to attend to its peculiar features, lest in viewing the subject in the light in which similar questions, when agitated between nations, are regarded, an error fatal to us be made. The question is not whether a community already possessing sufficient territory for a "healthful existence," shall be allowed to extend the line of its boundary — nor whether a country moved only by a greedy ambition, shall grasp a point where it can effect no object of general good to the human family, and which the equal interest of all requires to be maintained free and unappropriated, but whether this colony planted by Christian philanthropy, with the highest and holiest of purposes, shall be allowed any longer to have an existence. The question involves nothing less than the existence of the colony. If it be astricted to its original limits, all its former efforts will have been in vain. It must languish and drop a helpless abortion. Nor will it be of avail to extend its purchases along the coast, if within this line, there be intervening communities independent of its control, seeing the most salutary regulations — those which its very existence may require to be enforced, may, through these exempted points, be sadly weakened, and set at naught.

In whatever light the question is viewed, it teems with interest to us, and as its decision must be pronounced at some time, the present *seems as good as any other*. Our fate depends upon it; but if we should be driven hence, where shall we go? As it is in the power of neither our hand nor tongue to plead for us, may we not trust to our former circumstances and our present helplessness, to afford argument?

Now that the question is agitated, would it be improper for us to send a deputation to Europe and America, to ask a recognition of the colony? We are not aware of all the qualifications that entitle a people to such consideration. If regard be had to power, in the ordinary acceptation of the term — or to population and territorial extent, of course we have no claim. But if (and it seems more consonant with certain fundamental principles,) regard is had to the amount of good to be effected -- to the aggregate amount of evil and wretchedness to be prevented, then we may be permitted to plead. We throw out this by way of suggestion, in order to engage the attention of some of our more sapient friends.

97. Address Delivered Before the Liberia Lyceum

Carl Patrick Burrowes

Gentlemen, members of the Lyceum,

Called by your partiality to preside over your association for the present year, it has become my duty, in obedience to your expressed will on taking the chair, to address you on the occasion.[414]

When I look around me — met as my view is everywhere by many so much my superior in age [--] in experience, in talents, in short, in every qualification requisite to discharge, with dignity to themselves and advantage to the association, the duties of the office with which you have been pleased to honor me, I could not, were I so disposed, close my eyes to the extreme partiality with which you have regarded me. Accept therefore, gentlemen, my most hearty thanks, and permit me to assure you that, should my future course not sustain the high expectations which you have indulged, it shall not be for want of my most strenuous and unremitting endeavours.

In an address of the kind I am called upon to deliver, it would seem that the objects of this institution and the best mode of securing them should be assigned a prominent place. And although another subject[415] of deep, yea, of vital importance to our whole community hath engrossed nearly my whole attention, as I doubt not, gentlemen, it is a subject of deepest solicitude to you also, yet as the ability to discuss this subject successfully and to avail ourselves of all the benefits legitimately flowing from its successful discussion is one among the other purposes contemplated by your association, I proceed the more readily first to state the objects of the institution.

The constitution of the association in its 6th Article says "the object of this association shall be the diffusion of knowledge throughout the colony as the best method to advance not only general but individual improvement."

The object of our association then is the acquisition of knowledge. We have associated together that we may widen the field of our observation and extend the circle of our information on all subjects with which it is useful or ornamental to be acquainted. The opinions which we have formed and the sentiments we entertain whether derived from observation or imbibed from books, it is the object of this association to submit to a rigid scrutiny and to close and searching examination; being assured that principles and doctrines that will not endure a proper test should be at once abandoned. Thus our association is intended to have a reflexive action: to confirm us in the information which we fancy we already possess or to convince us of its futility and give it to the winds.

But we also seek to increase our knowledge. Knowledge is derived from without. After all that has been said about innate ideas and principles, it will, I think, be no easy matter for any one to show, that we have one single idea that we did not originally receive by perception or sensation. It is admitted that when ideas are once received into the mind by the avenues of the senses, they may be, and are by every individual, combined into forms in which they did not originally enter. What we mean to say is, that were it possible to resolve and analyse these mental combinations into their original and component parts they would be found to be ideas which could enter only by the senses. Mind, or rather the capacity of receiving ideas, is inherent in our nature; its development and improvement depend upon education and experience. The storehouse of knowledge is created with us; the ideas to adorn and enrich it are imported from abroad. It seems to be a law of our nature that every valuable acquisition is only to be obtained by labour. Eminently is this remark true of mental acquisitions. And as they are of all attainments the most valuable and ennobling so they demand the most constant labour and unwearied diligent study. It is the possession of mind — and its capacity of indefinite enlargement and improvement — which imparts to man his dignity. For apart from mind, wherein does he differ from the brute? The object of this institution is to educate and discipline this power –– to call it into vigorous exercise and to direct it to its legitimate objects, or — if I may use a figure — to levy a tribute on nature and art for the necessary furniture with which, by a judicious combination and arrangement, to adorn the apartment of knowledge.

We proceed in the next place to notice the means by which these objects will be most certainly attained.

The existence of our Lyceum indicates our conviction of the efficiency of associations. A little reflection will show that on this subject our opinion is not ill-founded. We are obeying the impulses of our nature. Man is a social being. God saw that it was not good for man to be alone and gave him woman — to soften down his asperity, to curb his wildness, to call out his sympathies into play and to perpetuate his species. Since men increased upon the earth we have ever found them driven to consocation as by the force of instinct. This disposition was implanted by our creator in the breast of his rational creatures for the most salutary purposes. Everywhere and evermore ["]union is strength["] has long since passed into a proverb. We must however confine our remarks to the influence of literary and scientific associations on the mind of the student.

In the first place they enlarge the stock of material for the mental artificer. The object of the modern philosophy is to collect facts, unlike the ancient which was to

Carl Patrick Burrowes

explain phenomena. At each meeting of our institution it is to be expected that each member will, in addition to the information which he may himself have collected in the interval since the last meeting, have the benefit of the industry and acquirements of every other member during the same period. Whatever each one and every one may have discovered, whether in morale or in politics, in law or in physics, whether in history or geography –– whether it concerns us as a distinct and separate people or as related to other nations, whatever the discovery may be, it is expected the Lyceum will have the full benefit of it. What an augmentation of power!! and into how many different departments of nature, and art, and science we may thus simultaneously walk! Suppose gentlemen our institution should number twenty-five industrious students — men who, while they move along in their daily walk, keep their eyes open and their brains at work, who attend regularly our meetings to hand over to the common stock their weekly gathering of facts and observations. Each member would, in every one week, have the benefit of twenty-five weeks of observation and study. Not only have we no assurance that any one member would in the space of twice twenty-five weeks reap the same collection of facts in the field of observation or gather them from meditation and reflection — the offspring of observation, but, on the contrary, the probability is strong against the supposition. Nature's book, it is true is every where open, presenting to the enquiring eye lessons of wisdom and goodness; but she does not teach systems, or rather her lessons are not given in a systematic form. Systems are ours. Their utility results from the feebleness of our powers and the contraction of our vision. Overcome by partial antipathies and bewildered by variety and profusion, we need the uniformity of classification and the simplicity of systematic arrangement in order to clear and distinct comprehension.

I have already remarked that all our knowledge is acquired originally by the senses. If this remark be true the world at large must be our field — not indeed the harvest field of matured fruit but the forest of Lebanon yielding abundant material to the skillful artisan, or the quarry whence to bring the [variegated] marble to adorn and beautify the edifice. It is characteristic of the student that his mind is ever in motion. Whether he be engaged in pursuits exclusively literary and directs his mind to the acquisition of languages, to their structures and idiomatic peculiarities, to philosophy, to history or to chronology, or whether he be more especially a student of nature and examines and analyses the material subsistances around him, ascertains their uses and powers as they are now found, or their effects in different combinations, still the world is his field.

The fixed employment of most men, restricting them as it necessarily does to a degree of sameness in their daily walk and daily train of thought, precludes the opportunity of regular extensive excursions and deplorably contracts their spheres of observation. The minds of men are differently constituted and diverse in their character. Facts and phenomena which would altogether elude minds of one class would be instantly detected by those of another. The poetry of nature awakens of devotion and kindles the rapture of one, the utility and benevolence of her arrangements feed the contemplation of another. The one revels in whatever is grand and whatever is beautiful, the other dwells with pleasure only on what is beneficent. Utility is the food of one, sublimity the element of the other. In the same field where the man of highly imaginative mind would kindle into ecstasy, the cold, frigid but equally intellectual man would find nothing to arouse his energies. The faculty of observation is not only strengthened by exercise but becomes stronger and keener in proportion as it is continuously directed to a particular subject; and each one will be found to possess a greater acuteness of perception of all the shades of phenomena which fall more especially within the particular province of study. Thus an association by bringing together men from various walks of life and engaging in different departments of study — men varied in their mental constitution and diverse in their habits and modes of thought, widens the sphere of observation to an extent altogether incalculable.

In examining the advantages offered by our society, I would by no means overlook the arena it presents for intellectual gladiatorship. In some respects the mind resembles some of the members of the body. Its energy and dexterity are both increased by exercise; and in no kind of exertion in which the mind is capable of enjoying does it find so great benefit as in collision of [the] mind. Much exertion it is contested is sometimes requisite to carry the works of some frowning proposition, and we occasionally find our patience, and our dexterity and acuteness too, heavily taxed to detect a subtle and specious written sophism — to strip it of its garb and to expose its hollowness and hypocrisy. But when in our opinion we have triumphed, the work is once and forever completed, and in the dethroned usurper at our feet we behold a trophy of our prowess. Wonderful victory! Frequently the mere maniac exultation of ignorance over its own folly, or the mad laugh of inanity at its own stolidity! Many such a visionary victory has no doubt quickened the pulse of the victor and circled a wreath of glory around his brow as he sat silently and complacently in his study!! A victory wrought in the field of actual combat may be, and frequently is, an altogether different thing from a victory achieved in the silent meditation of the study. In debate we encounter the living combatant, not the mere passive proposition. As anxious to defend as we are to overthrow, he parrays our blow and eludes its force — rapidly and dexterously changes his position, concentrates his whole force in the defense of the assailable points in his works, and frequently by an unexpected and furious sortie diverts our force and throws us on the defensive by becoming in his turn the assailant. "The mind of the controvertist," says an eloquent writer, "warmed and agitated is turned to every quarter." He explores the whole ground of debate, detects with readiness the weak points of an opposing argument and, like a skillful tactician, brings down upon them the whole pressure of his force.

It is to be regretted that, in the eager strife of debate, truth is too often forgotten in the anxiety for triumph. This is to be deplored; and it should become a maxim with every one to enter a discussion with no other design than to elicit truth, and to pursue it no further than the object demands. Frequent, protracted and violent struggles for the mere purpose of triumph — while at the same time our secret conviction is that truth lies on the opposite side — may operate to produce in our mind a deplorable confusion of ideas of the value of that which alone gives to victory its importance — namely truth. But after allowing to this and to every other objection which can be urged against debate and oral discourse all the force they are entitled to still, it must be conceded the benefits of such exercises are of the very first importance. It is a species of engagement in which the mind acquires dexterity of movement and elasticity of force, in which its faculty of perception is whetted and edged, and its facility of detecting differences and discovering analogies wonderfully increased. The enemy is met in the open field and grappled with hand to hand. The conspicuousness of the theatre, the gaze of congregated spectators, the fire of the eager eye and the hope of the approving award all combined, wakens in the mind an ardor and kindles in it an enthusiasm, and imparts to it an energy it can never hope to feel in the seclusion of the cloister. It is in these keen conflicts that the doublings and evasions of sophistry are unravelled and exposed, and specious and imposing paradoxes laid bare. It is in those shocks that the sparks of truth are pluck out.

It would seem proper that we should now glance — as all the time will allow us to do is merely glance — at some of the benefits resulting from a sound education, or from an improved, enlightened and disciplined mind.

I have already remarked that man is social being, and that in obedience to the law under which he is created he is everywhere found seeking the association of his kind. Convenience and utility have diversified their peculiar character in subordination to the great object of all which is the felicity and perfection of human nature. From these associations spring new and peculiar duties and obligations; and each political association, as a member of the great family of man, is reciprocally bound to all the others by the relation of a common nature, and to the discharge of the duties therefrom arising. The happiness of each individual of any association and as a consequence the felicity of the whole, will evermore be found in proportion to the fidelity with which each performs his appropriate duties and sustains his appropriate obligations. And when there is no defect in ability, it may be assumed as certain that each will faithfully perform his part in proportion as he is convinced of its personal utility. Ignorance is the hot-bed of vice, the rank and prolific soil in which most of the vices grow, which afflict society. It is the educated and disciplined mind that comprehends the whole system of duties, examines them in all their details, surveys them in all their relations and foresees the certain beneficial effect of their performance upon society. These are the subjects upon which the mind may expend all its force. Here is the element in which it may rise and soar and expatiate until it attains an angel's size, and an angel's elevation. For duty to our God[,] our neighbor and ourselves comprehend the sum of human obligation.

In the use of the term education however, I would not be misunderstood, and at the risk of taxing your patience a moment I must here explain myself.

I by no means use the term education in that sense in which it was used by the ancients and in which it is now used by many of the moderns. Holding the term in this sense you would, no doubt, confront me with many splendid exceptions, of both ancient and modern date. The present days present us with many unhappy instances of highly cultivated minds exerting a most disastrous influence upon the human family. And while it is acknowledged that no nation was more refined or highly cultivated than the Greeks, it will not be denied that none did less for the moral renovation of the world. The grand error of both the instances we have noticed here lies in this -- that while they pay all attention to mental cultivation, they entirely overlook man's moral nature or deplorably misconceive it. The ancients had, it is true, their ethics, their systems of morals. But having no certain first principles, firmly and authoritatively planted as a basis, the superstructures erected were insubstantial and insecure, and invariably yielded to the raging elements of unchastened human passions. Their systems were mere speculations, always vague, frequently contradictory and as numerous as their abettors. Modern sophists have assumed for disguise a more decent and unpretending title: They adopt for their motto the fitness of things, and which fitness we will find upon examination to depend entirely upon the taste of the writer.

I pass that numerous class of writers called novelists, to which the frivolity and sickly sentimentalism of the age pay such obsequious court and so much fulsome adulation, with the remark that while the mental vigor, close observation and commanding eloquence which some of them display are worthy of all admiration, their degenerate and licentious sentiments should be an inseparable barrier to their introduction into well ordered society. Many of Bulwar's most brilliant sentences are gilded infidelity and the production of Paul de Kock are gross licentiousness![416]

The education of which I speak regards man not only as an actor on the present scene, but relates to the whole duration of his being. It regards his future well being as dependent upon his present conduct, and it seeks to regulate his conduct accordingly. You will perceive then at once, that I entertain no sympathy for that system of education in which the principles inculcated in the bible have no place. Every such system is radically defective. Its teachings cannot penetrate into the depths of man's being — for as it is only in the moral nature that responsibilities are founded, so the only instruction that can permanently benefit him is that which enlightens his moral nature to sustain these obligations. To persuade men to do justly, love mercy, and walk humbly with God, should be the end of all instruction. Thus the education we recommend and advance is that which aims to prepare man for the duties of his station.

The advantages of sound education are so numerous that in adverting to them I know not scarcely where to begin. Not the least among them is the perennial source of pure and unsophisticated pleasure which it opens to the mind. The educated man is not wholly dependent on others for his happiness. His mind is already the repository of materials for which it is only necessary to make requisitions to rekindle the most delightful emotions. Images long since appropriated and treasured up in the storehouse of memory he has only to bring out, and by a skillful combination and arrangement, he can dispose them into endless forms to tempt and gratify the eye of contemplation. He needs not the living companion for instructive maxims and enlivening converse, not the living for example for incentive to action. In the voice of history he listens to the lessons of departed wisdom, while the recorded actions of departed virtue fans in his bosom the fire of a generous emulation. He can ascend to the infancy of nations, when abandoning the plains and forests where as individuals they roamed in all the wildness of an unrestrained freedom, they gradually coalesce into the form and compactness of political association -- contemplate them as they compose the elements and plant the basis of their future prosperity, move along with them as they advance step by step to their greatness, and look with interest and concern on the elements of destruction evolving in the working of their institutions, acquiring force with their expansion until they explode and scatter the nation to the winds. The pleasure derived from such contemplations are of a private character, the lessons deduced from them are of public utility.

The great destroyer of human institutions are the human passions. And human institutions have a wonderful effect in awakening the passions and in directing their movement, so that they contain a power of mutual generation and mutual destruction. That apparently simplest and certainly the most unstable of all forms of government, I mean a democracy, has been ever found among an ignorant people to be merely an expression of public impatience of control. The ferocity and licentiousness of opinion, the rage and rancor of party spirit -- the rapid struggle for place and power, the furious contention for spoil and the swarm of croaking demagogues which we ever find deforming such a constitution are alike its offspring and destroyer. The instability of this form of society and the evil resulting from it are undoubtedly owing to pride and ignorance, the high notions of natural equality — which in themselves are just, and ignorance of duty. This system awakens the passions, and ignorance arms them with fury. Enlighten the people, let them be no longer the dupes of unprincipled political blacklegs, and this system — which is now everywhere the symbol of strife and confusion — may become in practice, what it certainly is in theory: the most just and beautiful of all systems. Without deciding upon the claims of any particular form of government (which I by no means regard myself able to do), I feel at liberty to remark that, under all, ignorance is the great enemy of human happiness and human liberty, but that under none can a people be either unhappy or oppressed who are acquainted alike with their rights and their duties. The education of a people, then, should be an object of primary importance, as upon it depends in a very great degree their own happiness and the stability of their institutions.

Gentlemen, we have fallen on momentous times. We have been as asleep -- but, in the midst of pleasing dreams, we are aroused by the din of battle and the clanging trumpet calling us to arms.

Our position is of all positions the most difficult to describe -- it is altogether anomalous, and to the last degree perplexing. We have hitherto enjoyed privileges and exercised rights by sufferance under the patronage of the American Colonization Society. Up to the present period our colony and everything connected with it have been too insignificant to tempt the cupidity or call forth the opposition of foreign nations. The days of our infancy are passing away: A little one has become a thousand and a strong one a great nation; or, to drop the figure, the word Liberia begins to be heard abroad as a name designating a place whence valuable articles of commerce are exported, and which may at no distant day become a still wider door for the introduction of foreign production into Africa, and for the passage of African production into foreign countries. These considerations have no doubt prompted the question "Tell us by what authority thou dost these things." It were idle to enter on the discussion of right abstractedly or speculatively considered. Such arguments have no force with the selfish generations of the present day. We must conform at once to the maxims and settled usages of the world. We must define our rights and assume their correlative responsibilities. We must prepare to retain the one and demand the other. Imposing task, momentous enterprise. Imposing and momentous however as it may be, there is no discharge from this war except to certain death. Like the wanderers from Samaria, we shall find it certain death to remain here or to return to the city. Hope can be indulged only in going forward. Let us then not falter, because to falter is to yield. Let us fix our eye upon the prize and advance steadily toward it. It is a grand and noble object and worthy of the consecration of our entire time and talent. In the struggle union is strength. Let us sink all minor and personal differences in a general concern for the public good. Let all our feelings and all our sympathies be of a public character. Let there be perfect harmony in design, perfect unity in action, confident that the true interest of one is the true interest of all. Gentlemen, the present generation must not, cannot live for itself. It lives for generations yet to come. To lay broad and deep the foundations of the social edifice, to equal it in all its fair proportions to the generation that succeeds us would be an honor which no other age has witnessed and none but us can hope to enjoy. Rising to a full perception of the work to be accomplished and surveying with a steady eye the field around us, let us buckle on our armor for the conflict. "Every battle of the warrior is with confused noise and garments rolled in blood, but this is a keener, a moral conflict, a contest in which truth marshalls her legions against error, humanity against avarice and oppression, a contest in which the genius of our holy religion grapples with the powers of darkness."[417] Humanity is on our side -- and on our side are truth, morality and religion and all their influences. And God himself is on our side, and if God be for us who can be against us. Ye men of Liberia prove yourselves worthy of these holy alliances. Abandon your dissension -- forget your personal differences. Let there be but one heart and one throb in that heart, and one head and one design in that head. By order and decorum in our social intercourse, by a prompt excision of every excess, by ready submission to wholesome regulations, by a cherished goodwill for all God's rational creatures and by undue partiality for none -- by an entire system of well-appointed and well-sustained institutions under which justice tempered with mercy shall be equally meted to all, by our respect for constituted authority both here and abroad, by order, industry and virtue let us prove ourselves worthy of the booty we ask -- a name, a home, a place in the land of the living. Then pleading we shall be successful, and Liberia shall live before God and before the nations of the earth and become the focus where the rays of light emanating from other lands shall meet: hence they shall go out, diverging in every direction as they fly, piercing the darkness which for ages like a sable pall has mantled the generations of our fatherland until liberty and law and religion and love shall kindle a blaze of glory in this benighted land.

98. Anniversary speech, 1 December 1846

Fellow citizens,[418]

As far back towards the infancy of our race, as history and tradition are able to conduct us, we have found the custom every where prevailing among mankind, to mark, by some striking exhibition, those events which were important and interesting, either in their immediate bearing, or in their remote consequences upon the destiny of those among whom they occurred. These events are epochs in the history of man — they mark the rise and fall of kingdoms and of dynasties — they record the movements of the human mind, and the influence of those movements upon the destinies of the race; and whilst they frequently disclose to us the sad and sickening spectacle of innocence bending under the weight of injustice, and of weakness robbed and despoiled by the hand of an unscrupulous oppression; they occasionally display, as a theme for admiring contemplation, the sublime spectacle of the human mind, roused by a concurrence of circumstances, to vigorous advances in the career of improvement. To trace the operations of these circumstances from their first appearance, as effects from the workings of the human passions, until, as a cause, they revert with combined and concentrated energy upon those minds from which they at first evolved, would be at once a most interesting and difficult task; and, let it be borne in mind, requires far higher ability and more varied talent than he possesses who this day has the honour to address you.

The utility of thus marking the progress of time — of recording the occurrence of events — and of holding up remarkable personages to the contemplation of mankind, is too obvious to need remark. It arises from the instincts of mankind — the irrepressible spirit of emulation — and the ardent longings after immortality; and this restless passion to perpetuate their existence, which they find it impossible to suppress, impels them to secure the admiration of succeeding generations in the performance of deeds, by which, although dead, they may yet speak. In commemorating events thus powerful in forming the manners and sentiments of mankind, and in rousing them to strenuous exertion and to high and sustained emulation, it is obvious that such, and such only should be selected as virtue and humanity would approve; and that, if any of an opposite character be held up, they should be displayed only as beacons, or as a towering Pharos,[419] throwing a strong but lurid light to mark the melancholy grave of mad ambition, and to warn the inexperienced voyager of the existing danger.

Thanks to the improved and humanised spirit — or, should I not rather say, the chastened and pacific civilization of the age in which we live,— that laurels gathered upon the field of mortal strife, and bedewed with the tears of the Widow and the Orphan, are regarded now, not with admiration but with horror — that the armed warrior, reeking with the gore of murdered thousands, who, in the age that is just passing away, would have been hailed with noisy acclamation by the senseless crowd, is now regarded only as the savage commissioner of an unsparing oppression, or at best as the ghostly executioner of an unpitying justice. — He who would embalm his name in the grateful remembrance of coming generations — he who would secure for himself a niche in the temple of undying fame — he who would hew out for himself a monument of which his country may boast — he who would entail upon heirs a name which they may be proud to wear, must seek some other field than that of battle as the theatre of his exploits.

Still, we honour the heroes of the age that has passed. No slander can tarnish their hard-earned fame — no morbid sentimentalism sully their peerless glory — no mean detraction abate the disinterestedness of their conduct. They bowed to the spirit of the age: and, acting up to the light afforded them, they yielded to the dictates of an honest conscience. While assembled here to-day, on this festal occasion, to commemorate the event for which the founders of our infant Republic toiled, and fought, and bled, we seem to behold the forms of the departed ones mingling in our assembly: we seem to behold them taking their seats by the side of their venerable compeers yet spared among us: watching with intense anxiety the emotions which agitate our bosoms, and marking the character of the resolves which the occasion is ripening. Rest in peace, ye venerable shades! And ye, their living representatives —

calm be the evening of your days. We honour you. And though no sculptured marble transmit your fame, a nobler monument shall be yours — the happy hearts of unborn millions shall be the shrine in which your names will be treasured. In your high example — in your noble disinterestedness — in your entire subordination of every thought, and act, and scheme, and interest, to the heaven-born purpose of human regeneration and human elevation, we hear the language of encouragement.

Fellow citizens, — on this occasion, so big with subjects of profitable meditation — when it is so natural that the mind should oscillate between the events of the past and the prospects of the future, we can conceive of nothing more proper than the enquiry, how we can best execute the solemn trust committed to our hand — how we may challenge and secure the admiration and the gratitude of a virtuous and a happy prosperity, by transmitting to them the patrimony received from our fathers, not only in all its original entireness, but in vastly augmented beauty[,] order, and strength. In a word, how we may best conduct ourselves so as to incite them to high and sustained exertion in the cause of virtue and humanity.

In order to impress your minds with the propriety of this enquiry, there is, I trust, no need that I shall remind you of the peculiarity of our condition. It will suffice that I remark, that, should you succeed in rearing upon the foundation already laid, — or, to drop the figure — should you succeed in establishing a community of virtuous, orderly, intelligent, and industrious citizens, this very peculiarity must enter largely into every consideration on the amount of praise to which you shall be held entitled.

Let us, then, for a moment look back, that from the events of the past we may derive hope for the future.

We have not yet numbered twenty-six years since he who is the oldest colonist amongst us was the inhabitant — not the citizen — of a country — and that too the country of his birth — where the prevailing sentiment is, that he and his race are incapacitated, by an inherent defect in their mental constitution, to enjoy that greatest of all blessings, and to exercise that greatest of all rights, bestowed by a beneficent God upon his rational creatures — namely, the government of themselves. Acting upon this opinion — an opinion as false as it is foul — acting upon this opinion, as upon a self-evident proposition, those who held it proceeded with a fiendish consistency to deny the rights of citizens to those whom they had declared incapable of performing the duties of citizens. It is not necessary, and therefore I will not disgust you with the hideous picture of that state of things which followed upon the prevalence of this blasphemous opinion. The bare mention that such an

Carl Patrick Burrowes

opinion prevailed would be sufficient to call up in the mind, even of those who had never witnessed its operation, images of the most sickening and revolting character. Under the iron reign of this crushing sentiment, most of us who are assembled here to-day drew our first breath and sighed away the years of our youth. No hope cheered us: no noble object looming in the dim and distant future kindled our ambition. Oppression — cold, cheerless oppression, like the dreary region of an eternal winter, chilled every noble passion and fettered and paralysed every arm. And if among the oppressed millions there were found here and there one in whose bosom the last glimmer of a generous passion was not yet extinguished — one, who, from the midst of the inglorious slumbers in the deep degradation around him, would lift his voice and demand those rights which the God of nature hath bestowed in equal gift upon all His rational creatures, he was met at once by those who had at first denied and then enforced, with the stern reply, that for him and for all his race — Liberty and Expatriation are inseparable.

Dreadful as the alternative was — fearful as was the experiment now proposed to be tried, there were hearts equal to the task — hearts which quailed not at the dangers which loomed and frowned in the distance, but calm, cool, and fixed in their purpose, prepared to meet them with the watchword — Give me liberty or give me death.

On the 6th day of February, in the year of Our Lord One Thousand Eight Hundred and Twenty, the ship *Elizabeth* cast loose from her moorings at New York, and on the 8th day of March, of the same year, the pilgrims first beheld the land of their fathers, the cloud-capped mountains of Sierra Leone, and cast anchor in that harbour. A few days afterwards they again weighed anchor, stood to the south, and debarked upon the low and deadly island of Sherbro. On the character of those who formed her noble company, I deem it unnecessary to remark. They are sufficiently commended to our esteem, as being the first to encounter the difficulties and to face the dangers of an enterprise, which, we trust, is to wipe away from us the reproach of ages — to silence the calumny of those who abuse us, and to restore to Africa her long-lost glory. I need not detain you with a narrative of their privations and sufferings: nor will I stop to tell you — though it would be a pleasing task to do so — with what happy hearts they greeted a reinforcement of pilgrims who joined them in 1821, by the *Nautilus*. Passing by intermediate events, which, did the time allow, it would be interesting to notice, we hasten to that grand event — that era of our separate existence, the 25th day of April, in the year of Grace 1822, when the American flag first threw out its graceful folds to the breeze on the heights of

Mesurado, and the pilgrims, relying upon the protection of Heaven and the moral grandeur of their cause, took solemn possession of the land in the name of virtue, humanity, and religion.

It would discover an unpardonable apathy, were we to pass on without pausing a moment to reflect upon the emotions which heaved the bosoms of the pilgrims, when they stood for the first time where we now stand. What a prospect spread out before them! They stood in the midst of an ancient wilderness, rank and compacted by the growth of a thousand years, unthinned and unreclaimed by a single stroke of the woodman's axe. Few and far between might be found inconsiderable openings, where the ignorant native erected his rude habitation, or, savage as his patrimonial wilderness, celebrated his bloody rites, and presented his votive gifts, to Demons. Already the late proprietors of the soil had manifested unequivocal symptoms of hostility, and an intention to expel the strangers, as soon as an opportunity to do so should be presented. The rainy season, that terrible ordeal of foreign constitutions, was about setting in; the lurid lightning shot its fiery bolt into the forest around them; the thunder muttered its angry tones over their head; and the frail tenements, the best which their circumstances would afford, to shield them from a scorching sun by day and drenching rains at night, had not yet been completed. To suppose that at this time, when all things above and around them seemed to combine their influences against them, to suppose they did not perceive the full danger and magnitude of the enterprise they had embarked in, would be to suppose, not that they were heroes, but that they had lost the sensibility of men. True courage is equally remote from blind recklessness and unmanning timidity; and true heroism does not consist in insensibility to danger. He is a hero who calmly meets, and fearlessly grapples the dangers which duty and honour forbid him to decline. The pilgrims rose to a full perception of all the circumstances of their condition. But when they looked back to that country from which they had come out, and remembered the degradations in that house of bondage out of which they had been so fortunate as to escape, they bethought themselves; and, recollecting the high satisfaction with which they knew success would gladden their hearts, the rich inheritance they would entail upon their children, and the powerful aid it would lend to the cause of universal humanity, they yielded to the noble inspiration and girded them to the battle, either for doing or for suffering.

Let is not be supposed, because I have laid universal humanity under a tribute of gratitude to the founders of Liberia, that I have attached to their humble achievements too important an influence, in that grand system of agencies which is now at work, renovating human society, and purifying and enlarging the sources of its enjoyment. In the system of that Almighty Being, without whose notice not a sparrow falls to the ground:

"Who sees with equal eye, as God of all,
A hero perish, or a sparrow fall:
Atoms or systems into ruin hurled,
And now a bubble burst, and now a world;"[420]

In the system of the Almighty One, no action of a mortal being is unimportant. Every action of every rational creature hath its assigned place in his system of operations, and is made to hear, however undersigned by the agent, with force upon the end which His wisdom and goodness have in view to accomplish.

On the morning of the 1st day of December, in the year of Our Lord One Thousand Eight Hundred and twenty-two; on that morning, just when the gloom of night was retiring before the advancing light of day, the portentous cloud which had been some time rising upon the horizon of Liberia, increasing and gathering blackness as it advanced, filling all hearts with fearful apprehension, burst upon the Colony with the force of a tornado. The events of that day have marked it as the most conspicuous in our annals, and it is the anniversary of that day we are here assembled to celebrate.

And what fellow citizens are the particular circumstances of that most eventful day which more than others awaken our exultation? On which one amongst them all is our attention most intensely fixed? Is it on that our fathers fought, and fought bravely, and strewed the ensanguined plain with the dead bodies of their savage assailants? Is it on the bloody lesson of their superiority which they taught them in the hoarse thunder of the murderous cannon? Is it on that greater skill they displayed in the inglorious art of slaughter and death? I trust not. These trophies of their valour serve not to awaken exultation, but to call up a sigh of regret. It was as the possessors of far higher and nobler virtues they desired to be remembered; as such we tenderly cherish the remembrance of them; and to exult over the fallen foe would be to grieve the pure spirit of those by whose arm the savage fell. Necessity, stern necessity, unsheathed their sword and forced upon them an alternative from which all the feelings of their heart turned with instinctive recoil.

But there is a circumstance connected with the events of that day, with which our hearts cannot be too deeply impressed, as it will serve, on each appropriate occasion, as a check upon presumption and an antidote against despair. Think upon the number of the assailants, and compare it with the number of the assailed, and then say whether any scepticism short of downright, unblushed Atheism, can doubt the interposition, in the events of that day, of an overruling Providence. Most emphatically does the issue of that contest declare "The battle is not to the strong." The Lord was a shield around them, so that when their foes rose up against them, they stumbled and fell. To the interposition of an ever-gracious Providence, manifested in no ordinary way, we owe the privileges and pleasure of this day.

At this epoch we date the establishment of the Colony.

Having sustained and repulsed every external attack, and maintained its ground against the combined and concentrated forces of the country, it had now to commence its onward career. If there were any, who, because the colonists had repulsed the natives, supposed they had passed the greatest danger, and overcome the most formidable obstacles; they gave, in this very supposition, evidence of a deplorable ignorance of human nature and of human history. It is from within, that the elements of national overthrow have most commonly evolved: and the weakness under which nations expire, generally results from disease of the national heart. Luxury and ambition, oppression on the one side and insubordination on the other; these are the fatal elements which, with more than volcanic force, rend to atoms the fabric of human institutions. A common danger, a danger equally menacing all, is almost sure to sink every minor and merely personal consideration, and to be met by a combination of energy, concentration of effort, and unity of action: and in proportion as the pressure of the danger is great, will there be want of scope for those passions which, in a certain class, possess such fearful and disorganising potency.

From the period of their landing, up to the moment of which have just spoken, all minds had been possessed by an undefined apprehension of impending danger, and the first and the constant lesson which their critical position inculcated upon them was Union and Subordination. The pressure was now taken off, the angry cloud had now passed away, the heavens shone bright and clear, the face of nature was calm and placid, and on every breeze was wafted the fragrance from the surrounding groves. All breathed freely. Each one had time to look around him, to contemplate with calmness and composure the circumstances of his condition, and to select that particular mode of operation, and line of conduct, which was most congenial with his disposition. All were free -- All were equal. Here was unbounded scope for the operation of the passions. Will they, who have been declared incapable of enjoying liberty without running into the wildest excesses of anarchy — Will they, now the gift is enjoyed in its largest extent, restrain themselves within the bounds of a rational and virtuous freedom? Will they connect those two ideas which are at one and the same time the base and the summit of all just political theories, and which can never be separated? Will their liberty be tempered by just and wholesome law? Is it to be expected that a people just set free from the chains of the most abject oppression and slavery, can be otherwise than turbulent, insubordinate, and impatient of the least restraint? Is it among the things to be hoped, that they into whose minds the idea of political action had not been allowed to enter, will not, now political power is entrusted to their hands, rush into the wildest extremes of crude legislation?

Fellow Citizens! the voice of twenty-four years this day gives the answer; and we are assembled to hear it, and let those who abuse us hear it; let them hear it and be for ever silent, when they hear that Liberty regulated by Law, and Religion free from Superstition, form the foundation of which rests the cement which unites, and the ornament which beautifies, our political and social edifice.

Let us now turn from those who preceded us, and ask, What are the peculiar obligations which rest upon us: what the particular duties to which we are called? Let us not suppose, that because we are not called upon to drive the invading native from our door — that because we can lie down at night without fear — because the savage war-whoop does not now ring upon the midnight air, — therefore we have nothing to do. No mistake can be more fatal. Ours is a moral fight. It is a keener warfare, a sharper conflict.

For after indulging to the utmost allowed extent in hyperbolical expression and figurative declamation, still we are forced to confess, the work is but just commenced. The nervous arm of our predecessor marked out the site, and laid the foundation, and reared the walls, of the edifice. The scaffold is still around it. It is ours to mount it — to commence where they ended, and to conduct it on towards a glorious completion. How shall we execute our trust — how shall we conduct ourselves so as to stand acquitted before the bar of coming generations, and obtain from them a favorable and an honourable verdict? By what means shall we secure and perpetuate our own prosperity, and transmit it an inheritance to our children? These are questions which seem peculiarly appropriate to this interesting occasion. And let me congratulate you, fellow-citizens, that you have the experience of others to guide you. The art of government is now elevated to the dignity of a science. The most gifted minds — minds which do honour to human nature, have long been turned to the subject: and maxims and propositions which, consecrated by time, had grown into the strength of axioms — maxims which had obtained universal assent and universal application — maxims which would have overwhelmed him who should have doubted them, with more than sacrilegious turpitude and sent him to atone for his presumption upon the scaffold, or in the gloomy depths of a dungeon — maxims the legitimate offspring of ignorance and oppression, have been successfully explored and the human mind disenthralled. That more than magical phrase, in the hand of the despot, "the divine rights of kings," has lost its power to charm; and frequent examinations into the foundations of society have at length taught men the interesting truth, that the duties and rights of magistrate and subject are correlate — that government is made for the people, and not the people for the government: thus establishing the eternal truth first enunciated in the Declaration of American Independence, "That all men are free and equal." The bare utterance of those ever-memorable words, by the immortal Jefferson, whilst it struck the fetters from the human mind, and sent it bounding on it a career of improvement, wrested the sceptre from the tyrant's hand and dissolved his throne beneath him. "Magna est veritas et prœvalebit."[421] Truth threw a strong and steady light where there was naught but darkness before: man beheld his dignity and his rights, and prepared to demand the one and sustain the other. But I return. By what means shall we advance our prosperity?

The first requisite, to permanent advancement, if I may so speak, is order. Order is heaven's first law. It is this which imparts stability to human institutions, because, while like the laws of nature it restrains each one in his proper sphere, it leaves all to operate freely and without disturbance. Here will be no jostling. When I say order, I mean not to restrict the term to the ordinary occupations of life; I extend the word to mean, a strict and conscientious submission to established law. It is said to be the boast of that form of government under which we live, that no man, however high in office, can violate with impunity the sacred trust committed to his hand, and long insult the people by trampling upon their rights: that the distinguishing excellence of a republican form of government is, that, under it, oppression can have no place. This opinion I am not disposed to combat; but as it is a fact, that a safe and constitutional remedy for all grievances of this kind is in the hands of the people, this circumstance alone should dispose every one to submit, for a time, to some inconvenience rather than apply a rash and violent corrective. I admit, there are cases in which the minions of office become so intoxicated with a little brief power — that, forgetting all men are free and possess certain constitutional privileges, and forgetting also, that they were elevated to office not to be oppressors but conservators, their haughty, vexatious, and oppressive conduct, becomes intolerable. In such cases as these, let the strong indignation of an outraged public, calmly but firmly expressed, awaken the dreamer from his vision of greatness, and send him back to re-enact his dream in his original obscurity.

Another argument for order and subordination lies in the fact, that the laws are in the hands of the people. Legislators are not elevated to office for their private emolument and honour, but for the nobler purpose of advancing and securing the happiness of their constituents: and they are bound — by the most solemn considerations — they are bound, to enact such laws, and such laws only, as are suited to the genius and circumstances of the people. If they betray the high trust committed to them, and enact laws either oppressive or partial, the corrective is equally in the hands of the people. They have only to apply the constitutional remedy. Here, then, is no apology for disorder. Order, then, must be our rule; for without subordination, and prompt and constant and conscientious obedience to wholesome law, there can be no security for person nor property. The bands of society would be untwisted, and the whole fabric exposed to ruin on the first popular outbreak. Be it, then, fellow-citizens, our first concern to sustain our officers in the proper discharge of their constitutional duties; to secure obedience to the laws, and to preserve them from violation with the same jealousy with which we watch the first encroachment of power.

I observe in the second place that union among ourselves is absolutely necessary to prosperity. The idea of prosperity and stability where disunion reigns, where the elements of discord are actively at work; the idea of prosperity and stability, in such circumstances, can only serve to mislead. Can that army, in which faction triumphs among the soldiers and disunion and jealousy distract the counsels of the officers, hope to succeed in a campaign? Where each is afraid of the other, where no one has confidence in any, where every one regards every other one with feelings not only of jealousy but of positive hostility, how can there be any hope to bring an unbroken front to bear with undivided force upon any single point? I would observe also, that the complexion of the soldiers' mind will be sure to be tinged by that of their officers. In every community there will be found some few to whom the mass will look up with unenquiring deference. Mankind generally are averse to the labour of thinking. This circumstance separates those who should be very friends, and men file off under different leaders as fancy or caprice may dictate. Each party ranges itself under the banner of a leader whom it invests with all perfection of political sagacity and political integrity. To his semi-brutal followers his word is law; his decisions an oracle. *Finding* in him every attribute of perfection they abandon the reins to his hand; yield up the glorious privileges of thinking and examining, and prepare to follow with a blind and implicit obedience. This unworthy abandonment of the public interests, this surrender of a privilege to which every man is born, and which every man should exercise, is the capital of intriguing politicians and unprincipled political demagogues. And, let me ask you, fellow-citizens, what scheme, however mad and absurd, which has been set on foot by these unprincipled leaders, has not had among the masses its advocates and adherents? Bad, however, as human nature is, alluring and fascinating as are the glitter and privilege of place and power, this confidence has not been always abused. We could easily point out instances, in which the influence which this disposition we have been adverting to has given to men, has been exerted wholly and exclusively for the public good. But we must take human nature as we find it; and as we find this disposition every where prevalent, the duty becomes imperative on all who have influence, to exert it for the public good. The root of the jealousies and divisions among public men will, generally speaking, be found planted in the soil of selfishness and ambition: not in any real and sincere disagreement as to the proper measures for the public good. This, I admit, is always the avowed, the ostensible, but I am bold to say, not the real cause.

It is envy of place and emolument — it is ambition of power, that array public men in a hostile attitude, and range their infatuated followers under their opposing banners. In the infancy of our political existence, let those amongst us who have credit with the people and influence over them, beware of so great infatuation. Let us recollect, that all cannot govern: that from the division and order into which society naturally resolves itself, all even of those who are worthy, cannot stand in the foremost ranks. Let us remember, that we equally serve our country, whether we sit in the gubernatorial or presidential chair; whether we deliberate in the Hall of the Legislature or preside in the sanctuary of Justice; that we equally serve our country, whether from the shades of cloistered retirement we send forth wholesome maxims for public instruction, or in the intercourse of our daily life we set an attracting example of obedience to the laws; that we equally serve our country, whether from the sacred desk we inculcate lessons of celestial wisdom, exhibit the sanctions of a heaven-descended religion and hurl the thunders of an incensed Jehovah, or in the nursery of learning unfold the mysteries and display the glories of science, recall and reenact the deeds and the achievements of the past, and call back upon the stage the heroes, the patriots, and the sages of antiquity, to kindle the ardor[,] nerve the virtue, awaken the patriotism, elevate and purify the sentiment, and expand the mind, of the generous and aspiring youth. Humble as many of those offices of which I have spoken are esteemed to be, — obscure and concealed from vulgar gaze and destitute of the trappings are, it is, nevertheless, fellow-citizens, not within the reach of our judgment to determine which one of them exerts the greatest influence on the destinies of our race. True dignity, and, I may add, true usefulness, depend not so much upon the circumstances of office as upon the faithful discharge of appropriate duties.

Honour and fame from no condition rise;
Act well your part — there all true honour lies.

He who does the best his circumstances allow,
Does well, acts nobly: Angels could do no more. [422]

It is the false notion of honour which has unhappily possessed the minds of men, placing all dignity in the pageantry of state and the tinsel of office, which produces those collisions, jostlings, and acrimony of contending factions which sometimes shake the fabric of society to its very foundations: it is by the maddening influence of this false notion that men, whose claim to respectful notoriety is inversely as their desire to be conspicuous, are sometimes urged to abandon their obscure but appropriate position in the line, and to rush into the foremost ranks. When men shall have learned wherein true honour lies — when men shall have formed correct ideas of true and sober dignity, then we shall have formed correct ideas of true and sober dignity, then we shall see all the ranks of society united as by a golden chain — then Ephraim shall not envy Judah, nor Judah vex Ephraim; — then the occupant of the palace and he of the cottage — then the man in lawn and the man in rags will, like the parts of a well-adjusted machine, act in perfect unison. Considering, then, the influence which in every community a few men are found to possess — considering, also, that each one of these influential men is sure to be followed by a party, we can hardly appreciate the obligation which rests upon them, to abandon all jealousies and suspicions — to merge every private and personal consideration in thoughts for the public good — and to bring a mind free from envy and untrammelled by party predilection to a solemn deliberation on the great objects of public utility.

The education of our youth is the next subject to which I would direct your attention. "Knowledge is power" — is an old proverb — but not the less true because it is old. This is the spring that regulates the movements of society — this is at once the lever and the safety-valve of human institutions. Without it society will either not move at all, or, like an unbalanced, unhelmed ship move in a direction and at a rate that must eventually destroy it. Education corrects vice — cures disorders — abates jealousies — adorns virtue — commands the winds — triumphs over the waves — scales the heavens. In a word, education lays all nature under tribute, and forces her to administer to the comfort and happiness of man. Nor is this all that education does. It ennobles and elevates the mind, and urges the soul upward and animates it to deeds of high and lasting renown. Education opens sources of pure[,] refined, and exquisite enjoyment — it unlocks the temple of nature, and admits the awe-stricken soul, to behold and admire the wondrous works of God. An ignorant, vicious[,] idle community has the elements of destruction already in its bosom. On the very first application of a torch they will explode and lay the whole fabric in ruins. A virtuous, orderly, educated people, have all the elements of national greatness and national perpetuity. — Would we be happy at home and respected abroad, we must educate our youth.

In professing to notice those things which are necessary to our prosperity — to the advancement of our prosperity, and the perpetuity of our prosperity, it is natural that you should expect that agriculture industry will be brought prominently into view. I think it may be safely affirmed, that the virtue and independence of a people will be inversely as their attention is wholly given to commerce — that their virtue and independence is evermore to be measured by their pursuits of the wholesome and pleasing and primitive employment of agriculture and husbandry. Go into the countries of Europe — examine their large manufacturing and commercial towns and cities. Then visit the rural, agricultural districts — compare the quiet, tranquillity, order, virtue, plenty of the latter, with the bustle, confusion, vice, and general dependence and poverty of the other, and you cannot fail to be struck, and deeply affected, by the frightful contrast. And wherefore? Is not commerce called the great civiliser of the world? Is it not the means by which nations become acquainted and hold communion with each other? Is it not by this means that the great and master-minds of one nation commune with kindred minds of other nations? Is it not the channel through which improvements in art, in science, in literature, in all that adorns, dignifies, and enables human nature, flow as on the wings of the wind from country to country? Grant it. It is not my purpose to pronounce a wholesale anathema upon commerce. I appreciate its high importance in improving our race. It is excess I would discourage — it is the wretched deteriorating influence it will exert upon a people, when, by adsorbing their whole attention, it keeps them looking constantly abroad to the neglect of the improvement of their own country. It is to this I would call your attention. Again: — Let it not be forgotten, that if commerce imports improvements, it imports vices also. It offers the same facility for the transmission of both. The same vessel that brings us the Book of God brings us also the Age of Reason — and in one and the same ship, we not unfrequently find the devoted self-sacrificing missionary, and that accursed thing which a celebrated orator with characteristic energy has styled "liquid fire and distilled damnation."

In the natural, or, more properly, vegetable world, we have sometimes seen exotics outstripping in rapidity of growth the natural spontaneous productions of the soil. In this we have not a very unhappy illustration of the rank growth of imported vices. These baneful exotics, grafted on the tree of indigenous corruption, seem to receive and impart unwonted vigour from the contact: and the result is, a fruit of the most disorganising potency. An examination into the moral state of towns and districts, wholly given to commerce and manufactures, will fully sustain this remark. How, let me ask you, can there be order, where the very nature of the pursuits which engross all minds demand ceaseless hurry [,] bustle, and confusion? — Where to stop to breathe is to be at once outdone, and where he who can move the most swiftly amid the greatest confusion is thought to be the smartest man! In respect of virtue, — Is it to be thought of, except for the purpose of holding it up to ridicule, in a place where the vicious of all countries meet; and where females of every class and character, far from the watchful eye of parental solicitude, are huddled together in one promiscuous throng, and dependent for their daily bread upon the freaks and fancies of unprincipled employers! Lowell, in America, is, I believe, the only large manufacturing town where virtue is held in the least esteem. What shall I say of honesty and integrity, where the lowest, basest arts, are practised for gain; where all is intrigue and circumvention — where the maxim prevails, "all is fair in trade" — where each regards the other as lawful game — where one can gain only by the loss of the other — where, in a word, rascality is fair-play, and [villainy] systematic; where, fellow-citizens, let me ask you, where, in such a community, is there room for honesty? Can the heart fail, in such circumstances, to become deadened to every feeling of humanity — steeled against every kindly, generous, and ennobling impulse? I will not venture to affirm, that the result we have just now noticed is universal. I admit, with pleasure, there are honourable exceptions — but I do affirm, that what I have said forms the general rule.

But let us turn from these scenes of noise and smoke and deep depravity, and visit the quiet abode of the farmer and the husbandman. What tranquillity reigns here, and order, and peace, and virtue!! Behold the farmer, as he goes forth in the morning to this daily task; — how firm and elastic his step; how cheerful his sun-burnt countenance; how active his athletic arm!! Behold how cheerfully he labors; how the fat valleys around him laugh with corn; how the spacious plains teem with grain, and the ancient forests fall beneath his resounding axe!!! Follow him, when the labor of the day is over; follow him to his humble home. See him surrounded by an affectionate, industrious, frugal wife, unsophisticated by the vices and dissipations of the fashionable world, and by a prattling progeny blooming in health, and big with promise of future usefulness. No cankering cares gnaw his peaceful bosom; no uncertain speculation disturbs his quiet slumbers; no revolutions in foreign lands, damming up the channels of trade, cloud the calm serenity of his brow. Oh! if there be a spot on earth, where true happiness is to be found, here is that spot.

But we take a higher and a more extended view of this subject, and regard it in its bearing on political economy. And my first remark is, that no nation can be independent which subsists wholly by commerce. And here let it be observed, once for all, that I use the word independent in a sense altogether distinct from sovereignty. I admit that there may be a temporary prosperity; that so long as peace prevails amongst nations connected by commercial and diplomatic relations, — so long as each acts in perfect faith, and maintains in all their entireness and in all their integrity his treaty stipulations, there may not be felt a want of the necessaries or even of the luxuries of life. There may, perhaps, be a large influx of the precious metals. Nothing, however, could be more fallacious, than to regard this activity as an indication of independence or permanent prosperity. For I remark, in the second place, that so uncertain are the operations of trade — so suddenly are its channels and outlets closed by misunderstandings and ruptures between rival nations — so liable is it to paralysing shocks from intriguing cabinets and wily politicians[,] the operations of one year scarcely afford any ground for conjecture in regard to the operations of the next. Let us illustrate our position by an humble supposition.

Suppose the surrounding country should suddenly relent [and] throw wide its doors, and shake its teeming wealth of gold and ivory and wood and dye into our lap — and the native African patient of labor and of travel, should supply us at the most accommodating rates with all the coarser food for our consumption: Suppose vessels should flock, as under such circumstances vessels would most assuredly flock, to our shores, offering us in exchange for the produce thus liberally poured in upon us, the conveniences, elegances, and luxuries of foreign countries. Suppose every man desert his farm, and betake himself to trading as the more easy and the more speedy road to wealth. There would certainly be great activity and great prosperity. But would we be independent. One more supposition, and the important and interesting problem is solved. Suppose the paths to the interior are

Carl Patrick Burrowes

suddenly blocked up by feuds among the tribes; all ingress cut off and trade suspended. Where, then, are our supplies? Should we be able to return to our farms, and draw thence articles of exchange with foreign nations? By no means. In the mania for trade our farms have been deserted, and like the land on which [a] curse rests have long laid fallow. Think you fellow citizens that our trade once gone, we should again behold the French, the Bremen,[423] the American, and the English flag floating to the breeze in our harbour. From that hour you might bid a long adieu to every white face but that of a missionary. Fellow Citizens! our prosperity and independence are to be drawn from the soil. That is the highway to honour, to wealth, to private and national prosperity.

Liberians! do not disdain the humble occupation! It commends itself to our attention ennobled and sanctified by the example of our Creator. "And the Lord planted a garden eastward in Eden; and there he put the man whom he had formed. And out of the ground made the Lord God to grow every tree that is pleasant to the sight, and good for food. [..] And the Lord God took the man and put him into the garden of Eden, to dress it and to keep it."[424] Never, never, until this degenerate age, has this simple[,] primitive[,] patriarchal occupation been despised.

> In ancient times, the sacred plough employed.
> The kings and awful fathers of mankind;
> And some, with whom compared your insect tribes
> Are but the beings of a summer's day,
> Have held the scale of empires, ruled the storm
> Of mighty war; then, with unwearied hand,
> Disdaining little delicacies, seized
> The plough, and greatly independent lived.[425]

Thus sings the author of the Seasons, one of Britain's sweetest bards.

The last remark time will allow me to make under this head, is, that "Righteousness exalteth a nation; but sin is a reproach to any people."[426] All attempts to correct the depravity of man, to stay the head-long propensity to vice — to abate the madness of ambition, will be found deplorably inefficient, unless we apply the restrictions and the tremendous sanctions of religion. A profound regard and deference upon God, and of our obligation and accountability to Him; an ever-present, ever-pressing sense of His universal and all-controlling providence, this, and only this, can give energy to the arm of law, cool the raging fever of the passions, and abate the lofty pretensions of mad ambition. In prosperity, let us bring out our thank-offering, and present it with cheerful hearts in orderly, virtuous, and religious conduct. In adversity, let us consider, confess our sins, and abase ourselves before the throne of God. In danger, let us go to Him, whose prerogative it is to deliver; let us go to Him, with the humility and confidence which a deep conviction that the battle is not to the strong nor the race to the swift, is calculated to inspire.

Fellow citizens! we stand now on ground never occupied by a people before. However insignificant we may regard ourselves, the eyes of Europe and America are upon us, as a germ, destined to burst from its enclosure in the earth, unfold its petals to the genial air, rise to the height and swell to the dimensions of the full-grown tree, or (inglorious fate!) to shrivel, to die, and to be buried in oblivion. Rise, fellow-citizens, rise to a clear and full perception of your tremendous responsibilities!! Upon you, rely upon it, depends in a measure you can hardly conceive, the future destiny of your race. You, you are to give the answer, whether the African race is doomed to interminable degradation, — a hideous blot on the fair face of Creation, a libel upon the dignity of human nature, — or whether they are incapable to take an honourable rank amongst the great family of nations! The friends of the colony are trembling; the enemies of the Coloured man are hoping. Say, fellow-citizens, will you palsy the hands of your friends and sicken their hearts, and gladden the souls of your enemies, by a base refusal to enter upon the career of glory which is now opening so propitiously before you? The genius of universal emancipation, bending from her lofty seat, invites you to accept the wreath of national independence. The voice of your friends, swelling upon the breeze, cries to you from afar — Raise your standard! assert your independence!! throw out your banners to the wind!! And will the descendants of the mighty Pharaohs, that awed the world — will the sons of him who drove back the serried legions of Rome and laid siege to the "eternal city" — will they, the achievements of whose fathers are yet the wonder and admiration of the world — will they refuse the proffered boon, and basely cling to the chains of Slavery and dependence? Never! never!! never!!! Shades of the mighty dead! —— spirits of departed great ones! inspire us, animate us to the task — nerve us for the battle! Pour into our bosom a portion of that ardour and patriotism which bore you on to battle[,] to victory, and to conquest.

Shall Liberia live? Yes; in the generous emotions now swelling in your bosoms — in the high and noble purpose now fixing itself in your mind, and ripening into the unyieldingness of indomitable principle, we hear the inspiring response — Liberia shall live before God, and before the nations of the Earth.

The night is passing away, the dusky shades are fleeing, and even now

"Jocund day stands tiptoe
On the misty mountain top."[427]

99. Liberia's Declaration of Independence

We the representatives of the people of the Commonwealth of Liberia, in Convention assembled, invested with authority for forming a new government, relying upon the aid and protection of the Great Arbiter of human events, do hereby, in the name, and on the behalf of the people of this Commonwealth, publish and declare the said Commonwealth a FREE, SOVEREIGN, AND INDEPENDENT STATE, by the name and title of the REPUBLIC OF LIBERIA.[428]

While announcing to the nations of the world the new position which the people of this Republic have felt themselves called upon to assume, courtesy to their opinion seems to demand a brief accompanying statement of the causes which induced them, first to expatriate themselves from the land of their nativity and to form settlements on this barbarous coast, and now to organize their government by the assumption of a sovereign and independent character. Therefore we respectfully ask their attention to the following facts.

We recognise in all men, certain natural and inalienable rights; among these are life, liberty, and the right to acquire, possess, enjoy and defend property. By the practice and consent of men in all ages, some system or form of government is proven to be necessary to exercise, enjoy and secure those rights; and every people have a right to institute a government, and to choose and adopt that system or form of it, which in their opinion will most effectually accomplish these objects, and secure their happiness, which does not interfere with the just rights of others. The right therefore to institute government, and to all the powers necessary to conduct it, is, an inalienable right, and cannot be resisted without the grossest injustice.

We the people of the Republic of Liberia were originally the inhabitants of the United States of North America.

In some parts of that country, we were debarred by law from all the rights and privileges of men — in other parts, public sentiment, more powerful than law, frowned us down.

We were every where shut out from all civil office.

We were excluded from all participation in the government.

We were taxed without our consent.

We were compelled to contribute to the resources of a country, which gave us no protection.

We were made a separate and distinct class, and against us every avenue to improvement was effectually closed. Strangers from all lands of a color different from ours, were preferred before us.

We uttered our complaints, but they were unattended to, or only met by alleging the peculiar institutions of the country.

All hope of a favorable change in our country was thus wholly extinguished in our bosoms, and we looked with anxiety abroad for some asylum from the deep degradation.

The Western coast of Africa was the place selected by American benevolence and philanthropy, for our future home. Removed beyond those influences which depressed us in our native land, it was hoped we would be enabled to enjoy those rights and privileges, and exercise and improve those faculties, which the God of nature has given us in common with the rest of mankind.

Under the auspices of the American Colonization Society, we established ourselves here, on land acquired by purchase from the Lords of the soil.

In an original compact with this Society, we, for important reasons delegated to it certain political powers; while this institution stipulated that whenever the people should become capable of conducting the government, or whenever the people should desire it, this institution would resign the delegated power, peaceably withdraw its supervision, and leave the people to the government of themselves.

Under the auspices and guidance of this institution, which has nobly and in perfect faith redeemed its pledges to the people, we have grown and prospered.

From time to time, our number has been increased by migration from American, and by accessions from native tribes; and from time to time, as circumstances required it, we have extended our borders by acquisitions of land by honorable purchase from the natives of the country.

As our territory has extended, and our population increased, our commerce has also increased. The flags of most of the civilized nations of the earth float in our harbors, and their merchants are opening an honorable and profitable trade. Until recently, these visits have been of a uniformly harmonious character, but as they have become more frequent, and to more numerous points of our extending coast, questions have arisen, which it is supposed can be adjusted only by agreement between sovereign powers.

For years past, the American Colonization Society, has virtually withdrawn from all direct and active part in the administration of the government, except in the appointment of the Governor, who is also a colonist, for the apparent purpose of testing the ability of the people to conduct the affairs of government, and no complaint of crude legislature, nor of mismanagement, nor of mal-administration has yet been heard, In view of these facts, this institution, the American Colonization Society, with that good faith which has uniformly marked all its dealings with us, did by a set of resolutions in January, in the Year of Our Lord One Thousand Eight Hundred and Forty-Six, dissolve all political connexion with the people of this Republic, returned the power with which it was delegated, and left the people to the government of themselves.

The people of the Republic of Liberia then, are of right, and in fact, a free, sovereign and independent State; possessed of all the rights, powers, and functions of government.

In assuming the momentous responsibilities of the position they have taken, the people of this Republic, feel justified by the necessities of the case, and with this conviction they throw themselves with confidence upon the candid consideration of the civilized world.

Liberia is not the offspring of grasping ambition, nor the tool of avaricious speculation.

No desire for territorial aggrandizement brought us to these shores; nor do we believe so sordid a motive entered into the high considerations of those who aided us in providing this asylum.

Liberia is an asylum from the most grinding oppression.

In coming to the shores of Africa, we indulged the pleasing hope that we would be permitted to exercise and improve those faculties, which impart to man his dignity — to nourish in our hearts the flame of honorable ambition, to cherish and indulge those aspirations, which a beneficent Creator had implanted in every human heart, and to evince to all who despise, ridicule and oppress our race, that we possess with them a common nature, are with them susceptible of equal refinement, and capable of equal advancement in all that adorns and dignifies man.

We were animated with the hope, that here we should be at liberty to train up our children in the way they should go — to inspire them with the love of an honorable fame, to kindle within them, the principles of humanity, virtue and religion.

Among the strongest motives to leave our native land — to abandon forever the scenes of our childhood, and to sever the most endeared connexions, was the desire for a retreat where, free from the agitations of fear and molestations, we could, in composure and security approach in worship, the God of our fathers.

Thus far our highest hopes have been realized.

Liberia is already the happy home of thousands, who were once the doomed victims of oppression, and if left unmolested to go on with her natural and spontaneous growth; if her movements be left free from the paralysing intrigues of jealous, ambitious, and unscrupulous avarice, she will throw open a wider and yet a wider door for thousands, who are now looking with an anxious eye for some land of rest.

Our courts of justice are open equally to the stranger and the citizen for the redress of grievances, for the remedy of injuries, and for the punishment of crime.

Our numerous and well attended schools attest our efforts, and our desire for the improvement of our children.

Our churches for the worship of our Creator, every where to be seen, bear testimony to our piety, and to our acknowledgment of His Providence.

The native African bowing down with us before the altar of the living God, declare that from us, feeble as we are, the light of Christianity has gone forth, while upon that curse of curses, the slave trade, a deadly blight has fallen as far as our influence extends.

Therefore in the name of humanity, and virtue and religion — in the name of the Great God, our common Creator, and our common Judge, we appeal to the nations of Christendom, and earnestly and respectfully ask of them, that they will regard us with the sympathy and friendly consideration, to which the peculiarities of our condition entitle us, and to extend to us, that comity which marks the friendly intercourse of civilized and independent communities.

Abbreviations

ACS	=	*Annual Report of the American Colonization Society*
AL	=	*Africa's Luminary*
ALL	=	*Acts Passed by the Legislature of the Republic of Liberia*
AR	=	*African Repository*
BPP	=	*British Parliamentary Papers*
LH	=	*Liberia Herald*
MCJ	=	*Maryland Colonization Journal*
MSA	=	*Mutual Assurance Society, Richmond, City, Virginia*
SBHLA	=	*Southern Baptist Historical Library and Archives*
WPA	=	*Work Projects Administration*

Endnotes

1. Geertz, *Interpretation*, 5, 212. One means of gauging scholarly influence quantitatively is the ISI Web of Knowledge Cited Reference Index. As of 24 October 2007, ISI listed 242 references just to the version of Geertz's "Ideology as a Cultural System" that appeared in David Apter's *Ideology and Discontent.*
2. Appleby, *Liberalism*, 125.
3. Gramsci, *Prison Notebooks*, 323.
4. Mintz and Price, *Birth of African-American Culture.*

5. In the field of anthropology and the writing of history (both of which involve scholars from one society or time period recovering the mentality and lived experiences of people living in another), scholars are trained to set aside their own "etic" perspectives in order to recognize and recover the "emic" perspectives of their subjects. The emic perspective focuses on the intrinsic cultural distinctions that are meaningful to the members of a given society, while the etic perspective relies on the extrinsic concept and categories that have meaning for scientific observers.

6. For example, see H. A. B. Jones ("Struggle," 163-207, especially 165) who, although trained as a historian, wrote an entire chapter on "Blyden and Unification," relying almost entirely on Blyden and without citing a single critic.

7. Williamson, *New People*.

8. Holden, *Blyden*, 649, emphasis added.

9. Ibid, 45, 82-95; Lynch, *Edward Wilmot Blyden*, 15.

10. R. M. Miller, *Dear Master*, especially 30; Wiley, *Slaves No More*. For the West Indian system of complexional distinctions among blacks and its impact on the United States, see Berlin, *Slaves Without Masters*, 99, 196-199, and Horton, *Free People of Color*, 122-144.

11. Edward S. Morris, "The Hon. Hilary Teage," *AR*, June 1865, 181; Lapsansky-Werner and Bacon, *Back to Africa*, 300 (emphasis in the original). For Blyden's invocation of Teage's poem, "Land of the Mighty Dead," during a visit to the pyramids in Egypt, see Holden, *Blyden*, 141. For Blyden's "genius" characterization, see Edward W. Blyden to William Coppinger, 3 June 1878, in Blyden, *Selected Letters*, 270.

12. For example, see Gurley, *Life of Jehudi Ashmun*.

13. Syfert, "Liberian Coasting Trade," 224, 234.

14. Syfert, "History of the Liberian Coasting Trade," esp. 114-6, 126-7; Syfert, "Liberian Coasting Trade," 280-281; "Notice [concerning proposed soap manufacturing], *LH*, 24 November 1848, 3; July, *Origins*, 96. For the claim that "Teage did not prosper in any of his occupations, as merchant, minister, or editor," see Marie Tyler-McGraw, "Hilary Teage: Discord and Nostalgia," Virginia Emigrants to Liberia, 27 September 2008

15. Foner, Free Land, Free Labor.

16. Garrison, *Thoughts*, 25.

17. Sawyer, *Emergence of Autocracy*, 38. This attempt to condemn the colonization effort based on its lack of access to ethnographic literature seems elitist and particularly self-serving since only intellectuals, such as Sawyer, could undertake the "thorough and systematic study" needed to tease the tidy constitutional implications out of such messy ethnographic facts. Such study is also utopian, since it has never guided the establishment of any nation, not even Plato's imagined republic. By this definition, every society along the rim of the Atlantic Ocean would be fatally flawed, especially those of the New World, whose founders possessed less information about the indigenous societies of the Americas than Liberians had of Africa – and less cultural affinity. Idealist also is Sawyer's insistence that ethnography mysteriously precede exploration, a proposition without precedent in human history. Paradoxically, in this quote Sawyer condemns "the idea of Liberia" based on his having discovered information on

"the social and cultural life of the peoples of the region" third-hand through various ethnographers and ethnohistorians, whose analyses relied on facts collected firsthand by colonizationists and repatriates, including Hilary Teage.

18. For example, see Wilson, *Origins*, 19.

19. Liebenow, *Liberia*, v.

20. For example, see Van der Kraaij, *Open Door Policy*, 10; Anyang' Nyong'o, *Popular Struggles*, 214.

21. "Framing and establishment: "The Late Hilary Teage, of Liberia," *AR*, October 1853, 316-17; "a graduate" and "calumny": Armistead, *Calumny*, 8; "superior man" and "black man": Lapsansky-Werner and Bacon, *Back to Africa*, 300.

22. "Reward of Merit," *MCJ*, August 1846, 220-221; Harris, *Paul Cuffe*; West, *Back to Africa*, 40-51; July, *Origins*, 48-66. I have followed Harris in spelling the name as "Cuffe."

23. Great Britain Foreign Office, *Liberia*, 24; Smyke, "Nathaniel V. Massaquoi;" Wilson, *Imperial Experience*, 95-97; Uche, "Ebony Kinship," 224; Buell, *Native Problem*, 790; van der Kraaij, *Open Door Policy*, 28; T. J. Jones, *Education*, 295.

24. Notable exceptions are July, *Origins*, 93-100; M. A. G. Brown, "Some Liberian Intellectuals;" and Poe, "Not Christopolis," 538-539.

25. Appleby, *Liberalism*, 125. For an alternative explanation of this commitment — one that is complimentary but more structuralist, see Haskell ("Capitalism," 107-35, especially 111) who credited the expansion of the market economy with initiating a shift in "perception or cognitive style." Also see: Tyler-McGraw and Kimball, *Bondage and Freedom*, 11-17; Isaac, *Transformation*, 243-268, and "The Late Hilary Teage, of Liberia," *MCJ*, October 1853, 71. The distinction between "vessel" and "content" of thinking, as well as the conception of ideology upon which it rests, are derived from the work of Geertz, *Interpretation*, 219. My dating of "the Golden Age" is derived from Moses's study of the African-American experience (*Golden Age*, especially 15-31), and finds broad confirmation in the work of July, *Origins* and Walker, *Black Loyalists*, 218-240, scholars of African history.

26. For various references to "cassado" as part of repatriate cuisine and horticulture, see "no cassado for breakfast," doc. 22; "raise something besides cassado," doc. 49; and "such as cassado, potatoes," doc. 63. This shrubby tropical plant, also called cassava or manioc, is valued in local indigenous cultures for both its edible leaves and starchy tuberous roots. For African cultural practices, see "inspiring song," doc. 57; "gracious reception," doc. 61; and "A Beautiful Custom," doc. 65.

27. "The Lyceum and the Lectures" and "For *Africa's Luminary*: The Liberia Lyceum," *AL*, 7 August 1840, 38-39; Shick, *Behold*, 162n50; Holden, *Blyden*; Lynch, *Edward Wilmot Blyden*; Blyden, *Selected Letters*. For examples of addresses before the Lyceum, see doc. 97 and [Joseph Jenkins Roberts], "From *Africa's Luminary*: Address," *LH*, 5 October 1845, 6-7.

28. Cassell, *Liberia*, 166.

29. For evidence regarding the relative openness of the political system to participation by whites of all economic stations, see R. E. Brown and B. K. Brown, *Virginia*; Isaac, *Transformation*, 131-135. For Teage's reference to "the immortal Jefferson, see doc. 98.

30. For example, see Garrison, *Thoughts*.

31. Due to the lack of standardized spelling during this period, the name was also rendered as "Teague," "Tigue," and "Teag."

32. U. S. Bureau of the Census, *Heads of Families*, 102; W. A. Jones, *Douglas Register*, 399; Holmes, *Nine Generations*; Nicholson, "Nicholson Family;" Evans, "Nicholson Family," esp. 57.

33. A term widely used by historians, "manumitted" means "legally freed from slavery." For migration and population information, see R. S. Dunn, "Society in the Chesapeake," 59; U. S. Census Office, *Census for 1830*; Walsh, "Slave Life," 171. Most Teages in the U.S. South and Midwest are thought to be descendants of William Teague, who lived in Frederick County, Virginia, between 1714 and 1751, when he disposed of his land holdings and moved to North Carolina; see E. J. Wood, Sarrett and Cook, *Ponder-Teague*, 273-279, 295-296.

34. Pinchbeck, *Virginia Negro Artisan*, 47-49, 50; "Reward of Merit," *MCJ*, August 1846, 220-21; Genovese, *Roll, Jordan, Roll*, 391; "The Late Hilary Teage, of Liberia," *AR*, October 1853, 316-17; "Reward of Merit," *MCJ*, August 1846, 220. For information on the slave quarters, see Isaac, *Transformation*, 30-32; Blassingame, *Slave Community*, 249-83; Genovese, *Roll, Jordan, Roll*, 524-34; and Rawick, *From Sundown*, 70-71, 77, 84. For the existence of an autonomous status structure among slaves and the place of artisans in it, see Blassingame, "Status," 141-42, 150; Genovese, *Roll, Jordan, Roll*, 388-98; and Escott, *Slavery Remembered*, 59-70. For slave prices in Virginia, see Pinchbeck, *Virginia Negro Artisan*, 47-49, 50. For the privileges of artisans, see Kulikoff, *Tobacco and Slaves*, 393. For the implications of plantation size for the autonomy of slave culture, see Fogel, *Without Consent*, 45-98. For the impact of republicanism on Richmond blacks, see Tyler-McGraw and Kimball, *Bondage and Freedom*, 61-72; Egerton, "Gabriel's Conspiracy"; and Mullin, "Gabriel's Insurrection."

35. WPA, Writers' Program of Virginia, *Virginia*, 53; Isaac, *Transformation*, 146, 204, 248; G. S. Wood, *Creation of the American Republic*, 314; Appleby, *Liberalism*, 119; McDonald, *Novus Ordo Seclorum*, 28.

36. WPA, Writers' Program of Virginia, *Virginia*, 53. See also McDonald, *Novus Ordo Seclorum*, 10, G. S. Wood, *Creation of the American Republic*, 314. According to Dabney (*Richmond*, 50-51), this slogan would come to serve as a rallying cry for blacks connected with Gabriel's rebellion. It was also cited by Hilary Teage in urging Liberians to declare their independence; see "give me Liberty or give me death," doc. 98.

37. R. S. Dunn, "Society in the Chesapeake," 49; Appleby, *Capitalism*, esp. 83. See also Sheldon, *Political Philosophy*; G. S. Wood, *Creation of the American Republic*; McDonald, *Novus Ordo Seclorum*.

38. Egerton, "Gabriel's Conspiracy," 199-202. The work with which to begin any study of the Haitian Revolution remains James, *Black Jacobins*. For the international consequences of the revolution and the response of Americans to it, see R. S. Dunn, "Society in the Chesapeake," 80-81; Babcock, "Manumission in Virginia," 7-19; Dabney, *Richmond*, 50-51; Kulikoff, *Tobacco and Slaves*, 416-420; Knight, "American Revolution and the Caribbean;" D. B. Davis, *Problem of Slavery*, 557-564; Davis, "American Slavery;" Quarles, "Revolutionary War," 283-301; J. C. Miller, *Wolf by the Ear*, 133-141. The American Revolutionary War also served to expand the horizons of those slaves who were forced to travel with their master in the Continent Army.

39. Babcock, "Manumission in Virginia," 20-21.

40. ; Egerton, *Gabriel's Rebellion*, 10. See also J. C. Miller, *Wolf by the Ear*; Appleby, *Capitalism*, 102; D. B. Davis, *Problem of Slavery*, especially 255-284; Jordan, *White Over Black*, 429-481; McColley, *Slavery and Jeffersonian Virginia*; Berlin and Hoffman, *Slavery and Freedom*; Klein, *Slavery in the Americas*, 172-173; G. W. Sheldon, *Political Philosophy*, 129-140; Isaac, *Transformation*, 13, 19-22, 135; Sheldon, *Political Philosophy*, 112-113; McColley, *Slavery and Jeffersonian Virginia*, 7-33; Daniel, "Virginia Baptists;" Essig, "Very Wintry Season."

41. Will of Joshua Nicholson, 1796, in *The Douglas Register*, Book 17, p 28; Evans, "Nicholson Family," 57; "Willis vs. Willis," *William and Mary College Quarterly* (Vol. 6, Series 1), 259.

42. *Ibid.*

43. Nicholson Family Bible (microfilm); Virginia State Library, Archives Branch, Richmond, arc. 30754, filed misc., reel 775 in Nicholas Family, 1787-1820; Will of Joshua Nicholson, 1796, in *The Douglas Register*, Book 17, p 28; *William and Mary College Quarterly* (Vol. 6, Series 1), 258-259. A pattern of intermarriage among the Virginia gentry was especially evident among John's descendants. His son Howell and his daughter married two siblings, both children of Maj. Charles and Sallie Andrews Briggs. A son of Howell married his double first cousin, Julia Anne Briggs.

44. McGinnis, *Virginia Genealogy*, 179; U. S. Bureau of the Census, *Heads of Families*, 9; WPA, Writers' Program of Virginia, *Virginia*, 62.

45. R. S. Dunn, "Society in the Chesapeake," 49, 50n4, 59; Klein, *Slavery in the Americas*, 166, 177, 230; Kulikoff, *Tobacco and Slaves*, 319; Egerton, *Gabriel's Rebellion*, 8; P. D. Morgan, *Don't Grieve*, 15, 18; Kulikoff, "Origins of Afro-American Society;" Kulikoff, "Uprooted Peoples," 149, table 1.

46. Sobel, *Trabelin' On*, 31. See also Escott, *Slavery Remembered*, 18-35; Holloway, *Africanisms*, ix-18; Mintz and Price, *Birth of African-American Culture*; Parish, *Slavery*, 64-96; Rawick, *From Sundown*, 14-52; Stuckey, *Slave Culture*, 3-97.

47. R. S. Dunn, "Society in the Chesapeake," 59. See also Holloway, *Africanisms*; Sobel, *The World They Made*; Sobel, *Trabelin' On*; Kulikoff, "Origins of Afro-American Society;" Isaac, *Transformation*, 80-87.

48. "Slow procession": P. D. Morgan, *Don't Grieve*, 20; "quasi-African body": Sobel, *Trabelin' On*, xxi. See also Goldfield, "Black Life," 147; Berlin, "Time, Space and the Evolution;" Gutman, *Black Family*, 45-100, 185-229; Holloway, *Africanisms*, ix-18; Parish, *Slavery*, 89-90; Rawick, *From Sundown*, 30-52; Stuckey, *Slave Culture*, 3-97. The importance attached to funerals might explain the attraction of blacks to the Masons and other fraternal groups that emphasized burial rituals.

49. Klein, *Slavery in the Americas*, 179; Walsh, "Slave Life;" Robert, *Tobacco Kingdom*, 32-50; Isaac, *Transformation*, 22-30. For a discussion of the black work ethic and the myth of black laziness in the context of slavery, see Genovese, *Roll, Jordan, Roll*, 285, 324.

50. Fore example, see "oppression," doc. 90.

51. Klein, *Slavery in the Americas*, 236; Kulikoff, *Tobacco and Slaves*, 373, 393, 402; Walsh, "Slave Life," 178-187, 190; P. D. Morgan, *Don't Grieve*, 23; R. S. Dunn, "Society in the Chesapeake," 80-81; Babcock, "Manumission in Virginia," 36, 50-55; Jackson, "Manumission"; Genovese, *Roll, Jordan, Roll*, 391; Schwarz, "Emancipators"; Matison, "Manumission by Purchase."

52. Evans, "Nicholson family," 55; Will Book 3, p. 330, Circuit Court, Southampton County, Courtland, Virginia. For the death of Joshua's mother, see Evans, "Nicholson family," 55. According to K. B. Williams (Marriages of Goochland County, 64), the only Nicholson marriage listed in the records of Goochland County between 1733 and 1815 was that of Mary Nicholson to Joseph Royall Morris of Henry County on 23 November 1799. See also "Reward of Merit," *MCJ*, August 1846, 220-221. This obituary seems to have been written by Hilary Teage, given the writer's intimate knowledge of the details of Colin's life, as well as the sardonic reference to American republican claims, similar to some of his other writings. See also Shick, *Emigrants*, 96.

53. WPA, Writers' Program of Virginia, *Virginia*, 89, 90, 92. It was not until 1812 that the first turnpike company was chartered to build a proper thoroughfare between the two towns, for the use of which the company was allowed to charge a toll.

54. G. W. Sheldon, "Black-White Relations," 27; Goldfield, "Black Life," 136. For the relatively privileged status of skilled blacks, see Berlin, *Slaves Without Masters*, 219; and Genovese, *Roll, Jordan, Roll*, 390.

55. Dabney, *Richmond*, 50-51. See also WPA, Writers' Program of Virginia, *Virginia*, 79; Tyler-McGraw and Kimball, *Bondage and Freedom*, 11-17.

56. Dabney, *Richmond*, 50-51; Berkeley, "Prophet Without Honor," 180-190.

57. Sparacio and Sparacio, *Virginia County Court Records*, 97. See also MAS, no. 162, 13 April 1796; Scott, *Old Richmond*, 131.

58. Scott, *Old Richmond*, 131. See also Bill of Bell & Shiphard [to John Preston for assorted leather items 1794], John Preston Papers, 1732-1907, Virginia Historical Society.

59. "Reward of Merit," *MCJ*, August 1846, 220.

60. Ibid; MAS, no. 2835, 23 November 1820; MAS, no. 4591, declaration no. 1033, 13 July 1822. For information on Shiphard's properties, see MAS, no. 985, 22 March 1809; no. 10150, declaration no. 6887, 1 December 1836; MAS, no. 2787, declaration no. 947, 15 May 1820; no. 5221, declaration no. 946, 15 July 1822.

61. P. D. Morgan, *Don't Grieve*, 20. See also Daniel, "Virginia Baptists"; Essig, "Very Wintry Season;" Jackson, "Religious Development." On Baptists in Virginia generally, see Isaac, *Transformation*, 161-177.

62. The version of Christianity proffered to blacks by plantation ministers, often with the sponsorship of masters, emphasized lessons on "humility, patience and fear of sin," such as the apostle Paul's letters in the New Testament. It decried materialism in favor of obedience in the present, which would lead to rewards in the hereafter. African-Americans were said to be descendants of Ham, forever cursed to be "hewers of wood and drawers of water": Levine, *Black Culture*, 43-53. See also Curry, *The Free Black*, 177; Stuckey, *Slave Culture*, 3-97; Harding, *There Is a River*, 52-74.

63. From Gillfield evolved the Elam Baptist Church, founded in 1810 in nearby Charles City and led the free black pastor Abram Brown. It is interesting to note that in the early 1990s the church was being led by the Rev. Ned Cary, a fifth-generation descendant of Lott Cary, who accompanied the Teage family to Liberia. See Blackwell, "Honoring of Cary Termed Overdue."

64. B. S. White, *First Baptist Church*, 19, also 11, 18, 219-220.

65. B. S. White, *First Baptist Church*, 12; Jackson, "Religious Development," 188, 193, 195, 202n. 95b, 216-217; Sobel, *Trabelin' On*, 190-191; Shick, *Emigrants*, 86; P. D. Morgan, *Don't Grieve*, 40; WPA, Historical Records Survey of Virginia, *Inventory*, 104; Reynolds, *Hymns of Our Faith*, xix, xxxi; Richmond *Times-Dispatch*, 28 August 1955. The church building at H and Fifteenth Streets would be ceded in 1841 to black members, who came to operate the First African Baptist Church.

66. U. S. Bureau of the Census, *Heads of Families*, 36. Having put aside the name of his former owner upon emancipation, Cary might have taken his last name from the street on which this church was located or from Lott, the Old Testament prophet who was sent to warn the residents of Sodom to turn away from their sinful conduct but was rebuffed. The 1810 Census lists a William Christian in Charles City County with only eleven slaves. According to Hopkins (*Some Wills*, 107), a William Christian of New Kent left a plantation in Charles City County to his daughter Elizabeth in a will that was dated 2 December 1801 and probated 14 January 1802. This transference might have precipitated the hiring out of Cary. Given the relative mobility enjoyed by artisans, the two men might have had contacts or family ties before coming to the capital, especially since Cary's home county abutted Goochland County, where Teage was raised, and was only thirty miles from Richmond. It is possible that Teage's wife, Frances, was Cary's sister; Cary had a daughter, born in 1806, named Frances, and one of his grandsons would later be taken into Hilary Teage's household. See Shick, *Emigrants*, 20; U. S. Senate, *U. S. Navy Department*, 310; Taylor, *Biography*, 10; Fisher, "Lott Cary," 381-82. For the privileges of artisans, see R. S. Dunn, "Society in the Chesapeake," 69, and Babcock, "Manumission in Virginia," 19.

67. Gurley, *Life of Jehudi Ashmun*, 147; Fisher, "Lott Cary," 382; Ryland, "Reminiscences," 248-49; Taylor, *Biography*, 13, 19. According to Sobel (*Trabelin' On*, 160), exhorting or lay preaching was common among black Baptists because, although converts generally felt called to preach, few blacks were licensed. In contrast to trained preachers, exhorters relied heavily on "metaphors, parables, and allegories based on life rather than on book learning."

68. Taylor, *Biography*, 13, 19; MSA, no. 2026, declaration no. 2025/2026, 24 December 1818; Burrows, *Christian Merchant*, 3, 7-9.

69. Burrows, *Christian Merchant*, 3, 7-9, 10; B. S. White, *First Baptist Church*, 31.

70. Taylor, *Biography*, 13-14, 19. See also "Reward of Merit," *MCJ*, August 1846, 220.

71. Genovese, *Roll, Jordan, Roll*, 392; Taylor, *Biography*, 14, 18. See also Gurley, *Life of Jehudi Ashmun*, 148.

72. "Reward of Merit," *MCJ*, August 1846, 221.

73. "Died!", Richmond *Enquirer*, 14 August 1827.

74. "Judgment" and "keenness of penetration": William Crane to the Rev. O. B. Brown, 28 March 1819, in Taylor, *Biography*, 17-18; "magnetic personality": Graham, "Century of Development," 20-22; "ideas would sometimes burst": Gurley, *Life of Jehudi Ashmun*, 148. See also Taylor, *Biography*, 12, 25.

75. U. S. Census Office, *Fourth Census of the United States for 1820*, 212, 217; Jackson, *Free Negro Labor*, 143, 146, and J. H. Brewer, "Negro Property Owners." On 12 March 1812, Colin leased a thirty-

by-sixth-foot property on the east side of Eighteenth Street from Hannah Lovall Jones for $25 per year. This transaction was recorded in court as a deed, leading Jackson (*Free Negro Labor*, 146) to mistakenly include Colin among free black property owners.

76. Gatewood, *Aristocrats*, 9,18; Genovese, *Roll, Jordan, Roll*, 399, 401; Russell, *Free Negro*, 66, 146-53; Guild, *Black Laws*, 137; Klein, *Slavery in the Americas*, 242; DuBois and Dill, *Negro American Artisan*, 28-37. Although the social structure that had existed among slaves probably determined the behavior of individuals drawn from that milieu, the standards of free blacks probably prevailed at the formal and institutional levels. Very likely, those elements that were present in both status structures would have reinforced one another, resulting in a high valuation of literacy, church leadership and service to others, while elements that were not shared by free blacks would have fallen away.

77. Slaughter, *Virginian History*; Russell, *Free Negro*, 73; Tyler-McGraw, "Richmond Free Blacks," 217; Egerton, "'Its Origin," 463-80.

78. Fisher, "Lott Cary," 385-88; Burrows, *Christian Merchant*, 36-37; Tupper, *First Century*; B. S. White, *First Baptist Church*, 27.

79. This reading must have occurred sometime between 1815, when the Richmond African Baptist Missionary Society was organized, and 1819, when William Crane revealed its plans to the American Baptist Foreign Mission Society. See Fisher, "Lott Cary," 385-387; Ryland, "First African Church," 71; Poe, "Not Christopolis," 536-37. For information on the movement of black Virginia loyalists to Sierra Leone, see Harris, *Paul Cuffe*; West, *Back to Africa*, 40-51; July, *Origins*, 48-66; and J. W. S. G. Walker, *Black Loyalists*.

80. Gurley, *Life of Jehudi Ashmun*, 148-49. See also Fisher, "Lott Cary," 390n53; Taylor, *Biography*, 21; Tracy, *History of American Missions*, 439; Sobel, *Trabelin' On*, 204, 226-27; B. S. White, *First Baptist Church*, 30.

81. "I am an African": Gurley, *Life of Jehudi Ashmun*, 148-49; importance of literacy: Fisher, "Lott Cary," 388. Also see Tyler-McGraw, "The Prize I Mean," 357; Tyler-McGraw, "Richmond Free Blacks," 212-15.

82. Leslie, *New and Exact Account*, 323. See also Harding, *There Is a River*, 18; Stuckey, *Slave Culture*, vii-97.

83. Higginbotham, In the Matter of Color.

84. Curtin, *Atlantic Slave Trade*, 359-60; H. H. Bell, "Introduction," to *Search for a Place*, 2-3.

85. H. H. Bell, "Introduction," to *Search for a Place*, 2-3; West, *Back to Africa*.

86. The quote is from the unsigned introduction to Coker, *Journal*, v. See also H. H. Bell, ""Introduction," to *Search for a Place*, 2-4; Harris, *Paul Cuffe*, 13-72; Katz, "Earliest Responses," i-xiv; Tyler-McGraw, "Richmond Free Blacks," 220-221; Mills, "Abstract of a Journal," 5-7; Payne, *History of the African Methodist Episcopal Church*, 14. With funding from the U. S. government and escorted by a U. S. Navy warship, eighty-eight blacks sailed for Africa on the *Elizabeth*. Aboard were free blacks from Virginia, Maryland, Washington, DC, Pennsylvania and New York, mostly women and children, many of whom had "long contemplated a settlement in Africa." They included Frederick James, a carpenter from Virginia who had lived for years in Washington, D.C. and Philadelphia; Nathaniel Peck, a mill owner from Baltimore;

and the Rev. Daniel Coker, who was elected the first bishop of the African Methodist Episcopal denomination in 1818, but declined the position due to his colonizationist interest.

87. Bracey, Meier and Rudwick, *Black Nationalism*; Moses, *Golden Age*, 15-55.

88. Quoted in Dann, *Black Press*, 35. This was probably written by the co-editor of *Freedom's Journal's* John Russwurm (1799-1851), who emigrated to Liberia in 1829.

89. Sherwood, "Early Negro Deportation Projects"; Egerton, *Gabriel's Rebellion*, 13-15. In contrast to the Virginia schemes, which often called for government involvement, northern whites generally proposed plans for colonization that depended on private benevolence and were linked to abolition or widespread manumission. For a detailed discussion of Jefferson's paradoxical position on slavery, see J. C. Miller, *Wolf by the Ear*; also Jordan, *White Over Black*.

90. Peterson, Portable Thomas Jefferson, 185-88.

91. ibid.

92. Egerton, "'Its Origins.'" For the political character of Gabriel's rebellion and the norms of the American Revolution that it embodied, see Mullin, "Gabriel's Insurrection," 53-73.

93. Egerton, "'Its Origins.'"

94. Harris, *Paul Cuffe*, 69-71; Sherwood, "Early Negro Deportation Projects," 508; Egerton, "'Its Origins.'"

95. Berlin, *Slaves Without Masters*, 182-216, especially 201; Foster, "Colonization of Free Negroes," 44-45; Fox, *American Colonization Society*, 8-34; Fredrickson, *Black Image*, 1-42; Katz, "Earliest Responses," i-xi; Kocher, "Duty"; R. M. Miller, *Dear Master*, 26-27; Sherwood, "Early Negro Deportation Projects," 507; Staudenraus, *African Colonization Movement*.

96. Allen, "'All of Us Are Highly Pleased,'" 104-6; Berlin, *Slaves Without Masters*, 204-7; Jay, *Inquiry*; Katz, "Earliest Responses"; McClaughlin, "Sectional Responses"; Mehlinger, "Attitude of the Free Negro." Although well attended such meetings did not signal universal opposition to colonization by free blacks. They reflected, instead, a fear that colonization under the ACS, given the national influence of its leaders, would culminate in forced deportations. Several of the anti-ACS resolutions issued at these meetings specifically left open a door to emigration. Meeting in 1817, free blacks in Richmond indicated their preference for settlement anywhere on the North American continent over Africa. However, while rejecting colonization in 1831, an assembly in Baltimore retained the option to emigrate at a later date of its members' own free will. Well into the twentieth century, emigration would endure as a significant concern among African Americans, often with Liberia as the focus. See Kinshasa, *Emigration vs. Assimilation*; Mehlinger, "Attitude of the Free Negro," 277, 283; F. J. Miller, *Search*; Redkey, *Black Exodus*.

97. Jay, *Inquiry*, 16-17. The phrase "a stain upon our escutcheon" means a dishonor to white America's reputation. Also see Tyler-McGraw, "'The Prize I Mean'," 359; Berlin, *Slaves Without Master*, 201-216. The colonizationists' emphasis on the social environment is from Fredrickson, *Black Image*, 1-42.

98. D. E. Dunn, Beyan and Burrowes, *Historical Dictionary*, 3-6, 18-19, 124. For the effacing of free-black agency, see Fox, *American Colonization Society*; Beyan, *American Colonization Society*.

99. Gurley, *Life of Jehudi Ashmun*; Burrowes, "Black Christian Republicanism"; F. J. Miller, *Search*, 68; D. E. Dunn, Beyan and Burrowes, *Historical Dictionary*, 62-63; Shick, *Emigrants*, 96; "Reward of Merit," *MCJ*, August 1846, 220-221; "Death of Hon. Hillary Teage," *MCJ*, August 1853, 47; [R. R. G. [Ralph Randolph Gurley], "The late Hilary Teage, of Liberia, *AR*, Oct. 1853, 316-317.

100. For Cary's reading of *The Wealth of Nations*, see Gurley, *Life of Jehudi Ashmun*, 148.

101. "Proprietors of the soil": Huberich, *Political and Legislative History*, 1: 839; "if only we could share in them" and "i wish to Goy to Liberia": Woodson, *Mind of the Negro*, 2, 93. Also see Berlin, *Slaves Without Masters*, 303-309.

102. Allen, "'All of Us Are Highly Pleased'," 105-107; McClaughlin, "Sectional Responses"; R. M. Miller, *Dear Master*; Wiley, *Slaves No More*.

103. Wiley, *Slaves No More*, 9.

104. R. M. Miller, "'Home as Found,'" 72-73; Gurley, *Life of Jehudi Ashmun*, 194-196; "Death of Hon. Hillary Teage," *MCJ*, August 1853, 47; Jackson, "Religious Development," 188, 193, 195, 202, especially n. 95b, 216-217; Shick, *Emigrants*, 86; Wold, *God's Impatience*, 61; Huberich, *Political and Legislative History*, 1: 638-9, 641, 646, 647 n. 1. Gillfield was so financially secure that it aided a white congregation in the same town in building its own church.

105. "Constitution and Laws of the Commonwealth of Liberia," *AR*, December 1843, 379-380; Teage, *Constitution and Laws of the Commonwealth of Liberia*; Hilary Teage, "The Colony of Liberia [Part 1]," *AR*, September 1844, 257-61; Hilary Teage, "The Colony of Liberia [Part 2]," *AR*, January 1845, 13-17; ["Treatise on Self Government"], doc. 96; "Death of Hon. Hillary Teage," *MCJ*, August 1853, 47; "The Late Hilary Teage, of Liberia," *AR*, October 1853, 316-317; "The Election," *AL*, 3 January 1840; Syfert, "History of the Liberian Coasting Trade," 280-281; Holden, *Blyden*, 36. When Teage resigned from the colonial government in 1835, he had a salary $600 as colonial secretary and $300 as editor of the *Liberia Herald*; see [Thomas Buchanan], "Despatches from Liberia," *AR*, 1 March 1840, 72. According Richardson (*Liberia's Past and Present*, 59, n*) who worked at the Liberian State Department and had full access to official records, Teage also served as the first secretary of that department.

106. This evocation of the ancestors, which became an element in Liberian civic religion, was evident in the thinking of another Baptist, John N. Lewis, who ended a speech to the Liberia Lyceum in a similar vein: "Let us invoke the spirits of our fathers that have finished their labor and are now, we hope, enjoying the happiness of another and blessed world. And easily we imagine that we see them hovering over us, in the likeness of a Carey, Benson, Waring, Devany, Teage and Barbour;" see [John N. Lewis,] "From *Africa's Luminary*, Address," *LH*, 7 November 1845, 14-15.

107. Berlin (*Slaves Without Masters*, 315n4; also 297-298) defined "the North as the states which made provisions for emancipation following the American Revolution or which later entered the Union as free states. Delaware, Kentucky, Maryland, Missouri, North Carolina, Tennessee, Virginia, and the District of Columbia constitute the Upper South; Alabama, Arkansas, Florida, Georgia, Louisiana, Mississippi South Carolina, and Texas the Lower South." Political passions in Liberia seem to have flowed along the regional lines outlined by Berlin, except for those of Kentuckians, who acted in concert with blacks from the Lower South.

108. Blassingame, "Status," 146-147. See also P. Campbell, *Maryland in Africa*, 196-203, 236; D. E. Dunn, *History of the Episcopal Church*, 74; Tyler-McGraw, "Richmond Free Blacks," 220-221.

109. Berlin, *Slaves Without Masters*, 308, 312.

110. "A little lifted up": John B. Russwurm to R. R. Gurley, Liberia, 6 August 1833, cited in P. Campbell, *Maryland in Africa*, 51; "in the hands of a class": Wiley, *Slaves No More*, 313n1, Letter 1. See also R. S. Dunn, "Society in the Chesapeake," 49; A. B. Williams, *Liberian Exodus*, 53, 49; Rogers, "Liberian Journalism," 92-93 and 108n131, citing Samuel F. McGill to Moses Sheppard, Monrovia, 16 June 1855, located at the Friends Historical Library, Swarthmore College, Pennsylvania.

111. Burrowes, "Black Christian Republicans," 76-80, 88; S. A. Davis, "Hilary Teage," 72; Huberich, *Political and Legislative History*, 1: 389, n. 5; Horton, *Free People of Color*, 144; Berlin, "Structure of the Free Negro Caste," 314. Although systematic data on complexion were not kept for repatriates, it is possible that mulattos accounted for 50 percent of the population.
After all, early Liberians were disproportionately free blacks from Virginia, where persons of mixed racial ancestry constituted 65 percent of the free black population (Horton, *Free People of Color*, 125). If mulattos were half of the repatriate community, their success in politics and business could hardly be credited to preferential treatment by whites (e.g., Beyan, *American Colonization Society*) or their own conspiratorial machinations (e.g., Blyden, "Mixed Races in Liberia"), unless the degree of their success could be shown to have exceeded their numbers in the population. Dark-complexioned presidents were Stephen Allen Benson (1856-1864), Liberia's second president; Daniel B. Warner (1864-1868), the third; and Edward James Roye (1869-1871) the fifth. Their light-skinned counterparts were Joseph Jenkins Roberts (1848-1856), the first president; and James Spriggs Payne (1868-1870), the fourth. For photographs and painted portraits of these men, see Richardson, *Liberia's Past and Present*, 86-88, and Shick, *Behold*, 44, 117, 119. For a contemporaneous description of Benson, Warner and Teage as dark-skinned, see Benjamin Coates, introduction to E. W. Blyden, "The Negro in Ancient History," *Methodist Quarterly*, July 1869, cited in Holden, *Blyden*, 166.

112. "Extracts of a Letter Dated New Georgia, Liberia, 17th of August, 1834, from Mr. James Eden, a Colored Teacher at Liberia," *AR*, March 1835, 88-89; "Journal of an African Cruiser," *MCJ*, December 1845, 92-93. For Colin Teage's service as pastor of the Second Baptist Church in Monrovia, see Tracy, *History of American Missions*, 558.

113. Egerton, *Gabriel's Rebellion*, 23; William Davis, phone interview by author, 18 June 1995. Davis, a descendent of Colinette Teage, kindly provided information on various Teage family properties, while the address of the *Herald* during the colonial period is taken from Slaughter, *Virginia History*, 110. A letter from James Eden, a teacher in Monrovia, reported two Baptist churches in the city, with the Second Baptist pastored by Colin Teage and the First Baptist led by the Rev. Colston Waring. However, Eden did not give the locations of these two churches, and no other source confirms the existence of two separate congregations. Furthermore, it seems unlikely that Colin Teage, who arrived before Waring, would lead the "second" church, unless this congregation was a missionary effort, in keeping with his original motivation for coming to Africa.

[114]. A "kroo" was a unit of measurement in nineteenth-century Liberia that was equivalent to four imperial gallons or a half bushel.

115. U. S. Senate, *U. S. Navy Department*, 376. These population figures are from a census taken in 1843.

116. Taylor, *Biography*, 19. See also Tyler-McGraw, "Richmond Free Blacks," 213; Tyler-McGraw and Kimball, *Bondage and Freedom*, 55, 63; Dabney, *Richmond*, 77; Taylor, *Biography*, 19. Before his parents settled permanently in Liberia in 1826, Hilary might have spent an extended period in England, where he could have furthered his education. In an 1851 letter he would say, "I have tried England & America and Africa, but I am free to confirm I breathed freely and saw clearly no where but in Africa;" see "I have tried England" (doc. 54); see Poe, "Not Christopolis," 538. Close ties between the Teage and Crane families continued long after the Teages emgrated, as indicated by the service of William Crane, Esq., as the agent of the *Herald* in Baltimore, Maryland, for several years. See "From the *Liberia Herald*," *AL*, 18 October 1839, 58, and "Agents for the *Liberia Herald*," *LH*, 5 November 1847, 93.

117. [Richard E. Murray], "Good Testimony," *AR*, November 1851, 336. Richard E. Murray (1798-1856) was an ACS agent in Sinoe County from 1844 to 1856.

118. Syfert, "Origins of Privilege," especially 114-6, 126-7; Syfert, "History of the Liberian Coasting Trade," 280-281; "Notice," *LH*, 24 November 1848, 3; July, *Origins*, 96; Davis interview. Listed as Teage's partners in the soap business were J. S. Payne, John N. Lewis and D. T. Harris.

119. "We speak advisedly": "From the *Liberia Herald*," *AL*, 18 October 1839, 58, and "the privilege of arraigning and abusing": "*Liberia Herald*," *AR*, April 1837, 131-132.

120. "Our Wants," *LH*, 25 June 1849, 31.

121. James C. Minor to ACS Agent, Monrovia, 27 August 1852, Letter 14, in Wiley, *Slaves No More*, 28-29.

122. A. F. Russell, "For the *Liberia Herald*: Liberia, No. 1," *LH*, 6 November 1846, 7; reprinted in *AR*, February 1847, 48-53. "Notice, the Undersigned Have Formed Themselves into a Company for the Manufacture of Soap," *LH*, 29 December 1848, 15. For Teage's role as president of the Lyceum during this period, see doc. 97.

123. "For the *Liberia Herald*: Liberia, No. 1," LH, 6 November 1846, 7-9.

124. D. T. H., "*Liberia Herald*," *LH*, 1 October 1850, 19. D. T. H. was probably Dessalines T. Harris. See also Shick, *Behold*, 162n50; Wiley, *Slaves No More*, 29-30, Letter 15; A. W. A., "Communication," *LH*, 5 October 1845, 6-7.

125. Syfert, "Origins of Privilege," especially 114-6, 126-7; Syfert, "History of the Liberian Coasting Trade," 271, 280-281, 283; July, *Origins*, 96. Registered on 23 July 1852, the sale transferred Lot 26 from Hilary and his wife, Mary, to Smith for $150 (Land Register, Monrovia, Montserrado County, Republic of Liberia). Since there is no evidence that Teage was married more than once, it seems likely that "Mary" was the middle name of Eliza M., whom he married sometime before 1843.

126. "He does not set up as lawyer" is from "Notice, the subscriber hereby gives notice ...," *LH*, 24 November 1848, 3; "Here we are, at it again!" is from "Here We Are," p. 161. Teage used capsicum, the scientific term for pepper, to remind readers of the "heat" which he could

unleash for not paying their subscription, in place of this gentle chiding. See "planting potatoes and collecting pepper," p. 162; also "20 acres of land under cultivation," p. 246, where Teage reported his cultivation of rice, cassava, potatoes, corn, pepper and ginger.

127. "Eliza M." was probably Eliza Jackson, who traveled on the Elizabeth with Edward (19), Jane (17), and Rachel (20), all free black Jacksons from New York. Both Eliza and Rachel were literate (Shick, *Emigrants*, 48-49). George was the orphaned son of Jesse Shaw, an early immigrant to Liberia and military hero. Sally, the only person listed as a servant, bore the last name of Hilary's brother-in-law, George. William was the grandson of Lott Cary, and Levy was the son of John James from North Carolina, another early immigrant and military hero. See Shick, *Emigrants*, 20, 27, 50, 59, 66, 87, 310, 312; H. D. Brown, *Character Sketches*; U. S. Senate, *U. S. Navy Department*, 310, 312. The 1843 census lists an apprentice named David Teage with no education and no apparent connection to the families of Hilary or his mother. According to the Acts of the Liberian Legislature for 1898, there was Hilary Teage serving as deacon of the first Good Hope Baptist Church of Marshall in Montserrado County. If this was the son of Hilary, he would have been born between 1843 and 1853, the latter being the year Hilary died. It is possible that Teage and his wife could have had a son in this ten-year period, as she was 30 in 1843, but it is highly unlikely since this would have been her first child, at least by Teage. If this other Hilary was born during that period, he would have been between 45 and 55 years old at the time of the church's incorporation, a probable age for a deacon (U. S. Senate, *U. S. Navy Department*, 356; *ALL*, 1898, 4).

128. Boles, *Masters and Slaves*, 2.

129. Curry, *The Free Black*; Woodson, *Education of the Negro*, 206-19; D. E. Dunn, Beyan and Burrowes, *Historical Dictionary*, 123-24.

130. "[John Day], "To the Free People of Color," *MCJ*, January 1854, 123-125. John Day (1797-1861) was superintendent of the Baptist mission in Liberia. For the importance of the lyceums in mass education, see J. W. Lugenbeel, "Latest from Liberia," *AR*, Nov. 1845, 21-23.

131. Burrowes, "Press Freedom in Liberia," 716-17.

132. W. M. Brewer, "John B. Russwurm"; P. Campbell, *Maryland in Africa*; Kinshasa, *Emigration vs. Assimilation*; Sagarin, *John Brown Russwurm*; Moses, *Destiny and Race*; Moses, *Alexander Crummell*; Rigsby, *Alexander Crummell*; Holden, *Blyden*; Lynch, *Edward Wilmot Blyden*; Blyden, *Selected Letters*; Delany, "Official Report;" Sterling, *Making of an Afro-American*; Ullman, *Martin R. Delany*; Chester, *Thomas Morris Chester*; Stuckey, *Slave Culture*, 138-92. Although Chester originally came to Liberia as a repatriate and even served as an emissary for his adopted country during his seventeen-year stay, he resettled in the United States where he served as a Civil War correspondent as well as a politician and public official during Reconstruction. For information on Garnet's brief service as U. S. resident minister to Liberia, see Skinner, *African Americans and U. S. Policy*, especially 106-108.

133. "Remarkable for his abilities": "The Late Hilary Teage, of Liberia," *MCJ*, 1853, 71-72; "one of the ablest": "Death in Liberia," *MCJ*, August 1853, 47; "brightest and most cultivated": "Death of Hon. Hillary Teage," *MCJ*, 1853, 47; "genius": Edward W. Blyden to William Coppinger, 3 June 1878, in Blyden, *Selected Letters*, 270; "organic intellectual" and "permanent persuader": Gramsci, *Prison Notebooks*, 5-23, especially 10.

134. For fuller discussion of this aspect of Teage's thinking, see the following section of this introduction entitled "The Grand Object of a Republic on Africa's Soil." See also Tillotson, Fussell and Waingrow, *Eighteenth-Century English Literature*, 18.

135. Sullivan, *British Literary Magazines*, 424-433; Schwarzlose, Newspapers; also "extract from our journal," p. 274; "The Late Hilary Teage, of Liberia" *MCJ*, October 1853, 71-72. The use of pseudonyms, common in pre-Civil War American journalism, especially in the southern states, would remain a feature of Liberian political commentary at least through the 1960s. Teage's sermons include "The Proceedings of the Liberia Providence Baptist Association" (1839), a pamphlet edited with a pastoral address by him; see "Baptist Association," *AL*, 19 April 1839, 10.

136. Cornford, *Edward Young*, ix; also Noyes, *English Romantic Poetry*, xxiii. For a reference by Teage to "Night Thoughts," see "Tis greatly wise to talk," p. 127. This attraction may have rested upon Teage's recognition of similarities between his environment and the England about which Young had written. Both places were characterized by high mortality due to disease and violent death. For mortality in nineteenth-century Liberia and eighteenth-century England, respectively, see Shick, *Behold*, 19-41, and Tillotson, Fussell and Waingrow, *Eighteenth-Century English Literature*, 7.

137. See "theatre of his exploits," p. 397.

138. For example, see "friends of morality," doc. 15, and "what a host of titles!," doc. 16.

139. See "extract from our journal," doc. 61, and "The Late Hilary Teage, of Liberia," *MCJ*, October 1853, 71-72. Teage's sermons include *The Proceedings of the Liberia Providence Baptist Association*, a pamphlet edited with a pastoral address by him. See "Baptist Association," *AL*, 19 April 1839, 10.

140. Liberia, *Independent Republic*.

141. [Hilary Teage], "The *Liberia Herald* with Regard to Independence," *ACS*, 1847, 21. While this motivation may not have been shared by all repatriates, it had certainly animated free blacks, such as Colin Teage, who had provided alternative leadership to the colony while organizing its second-largest denomination, the Baptist Church, with little support from abroad. For the importance of institution building to blacks in the United States after emancipation, see R. T. Smith, "Race, Class, and Gender," esp. 277.

142. The major source of common-law reasoning was Sir William Blackstone's *Commentaries on the Laws of England*. Also called civic humanism, republicanism included the political philosophies of Aristotle, Cicero, Charles-Louis de Secondat Montesquieu (known as Montesquieu), and James Harrington. Primary exponents of liberal republicanism were Thomas Hobbes, who contributed a theory of sovereignty, and especially John Locke, whose empiricism and theory of the origin of rights proved influential. See McDonald, *Novus Ordo Seclorum*, xii, 1, 7, 60-67, 80-83, 164n40; G. W. Sheldon, *Political Philosophy*, 7, 27; G. S. Wood, *Creation of the American Republic*, 7-8, 10, 14, 16, 19, 48, 64, 264-65, 290, 348, 371, 414; and Appleby, *Capitalism*, 17, 19-23, 95. Notable among other traditions was the Scottish common sense school, which held that all adult human beings were endowed with a moral sense; see McDonald, *Novus Ordo Seclorum*, 54-55. For the possible impact of this school on Teage, see "Letter to William McLain," p. 257. Also see Liberia, *Independent Republic*, 13; Alexander, *History of Colonization*, 537-8. These sources

indicate the reading interests of Samuel Benedict, the first chief justice of Liberia, which included Blackstone and Montesquieu.

143. McDonald, *Novus Ordo Seclorum*, 70-71; "Black Christian Republicans." According to McDonald (*Novus Ordo Seclorum*, 74-75; also Peterson, *Portable Thomas Jefferson*, xxi.), in the thinking of Jeffersonian republicans, "ownership of the land begat independence, independence begat virtue and virtue begat republican liberty." For Jefferson's ideas on black colonization, see Peterson, *Portable Thomas Jefferson*, 185-88. The Republican label for Liberia's first party is from H. H. Johnston, *Liberia*, 1: 230. The choice of this name carried a double implication. On the one hand, it reflected the members' socialization in the Upper South, where a party by the same name had dominated. Within the Liberian context, it underscored the priority this group assigned to the creation of a secular state, in contrast to the country's first opposition party, which was based in the Methodist Church. For the religious dimensions of early Liberian politics and the secular-sacred tensions, see Poe, "Not Christopolis," 535, and Shick, "Rhetoric and Reality." Although no evidence of Teage's membership in the Republican Party has been found, this inference regarding his association is derived from three factors: his service in Republican administrations; his business association with leading Republicans, such as James S. Payne; and the predominance of fellow Virginians in the leadership of the party.

144. See also "of sense and perseverance," doc. 10.

145. Teage's standard was similar to a law from the colonial period that considered citizenship a privilege earned through "responsible" conduct, as verified by three disinterested citizens. A responsible citizen was a homeowner who, over the course of at least three years, had consistently attended church services, dressed in Western clothes, and cultivated two acres. See Huberich, *Political and Legislative History*, 2: 1029; J. Martin, "How to Build a Nation," 18-19, citing A. F. Russell to Richard Duane, 1 January 1876 [?]. While these criteria for citizenship may seem elitist by today's standards, they were quite radical at the time. Instead of a social order that fixed one's place at birth, this one would allow individuals to ascend the social hierarchy through talent (property-ownership) and virtue (Christianity and public service). Similar notions of "citizenship" as the privilege of property holders existed in many indigenous Liberian cultures, although wealth was measured not in land but in wives, clients, and prestige goods.

146. Horton, *Free People of Color*, 117. At least two women, Mary Benedict and Harriet Brander, were publicly identified with the Anti-Administration Party during the colonial era. Both Mary, the wife of Superior Court Judge Samuel Benedict, and Harriet, who was married to Judge Nathaniel Brander, signed an 1840 petition in support of the Rev. John Seys, superintendent of the Methodist Mission, who was then locked in a political contest with the colonial government. The leaders of that petition drive, along with several signatories, would later emerge as candidates on the Anti-Administration ticket. Mrs. Brander also testified for the defense when Seys was tried for non-payment of import duty. See "To All Whom It May Concern," *AL*, 6 November 1840, 63. The recognition of women's economic rights in Liberia,

which went against the grain of Anglo-Saxon tradition, can be explained in light of the local demographic picture. Although an almost equal number of men and women immigrated between 1820 and 1843, there was a much higher mortality rate among men. Between ages 26 and 45, the central death rate (deaths per thousand per year) was 89 for males and 72 for females. For ages 46 to 98, the rates rose to 201 for males compared to 153 for females (Shick, *Emigrants*, 46, 51). The celebration of valor when associated with women was evident in the celebration of 1 December as Matilda Newport Day, in honor of a woman who allegedly drove attackers away from the colony when it was most vulnerable, by lighting a canon with a flint from her pipe. While without parallel in Euro-American and European societies, the consecration of Newport as the veritable mother of the nation bears striking similarity to the veneration of "Gen." Harriet Tubman in African-American society and of Nanee, the leader of a nineteenth century slave revolt, in Jamaica. According to Karnga (*Negro Republic*, 20), a woman named Newby was similarly celebrated in Edina, but her significance — recognized only at the local level — seems to have faded with time.

147. This reference is to Lovell, Massachusetts, was a company town where textile was produced. The employees, mostly former farm girls, had their lives closely regulated, with particular attention given to their moral education by the company owners. For the contrast between the market (regarded as beneficial) and wage labor and commodification (distrusted as potentially alienating) in nineteenth-century thought, see Ashworth, "Relationship Between Capitalism and Humanitarianism."

148. [Joseph Jenkins Roberts], "Address …," *LH*, 5 October 1845, 6-7. The partial quotes are drawn from two distinct Old Testament passages. In the first, Exodus 5:7, the Israelites requested leave from Egypt, only to be denied permission and punished with the additional task of finding the straw with which to make bricks for the pharaoh. The second passage, Samuel 1: 19-20, follows David's slaying of the Amalekite who brought him news of the death of Saul and his son Jonathan. Drawn from Samuel 1:20, the passage: "The beauty of Israel is slain upon thy high places: how are the mighty fallen! Tell it not in Gath, publish it not in the streets of Askelon; lest the daughters of the Philistines rejoice, lest the daughters of the uncircumcised triumph." Applying these two passages to the conditions of his day, Roberts recast blacks as the Israelites and Jefferson as the pharaoh who, in the name of national security, would punish his bondmen if they dared to report that the mighty, indeed, had fallen.

149. For example, see Garrison, *Thoughts*.

150. Moses, *Wings of Ethiopia*, 351; Lynch, *Edward Wilmot Blyden*; July, *Origins*; Stuckey, *Slave Culture*; Wilson, *Origins*. For references in Teage's writings to the existence of slavery and the slave trade in local societies, see "slaves of which the Baracoons were crammed," doc. 13; "seat of an extensive slave dealer," doc. 59; "Manah's slaves," doc. 59; "vessels coming for slaves," doc. 60; "payment of twenty slaves," doc. 61; "accursed traffic is wholly destroyed," doc. 67; and "destroy this abominable traffic," doc. 75. For independent confirmation of some of the activities Teage describes by someone who participated in the trade, see Conneau, *Slaver's Log Book*.

151. For example, see "permanent and wealthy and polished," doc. 5, and "Here science once displayed," doc. 90.

152. M. A. G. Brown, "Education and National Development," 87-88, 95n21; d'Amico, "Spiritual and Secular Activities," 121-122; H. D. Brown, *Character Sketches*; Wold, *God's Impatience*, 64. A lack of foreign support would make the Baptists the country's most self-supporting denomination, but also hampered their expansion into the interior. Recaptured Africans may have been receptive to assimilation, given their displacement largely from the Congo. If that was so, the Congo people may have been particularly attracted to Baptist theology's juxtaposition of a "disorderly" secular world with an "orderly" life in Christ. In contrast, converts from African communities neighboring Liberia often retreated to home villages after years of living by Liberian cultural standards. For more on this aspect of Baptist thinking, see Isaac, *Transformation*, 170.

153. Although this article was signed "Observer," the author was evidently Teage, given away by his reference to his association with the paper as having begun in 1835 and ended only recently. Teage refers here to Jacob Vonbrumn, a Bassa Baptist preacher who was supported by the American Baptist Board until his death in 1876. See D. E. Dunn, *History of the Episcopal Church*, 119-120; Cason, "Growth of Christianity," 187-188.

154. For Teage's denunciation of slavery, see also "slaves of which the Baracoons were crammed," doc. 13; "now that the slave trade has been abolished," doc. 68; "the British people regard themselves pledged," doc. 75; "suffering one general decree of oppression," doc. 76; and "oppression's cursed yoke," doc. 90.

155. For similar sentiments in an open letter from Liberians to free blacks in the United States, see Liberia, *Independent Republic*.

156. See "professing as the English do," doc. 40; "Gratitude to the British," doc. 75; and "addressed to Queen Victoria," doc. 76. On Haiti, see Genovese, *From Rebellion to Revolution*, 84, also xix.

157. [Hilary Teage], "The *Liberia Herald* with Regard to Independence," ACS, 1847, 21.

158. To compare the theory of government formation implicit in this passage with that presented by Locke, who traced the origin of the state to the preservation of property, see Locke, *Two Treatises*, 341-342, 348-369.

159. Huberich, *Political and Legislative History*, 1: 647n2, 849; "Constitution and Laws of the Commonwealth of Liberia," *AR*, December 1843, 379. The statutes published in 1856 may have been collected by Teage during the last year of his life. The phrase "the pedant and the votary of mystery" (doc. 52) seems to have been a swipe at Samuel Benedict, then serving as chief justice and a perennial political opponent of Teage's political faction from the colonial days. For a similar rejection of pedantry by a generation of British writers influenced by Lockean empiricism and psychology, see Tillotson, Fussell and Waingrow, *Eighteenth-Century English Literature*, 3.

160. A fear of luxuries and political corruption was one strand in early American political thinking, brought over from the country-party tradition of British Whigs, but it found little expression among Jeffersonians, according to Appleby (*Capitalism*, 90, 93). Because liberal republicans believed the future offered limitless possibilities for growth, they sought to equalize society more by raising the living standards of persons at the bottom of society than by tearing down those persons at the top. For evidence of a similar pillaging by American

intellectuals during the struggle for independence of the "records of all peoples in all situations" in search of "constant and universal principles of human nature," see G. S. Wood, *Creation of the American Republic*, 8, also 29, 34-35. Teage might have idealized the elections of the colonial period, which were contested by individuals, each risking rise or fall on the basis of his achievements and reputation. For a similarly negative view of political parties, as "signs of sickness in the body politic," as held by leaders of the American Revolution, see G. S. Wood, *Creation of the American Republic*, 55-65.

161. "Additions to Baptist Churches in the Last Five Months," *AR*, August 1848, 234. Although the Baptists and their progenitors among the Anabaptists had placed a premium on the separation of leadership roles in church and state, this element was neglected by Teage, his father and Lott Cary, all of whom played roles in both institutions simultaneously. For Baptist theology and history, see Lincoln and Mamiya, *Black Church*, 3-4; and Poe, "Not Christopolis." For an example of Teage's view of social ethics, see "their christian welfare," doc. 68, "who taught our hands to fight," doc. 89, and "this colony planted by Christian philanthropy," doc. 96.

162. Lienesch, *New Order of the Ages*, 197; Poe, "Not Christopolis;" Lincoln and Mamiya, *Black Church*, 22.

163. Sobel, *Trabelin' On*; D. B. Davis, *Slavery and Human Progress*, 5-153; Poe, "Not Christopolis," 537; Liberia, *Independence*, end page. Genovese (*Roll, Jordan, Roll*, 252-255) argues that the personas of Moses and Jesus were conflated in African-American Christianity of the pre-Civil War period. This suggests that Liberians' deemphasis of Christ was rooted in African-American theology. It is not possible at this time to comment on the Liberians' image of Moses, given the paucity of sources and the absence of any overt references to the Old Testament leader in those sources that are available. The absence of any reference to Jesus in early Liberian hymns contrasts sharply with the Christ-centered writings of Jehudi Ashmun, the white ACS agent who governed Liberia from 1822 to 1828, as presented in Gurley's *Life of Jehudi Ashmun*.

164. Following Giddens (*Consequences of Modernity*), I use "modernity" to cover the nexus of ideas and dispositions that are normally identified with the Scientific Revolution, as well as the institutional arrangements associated with capitalism and industrialization.

165. This acceptant attitude toward pidgin contrasts sharply with the attitude of later "civilizationists" such as Edward Wilmot Blyden and Alexander Crummell.

166. Mathews, *Religion in the Old South*, 190. See also Poe, "Not Christopolis."

167. For the democratic orientation of Virginia Baptists from 1740 to 1790, see Isaac, *Transformation*, 165-171, 300-308. For the significance of the conversion experience among them, see Lincoln and Mamiya, *Black Church*, 6-7; Lippy, "Religious Experience," 92. The black members of Teage's former church in Richmond showed a preference for these spirituals over European hymns. See Epstein, *Sinful Tunes*, 206-7.

168. See "spirit of improvement," doc. 5; "effort itself to be made by us," doc. 47; "a portion was of our own production," doc. 41; "stocking mania," doc. 4; and "when we raise groundnuts," doc. 49. For information on the political career and authoritarian philosophy of Russwurm, see Sagarin, *John Brown Russwurm*, as well as editorials by Russwurm cited in Staudenraus, *African Colonization Movement*, 167-168; and Dann, *Black Press*, 39. For Crummell, see Moses, *Destiny and Race*; Moses, *Alexander Crummell*, especially 5; Oldfield, "Protestant Episcopal Church";

Oldfield, *Alexander Crummell*. For Blyden, see Lynch, *Edward Wilmot Blyden*.

169. R. R. G. [Ralph Randolph Gurley], "The Late Hilary Teage, of Liberia," *MCJ*, 1853, 71-72.

170. Marcus Garvey, "The True Solution of the Negro Problem," in Bracey, Meier and Rudwick, *Black Nationalism*, 209-210; Moses, *Golden Age*, 19; McCall, "Liberia," 9; Azikiwe, *Liberia in World Politics*; Lynch, *Edward Wilmot Blyden*, 249; Hilary Teage to the Rev. J. B. Pinney, Monrovia, 27 August 1852, in ACS, January 1853, 17-18. The duality of social ethics and Lockean liberalism is taken from Sheldon (1991, 14, 43), who applied it to Jefferson. Unlike Teage, who insisted that the state possess a republican character, Garvey was inclined toward the construction of an empire.

171. Isaac (*Transformation*, 171n*) identified an "ambivalence" between communitarianism and individualism in the Baptist worldview. In Teage's thinking, however, the two were interdependent, the one serving to reinforce the other, reflecting the "dialectic between the communal and the privatistic" identified in the black sacred cosmology by Lincoln and Mamiya (*Black Church*, 13, also 11). For evidence of a similar dialectic in white southern conservatism, see Genovese, *Southern Tradition*.

172. For example, see "we feel confident that these dangers," doc. 43, and "the great object which at first brought us," doc. 45.

173. Cassell, *Liberia*, 264, 276-278, 351. One factor precipitating the civilian overthrow of the Edward James Roye government (1870-1871) was his insistence on lengthening his term of office.

174. For the stereotyping of black Reconstruction leaders, see Stampp, "Tragic Legend"; Rabinowitz, *Southern Black Leaders*, xi-xxiv; Foner, "Black Reconstruction Leaders." For similar myths in the context of Liberian studies, see Burrowes, *Americo-Liberian Ruling Class*, 13-18. Regarding the general ignoring of repatriate motivations and ideas, notable exceptions include F. J. Miller, *Search*; R. M. Miller, *Dear Master*; Wiley, *Slaves No More*; Tyler-McGraw, "Richmond Free Blacks"; Tyler-McGraw, "'The Prize I Mean'." Prominent among those who left Liberia were Edward Wilmot Blyden and Alexander Crummell, noted for their bitter criticism of Liberia.

175. Cassell, *Liberia*, 292; J. Martin, "How to Build a Nation"; "Resolution," *ALL*, 1874, 6-10; "An Act Granting," *ALL*, 1875, 20; "An Act Supplementary," *ALL*, 1884, 7, 10-11; "An Act Authorizing," *ALL*, 1891, 19-20; Lynch, *Edward Wilmot Blyden*, 248; Blyden, *Selected Letters*, 492.

176. Mudimbe, *Invention of Africa*. See also Wilson, *Imperial Experience*, 116-118, 127; Lynch, *Edward Wilmot Blyden*, 119-125.

177. Although Liberian Republicans and their True Whig opponents both extolled the need for virtuous citizens, the former seem to have drawn upon Aristotle for their conceptualization, while the latter leaned toward Plato. As explained by G. W. Sheldon (*Political Philosophy*, 163-164), "Plato's conception of virtue, or *areta*, was a functional standard — a thing was virtuous because it possessed qualities enabling it to function well or effectively ... Plato applied this functional standard of virtue to society through his division of the Republic into classes possessing specific virtues. ... Public virtue for Plato is made up of the virtue of different functionaries in society. ... (Aristotle added the concept of moral virtue, or *ethike*), which governs purely human relations apart from individuals' social functions and requires a

different kind of excellence. … The knowledge of moral virtue requires friendship and citizenship, or participation in public life."

178. This categorization of various forms of action in Teage's thinking relies on Max Weber, who distinguished between four types: traditional (performed simply because it was in the past), affectual (performed simply as an expression of emotion), instrumental (performed after the actor has compared different means to a goal and perhaps after assessing the goal itself), and value-rationality (where the goal and perhaps the means are unexamined. See "Action Theory," in Abercrombie, Hill, and Turner, *Dictionary of Sociology*, 13-15.

179. The tradition of appeals to the reputation of widely accepted authorities seems to have resulted from a merger of Victorian British education and certain African modes of panegyric, but further research on this point is clearly in order. The original meaning of the Greek term sophistes was "expert." The sophists, who were influential in Greece around 400 B. C., emphasized expertise in oratory, above logic, for which they fell into lasting disrepute. For an analysis of the idealist, anti-empiricist and authoritarian philosophy of Alexander Crummell, see "'Cambridge Platonism' in the Republic of Liberia," in Moses, *Wings of Ethiopia*, 79-95, For Blyden's education, see Lynch, *Edward Wilmot Blyden*, 13-14, and Holden, *Blyden*, 50-64. Although Teage used Greek and Roman references in his writings, he cited the wanton sensuality and revelry of the ancients as evidence of their degeneracy; for example, see "with the ancient Greek sensuality," doc. 60.

180. References to Teage's ill health appeared in several issues of the *Herald*, including the editions of 31 October 1842 and 29 December 1849, 10. Two years before his death, he ended a letter to an ACS official with "I now close, by soliciting an interest in your prayers. Yours, in affliction." Hilary Teage to the Rev. J. B. Pinney, Monrovia, 17 May 1851, *AR*, September 1851, 269.

181. "A great star": "Death in Liberia," *MCJ*, 1853, 47; "Chiefest luminary" and "melancholy spirit": Daniel B. Warner, *LH*, 15 June 1853, 86; and "Superior genius and talents": Joseph Jenkins Roberts, "Annual Address of President Roberts, *AR*, April 1854, 43.

182. This letter is from ACS Records, Series IB, vol. 1, reel 153, item no. 99068-71. It was sent by Ezekiel Skinner (1777-1855), an ACS agent in the colony from 12 August 1835 to 25 September 1836 (Huberich, *Political and Legislative History*, 1: 477-515). Its addressee was Ralph Randolph Gurley (1797-1872), ACS agent and secretary (from 1822 to 1872) and U. S. provisional agent to Liberia in 1824, at which time he drafted the colony's first Plan of Civil Government. A native of Connecticut, Gurley from graduated Yale College in 1818 and moved to Washington, DC. Although a licensed Presbyterian clergyman, he was never ordained, devoting his life mainly to African-American colonization (*National Cyclopædia*, 2: 252). See also ["Gurley's Mission to England"], doc. 70.

183. Hosting facilities for new immigrants.

184. John Brooke Pinney (1806-1882), was a missionary to Liberia in 1833, ACS agent in Liberia from 1 January 1834 to 10 May 1835, ACS agent for the New England states after his return from Africa, editor of the *New York Colonization Journal* from 1850 to 1858, and Liberian consul general to the United States in 1860. Born near Baltimore, Maryland, Pinney graduated from the University of Georgia at Athens in 1828 and was admitted to the Georgia bar. He later studied theology at Princeton Seminary and was ordained by the Presbyterian Church in 1832, devoting

all his life thereafter to African-American colonization (Huberich, *Political and Legislative History*, I: 478-479).

185. King Joe Harris was a Bassa chief who razed a Quaker settlement at Port Cresson in 1835 (R. M. Miller, *Dear Master*, 7 1n3).

186. Elliot Cresson was a Quaker businessman who led an internal effort to reform the ACS's shabby bookkeeping and management practices (Huberich, *Political and Legislative History*, 1: 569, 578; Staudenraus, *African Colonization Movement*, 125, 224, 234).

187. John Brown Russwurm (1799-1851) was the founding editor of the *Liberia Herald* newspaper, secretary to the ACS agent in the colony during the early 1830s, and governor of Maryland in Africa from 1836 to 1851 (Huberich, *Political and Legislative History*, 2: 437; for a fuller discussion of Russwurm's role in the press and politics of colonial Liberia, see Burrowes, "Press Freedom in Liberia," 153-220).

188. A reference to the colony of Mississippi in Africa, founded in 1835 by the Louisiana and Mississippi state colonization societies.

189. James Brown (1822?-1853), literate and freeborn, worked for several years with the druggist and chemist Todd & Co. in Washington, D.C., before emigrating in 1834. Within ten years he owned two buildings in Monrovia and held $500 in trade stock and $1,000 in personal property. He served as Sinoe County senator in 1848. In a letter to the ACS on 13 December 1840, Gov. Thomas Buchanan called Brown "one of the very best men in the colony … of good sense, considerable talent as a speaker." See "Despatches from Liberia: Agencies to America," *AR*, 15 March 1841, 89; also "Liberia [from the *National Intelligencer*, 16 August]," *AR*, September 1834, 218; "Arrival of the Liberia Packet," *AR*, April 1848, 97; "Losses of Liberia," *AR*, August 1854, 250; Syfert, "History of the Liberian Coasting Trade," 270).

190. The officers of the Ladies Benevolent Society included Teage's mother, Frances, and his sister, Colinette Johnson. See "An Act to Incorporate the Ladies' Benevolent Society of Monrovia," 1843, in Huberich, *Political and Legislative History*, 2: 1510-1511.

191. Born to a poor family in Albany, New York, Francis Burns was placed to work with a farmer at age four and indentured at eight. Allowed to obtain a formal education, he went as far as high school. Burns was already a lay preacher when he set out for Liberia in 1834. He traveled on the same ship as the Rev. John Seys, superintendent of the Methodist Mission, but relations between the two would soon cool, with Seys charging Burns with "insubordination" in 1840. While serving as pastor of the Upper Caldwell Methodist Church, Burns was c alled "the best preacher on all occasions that has ever resided in the colony. He is certainly a gentleman and a scholar, and his great usefulness as Principal of the Conference Seminary cannot be doubted." See [Editor, *Colonization Herald*], "*Africa's Luminary*," *AR*, August 1844, 240; also Drewel, "Methodist Education," 56, n. 20, quoting Burns, "Deceased Missionary Files," Methodist Missionary Library, New York; Groves, *Planting of Christianity*, 1: 296; U.S. Senate, *U.S. Navy Department*, 376, 395, 402, 405; "From Liberia," *AR*, July 1859, 221; "An Act Amendatory to the Act Entitled an Act Incorporating Liberia College, and the Supplement Thereto," *ALL*, 1862, 37-38; "An Act to Amend and Consolidate the Several Acts Concerning Liberia College," *ALL*, 1862, 87-90).

192. Tediously prolonged.

193. Teage touches here upon two issues that would prove contentious in twentieth-century studies of the slave trade: first, the primacy of European agency in the development of the trans-Atlantic trade and, second, the difference between European serfdom and systems of African enslavement in the Americas. For recent works that support Teage's implicit arguments, see Rodney, *How Europe Underdeveloped Africa*, on the first, and Genovese, *World the Slaveholders Made*, on the second.

194. Apparently from old French "rusty" (meaning rural) and "fief" (meaning chief).

195. Earlier spelling of "mosquito."

196. This is probably a reference to Sao Boso (d. 1837), founder of the Condo Confederation, who was also known as Boatswain. He originated in the area of what came to be called the Kwadu-Boni chiefdom and served as a ward to Litombo Seve, a Bandi leader, who sent Boso to Bopolu. See D. E. Dunn, Beyan, and Burrowes, *Historical Dictionary*, 45.

197. The quote is from Edward Young, "Night the Second" in *The Complaint, or Night-Thoughts on Life Death, and Immortality*, line 376. See Cornford, *Edward Young*, 61.

198. This apparently is an allusion to "The Flood of Years" by nineteenth-century American writer William Cullen Bryant; the poem compares life to a flood, which quickly passes into a quieter afterlife.

199. Uninhabited or uncultivated region; destroyed town.

200. The Italian god of gates and doorways, depicted with two faces looking in opposite directions.

201. This quote is from Psalm 107: 43. This psalm, entitled "Thanksgiving to the Lord for His Great Works of Deliverance," discusses God's salvation of His people from "bounds of iron."

202. This passage contains several words that are no longer widely used. These include "clime" for climate; "pusses" for a girl or young woman; "undentized" meaning without tooth; "variegated," meaning distinguished by variety, especially of colors; and "gew-gaws," meaning trinkets or trifles.

203. Relating to the Tuscany region of Italy.

204. Several phrases in this paragraph have fallen into disuse: "summum bonum," which is Latin for greatest or supreme good; "sumptuary," meaning regulating or limiting personal expenditures; and "animadversion," meaning criticism.

205. The number of immigrants arriving in Liberia in 1848 was 441, up from 51 in 1847 and 89 in 1846. "Table of Emigrants Sent by American Colonization Society," ACS, 1867, 59-60.

206. This nineteenth-century English word means recent.

207. This letter is from ACS Papers, series IB, vol. 2, reel 145, item no. 99178-79.

208. White, Hagar and Company, *Specimen*. A copy of this work is in the collection of the American Antiquarian Society in Worcester, Massachusetts.

209. Anthony David Williams (1799-1860) served as the acting governor of the colony from 25 September 1836 to 1 April 1839.

210. This letter is from ACS Papers, series IB, vol. 2, reel 145, item no. 99198-99. Its addressee is Samuel Wilkeson (1781-1848), New York judge, state senator and mayor of Buffalo. Entrusted in 1838 with the task of reorganizing the ACS's management practices and supervising its finances, Wilkeson instituted a line of packets — ships that brought cargo and mail from

Liberia to the ports of Baltimore and Philadelphia on a regular basis. He also edited the *African Repository* for two years. *National Cyclopædia*, 11, 414.

211. Property "lawfully" taken at sea in time of war.

212. The source of this letter is "Letter from Mr. Teage," *AR*, 15 March 1841, 95. Despite several searches, the original letter was not found among the ACS Papers.

213. The Rev. Squire Chase first served as a Methodist missionary to Liberia in 1837, but returned to the United States that year due to poor health. In 1842, he replaced John Seys as superintendent of the Methodist Mission and editor of the church's newspaper, *Africa's Luminary*. Rogers, Liberian Journalism, 81-83.

214. This paragraph contains several references needing fuller identification: "Dragooning" means to subjugate or persecute by the imposition of troops, while "eleemosynary" (from Medieval Latin) relating to or depending on charity. The "Mr. Baxter" mentioned here was probably George Baxter, a freeborn literate millwright from South Carolina and the only male adult with that last name listed in immigrant shipping records from 1820 to 1843. He arrived on 16 January 1833 with Ann (age 25), Daniel (8), Elizabeth (5), Eugenia (2), Henry (7), Jeremiah (3), Rose A. (4) and an infant. Shick, *Emigrants*, 5.

215. Although born a slave, Samuel Benedict (1792-1854) arrived from Savannah, Georgia, with a considerable collection of books and was a founding member of the Liberia Lyceum. In 1843, he held $3,000 in stock and four warehouses worth $1,000 each, as well as two farms planted with coffee, sugar cane and other crops. He served as a Superior Court judge in the colonial government, president of the Constitutional Convention of 1847 and first chief justice of the republic (1847--1854). An opposition party leader during the colonial period and in the early years of the republic, he ran unsuccessfully for the presidency against Joseph Jenkins Roberts in 1847 and again in 1852 (Burrowes, "Black Christian Republicans," 67-69). Nugent M. Hicks (1809?--18??) had been a slave and was somewhat literate when he arrived from Pennsylvania in 1830. He served as a colonel in the colonial militia and by 1843 owned three buildings with $1,000 in trade stock, held $2,500 in personal property and made an estimated commission of $18,500. He was declared an insolvent debtor in 1851 but supplied goods to British naval vessels in 1852 (Syfert, "History of the Liberian Coasting Trade," 275). James B. McGill (1820-1858) arrived from Maryland in 1831 in the company of his parents and siblings, all of whom were literate and freeborn. By 1843, he owned three buildings in Monrovia, $3,000 in trade stock, in $4,500 personal property, and two ships, Eliza Francis (1845-47) and Patsy (1848). He served as Montserrado County representative in 1848, speaker of the House in 1849, and Liberia College trustee in 1852 (Syfert, "History of the Liberian Coasting Trade," 277).

216. For an earlier use of the phrase "sly dalliance," see doc. 15.

217. John B. Gripon (1809-1847) was a literate freeborn carpenter who arrived from South Carolina in 1833. He was elected to the colonial legislature in December 1840 on the opposition ticket. In 1847, he was an associate judge of Montserrado County and head of the Methodist Liberia Conference Seminary. He died two months after being elected senator from Montserrado. Burrowes, "Black Christian Republicans," 70.

218. The Rev. Squire Chase, editor of *Africa's Luminary*.

219. The issue of the *Herald* that contained this article also carried on page 8 a letter from George S. Brown accusing Rev. Chase of refusing to pay a lawful bill, calling Brown a liar and black scoundrel, and threatening to hit him with a chair.

220. "Vouchsafed" means to condescend, to grant or to bestow; "nice" means wanton or profligate; obsolete.

221. "Bowers" means a private chamber in a medieval castle; "interior" refers to one's spiritual being or a boudoir. One meaning of "Sancho" in English is one's wife's or girlfriend's lover, which might have been a reference to Sancho Panza, Don Quixote's companion in the novel of the same name.

222. "Rapier" means a pointed sword; "squib" refers to a broken firecracker that burns but doesn't explode.

223. Having poor vision; slow in understanding of discernment; dull.

224. Obstinately disobedient or rebellious; insubordinate.

225. The original text refers to "crowns," but the context suggests that "crows" was intended.

226. Gotorah (also "Gotola" and "Goterah") was a Loma chief and an ally of the Condo Confederacy. He led an attack on the Methodist station at Heddington in 1840, but was repulsed by a Liberian force led by Sion Harris. A subsequent counterattack by the Liberia militia, which drove Gotorah from his fort, led several interior chiefs to sign peace treaties with the repatriates. R. M. Miller, *Dear Master*, 76-77n2.

227. "Kondah" is probably an alternative rendering of "Condo," the name of a powerful multi-ethnic confederation centered around Bopolu. Although the slave trade had provided the basis of Condo prosperity, the confederacy entered a strategic alliance with the early Liberian repatriates, defending them militarily against hostile Dei and Bassa neighbors and hosting a Methodist mission. D. E. Dunn, Beyan, and Burrowes, *Historical Dictionary*, 45.

228. Habitual untalkativeness, silence.

229. Not easily understood; obscure; hidden.

230. A person having a loud voice.

231. Pythi was the priestess of the Temple of Apollo at Delphi; she delivered the oracles.

232. This is probably a reference to the Rev. Squire Chase, editor of *Africa's Luminary*, who left Liberia in July 1843 for the United States, where he died a few months later. Rogers, "Liberian Journalism," 81-83.

233. This article was reprinted in *MCJ*, December 1845, 84-85. No copy could be located of the July 1847 issue of the *Herald*, from which this was reportedly taken.

234. Writing down.

235. Teage used "capsicum," the scientific term for pepper, to remind readers of the "heat" he that could unleash on them for not paying their subscriptions, in place of this gentle chiding.

236. Italics have been added to aid the reader in distinguishing the voice of one character from the other in this sketch.

237. Born to free parents on 2 September 1809, Beverly P. Yates left his native Richmond, Virginia, on 10 January 1829 for Liberia. In addition to establishing a major mercantile business, Yates rose to the positions of brigadier general in the militia, judge of the Court of Sessions, and

probate judge, and he was elected vice president of the republic. He was appointed financial agent of the Southern Baptist Mission Board in 1854 and as superintendent of the mission from 1859 to 1875. His correspondences with the Board were preserved in SBHLA, box 65 (*LH*, 29 June 1849, 31; Poe, "Not Christopolis," 540; Syfert, "History of the Liberian Coasting Trade," 282; Wiley, *Slaves No More*, 329, Letter 178, n. 2. For other references to Yates, see doc. 30.

238. Frederick B. James arrived in 1826 at age 8, accompanying his father, Jonathan (age 40), Keziah (11), Levi (3), Moore (6), and an infant. Following the death of Jonathan in 1832, Levi was taken into the household of Hilary Teage, who apprenticed him as a printer to the *Herald*. Shick, *Emigrants*, 50; U. S. Senate, *U.S. Navy Department*. See also "the station of brother F. B. James," doc. 26.

239. In 1845 the U. S. African Squadron captured the barque *Pons*, which was carrying more than over 900 slaves bound for Brazil. Some 756 survivors of the *Pons*, mainly Ibo and Congo, were resettled in Liberia. Many of the recaptured were apprenticed as farmers in the New Georgia area while others were taken into Liberian homes, which facilitated their absorption of Christianity and the cultural ideals of the repatriates. See "The Africans by the *Pons*," *AR*, January 1847, 25; Foote, *Africa and the American Flag*, 243-53; Gilliland, *Voyage to a Thousand Cares*.

240. Italics were added to aid readers in distinguishing between the two speakers.

241. This letter is from SBHLA, box 60. It was addressed to the secretary of the Foreign Mission Board, a position that was occupied by James Barnett Taylor for 26 years. Taylor wrote, among other books, *The Life of Lott Carey*. A native of Lincolnshire, England, Taylor lived for 12 years in New York, before moving in 1817 to Richmond, which remained his home until his death in 1871; see *Encyclopedia of Southern Baptists*, 2: 1347.

242. For more information on Frederick S. James, see doc. 23, and "the station of brother F. B. James," doc. 26.

243. This church was at Farmington, which is located on the Junk River. The person referred to as "Brother Smart" does not appear in the shipping records of the ACS, suggesting that he might have come out on his own. The only man with that last name and from that period, Francis Smart, emigrated on 10 July 1827 but is recorded as having died of a diseased brain in 1842. Shick, *Emigrants*, 88.

244. John T. Richardson, a literate farmer, was age 19 when, on 24 March 1829, he emigrated from Virginia with his family: Fountain (25), a farmer; Lucretia (60); Martha (16); Roxy (21); and Samuel (53), all emancipated. Richardson served the Southern Baptist Mission Board from 1849 to about 1862. His correspondence to the Board can be found in SBHLA, box 49, along with letters from several of his relatives (Shick, *Emigrants*, 79). Adam B. Anderson, a freeborn shoemaker, was age 29 when on 16 January 1833 he emigrated from Georgia on the *Hercules*. He served as assistant editor of the *Liberia Herald* and as acting editor at least once during Hilary Teage's absence (ibid, 1; *LH*, 5 September 1845, 2).

245. Henry Underwood, a freeborn native of Kentucky, emigrated in January 1847 at age forty-five. He served as a missionary with the Southern Baptist Mission Board from 1856 to 1872. R. T. Brown, *Immigrants to Liberia*, 59; SBHLA, box 61.

246. These brackets appear in the origin. David White, a freeborn native of North Carolina, was age 18 when, on 11 August 1827, he emigrated on the *Doris*, with his family: Essex (26), a farmer; Faithy (22); and Jane (21), all freeborn (Shick, *Emigrants*, 104). The adult male from this period in the ACS shipping records most closely matching the last name "Lockhart" is "Adam Locket," who emigrated from Mississippi to Millsburg on the *Rover* at age 30 with his family: Bernard (13); Carolina (10); Charlotte (33); David (12); Eliza (8); and Samuel (4). *ibid*, 59.

247. L. K. Crocker, who was Bassa by birth, served as a teacher and missionary with the Southern Baptist Mission Board from 1845 to 1875; his letters and other correspondence are preserved in SBHLA, box 15.

248. Monrovia.

249. Alternative spelling for "frenzied."

250. John 3:8.

251. John Benham replaced the Rev. Squire Chase as superintendent of the Methodist Mission. Just before leaving Liberia in 1847, Benham recommended to the Methodist headquarters in the United States that white missionaries no longer be sent to Liberia. That policy was adopted along with a decrease in financial support. D'Amico, "Spiritual and Secular Activities," 104-5.

252. For more information on Frederick S. James, see note 239 above and "Deacon F. B. James," doc. 23.

253. The original seems to read "which they have once unsettled the present established order of things."

254. This letter is from SBHLA, box 60. At its bottom is a note in a different style of handwriting: "Cape Mount an important missionary field. Grand Cape Mount. Inviting field. By the subjoined letter from Brother H. Teage, dated Monrovia Jan. 3, the attention of the Board is called to Cape Mount as a point which it is important at the earliest period to occupy. This position lies some fifty or sixty miles above Monrovia. Whether it shall be occupied by us or not depends upon the means which shall be funded by the churches. We have one hundred churches in the Southern country, any one of which might easily supply the necessary funds. Such supply we hope to realize. The letter thus refers to the subject. Cape Mount is an inviting field. See opposite."

255. This paragraph contains several words that have potentially confusing meanings: "lump" is a small cube of sugar; "pert" means flippantly cocky; and "waggish" means comic or foolish.

256. Aaron Davis, an emancipated literate blacksmith from Virginia, was age thirty-one when, on 9 December 1834, he emigrated on the *Ninus* to Bassa. He served as a missionary of the Southern Baptist Mission Board from 1847 to 1861. According to letters from B. Yates dates 20 May 1869 and 5 October 1869, Davis drowned in 1869 in the St. John's River, near the spot where John H. Chesseman had drowned (Shick, *Emigrants*, 26; SBHLA, box 16). John Day was born on 18 February 1797 in Hicksford, Virginia, and emigrated to Liberia in 1830. He founded Hope High School in Monrovia before moving to Bexley where he operated a school for twenty pupils and a press that published at least two primers in the Bassa language. Day was already an ordained Baptist pastor at Bexley, Grand Bassa, when, on 7 September 1846, the Southern Baptist Mission Board appointed him to serve as the superintendent of its Liberia mission. He served in that

position until his death on 15 February 1859. The extensive correspondences of Day and three of his sons who served with the Board are preserved in SBHLA, box 17.

257. This letter is from SBHLA, box 60. It was marked "Recd. May 11, 1848." Boston J. Drayton (11 August 1817-??), a freeborn native of South Carolina, emigrated in November 1845 on the *Roanoke*. He was appointed as a missionary to Liberia and Nigeria by the Southern Baptist Mission Board on 3 January 1848 –– the first black given such an appointment. Drayton maintained his connection to the Board, even after he was elected governor of Maryland in Africa in 1857. He ran unsuccessfully for the presidency of the republic in 1863, while serving as pastor of the Baptist church in Cape Palmas and head of the national Liberia Providence Baptist Association. He was serving as chief justice of the Supreme Court of Liberia at the time of his death in 1866. His letters to the Board, as well as letters from his wife Catherine, herself a missionary to Liberia and Sierra Leone, are preserved in SBHLA, boxes 17 and 18. See also R. T. Brown, *Immigrants to Liberia*, 22; Poe, "Not Christopolis," 540. William Andrew Johnson later served as acting secretary of the treasury (1875) and secretary of state (1869-70).

258. Teage implies here that each biblical passage offers multiple meannings, and even a single reader might derive different interpretations at each reading. His view stands in sharp contrast to many contemporary Christian fundamentalists who view each biblical passage as having one meaning which does not change.

259. This letter is from SBHLA, box 60. A note on the back of the letter in another handwriting reads "Recd. Aug. 7."

260. This letter is from SBHLA, box 60. According to a marginal note in another handwriting, this letter was "Recd. Aug. 7."

261. "Ult." was a widely used abbreviation for ultimo mense, Latin for "in the previous month."

262. Three Baptist clergy was mentioned in this passage: John N. Lewis (1791-1876) was a freeborn Virginian who arrived in 1824 with a family of six. He was elected to the Colonial Council in 1834, appointed colonial secretary in 1840, and appointed Montserrado County senator in 1847. He published the first digest of statutes in 1841 and was a member of the fraternal order of Free Ancient and Accepted Masons in 1867. Lewis served as secretary of state under four presidents, namely Joseph Jenkins Roberts (1848-54); Stephen A. Benson (1858-60); James S. Payne (1868-69); and Edward J. Roye (1870-71). Convicted of treason for his part in the fateful British loan of 1871, which contributed to the overthrow of the Roye regime, his death sentence was commuted by President Roberts upon his return to office (Burrowes, "Black Christian Republicans," 73-74). As for Nathaniel Brander, a few of his letters are preserved in SBHLA, box 9. James C. Minor served as printer of the *Liberia Herald* and in a letter to an ACS agent dated 27 August 1852 styled himself "conductor of that paper" on behalf of the proprietors. He was a member of the first independent Masonic Order of Liberia, formed in 1851 (Rogers, "Liberian Journalism," 72-74; Shick, *Behold*, 162n50).

263. For other references to Beverly P. Yates, see "Colonel B. P. Yates," doc. 23, and "Messers Payne and Yates," doc. 86.

264. Moore Worrell, a freeborn carpenter from North Carolina, was age 47 when in May 1848 he emigrated on the *Amazon*. He was followed two years later on the *Liberia Packet* by Betsey Worrell (48) and Moore Worrell (8), both emancipated (R. T. Brown, *Immigrants to Liberia*, 65).

265. A scolding or sharp rebuke.

266. This letter is from SBHLA, box 60.

267. This item is from SBHLA, box 60.

268. Taylor had already published his *Biography of Elder Lott Cary* (1837), which was destined to influence most other writings on Cary. The author, perhaps in the process of preparing a revised version of his book, apparently had solicited information on Cary from several persons. See also N. E. Brander, Monrovia, 17 May 1849, to Rev. J. B. Taylor, Richmond, in SBHLA, box 9.

269. For an earlier article on Colin Teage, which might have been written by Hilary, see "Reward of Merit," MCJ, August 1846, 221.

270. Happening in the current month.

271. This letter is from SBHLA, box 60. Its reverse side bears a postmark of "Baltimore, July 3," which seems to confirm that it indeed was mailed by Teage during his U. S. visit, but the sender's information is given, in a different handwriting, as "B. J. Drayton, April 12, 1849." Gurley's *Life of Jehudi Ashmun* includes a character sketch of Lott Cary, which claims that he had apologized for his role in the rebellion of 1823.

272. Eli Ayers, agent of the ACS (1821-24), signed the Treaty of Mesurado with local rulers, which resulted in the transference of the first group of repatriates from Sierra Leone to the Cape Mesurado region.

273. This letter is from SBHLA, box 60. Badagry, Nigeria, is a town along the Atlantic coast that lies east of Cotonou, Benin, and west of Lagos. The "mission to Central Africa" included Thomas Jefferson Bowen, Hervey Goodale and Robert F. Hill. One of the most celebrated American Baptist missionaries of the nineteenth century, Bowen was born on 2 January 1814 in Jackson County, Georgia. He was commissioned as a missionary to Africa on 22 February 1849, where he served for seven years. In 1853, he was joined in the field by his wife, Lurenna Henrietta Davis, a native of Greensboro, Georgia, and graduate of the Georgia Female College. Hill, a black Virginian, opted to remain in Liberia, while his white companions proceeded to Nigeria, where Goodale died. After returning to the United States in 1867, Hill delivered an address to the convention of the American Baptist Missionary Union, which is credited with helping to generate renewed missionary interests in Africa among northern Baptists. S. D. Martin, "Black Baptists," 71-72.

274. This was the wife of the Rev. N. S. Bastion, superintendent of the Methodist Mission in Liberia from September 1849 to August 1850, during which time he suspended the publication of *Africa's Luminary*, the Methodist paper that had long been a rival to the *Liberia Herald*. After Bastion's departure, the leadership of the Methodist church devolved to a Liberian for the first time. D'Amico, "Spiritual and Secular Activities," 106-107.

275. An earlier letter from Teage had already alerted Taylor to this development; see: Hilary Teage, Monrovia, 24 May 1852, to Rev. J. B. Taylor, Richmond, in SBHLA, box 60. A native of New England, Eli Ball (1776-1853) moved to Virginia in 1823. Having served first as pastor of the Baptist Church of Lynchburg, he moved to Richmond in 1826, where he became especially active with the various Baptist missionary boards. In 1852, he was sent to Liberia by the

Foreign Mission Board to prepare a survey of the work there and make recommendations. Burrows, *First Century*, 87-88.

276. This is probably John T. Richardson.

277. See the letter from H. Standish [?], 18 October 1850, to Hilary Teage, in SBHLA, box 60.

278. Lt. Andrew H. Foote was commander of the U.S. brig Perry in 1850-51, when it visited the coast of Africa. For his recollection of that visit, which includes a positive portrayal of Teage, see Foote, *Africa and the American Flag*.

279. This was probably the wife of the Rev. William Crocker, who is mentioned in doc. 68.

280. Past tense of dare.

281. "Mr. Harding" is a reference to Joseph M. Harden, a native of Baltimore, Maryland, who was appointed a missionary of the Southern Baptist Mission Board on 11 December 1850. He served as a pastor at New Virginia, Liberia, from 1850 to 1855, when he transferred to Nigeria. Together with his wife, the former Sarah Marsh, Harden is credited with organizing the First Baptist Church of Lagos, erected at their own expense, as well as the Lagos Baptist Academy, a school for both boys and girls. After Harden died in 1864, his widow continued to serve the Nigerian mission. Their son, Samuel, became principal of the academy, after furthering his education in the United States. Harden's correspondence with the Board can be found in SBHLA, box 26. Jacob Vonbrun, a Bassa chief and Baptist preacher who was supported by the American Baptist Board until his death in 1876; see "Now a Harriss, a Vonbrumn," doc. 68.

282. "Brother Scott" is probably Isaac Scott, a freeborn preacher from North Carolina, who was age 50 when in November 1852, he emigrated on the *Linda Stewart* with his family: Ann (6); Franklin (8); Isaac (22); James (4); Willy (36); Polly (13); and Theosphilu (15), all freeborn (R. T. Brown, *Immigrants to Liberia*, 53). "Mr. Campbell" is referring to Alexander Campbell (1788-1866) or his father Thomas (1763-1854), who together founded the Disciples of Christ (1809), which rejects denominational creed.

283. This letter is from SBHLA, box 60. It is recorded as recorded as "Recd. May 10. Answered." Although Taylor's name does not appear on this letter, it was probably sent to him in his capacity as corresponding secretary of the Southern Baptist Convention, as were the majority of letters from Teage that were found in the convention's archives.

284. From "Hymn 129: Submission and Deliverance" by Isaac Watts, first published in *Hymns of Isaac Watts* (1707).

285. This letter is from ACS Papers, series IB, vol. 2, reel 154, item no. 99188 90.

286. "Fur articles" is a reference to animal skins. They were apparently sent to the American Institute of the City of New York which hosted an annual fair celebrating agriculture and industry from 1833 to 1848. The Institute was located at Liberty and Broadway from 1833 to 1834, at 41 Cortlandt Street from 1834 to 1836, at 187 Broadway from 1836 to 1839, and at City Hall in the Park, from 1839 to 1848. It had proposed an exhibition of "the Works of Industry of all Nations" to be held in London in May 1851.

287. His father, Colin Teage, died while returning from that visit to the United States. See the letter from Peyton Skipworth to John Hartwell Cocke, 22 April 1840, in R. M. Miller, *Dear Master*, 72-77.

288. This letter is from ACS Papers, series IB, vol. 2, reel 154, item no. 99287-88. The suit discussed here was brought against the colonial government by the Methodist Mission challenging a recently instituted tax on goods brought into the Colony by the churches (*AL*, 18 September 1840; d'Amico, "Spiritual and Secular Activities," 123. For a fuller discussion of this case, see Burrowes, "Press Freedom in Liberia," 153-220. John Seys (1799-1872), a white West Indian, was superintendent of the Methodist Episcopal Church from 1834 to 1840 and founding editor of the *Africa's Luminary*. He left the Colony in 1840, after the opposition group he led, the Seys Party, was defeated in the elections by supporters of the colonial government. He returned as U. S. agent to Liberia in 1858 and later served as U. S. resident minister (Huberich, *Political and Legislative History*, 1: 728).

289. Archaic; used here to mean "before."

290. Latin for "extreme law is the greatest injury."

291. The number of immigrants arriving in Liberia in 1845 was 187, up from 170 in 1844 and 85 in 1843 ("Table of Emigrants Sent by American Colonization Society," *ACS*, 1867, 59.)

292. Two words in this sentence are archaic: "benisons," meaning blessings or benedictions (from Middle English), and "enervate," lacking physical, mental, or moral vigor.

293. This is probably L. T. Jones, who was captain of the HMS *Penelope*, under the command of Commodore Sir Charles Hatham, when the factories and barracoons were destroyed at Dombocorro Island in Gallinas territory in 1849. From 1844 to 1846, he was placed in command of the British squadron, which numbered from 12 to 21 ships, including his flagship, the *Penelope*, a steamer with 21 guns. Ward, *Royal Navy*, 183-185; Lloyd, *Navy and the Slave Trade*, 161. For another references to the *Penelope*, see "the frigate Penelope, doc. 73.

294. Boastfulness or bravado.

295. Boats.

296. The lower counties were Grand Bassa and Sinoe. When a referendum on independence was called in 1847, Sinoe did not participate and voting was disrupted in Bassa, where all of the 49 collected ballots were opposed. As a result, ballots were cast by only 269 of the colony's approximately 600 eligible voters. See J. W. Lugenbeel [colonial physician, Monrovia] to William McLain [ACS secretary, Washington, D. C.], 14 October 1847, ACS Papers, Letters from Liberia, 1844-1850, cited in Huberich, *Political and Legislative History*, 1: 845-46. For more on the opposition of the lower counties to the movement for independence, see "The members of the lower counties," doc. 44.

297. In this passage, Teage criticizes the reasoning of local opponents to Liberia's independence. He implies that their approach is deductive or top-down, reasoning from theory through hypothesis and observation to confirmation. Instead, he recommends an inductive or bottom-up approach, one that begins with observation then moves up through pattern and tentative hypothesis to theory.

298. A similar tension existed between localism and nationalism in the American legislative process; these undergirded two contrasting conceptualizations of legislator-constituent relations called "petitioning" and "instructing." As described by G. S. Wood (*Creation of the American Republic*, 189), "Petitioning implied that the representative was a superior so completely possessed of the

full authority of all the people that he must be solicited, never commanded, by his particular electors and must speak only for the general good and not merely for the interests of his local constituents. Instructing, on the other hand, implied that the delegate represented no one but the people who elected him and that he was simply a mistrusted agent of his electors, bound to follow their directions. The use of instructions — directions drawn up by a body of constituents to their particular representatives — had long been common in colonial politics, especially in New England."

299. Printed under the title "Independence of Liberia," the article was preceded by this note: "In the following article there are two misapprehensions, or misconceptions of the facts in the case. The first regards the nature of the proposition made to the commonwealth of Liberia by the Society. The article says the proposition was unaccompanied by a single word of explanation or stipulation; while the fact is, and whoever reads the article of the Board of Directors at their last meeting, will perceive it, the Board offered to Liberia the privilege of assuming the entire control of its affairs, and the Legislature of Liberia was requested to appoint a commissioner or commissioners to confer and make definite arrangements with the Executive Committee touching all the matters connected with the future condition and relations of Liberia with the Society. We are therefore much astonished that any person of as much shrewdness as the editor of the *Liberia Herald*, should have blundered as much as he has in the following article on this point. The other point of misconception is contained in the last sentence of the article, where the impression is made that the Society acted first, and thus threw on the people of Liberia the necessity of acting; while the truth is that the subject was brought before the Board of Directors at their last meeting, but the action of the Colonial Legislature at their meeting the year preceding. It is therefore rather late for them to pretend that they have been crowded into the consideration of this subject. They stirred the matter first, and it then being as it were, a great way off, excited little fear for the consequences. But now the responsibility is on them, and they would fain throw it off. But they cannot, and they need not. All will be right, we doubt not." An extract from this article appeared as "The *Liberia Herald* with regard to independence," *AR*, March 1847, 81-82. Although it was first published in the *Liberia Herald*, that issue of the paper has not been found. For more on the opposition of the lower counties to the movement for independence, see "the course which rumor says," doc. 43.

300. William L. Weaver (1796?-18??), freeborn and with some literacy, arrived from Virginia in 1824. He served as a military captain in 1827, councilor for Grand Bassa County in 1847 and Grand Bassa senator in 1848. In 1835 he sold goods in New York worth $5,000 to $6,000, and by 1843 he owned two buildings at Edina, $600 in trade stock and $2,000 in personal property with commissions of about $8,000. From 1844 to 1868, he operated two trading vessels along the West African coast. Syfert, "History of the Liberian Coasting Trade," 281.

301. "Proximo," short for the Latin phrase proximo mense, means "occurring during the next month."

302. Prosperity, happiness or in the common good.

303. Atmosphere of social harmony.

304. Kind, gracious.

305. Teage refers here to two British and two American legislators: Peel (1788-1850) helped pass the Catholic Emancipation Act while serving as British home secretary (1822-27 and 1828-30) and later served as prime minister (1834-35 and 1841-46); Russell (1792-1878), an advocate of parliamentary reform while serving as prime minister (1846-1852 and 1865-1866); Daniel Webster (1782-1852), an American lawyer renowned for his oratory, who served in Congress (1813-30) and as secretary of state (1840-43); and John Calhoun (1782-1850), called the voice of the South for his leadership of the states-rights' movement while representing South Carolina in Congress (1832-44) and was regarded, with Webster, as one of America's greatest orators.

306. This letter is from ACS Papers, series IB, vol. 3, reel 154, item no. 99501-2.

307. Used in this context as a synonym of "something."

308. Thomas Buchanan served from 1 January 1836 to August 1837 as governor of Bassa Cove, a colony of the Pennsylvania and New York auxiliaries of the ACS, and from December 1838 until his death on 3 September 1841 as the first governor of the commonwealth of Liberia. Born in Franklin County, New York, Buchanan became interested in the antislavery cause early in life but by age twenty-seven was a confirmed colonizationist. Teage delivered the funeral oration for Buchanan, who died at Bassa Cove; see "Sermon on the Death of Gov. Thomas Buchanan," doc. 94.

309. Three pages in this issue of the *Herald* were mislabeled as page 3. The correct pagination was discerned by referring to the numbering of pages in the previous and the subsequent issues.

310. "An Act Authorizing a Loan, and Fixing the Currency of the Republic, and Authorizing the Appointment of Sub-Treasurers in the Counties of Grand Bassa and Sinoe; Laws Enacted by the Senate and House of Representatives of the Republic of Liberia, Passed at Their First Session, Held in Monrovia, in January and February, 1848," *AR*, November 1848, 329-30.

311. Both the *Colonization Herald* of February 1852, and the *Liberia Herald* of 6 October 1852, announced the publication that year of a "Compilation of Laws," credited to Teage, who was then serving as attorney general. Unfortunately, no copy has been traced. That document might have been incorporated into Killian, *Statute Laws of the Republic*. Killian, it should be noted, was one of the *Liberia Herald* printers during Teage's tenure as editor. For a similar code compiled by Teage during Liberia's colonial period, see Teage, *Constitution and Laws*.

312. A shrewd attorney adept at the discovery and manipulation of legal technicalities.

313. The first four men listed here are obviously these British writers: John Milton (1608-1674), acclaimed for his *Paradise Lost* and *Paradise Regained*, in which reason triumphs over passion; Edmund Burke (1729-1797), the Irish philosopher renowned for his defense of constitutional government against prevailing abuses; Isaac Newton (1642-1727) renowned for his discovery of gravity and study of optics; and James Hall (1761-1832), the Scottish founder of experimental geology. The reference to "Chalmers" is more ambiguous, however, indicating one of two Scottish writers: Alexander (1759-1834), a journalist noted for his thirty-two-volume *General Biographical Dictionary*, published between 1812 and 1817, or George (1742-1825), renowned for his biographies of Daniel Defoe, Thomas Paine and Mary, Queen of Scots. Teage's preference for Scottish writers, which was in keeping with the intellectual milieu of antebellum Virginia,

might have received reinforcement from several Scotsmen with whom he was in contact during early childhood, including the Rev. Jacob Gregg of the First Baptist Church and his father's second owner, Robert Bell. The only Americans included on this list were the signatories of the Declaration of Independence, a choice probably determined in part by Teage's republican proclivities.

314. This last snide remark seems to have been a reference to Samuel Benedict, then serving as chief justice and a perennial opponent of Teage's political faction from the colonial days.

315. Teage is referring to his tenure as editor of the *Liberia Herald*.

316. Maryland in Liberia, about two hundred miles eastward of Monrovia on the coast, was founded in 1831 by the Maryland State Colonization Society. Although an auxiliary of the ACS, the Maryland Society administered its colony separately from other repatriate settlements, in protest of the national organization's administrative and financial problems. The colony declared its independence in 1853 — the year Teage died, but four years later voted to relinquish its sovereignty and join Liberia. P. Campbell, *Maryland in Africa*.

317. Teage seems here to be alluding to what might have been the influence of the Poro, a male power association responsible for the enculturation of young men as well as the adjudication of asocial and interethnic issues. The Poro was most active in central and western Liberia, particularly among the Gola, Vai, Bandi, Mende, Loma, Kpelle and part of the Ma. D. E. Dunn Beyan, and Burrowes, *Historical Dictionary*, 268.

318. This letter is from ACS Papers, series IB, vol. 4, reel 155, item no. 99770-71.

319. Anthony J. Woods was a freeborn, literate blacksmith, who arrived from the state of Maryland in January 1828, with Garreston (1); and Julian (28) (Shick, *Emigrants*, 109). Beginning with "We have one Doctor" and ending with "a cabin passage," a line was drawn through the section on A. J. Woods, but it seems to have been done after the letter was sent.

320. This article is from *AR*, July 1837, 193. No copy was found of the January 1837 issue of the *Liberia Herald*, in which this article first appeared.

321. Supplies.

322. Someone who was subject to surveillance.

323. Siaka of Gendama was the ruler of Gallinas country and head of the Massaquoi family in the early nineteenth century. His involvement in the slave trade led to a British blockade of the Gallinas in 1826, which was lifted one year later. Siaka, who lived with his sons in European-style houses in a well fortified town, died in the late 1840s. He was succeeded by a son, Prince Mana. For more on the role of Mana (also rendered "Manah"), see "'Prince Manah' the commander-in-chief," doc. 59, and Foray, *Historical Dictionary*, 194.

324. This passage describes three forms of trial by ordeal once sanctioned by some local cultures, especially in western Liberia, for uncovering guilt or malevolence. The first — and most prevalent — involved the drinking of a poisonous decoction from the bark of Erythrophlaeum guineeuse. If the accused person died from the draught, that was taken to be proof of guilt, whereas survival was evidence of innocence. The word "saucy," a form of West African pidgin sometimes rendered as "sassy," is thought to be derived from the Anglo-French word "sauce," which was used by sailors in the eighteenth century to describe something spicy or pungent.

The second test involved plunging one's hand and arm into boiling palm oil. In the third, a hot cutlass would be placed against the skin of the accused person. H. H. Johnston, *Liberia*, 2: 1065-66.

325. A judicial proceeding whose purpose is to obtain relief at the hands of a court.

326. This is a reference to smooth, fine clay taken from the hills of termites, known locally as "bug-a-bugs." For a description of these termites by Teage, see "Bug-a-bugs," doc. 83.

327. Italics have been added to aid the reader in distinguishing the voice of one character from the other in this sketch.

328. A horsetail is the symbol of political authority in many local cultures.

329. Teage seems to use "our friend" sarcastically in reference to Lake. Testifying in January 1831 concerning slave trading at Gallinas, Lake, a merchant at Freetown, reported seeing a money bag stamped with the name of a slave vessel, "Mauzanares," in the hands of Teage, a former trading partner, suggesting that he was involved in the slave trade. "Sierra Leone: Charge delivered by Mr. Justice Jeffcot relating to the Slave Trade 1831-32," *British Parliamentary Papers*, 80: 489; "John Dean Lake I owed sixty pounds," doc. 80.

330. Zolu Duma (??-d. 1827) was also known as Peter Softly or Peter Careful. Although of Gola origin, he was reared by a Bassa trader, Wuling, who introduced him to the Vai coast. From there, Duma traveled to Europe where he remained briefly. After returning to the pre-Liberian coast, he established himself at Gohn, a town near a coastal creek that served as a transshipment point to the interior. He eventually gained control of the coastal Vai in the Gawula and Tombe areas, the southwest Gola, north of the Lofa River, and some Dei, on the basis of his prosperity in trading slaves, camwood, rice, ivory, and locally woven cloth. The Liberian repatriates established a Baptist mission at his well-fortified town, but it was closed following his death in 1826. Holsoe, "A Study of Relations," 334; Dunn, Beyan, and Burrowes, *Historical Dictionary*, 116.

331. Chief Jenkins, also known as Fan Fila Yenge was a Gola ruler who, in 1833 broke away from the Gola confederation centered at Gon. After the death of Zolu Duma, some of his followers had shifted their allegiance to Yenge. From Yenge's headquarters at Bopolu, he fought against the confederacy and undertook a war on the Dei between 1837 and 1838, capturing two hundred persons in one campaign, all of whom were reportedly murdered. See R. M. Miller, *Dear Master*, 67n1; "From the Lieutenant Governor, Anthony D. Williams," *AR*, March 1838, 65-67.

332. Jalla Fingue (also Prince Peter) was the son and successor of Zolu Duma; see Holsoe, "Study of Relations," 347.

333. This journey is explained further in a report from Gov. Joseph J. Roberts [Monrovia] to William McLain [ACS Secretary, Washington, D.C.], dated 2 April 1845 and published as "Journal of Messrs. Teage and Brown," *AR*, July 1845, 211-213.

334. Jonas Cary (1804?-18??) was the somewhat literate son of Lott Cary, who arrived with his parents and siblings from Virginia in 1821. By 1843 he owned one building at Marshall, $800 in personal property and $300 in trade stock. An official list of persons in his household included five children, including three adopted sons, but no wife (Syfert, "History of the Liberian Coasting Trade," 270; U. S. Senate, *U. S. Navy Department*, 357). Bah Gay, a Bassa chief, was an ally of Chief Prince, and both were dependent on the slave trade. After a Liberian volunteer

force, aided by a British naval ship, captured a barracoon in his territory and freed the slaves, Bah Gay ceded jurisdiction of Little Bassa to Liberia sometime between 1839 and 1840; see "Despatches [from] Liberia," *AR*, October 1839, 277-282; "Message of Gov. Buchanan," *AR*, 1 February 1840, 35-36).

335. The mouth of a river.

336. Assembly of Roman Catholic cardinals presided over by the pope.

337. Something that binds, snares or entangles.

338. An official emissary of the devil.

339. Calling down of a curse.

340. Enclosing as if in a bower.

341. From "Childe Harold's Pilgrimage, Canto the Fourth," first published in 1816 by Lord Byron (1788-1824), an associate of the poet Percy B. Shelley. Noyes, *English Romantic Poetry*, 781-788; McGann, *Lord Byron*, 184.

342. A unit of length equal to six feet.

343. Alonzo Ferguson, a carpenter, arrived from South Carolina in 1848 at age 36, with Alonzo (2); Edward (36); Elizabeth (33); Elizabeth (4); Josephine (3); Rosena (26); and Samuel (6). An Alonzo Ferguson, probably his son, owned the *Mary* and the *Sarah* in 1871, while his other son, Samuel, went on to become the first black bishop of the Episcopal Church of Liberia. R. T. Brown, *Immigrants to Liberia*, 26; Syfert, "History of the Liberian Coasting Trade," 273.

344. The April 1845 issue of the *Herald*, in which this story would likely have been continued, was not located.

345. Captain C. H. Bell piloted the ship that brought 756 survivors of the *Pons*, mainly Ibo and Congo, for resettlement in Liberia. "Protagees" in the original text is probably a rendering of "protégés."

346. Sartorius, meaning the cross-legged position of a tailor at work.

347. These lines are from "Fable XLII: The Jugglers," by John Gay (1685-1732), an English writer noted for his satirical comedy and an associate of Alexander Pope and Jonathan Swift. Tillotson, Fussell and Waingrow, *Eighteenth-Century English Literature*, 492-494.; Faber, *Poetic Works*, 267-268.

348. Having the power to cure; healing or restorative.

349. Bopolu, a trading town in northwestern Liberia, was a major transshipment point between the coast and interior and served as the central location of the Condo Confederation in the early nineteenth century.

350. Accompanied by bloodshed; bloodthirsty.

351. An inn for accommodating caravans of traders.

352. This was probably the Mende ethnic group, given the direction from which the attack was launched and the rendering of the name.

353. This paragraph includes several words that are not well known: "lenity," the quality of being lenient; "the Kondays," a reference to the multi-ethnic Condo confederation; and "circumvallation," a surrounding rampart.

354. A West African pidgin phrase meaning "to be literate," from the Portuguese "saber" (to know). See Todd, *Pidgins and Creoles*, 15.

355. The meaning of "wallet" that seems most applicable here is knapsack.

356. This is probably the French frigate *Penelope*, which arrived in Monrovia on 22 February 1849, accompanied by another cruiser. Placed at the disposal of the Liberian government, these ships, together with several British cruisers and the U. S. sloop of war *Yorktown*, transported four hundred Liberian soldiers, including President Joseph Jenkins Roberts, to New Cesters, which was annexed after thirty slaves were liberated from the Spanish-owned slave station (Foote, *Africa and the American Flag*, 182-184. For more information on a visit to Liberia by the *Penelope*, see doc. 73.

357. This article was signed "Observer," a designation used by Teage on another published item after he had resigned as editor.

358. Teage's assumption that the Bassa and other African peoples would evolve to higher stages of "civilization" contrasted sharply with the view, then gaining ascendancy in the white world, that blacks were genetically inferior and their cultures hopelessly stagnant (Adas, *Machines as the Measure*, 196-198, 310-315). Although this might seem like a distinction without a difference when viewed through the cultural relativistic lens of the twentieth century, it was significant in the context of the nineteenth century.

359. For a fuller discussion of sassywood and other forms of trial by ordeal, see "the all discovering ordeal was resorted to," doc. 58.

360. The Rev. William Crocker, the Rev. William Mylne and the Rev. Ivory Clarke (also spelled "Clark") were white American Baptists who maintained a mission at Edina and reduced the Bassa language to writing. Crocker and Mylne came to Liberia in 1835, learned Bassa with the help of a bilingual repatriate, and converted some forty Bassa people; Clark arrived at Edina in January 1838. John B. Barton was a white Methodist who served in Liberia in the early nineteenth century. For information on John Day, see "Bro. Day," doc. 28; Tracy, *History of American Missions*, 560-571; Clarke, *West Africa*, 39; and "Baptist Mission at the Bassa," *AR*, July 1843, 215-216.

361. The "Harriss" referred to in this passage is not known, but the other two indigenous African clergy are Jacob Vonbrun, a Bassa chief and Baptist preacher who was supported by the American Baptist Board until his death in 1876, and Lewis Gary Crocker, chief of Little Bassa, who was educated with Vonbrun at a Baptist school at Bexley and supported by the Northern Baptist Board. Cason, *Growth of Christianity*, 187-188; Wiley, *Slaves No More*, 196, Letter 181.

362. This letter, one of the last written by Teage, was excerpted as "Letter from the Late Hilary Teage," *AR*, November 1853, 348-49. This full version is from ACS Papers, series IB, vol. 5 part 2, reel 155, item no. 00226.

363. Boombo, a Vai ruler at Little Cape Mount, conducted slave-raiding incursions into Dei territory, attacked towns presided over by Dwah-Be (also Dwar-loo-Beh), a Gola chief, and threatened Liberians at Little Cape Mount. For this breech of peace, he was seized by a Liberian expedition of about 250 men and imprisoned in March 1853 ("Late Intelligence [from] Liberia," *AR*, June 1853, 184-185; "Trial and Sentence of Boombo," *AR*, June 1853, 245-246; "Annual Message of Pres. Roberts," *AR*, April 1854, 100-102; "Little Cape Mount," *LH*, 2 February 1853; and "The Military Expedition," *LH*, 2 March 1853.

Carl Patrick Burrowes

364. This is a reference to Gurley, *Mission to England*. Gurley served as ACS secretary from 1823 to 1840 and again from 1841 to 1844; see doc. 1. For a summary evaluation of Gurley's mission and British reactions to it, see Blackett, *Building an Antislavery Wall*, 70-77.

365. Having no special distinction; grounds shared by all, as in a public park.

366. Whether willingly or unwillingly.

367. Meaning "see."

368. Not having one state but many powers contending over one region; a situation in which a state is unable to enforce its laws.

369. These lines are taken from "Verses Supposed to Be Written by Alexander Selkirk" by William Cowper (1731-1800), who was noted for his satirical and didactic poems, especially his paean to rural life, "The Task."

370. U. S. House of Representatives, *Report of Mr. Kennedy*. A review of this report was published as "Review of Mr. Kennedy's Report," *AR*, March 1844, 66-86.

371. In India, Britain had recently defeated the Muslim emirs of Sind, after they had refused to surrender their independence to the East India Company, while in South Africa the British had colonized Natal after expelling the Boers, who moved across the Vaal River.

372. This seems like a reference to the recent British taking of Natal.

373. From Greek, meaning "published every seven days." Despite several extensive searches, no record has been found of the *Weekly Elevator*.

374. A benefit bestowed, especially one bestowed in response to a request.

375. Hollings, J. H. *Ethel Woodville; or, Woman's Ministry: A Tale for the Times*. 2 vols. London: Hatchard, 1859, p. 101.

376. An Anglo-French treaty was signed in 1842, modeled after the Anglo-American treaty of earlier that year. The agreement, which lasted ten years, sought to moderate a growing rivalry between the two powers in West Africa. Each power agreed to deploy at least twenty-six cruisers against slavers and to respect treaties signed by the other with African chiefs. Miers, *Britain and the Ending of the Slave Trade*, 18-19.

377. For information on a visit to Liberia by the *Penelope*, see "the frigate *Penelope*," doc. 73.

378. In 1846, the command of the British naval squadron in the region underwent a change, passing from Captain L. T. Jones, whose lackluster tenure ended in January, to Commodore C. Hotham, who instituted an aggressive pursuit of slavers after taking over in October. Lloyd, *Navy and the Slave Trade*, 121.

379. Cheerfully optimistic, confident.

380. Shortly after being inaugurated in 1848 as Liberia's first president, Joseph Jenkins Roberts visited England, winning official recognition for Liberia as well as a personal audience with Queen Victoria.

381. This was *Herald* assistant editor John N. Lewis; see note 25 in the section "The Church" for information on Lewis.

382. To engage in negotiations, as to reach a settlement or agree on terms.

383. Act of despoiling or plundering.

384. The brig *Thistle*, a twelve-gun ship, was part of the British West African naval squadron created sometime around 1811 and consisting of two frigate and two or three sloops or brigs until 1831. Ward, *Royal Navy*, 113; Lloyd, *Navy and the Slave Trade*, 67.

385. Edward Wilmot Blyden, the West Indian native who would contribute significantly to the subsequent emigration of his fellow islanders, would arrive in Liberia one year after this invitation was published. Bylden's November 1862 visit to his native St. Thomas and a proclamation inviting West Indian immigrants to Liberia, issued in February 1864 by President Daniel B. Warner, are most often cited as the precipitants for the arrival of 346 Barbadians on the *Cora* on 6 April 1865. Lynch, *Edward Wilmot Blyden*, 34-35), but this article shows that the seeds for this locus of immigration date to Teage.

386. *MCJ*, September 1851, 269.

387. *MCJ*, January 1853, 17-18.

388. *MCJ*, February 1852, 47.

389. Published in the *AR*, May 1836, 159-160, this letter was preceded by the following note: "It seems that a Mr. John Dean Lake, made a statement before the British House of Commons, implicating Mr. Hilary Teage, now editor of the *Liberia Herald*, in a charge of having been engaged in the slave trade. The editor of the *Philadelphia Herald* wrote to Mr. Teage on the subject, and received from him a letter in answer, accompanied by a document, which was afterwards unfortunately mislaid. The Philadelphia editor delayed publishing the letter, in the hope of finding the document. The letter appeared in the *Christian Herald* of March 19, and is as follows."

390. Payments owed.

391. This article was accompanied by a note that it had been excerpted from the *Liberia Herald*, but the original was not found.

392. Entomology is the scientific study of insects, while ichthyology involves the study of fish.

393. Pressed together, especially in rows.

394. Camped temporarily.

395. Ambush.

396. The *Waterwitch* was a privately built ten-gun brig weighing 324 tons that was purchased by the British navy. It was one of fourteen sloops in the twenty-one ship British West African squadron captained by H. J. Matson from 1839 to 1843. Lloyd, *Navy and the Slave Trade*, 92, 101, 12).

397. Also rendered as "Timbo."

398. The firm of Payne and Yates, organized sometime in the 1840s, was owned by Francis Payne and Beverly Page Yates. By 1843, it had $4,000 in trade stock, $6,000 in personal property and $7,000 in commissions, plus one stone and three wooden buildings in Monrovia. Starting with one vessel, the *Peddler*, the firm later bought the *Spy*, *Liberia*, and *John E. Taylor*. By 1861, it operated a sawmill and two ships involved in trade along the West African coast, one of which traveled to England. Syfert, "History of the Liberian Coasting Trade," 286.

399. Three pages in this issue of the *Herald* were mislabeled as page "3." The correct pagination was discerned by referring to the numbering of pages in the previous and the subsequent issues.

400. In this passage, "mullet" refers to any of various stout-bodied edible fish of the Mugilidae family that inhabit coastal waters in the tropics, while "hiatus" means a gap or a short passage in an organ or a body part.

401. A dry, dusty wind that blows southwest from the Sahara Desert; derived from the Akan (Twi) word "haramata," meaning an evil thing.

402. This poem was printed with the following note, "Hymn composed by Mr. H. Teage, to be sung on the first of December, 1838."

403. These lyrics were set to the tune "Bermondsey"; see "Specimen of Liberian Poetry," *AR*, June 1843, 191-192, and *MCJ*, July 1843, 32.

404. Appearing beneath the poem was the notation "Nov. 21, 1845," possibly the date it was written.

405. An aromatic stem yielding an oil used in perfumery; flexible; stems used as a source of rattan.

406. "Classic Paly's" is possibly a reference to the bar that divides a heraldic coat of arms into equal parts.

407. Meaningless or deceptive language.

408. The Roman god of fire and metalworking.

409. The original text included the note "Tune Olivet," a reference to "Olivet (My Faith Looks Up To Thee), a hymn by Thomas Hastings and Lowell Masoni that made its appearance in 1831.

410. This speech was reprinted as "Extracts from a Sermon Delivered in the Methodist Episcopal Church, on Friday the 10th September, 1841, on the Death of His Excellency, Thomas Buchanan, Late Governor of the Commonwealth of Liberia, by Elder Hilary Teage," *AR*, 15 January 1842, 17-20.

411. This eulogy is taken from "Obituary," *AR*, August 1849, 245-248. This article appeared under the following note: "In writing the following notice, the undersigned was prompted alike by his own feelings of respect for the deceased, and by the suggestion of Rev. Mr. Wilson, and it was inserted in the *Luminary* as the more proper vehicle for its publication. Owing to some circumstance — probably to the illegibility of the copy — it appears there with so many errors, that it has been thought best to insert it here in a corrected form." All efforts to locate the issue of the *Luminary* in which this article was first published proved futile. Freeborn and literate, Elijah Johnson (c. 1787-1849) went to Africa to serve as a missionary. His birthplace is given variously as Maryland, New Jersey and New York. He sailed from New York in 1820 with his wife, a daughter and two sons on the *Elizabeth*, the first ship of emigrants sent out by the ACS. A veteran of the U. S. War of 1812, he led the colony's militia in battles at Bromley (1828 and 1832), Bassa Cove (1835) and Ringstown, thirty-five miles from Edina (1839). He served as ACS agent in 1822 and 1824. Burrowes, "Black Christian Republicans," 71-73.

412. This essay is taken from *AR*, September 1844, 258-261, and January 1845, 13-17; it was printed there in two parts. The journal noted that the essay was being reprinted from the *Liberia Herald*, but the issue that carried the original was not found.

413. A prediction; a prophecy.

414. This address is taken from *LH*, 31 May 1845, 9-10. It was presented in the Council Chamber on 21 May 1845.

415. The implicit reference could only be to the subject of independence which Teage and his compatriots had already broached in the *Herald* and other public forums.

416. Teage is referring here to Victorian British novelist Edward Bulwer-Lytton (1803-1873) and French novelist Charles Paul de Kock (1794-1871). Bulwer-Lytton, known for his alienation from social and political concerns, along with a fascination with metaphysics, was among the most popular and critically acclaimed writers of his day. De Kock faithfully portrayed the risqué aspect of middle-class Parisian life in his works, most notably Georgette (1820).

417. Author unknown.

418. This speech is taken from *LH*, 18 December 1846, 17-18, and 5 February 1847, 29-30. The speech was reprinted in Armistead, *Calumny Refuted*, 15-38.

419. A lighthouse off the coast of Egypt; one of the seven wonders of the ancient world.

420. The first two lines are from "An Essay on Man" (Epistle I, lines 87-90), by Alexander Pope (1688-1744); see H. Davis, *Pope*, 243. The second two lines are from Edward Young, lines 91-92.; see Cornford, *Edward Young*, 53.

421. "Truth is powerful, and will ultimately prevail." This quote did not appear in the version of this address that was published in the *Liberia Herald*.

422. These lines are from "An Essay on Man" (Epistle IV, lines 193-194), by Alexander Pope. See H. Davis, *Pope*, 274.

423. Bremen was a city with a major port on the Weser River southwest of Hamburg It retained its distinct identity while also a member of the German confederation (1815-71).

424. Genesis 2: 8, 9, 15.

425. These lines are from "Spring" (lines 58-65) in *The Season* by James Thomson (1700-1748), a Scottish poet renowned for his descriptive works on nature. Sambrook, *James Thomson*, 4-5.

426. Proverbs XIV: 34.

427. Romeo and Juliet, act 3, sc. 5, lines 9-10.

428. The Declaration is transcribed from Huberich, *Political and Legislative History*, 1: 828-32. According to an eyewitness, it was written by Teage and adopted by the Constitutional Convention of 1847 after "some" amendments. Unfortunately, no one to date has found the record of the convention, which might have noted specific amendments (Huberich, *Political and Legislative History*, 1: 821-834). Just as the American Declaration of Independence was directed to the king of England, this document — signifying a formal break with a former life — took conditions in the United States to be its focus. The "we" of the Liberian Declaration is obviously the repatriates from the United States, who constituted almost the entire population of de facto Liberia at the time this was written. Latter commentators have criticized this document for having excluded indigenous Africans (e. g., Wilson, *Origins*, 19). Blinded by presentism and good intentions, these writers fail to recognize that most contemporaneous Africans in the area now considered Liberia were members of other polities. To have referenced them in Liberia's Declaration would have been presumptuous and imperialistic. Such criticisms are akin to faulting American officials for not referencing California and Texas in their founding documents of 1779, a period when their authority was confined to thirteen colonies on the Eastern Seaboard.

References

Manuscript Records

Archives, Ministry of Foreign Affairs, Monrovia, Liberia

> Land Register, Monrovia, Montserrado County

Library of Congress, Washington, D. C.

> American Colonization Society, Records, 1792-1961

Library of Virginia Archives, Richmond

> First African Baptist Church, Richmond, Church Record Books. 3 vols.
> (Microfilm)

> Henrico County Deed Books, nos. 15 (1817) 501; 17 (1818) 605

> Mutual Assurance Society Record Books, Richmond, VA Richmond City. 229
> vols. and 52,103 items

> Nicholson Family Bible (microfilm), Arc. 30754. Filed misc. Reel 775 in
> Nicholson family, 1787-1820. Bible

> printed in 1800

> Richmond City Legislative Petitions, Petition of Slaves and Free Negroes for
> Church, 1823

> Richmond City, Virginia Hustings Court Deed Book II, 1792-1799. Indenture of
> John McKeand to Bell and

> Shiphard, July 8, 1793, pp. 79-81

Maryland Historical Society. Baltimore

> Maryland Colonization Society. Papers, financial records, reports of colonial
> agents, books on colonization, copies of the *Maryland Colonization Journal*
> (Baltimore, 1835-61) and the *Liberia Herald* (Monrovia, 1842-57)

Moorland-Spingarn Research Center, Howard University, Washington, D.C.

National Archives. Washington, D.C.

> U. S. State Department Records

Schomburg Center for Research in Black Culture, N.Y.

New York Public Library, Harlem, N. Y.

Southern Baptist Historical Library and Archives, Nashville

Letters of Samuel G. Day, Thomas Day and William J. Day in box 17

Letters of Joseph M. Harden in box 26

Letters of Hilary Teage in box 60

Virginia Historical Society, Richmond.

American Colonization Society, Virginia Branch, Records, 1823-1859. 2 vols.

Benjamin Brand Papers, 1790-1838. 417 items

First African Baptist Church, Richmond, Va., Minute Book, 1841-1857. 295 pages. Photocopy

Nicholson family papers, 1711-1877. 26 items

John Preston papers. Bill of Bell & Shiphard, 1794 [to John Preston for assorted leather items, 1794]

Richmond-Manchester Colonization Auxiliary and Virginia Colonization Society, Minutes

Shepard family papers, 1732-1907

Newspapers and Periodicals

African Repository (Washington, D.C.)

Africa's Luminary (Monrovia)

American Baptist Memorial: A Statistical, Biographical and Historical Magazine (New York)

Annual Report of the American Colonization Society (Washington, D.C.)

Enquirer (Richmond)

Liberia Herald (Monrovia)

Maryland Colonization Journal (Baltimore)

New York Colonization Journal (New York)

Religious Herald (Richmond)

Times-Dispatch (Richmond)

Tyler's Quarterly (Richmond)

Virginia Cavalcade (Richmond)

Virginia Gazette (Richmond)

Virginia Genealogist (Bowie, Maryland)

Virginia Magazine of History and Biography (Richmond)

William and Mary College Quarterly Historical Magazine (Williamsburg, Va.)

Primary Sources

Alexander, A. *A History of Colonization on the Western Coast of Africa*. Philadelphia: William S. Martien, 1847.

American Colonization Society. *Annual Report*, Vol. 1-91/93 (1818-1908/10). Reprint, New York: Negro Universities Press, 1969.

Armistead, Wilson. *Calumny Refuted by Facts from Liberia*. New York: Antislavery Office, 1848.

Benedict, Samuel. *Independent Republic of Liberia: Its Constitution and Declaration of Independence ... Issued Chiefly for the Use of the People of Color*. Philadelphia: William F. Geddes, 1848.

Blyden, Edward Wilmot. "Mixed Races in Liberia." *Smithsonian Institute Annual Report*. (1870): 386-89.

Blyden, Edward W. *Selected Letters of Edward Wilmot Blyden*. Edited by Hollis R. Lynch. Millwood, N.J.: KTO Press, 1978.

Brown, Henry D. *Character Sketches of the Early Settlers of Liberia*. Liverpool: Lionel Hart, 1891.

Burrows, J. C. *Christian Merchant: A Memoir of James C. Crane*. Charleston, S.C.: Southern Baptist Publication Society, 1858.

Burrows, J. C. "History of the Church." In *The First Century of the Baptist Church of Richmond, Virginia, 1770-1880*, edited by H. A. Tupper, pp. 43-105. Richmond: Carlton McCarthy, 1880.

Campbell, Robert. *A Pilgrimage to My Motherland: An Account of a Journey Among the Egbas and Yorubas of Central Africa in 1859-60.* New York: T. Hamilton, 1860. Reprinted, with an introduction by Howard H. Bell, in Search for a Place: Black Separatism and Africa, 1860. Ann Arbor, Mich.: Ann Arbor Paperbacks, 1971.

Chester, Thomas Morris. *Thomas Morris Chester: Black Civil War Correspondent.* Edited by R. J. M. Blackett. Baton Rouge: Louisiana State University Press, 1989.

Clark, James F. *Present Condition of the Free Colored People of the United States.* New York: American Antislavery Society, 1859.

Coker, D. *Journal of Daniel Coker, a Descendant of Africa.* Baltimore: Edward J. Coale, 1820. Reprint, Nendeln, Liechtenstein: Kraus, 1970.

Conneau, Theophilus. *A Slaver's Log Book or 20 Years' Residence in Africa.* New York: Avon Books, 1977.

Crummell, Alexander. *Selected Writings, 1840-1898.* Edited by Wilson J. Moses. Amherst, Mass.: University of Massachusetts Press, 1992.

Delany, Martin R. *Official Report of the Niger Valley Exploring Party.* New York: T. Hamilton, 1861. Reprinted, with introduction by Howard H. Bell, in *Search for a Place: Black Separatism and Africa, 1860.* Ann Arbor, Mich.: Ann Arbor Paperbacks, 1971.

Fitzhugh, George. *What Shall Be Done with the Free Negroes: Four Essays Written for the "Fredericksburg Recorder."* Fredericksburg, Va.: Recorder Office, 1851.

Foote, Andrew H. *Africa and the American Flag.* New York: D. Appleton, 1854.

Garrison, W. L. *Thoughts on African Colonization.* Boston: Garrison and Knapp, 1832. Reprint. New York: Arno Press, 1968.

Gurley, Ralph. R. *Life of Jehudi Ashmun.* Washington, D.C.: James C. Dunn, 1835. Reprint, New York: Negro Universities Press, 1969.

_____. *Mission to England on Behalf of the American Colonization Society.* Washington, D.C.: W. W. Morrison, 1841.

Historical Records Survey of Virginia, Works Projects Administration. *Inventory of the Church Archives of Virginia Negro Baptist Churches in Richmond.* Richmond: Historical Records Survey of Virginia, 1940.

Jay, William. *An Inquiry into the Character and Tendency of the American Colonization and American Antislavery Societies.* New York: American Antislavery Society, 1838. Reprint, New York: Negro Universities Press, 1969.

Killian, G. *The Statute Laws of the Republic of Liberia.* Monrovia, G. Killian, printer, 1856.

Leslie, Charles. *A New and Exact Account of Jamaica.* Edinburgh: R. Fleming, 1740.

Liberia. *Acts Passed by the Legislature of the Republic of Liberia.* Monrovia: Government Printing Office, 1847-.

Maddox, John. *The Richmond Directory, Register and Almanac for the Year 1819.* Richmond: John Maddox, 1819.

Martin, Joseph. *A New and Comprehensive Gazetteer of Virginia and the District of Columbia.* Charlottesville, Va.: W. H. Brockenbrough, 1835.

Miller, Randall M., ed. *Dear Master: Letters of a Slave Family.* Athens: University of Georgia, 1990.

Mills, Samuel J. "Abstract of a journal of the late Rev. Samuel John Mills." *ACS Second Annual Report* (1819): 18-67.

Mordecai, Samuel. *Richmond in By-Gone Days: Being Reminiscences of an Old Citizen.* Richmond: G. M. West, 1856.

Payne, D. A. *History of the African Methodist Episcopal Church.* Vol. 1. Nashville: AME Sunday-School Union, 1891.

Penn, Irvine Garland. *The Afro-American Press and Its Editors.* Springfield, Mass.: Willey, 1891.

Perdue, Charles L., Jr., Thomas E. Barden, and Robert K. Philips, eds. *Weevils in the Wheat: Interviews with Virginia Ex-slaves.* Bloomington: Indiana University Press, 1980.

Ryland, Robert. "First African Church: Celebration of the First Centenary." In *The First Century of the First Baptist Church of Richmond, Virginia, 1770-1880,* edited by H. A. Tupper, 247-72. Richmond: Carlton McCarthy, 1880.

_____. "Reminiscences of the First African Church." *American Baptist Memorial.* 14 (September-December 1855): 262-65.

Slaughter, Philip. *The Virginian History of African Colonization.* Richmond: MacFarlane and Fergusson, 1855. Reprint, Freeport, N.Y. Books for Libraries Press, 1970.

Taylor, J. B. *Biography of Elder Lott Cary, Late Missionary to Africa.* Baltimore: Armstrong and Berry, 1837.

Teage, Hilary. *Constitution and Laws of the Commonwealth of Liberia, Including an Abstract of Legal Principles and Rules with an Appendix of Forms. In Two Parts.* Monrovia: Hilary Teage, printer, 1843.

Tracy, Joseph, comp. *History of American Missions to the Heathen.* Worcester, Mass.: Spooner and Howland, 1840.

Tupper, H. A., ed. *The First Century of the First Baptist Church of Richmond, Virginia, 1770-1880.* Richmond: Carlton McCarthy, 1880.

U.S. Bureau of Census. *Seventh Census, Richmond City, 1850.* Washington, D.C.: Government Printing Office, 1850.

_____. *Fourth Census of the United States, 1820.* Virginia, Henrico County, ??98.

_____. *Census for 1820.* Washington, D.C.: Gales and Seaton, 1821.

_____. *Census for 1830.* Washington, D.C.: Green, 1832.

_____. *The Seventh Census of the United States 1850.* Washington, D.C.: Robert Armstrong, 1853.

_____. *Report on the Social Statistics of Cities, Part II. The Southern and the Western States.* Washington, D.C.: Government Printing Office, 1887.

U.S. House of Representatives. *Report of Mr. Kennedy, of Maryland, from the Committee of Commerce of the House of Representatives of the United States, on the memorial of the friends of Colonization assembled in convention in the city of Washington, May, 1842. To which is appended a collection of the most interesting papers on the subject of African Colonization, &, &.* Washington, D.C.: Government Printing Office, 1843.

U.S. Senate. *U.S. Navy Department, tables showing the number of emigrants and recaptured Africans sent to the colony of Liberia by the government of the United States ... together with a census of the colony and a report of its commerce, &c. September, 1843.* 28th Congress, 2d sess., Senate Document 150, 1845.

Walker, David. *David Walker's Appeal in Four Articles.* Boston, 1848. Reprint. New York: Arno Press, 1969.

White, Hagar and Company. *Specimen of Modern Printing Types Cast at the Foundry of White, Hagar and Co.* New York: G. G. Hopkins and Sons, 1835.

Wiley, Bell I., ed. *Slaves No More: Letters from Liberia, 1833-1869.* Lexington: University Press of Kentucky, 1980.

Williams, A. B. *The Liberian Exodus: An Account of the Voyage of the First Emigrants in the Bark "Azor."* Charleston, S.C.: News and Courier Book Presses, 1878.

Secondary Sources

Abercrombie, Nicholas, Stephen Hill, and Bryan S. Turner. *Dictionary of Sociology.* London: Penguin, 1986.

Abrahams, R. D. and J. F. Szwed. *After Africa: Extracts from British Travel Accounts and Journals of the Seventeenth, Eighteenth, and Nineteenth Centuries Concerning the Slaves, Their Manners, and Customs in the British West Indies.* New Haven, Conn.: Yale University Press, 1983.

Adas, Michael. *Machines as the Measure of Men: Science, Technology, and Ideologies of Western Dominance.* Ithaca, N.Y.: Cornell University Press, 1989.

Akpan, Monday B. "Liberia and Ethiopia, 1880-1914." In *Africa Under Colonial Domination, 1880-1935,* edited by A. A. Boahen, 249-82. *Vol. 7 of UNESCO General History of Africa.* Berkeley: University of California Press, 1985.

Allen, J. B. "'All of Us Are Highly Pleased with the Country': Black and White Kentuckians on Liberian Colonization." *Pylon* 43, no. 2 (1982): 97-109.

Anyang' Nyong'o, Peter. *Popular Struggles for Democracy in Africa.* London: Zed Books, 1987.

Appleby, Joyce. *Capitalism and a New Social Order: The Republican Vision of the 1790s.* New York: New York University Press, 1984.

_____. *Liberalism and Republicanism in the Historical Imagination.* Cambridge, Mass.: Harvard University Press, 1992.

Ashworth, John. "The Relationship Between Capitalism and Humanitarianism." In *The Antislavery Debate: Capitalism and Abolitionism as a Problem in Historical*

Interpretation, edited by Thomas Bender, 180-99. Berkeley: University of California, 1992.

Azikiwe, Nnamdi. *Liberia in World Politics.* London: A. H. Stockwell, 1934.

Babcock, Theodore S. "Manumission in Virginia, 1782-1806." M. A. thesis, University of Virginia, 1974.

Ballagh, James C. *A History of Slavery in Virginia.* Johns Hopkins University Studies in Historical and Political Science. Baltimore: Johns Hopkins Press, 1902.

Becker, Carl. *The Declaration of Independence: A Study in the History of Political Ideas.* New York: Random House, 1958.

Bell, H. H. Introduction to *Search for a Place: Black Separatism and Africa, 1860,* by Martin R. Delaney and Robert Campbell, pp. 1-22. Ann Arbor, Mich.: Ann Arbor Paperbacks, 1971.

Bell, John B. *Northampton County, Virginia: Tithables, 1720-1769.* Bowie, Md.: Heritage Books, 1993.

Bentley, Elizabeth Petty, comp. *Index to the 1810 Census of Virginia.* Baltimore: Genealogical Publishing, 1980.

Berkeley, Edmund, Jr. "Prophet Without Honor: Christopher McPherson, Free Person of Color." *Virginia Magazine,* 77 (April 1969): 180-90.

Berlin, Ira. *Slaves* Without Masters: The Free Negro in the Antebellum South. New York: New Press, 1974.

_____. "The Structure of the Free Negro Caste in the Antebellum United States." *Journal of Social History* 9, no. 3 (1976): 297-318.

_____. "Time, Space and the Evolution of Afro-American Society." *American Historical Review* 85, no. 1 (1980): 44-78.

Berlin, Ira, and Ronald Hoffman, eds. *Slavery and Freedom in the Age of the American Revolution.* Urbana: University of Illinois Press, 1986.

Beyan, Amos J. *The American Colonization Society and the Creation of the Liberian State: A Historical Perspective, 1822-1900.* Lanham, Md.: University Press of America, 1991.

Blackett, R. J. M. *Building an Antislavery Wall: Black Americans in the Atlantic Abolitionist Movement, 1830-1860.* Ithaca, N. Y.: Cornell University Press, 1989.

Blackwell, Lorraine. "Honoring of Cary Termed Overdue." *Richmond Times-Dispatch,* 26 November 1993, B1, B7.

Blassingame, John W. *The Slave Community: Plantation Life in the Antebellum South.* New York: Oxford University Press, 1979.

_____. "Status and Social Structure in the Slave Community: Evidence from New Sources." In *Perspectives and Irony in American Slavery,* edited by H. P. Owens, 137-51. Jackson: University Press of Mississippi, 1976.

Boles, John B., ed. *Masters and Slaves in the House of the Lord: Race and Religion in the American South, 1740-1870.* Lexington: The University Press of Kentucky, 1988.

Bracey, John H., Jr., August Meier, and Elliot Rudwick. *Black Nationalism in America.* Indianapolis: Bobbs-Merrill, 1970.

Breen, T. H. *Tobacco Culture: The Mentality of the Great Tidewater Planters on the Eve of Revolution.* Princeton, N.J.: Princeton University Press, 1985.

Breen, T. H., and Stephen Innes. *"Myne Owne Ground": Race and Freedom on Virginia's Eastern Shore, 1640-1676.* New York: Oxford University Press, 1980.

Brewer, James H. "Negro Property Owners in Seventeenth-Century Virginia." *William and Mary Quarterly* 3rd ser., vol. 12, no. 4 (1955): 575-580.

Brewer, W. M. "John B. Russwurm." *Journal of Negro History* 13, no. 4 (1928): 413-422.

Bristol Parish, Virginia. *Births from the Bristol Parish Register of Henrico, Prince George and Dinwiddie Counties, Virginia, 1720-1798.* Baltimore: Genealogical Publishing, 1990.

Brock, R. A. *The Vestry Book of Henrico Parish, Virginia, 1730-1773: From the Original Manuscript.* Bowie, Md.: Heritage Books, 1991.

Brown, Arthur Judson. *One Hundred Years: A History of the Work of the Presbyterian Church in the U.S.A.* New York: Fleming H. Revall, 1936.

Brown, Mary Antoinette Grimes. "Education and National Development in Liberia, 1800-1900." Ph.D. diss., Cornell University, 1967.

_____. "Some Liberian Intellectuals in the Nineteenth Century: An Appreciation." *Liberian Studies Journal* 6, no. 2 (1975): 162-175.

Brown, Robert E., and B. Katherine Brown. *Virginia, 1705-1786: Democracy or Aristocracy.* East Lansing: Michigan State University Press, 1964.

Brown, Robert T. *Immigrants to Liberia: 1843 to 1865 (an Alphabetical Listing)*. Philadelphia: Institute for Liberian Studies, 1980.

_____. "Simon Greenleaf and the Liberian Constitution of 1847." *Liberian Studies Journal* 9, no. 2 (1980-81): 51-60.

Brown, Stuart, Jr. *Virginia Genealogies*. Berryville: Virginia Book Co, 1967.

Buck, Dee A. *Northampton County, Virginia, Marriages, 1853-1992*. Bowie, Md.: Heritage Books, 1994.

Buell, R. L. *The Native Problem in Africa*. Vol. 2. New York: Macmillan, 1928.

Burrowes, Carl Patrick. *The Americo-Liberian Ruling Class and Other Myths: A Critique of Political Science in the Liberian Context*. Philadelphia: Department of African-American Studies, Temple University, 1986.

_____. "Black Christian Republicans: Delegates to the 1847 Liberian Constitutional Convention." *Liberian Studies Journal* 14, no. 2 (1989): 64-89.

_____. "Press Freedom in Liberia, 1830-1970: The Impact of Modernity, Ethnicity and Power Imbalances on Government-Press Relations." Ph.D. diss., Temple University, 1994.

Campbell, Penelope. *Maryland in Africa: The Maryland State Colonization Society, 1831-1857*. Urbana: University of Illinois Press, 1971.

Cason, J. W. "The Growth of Christianity in the Liberian Environment." Ph.D. diss., Columbia University, 1962.

Cassell, Christian Abayomi. *Liberia: History of the First African Republic*. New York: Fountainhead, 1970.

Chamberlayne, C. G., ed. *The Vestry Book and Register of St. Peter's Parish, New Kent and James City Counties, Virginia, 1706-1786*. Richmond: Virginia State Library and Archives, 1989.

Christian, W. Asbury. *Richmond: Her Past and Present*. Richmond: L. H. Jenkins, 1912.

Claiborne, John H. *Seventy-Five Years in Old Virginia*. Washington, D.C.: Neale, 1904.

Clarke, B. *West Africa and Christianity*. London: E. Arnold, 1986.

Clemens, William M. *Virginia Wills Before Seventeen Ninety-Nine: A Complete Abstract Register of All Names Mentioned in over 600 Recorded Wills*. Baltimore: Genealogical Publishing, 1986.

Cohen, David W., and Jack P. Greene, eds. *Neither Slave nor Free: The Freedmen of African Descent in the Slave Societies of the New World.* Baltimore: Johns Hopkins University Press, 1972.

Cole, Arthur C. *The Whig Party in the South.* Washington, D.C.: American Historical Association, 1913.

Cornford, Stephen, ed. *Edward Young "Night Thoughts."* Cambridge: Cambridge University Press, 1989.

Crozier, William Armstrong, ed. *Early Virginia Marriages.* Baltimore: Genealogical Publishing, 1968.

Curry, Leonard. *The Free Black in Urban America, 1800-1850: The Shadow of the Dream.* Chicago: University of Chicago Press, 1980.

Curtin, Philip D. *The Atlantic Slave Trade: A Census.* Madison: University of Wisconsin, 1969.

Dabney, Virginius. *Richmond: The Story of a City.* Garden City, New York: Doubleday, 1990.

d'Amico, John M. "Spiritual and Secular Activities of the Methodist Episcopal Church in Liberia, 1833-1933." Ph.D. diss., St. John's University, 1977.

Daniel, W. Harrison. "Virginia Baptists and the Negro in the Early Republic." *Virginia Magazine of History* 80 (1972): 60-69.

Dann, M. E. *The Black Press, 1827-1890: The Quest for National Identity.* New York: G. P. Putnam's Sons, 1972.

Davis, David Brion. "American Slavery and the American Revolution." In *Slavery and Freedom in the Age of the American Revolution,* edited by Ira Berlin and Ronald Hoffman, 262-280. Urbana: University of Illinois Press, 1983.

_____. *The Problem of Slavery in the Age of Revolution, 1770-1823.* Ithaca, N.Y.: Cornell University Press, 1975.

_____. *Slavery and Human Progress.* Oxford: Oxford University Press, 1984.

Davis, Herbert, ed. *Pope: Poetical Works.* Oxford: Oxford University Press, 1990.

Davis, Julia. *The Shenandoah.* New York: Farrar and Rinehart, 1945.

Davis, Stanley A. "Hilary Teage (pp. 72-77)." *This Is Liberia: A Brief History of This Land of Contradictions with Biographies of its Founders and Builders.* New York: William-Frederick Press, 1953.

Dixon, Christa K. *Negro Spirituals: From Bible to Folksong.* Philadelphia: Fortress Press, 1976.

Dorman, John Frederick. *Index to the "Virginia Genealogist," Volumes 1-20, 1957-1976.* Springfield, Va.: Genealogical Books in Print, 1981.

Dormu, A. K. *The Constitution of the Republic of Liberia and the Declaration of Independence with Notes by Alfonso K. Dormu.* New York: Exposition, 1970.

Dowdey, Clifford. *The Great Plantation: A Profile of Berkeley Hundred and Plantation Virginia from Jamestown to Appomattox.* New York: Rinehart, 1957.

Drake, St. Clair. *The Redemption of Africa and Black Religion.* Chicago: Third World Press, 1991.

Drewel, Henry John. "Methodist Education in Liberia, 1833-1856." In *Essays in the History of African Education,* edited by Vincent M. Battle and Charles H. Lyons, 33-60. New York: Teacher's College Press, Columbia University, 1970.

DuBois, W. E. Burghardt, and Augustus G. Dill, eds. *The Negro American Artisan. The Atlanta University Publications 17.* Atlanta: Atlanta University Press, 1912.

Duke, Maurice, and Daniel P. Jordan, eds. *A Richmond Reader, 1733-1983.* Chapel Hill: University of North Carolina Press, 1983.

Dunn, D. Elwood. *A History of the Episcopal Church in Liberia, 1821-1980.* Metuchen, N.J.: Scarecrow Press, 1992.

Dunn, D. Elwood, Amos J. Beyan, and Carl Patrick Burrowes. *Historical Dictionary of Liberia.* Metuchen, N.J.: Scarecrow Press, 2001.

Dunn, Richard S. "Society in the Chesapeake, 1776-1810." In *Slavery and Freedom in the Age of the American Revolution,* edited by Ira Berlin and Ronald Hoffman, 49-82. Urbana: University of Illinois Press, 1986.

"Edward James Roye: Fifth President of Liberia." *Negro History Bulletin* 16 (November 1952): 45.

Egerton, Douglas R. "Gabriel's Conspiracy and the Election of 1800." *Journal of Southern History* 56, no. 2 (1993): 191-214.

_____. *Gabriel's Rebellion: The Virginia Slave Conspiracies of 1800 and 1802.* Chapel Hill: University of North Carolina Press, 1993.

_____. "'Its Origin is Not a Little Curious': A New Look at the American Colonization Society." *Journal of the Early Republic* 5, no. 4 (1985): 463-480.

Encyclopedia of Southern Baptists. Nashville: Broadman Press, 1958–.

Epstein, Dena J. *Sinful Tunes and Spirituals: Black Folk Music to the Civil War.* Urbana: University of Illinois Press, 1977.

Escott, Paul D. *Slavery Remembered: A Record of Twentieth-Century Slave Narratives.* Chapel Hill: University of North Carolina, 1979.

Essig, James David. "A Very Wintry Season: Virginia Baptists and Slavery, 1785-1797." *Virginia Magazine of History and Biography* 88, no. 2 (1980): 170-85.

Evans, James D. "Nicholson Family of Virginia." *William and Mary Quarterly* 27th ser., vol. 12, no. 1 (1932): 49-66.

Faber, G. C. *The Poetic Works of John Gay.* New York: Russell and Russell, 1969.

Field, Barbara Jeanne. *Slavery and Freedom on the Middle Ground: Maryland During the Nineteenth Century.* New Haven, Conn.: Yale University Press, 1985.

Fisher, Miles Mark. "Lott Cary: The Colonizing Missionary." *Journal of Negro History* 7, no. 4 (1922): 380-418.

Fitts, Leroy. *Lott Carey: First Black Missionary to Africa.* Valley Forge, Pa.: Judson Press, 1978.

Fleet, Beverly. *Henrico County, Virginia, Records.* Vol. 21. Easley, S.C.: Southern Historical Press, 1944.

Fogel, Robert William. Without Consent or Contract: The Rise and Fall of American Slavery. New York: W. W. Norton, 1989.

Foley, Louise P. *Early Virginia Families Along the James River: Their Deep Roots and Tangled Branches: Charles City County, Prince George County.* Vol. 2, Baltimore: Genealogical Publishing, 1990.

Foner, Eric. "Black Reconstruction Leaders at the Grass Roots." In *Black Leaders of the Nineteenth Century*, edited by Leon Litwack and August Meier, 219-234. Urbana, Ill.: University of Illinois Press, 1988.

_____. *Reconstruction: America's Unfinished Revolution, 1863-1877*. New York: Harper and Row, 1988.

Foray, Cyril P. *Historical Dictionary of Sierra Leone*. Metuchen, N.J.: Scarecrow Press, 1977.

Foster, C. I. "The Colonization of Free Negroes in Liberia, 1816-1835." *Journal of Negro History* 38, no. 1 (1953): 41-66.

Fothergill, Augusta B., and John Mark Naugle. *Virginia Tax Payers, 1782-87, Other Than Those Published by the United States Census Bureau*. Baltimore: Genealogical Publishing, 1966.

Fox, E. L. *The American Colonization Society, 1817-1840*. Baltimore: Johns Hopkins University Press, 1919. Reprint, New York: AMS Press, 1971.

Fredrickson, George M. *The Black Image in the White Mind: The Debate on Afro-American Character and Destiny, 1817-1914*. New York: Harper Torchbooks, 1972.

Freeman, H. B. "The Vai and Their Kinfolk." *Negro History Bulletin* no. 16 (1952).

Gatewood, W. B. *Aristocrats of Color: The Black Elite, 1880-1920*. Bloomington: Indiana University Press, 1990.

Geddes, Jean. *Fairfax County: Historical Highlights from 1607*. Middleburg, Va.: Denlinger's, 1967.

Geertz, Clifford. "Ideology as a Cultural System." In *Ideology and Discontent*, edited by David Apter, 47-76. New York: Free Press, 1963.

_____. *The Interpretation of Cultures*. New York: Basic Books, 1973.

Genovese, Eugene D. *From Rebellion to Revolution: Afro-American Slave Revolts in the Making of the New World*. New York: Vintage, 1981.

_____. Roll, Jordan, Roll: The World the Slaves Made. New York: Vintage, 1974.

_____. *The Slaveholders' Dilemma: Freedom and Progress in Southern Conservative Thought, 1820-1860*. Columbia: University of South Carolina Press, 1992.

_____. The Southern Tradition: The Achievement and Limitations of an American Conservatism. Cambridge, Mass.: Harvard University Press, 1996.

_____. *The World the Slaveholders Made*. New York: Vintage, 1971.

Gershoni, Y. *Black Colonialism: The Americo-Liberian Scramble for the Hinterland*. Boulder, Colo.: Westview Press, 1985.

Gerster, Patrick, and Nicholas Cords. *Myth and Southern History*, Vol. 1: *The Old South*. Chicago: University of Illinois Press, 1989.

Giddens, Anthony. *The Consequences of Modernity*. Stanford: Stanford University Press, 1990.

Gilliland, C. Herbert. *Voyage to a Thousand Cares: Master's Mate Lawrence with the African Squadron, 1844-1846*. Annapolis, Md.: Naval Institute Press, 2004.

Gilreath, Amelia C. *Shenandoah County, Virginia, Abstract of Wills, 1772-1850*. Nokesville, Va.: W. L. Hopkins, 1980.

Goldfield, David R. "Black Life in Old South Cities." In *Before Freedom Came: African-American Life in the Antebellum South*, edited by Edward D. C. Campbell, Jr., with Kym S. Rice, 123-154. Charlottesville: University Press of Virginia, 1991.

_____. *Cottonfields and Skyscrapers: Southern City and Region, 1607-1980*. Baton Rouge: Louisiana State University Press, 1982.

_____. *Urban Growth in the Age of Sectionalism: Virginia, 1847-1861*. Baton Rouge: Louisiana State University Press, 1977.

Gooch, Brison D. *Europe in the Nineteenth Century: A History*. London: Macmillan, 1970.

Graham, A. A. "A Century of Development of Negro Baptists in Virginia," *Religious Herald*, 15 November 1923, 21-22.

Gramsci, Antonio. *Selections from the Prison Notebooks*. New York: International Publishers, 1973.

Great Britain Foreign Office, Historical Section. *Liberia*. Handbook No. 130. London: H. M. Stationery Office, 1920.

Greenberg, Michael S. "Gentlemen Slaveholders: The Social Outlook of the Virginia Planter Class." M.A. thesis, Rutgers University, 1978.

Greene, Jack P. *The Intellectual Heritage of the Constitutional Era*. Philadelphia: The Library Company of Philadelphia, 1986.

Gross, B. "Freedom's Journal and the Rights of All." *Journal of Negro History* 17, no. 3 (1932): 241-86.

Groves, C. P. *The Planting of Christianity in Africa*. 4 vol. London: Lutterworth Press, 1964.

Guild, June Purchell. *Black Laws of Virginia*. New York: Negro Universities Press, 1969.

Gutman, Herbert G. *The Black Family in Slavery and Freedom, 1750-1925.* New York: Vintage Books, 1976.

Hansard, James, and Luke Graves Hansard. *Irish University Press Series of British Parliamentary Papers.* Irish University Press Series. Shannon: Irish University Press, 1968-.

Harding, Vincent. *There Is a River: The Black Struggle for Freedom in America.* New York: Vintage, 1983.

Harris, Sheldon H. *Paul Cuffe: Black America and the African Return.* New York: Simon and Schuster, 1972.

Hart, Lyndon H., III, comp. *A Guide to Genealogical Notes and Charts in the Archives Branch, Virginia State Library.* Richmond: Virginia State Library, 1984.

Haskell, Thomas L. "Capitalism and the Origins of the Humanitarian Sensibility, Part 1." In *The Antislavery Debate,* edited by Thomas Bender, 107-135. Los Angeles: University of California Press, 1992.

Heinegg, Paul. *Free African Americans of North Carolina and Virginia.* Baltimore: Clearfield, 1994.

Henry, Charles P. *Culture and African American Politics.* Bloomington: Indiana University Press, 1992.

Higginbotham, A. L., Jr. *In the Matter of Color: Race and the American Legal Process: The Colonial Period.* New York: Oxford, 1978.

Historical Records Survey of Virginia, Division of Professional and Service Projects. *Inventory of the Church Archives of Virginia: Negro Baptist Churches in Richmond.* Richmond: Historical Records Survey of Virginia, 1940.

Holden, Edith. *Blyden of Liberia.* New York: Vantage, 1966.

Holloway, Joseph E., ed. *Africanisms in American Culture.* Bloomington: Indiana University Press, 1991.

Holmes, Janice Nicolson. *Nine Generations of Direct Descendants of the Robert Nicholson who Patented 500 Acres in Charles City County in the Virginia Colony on Jan. 3, 1655/56.* Forth Worth: Janice Nicolson Holmes, 1985.

Holsoe, Sven E. "A Study of Relations Between Settlers and Indigenous Peoples in Western Liberia, 1821-1847." *African Historical Studies* 4, no. 2 (1971): 331-62.

Hopkins, William L. *Some Wills from the Burned Counties of Virginia*. Richmond: W. L. Hopkins, 1987.

Horton, James Oliver. *Free People of Color: Inside the African American Community*. Washington, D.C.: Smithsonian Institution Press, 1993.

Howe, Daniel Walker. *The Political Culture of American Whigs*. Chicago: University of Chicago Press, 1979.

Huberich, C. H. *The Political and Legislative History of Liberia*. 2 vols. New York: Central Book Co., 1947.

Isaac, Rhys. *The Transformation of Virginia, 1740-1790*. New York: W. W. Norton, 1988.

Jackson, Luther P. "Free Negroes of Petersburg, Virginia." *Journal of Negro History* 12, no. 3 (1927): 365-88.

_____. *Free Negro Labor and Property Holding in Virginia, 1830-1860*. New York: Atheneum, 1969.

_____. "Manumission in Certain Virginia Cities." *Journal of Negro History* 15, no. 3 (1930): 278-314.

_____. "Religious Development of the Negro in Virginia from 1760 to 1860." *Journal of Negro History* 16, no. 2 (1931): 168-239.

_____. "Religious Instruction of Negroes, 1830-1860, with Special Reference to South Carolina." *Journal of Negro History* 15, no. 1 (1930): 72-114.

Jacobs, Sylvia M. *African Nexus: Black American Perspectives on the European Partitioning of Africa, 1880-1920*. Westport, Conn.: Greenwood Press, 1981.

_____, ed. *Black Americans and the Missionary Movement in Africa*. Westport, Conn.: Greenwood Press, 1982.

_____. "'Say Africa When You Pray': The Activities of Early Black Baptist Women Missionaries Among Liberian Women and Children." *Sage: A Scholarly Journal on Black Women* 3, no. 2 (1986): 16-21.

James, C. L. R. *The Black Jacobins: Toussaint L'Ouverture and the San Domingo Revolution*. New York: Vintage, 1963.

Jenkins, Williams S. *Pro-slavery Thought in the Old South*. Chapel Hill: University of North Carolina, 1935.

Johnston, Harry H. *Liberia*. 2 vols. New York: Dodd, Mead, 1906.

Johnston, James Hugo. *Race Relations in Virginia and Miscegenation in the South, 1776-1860.* Amherst: University of Massachusetts Press, 1970.

Jones, Hanna Abeodu Bowen. "The Struggle for Political and Cultural Unification in Liberia, 1837-1930." Pd.D. diss., Northwestern University, 1962.

Jones, T. J. *Education in Africa.* New York: Phelps-Stokes Fund, 1922.

Jones, W. Mac. *The Douglas Register.* Baltimore: Genealogical Publishing, 1966.

Jordan, Winthrop D. *White over Black: American Attitudes Toward the Negro, 1550-1812.* New York: Pelican Books, 1971.

July, Robert W. *The Origins of Modern African Thought: Its Development in West Africa During the Nineteenth and Twentieth Centuries.* New York: Frederick A. Praeger, 1967.

Kangas, M. N. and D. E. Payne. *Frederick County, Virginia, Wills and Administrations, 1795-1816.* Baltimore: Clearfield, 1992.

Karnga, A. *History of Liberia.* Liverpool: D. H. Tyte, 1926.

_____. *The Negro Republic on West Africa.* Monrovia: College of West Africa Press, 1909.

Katz, W. L. "Earliest Responses of American Negroes and Whites to African Colonization [Introduction]." *Thoughts on African Colonization,* by W. L. Garrison. Boston: Garrison and Knapp, 1832. Reprint, New York: Arno Press, 1968.

Kearney, Hugh. *Science and Change, 1500-1700.* New York: McGraw-Hill, 1971.

Kelso, William M. *Kingsmill Plantations, 1619-1800: An Archaeology of Country Life in Colonial Virginia.* Orlando: Academic Press, 1984.

Kinshasa, W. M. *Emigration vs. Assimilation: The Debate in the African-American Press, 1827-1861.* London: McFarland, 1988.

Klein, Herbert S. *The Middle Passage.* Princeton, N.J.: Princeton University Press, 1978.

_____. *Slavery in the Americas: A Comparative Study of Virginia and Cuba.* Chicago: University of Chicago Press, 1967.

Knight, Franklin W. "The American Revolution and the Caribbean." In *Slavery and Freedom in the Age of the American Revolution.*, edited by Ira Berlin and Ronald Hoffman, 237-261. Urbana: University of Illinois Press, 1983.

Kocher, K. L. "A Duty to America and Africa: A History of the Independent African Colonization Movement in Pennsylvania." *Pennsylvania History* 51, no. 2 (1984): 51-60.

Kulikoff, Allan. "The Origins of Afro-American Society in Tidewater Maryland and Virginia, 1700-1790." *William and Mary Quarterly* 3rd ser., 35, vol. 35, no. 2 (1978): 226-59.

_____. *Tobacco and Slaves: The Development of Southern Cultures in the Chesapeake, 1680-1800*. Chapel Hill: University of North Carolina Press, 1986.

_____. "Uprooted Peoples: Black Migrants in the Age of the American Revolution." In *Slavery and Freedom in the Age of the American Revolution*, edited by Ira Berlin and Ronald Hoffman, 143-171. Urbana: University of Illinois Press, 1986.

Lapsansky-Werner, Emma J., and Margaret Hope Bacon. *Back to Africa: Benjamin Coates and the Colonization Movement in America, 1848-1880*. University Park: Pennsylvania State University Press, 2005.

Latimer, Frances B. *Instruments of Freedom: Deeds and Wills of Emancipation, Northampton Co., Va., 1782-1864*. Bowie, Md.: Heritage Books, 1994.

_____. *The Register of Free Negroes: Northampton County, Virginia, 1853-1861*. Bowie, Md.: Heritage Books, 1992.

Lebsock, Suzanne. *The Free Women of Petersburg: Status and Culture in a Southern Town, 1784-1860*. New York: W. W. Norton, 1984.

Levine, Lawrence W. *Black Culture and Consciousness: Afro-American Folk Thought from Slavery to Freedom*. Oxford: Oxford University Press, 1977.

Lewis, Jan. *The Pursuit of Happiness: Family and Values in Jefferson's Virginia*. Cambridge: Cambridge University Press, 1983.

Lewis, Ronald L. *Coal, Iron, and Slaves: Industrial Slavery in Maryland and Virginia, 1715-1865*. Westport, Conn.: Greenwood Press, 1979.

Liebenow, J. Gus. *Liberia: The Evolution of Privilege*. Ithaca, N.Y.: Cornell University Press, 1969.

Lienesch, Michael. *New Order of the Ages: Time, the Constitution, and the Making of Modern American Political Thought*. Princeton, N.J.: Princeton University Press, 1988.

Lincoln, C. Eric, and Lawrence H. Mamiya. *The Black Church in the African American Experience*. Durham, N.C.: Duke University Press, 1990.

Lindsay, Joyce H., comp. *Marriages of Henrico County, Virginia, 1680-1808*. Easley, S.C.: Southern Historical Press, 1960.

Lippy, Charles H. "Religious Experience of Southern Blacks: Black-White Interaction in Southern Religion." In *Bibliography of Religion in the South*, 81-146. Macon, Ga.: Mercer University Press, 1986.

Litwack, Leon, and August Meier, eds. *Black Leaders of the Nineteenth Century*. Urbana: University of Illinois Press, 1988.

Lloyd, Christopher. *The Navy and the Slave Trade*. London: Frank Cass, 1968.

Locke, John. *Two Treatises of Government*. Cambridge: Cambridge University Press, 1967.

Logan, R. W. "Some New Interpretations of the Colonization Movement." *Pylon* 4 (1943): 328-34.

Lynch, Hollis R. *Edward Wilmot Blyden: Pan-Negro Patriot, 1832-1912*. New York: Oxford University Press, 1970.

Manarin, Louis H., and Clifford Dowdey. *The History of Henrico County*. Charlottesville: University Press of Virginia, 1984.

Martin, Jane. "How to Build a Nation: Liberian Ideas About National Integration in the Later Nineteenth Century." *Liberian Studies Journal* 2, no. 1 (1969): 15-42.

Martin, Sandy Dwayne. "Black Baptists, Foreign Missions, and African Colonization, 1814-1882." In *Black Americans and the Missionary Movement in Africa*, edited by Sylvia M. Jacobs, 63-76. Westport, Conn.: Greenwood Press, 1982.

Mathews, Donald G. *Religion in the Old South*. Chicago: University of Chicago Press, 1977.

Matison, Sumner Eliot. "Manumission by Purchase." *Journal of Negro History* 33, no. 2 (1948): 146-67.

McCall, Daniel F. "Liberia: An Appraisal." *Annals of the American Academy of Political and Social Science* 306 (1956): 88-97.

McClaughlin, T. L. "Sectional Responses of Free Negroes to the Idea of Colonization." *Research Studies* 34, no. 3 (1966): 123-34.

McColley, Robert. *Slavery and Jeffersonian Virginia*. 2d ed. Urbana: University of Illinois, 1973.

McDaniel, Antonio. *Swing Low, Sweet Chariot: The Mortality Cost of Colonizing Liberia in the Nineteenth Century*. Chicago: University of Chicago Press, 1995.

McDonald, Forrest. *Novus Ordo Seclorum: The Intellectual Origins of the Constitution*. Lawrence: University of Kansas Press, 1985.

McGann, Jerome J., ed. *Lord Byron: The Complete Poetical Works*. Vol. 2, *Childe Harold's Pilgrimage*. Oxford: Oxford University Press, 1980.

McGinnis, Carol. *Virginia Genealogy: Sources and Resources*. Baltimore: Genealogical Publishing, 1993.

Mehlinger, Louis R. "The Attitude of the Free Negro Toward African Colonization." *Journal of Negro History* 1, no. 3 (1916): 276-301.

Miers, Suzanne. *Britain and the Ending of the Slave Trade*. New York: Africana Publishing, 1975.

Mihalyka, Jean M. *Marriages of Northampton County, Virginia, 1660-1 to 1854*. Bowie, Md.: Heritage Books, 1990.

Mihalyka, Jean M., and Alice B. Deal, eds. *Gravestone Inscriptions in Northampton County, Virginia*. Bowie, Md.: Heritage Books, 1984.

Miller, Floyd J. *The Search for Black Nationality: Black Emigration and Colonization, 1787 to 1863*. Urbana: University of Illinois Press, 1975.

Miller, John C. *The Wolf by the Ear*. New York: Free Press, 1977.

Miller, Randall M. "'Home as Found': Ex-slaves and Liberia." *Liberian Studies Journal* 6, no. 2 (1975): 92-108.

Miller, T. M. "'Out of Bondage': A History of the Alexandria Colonization Society." *Alexandria History* 7 (1987): 15-30.

Minchinton, Walter E., Celia King, and Peter Waite, eds. *Virginia Slave-Trade Statistics, 1698-1775*. Richmond: Virginia State Library, 1984.

Mintz, Sidney W. "History and Anthropology: A Brief Reprise." In *Race and Slavery in the Western Hemisphere: Quantitative Studies*, edited by Stanley L. Engerman and Eugene D. Genovese, 477-494. Princeton, N.J.: Princeton University Press, 1975.

Mintz, Sidney W., and Richard Price. *The Birth of African-American Culture: An Anthropological Perspective.* Boston: Beacon Press, 1992.

Morgan, Edmund S. *American Slavery, American Freedom: The Ordeal of Colonial Virginia.* New York: W. W. Norton, 1975.

Morgan, Philip D., ed. *Don't Grieve After Me: The Black Experience in Virginia, 1619-1986.* Hampton, Va.: Hampton University, 1986.

Moses, Wilson J. *Alexander Crummell: A Study of Civilization and Discontent.* Amherst: University of Massachusetts Press, 1992.

_____. *The Golden Age of Black Nationalism, 1850-1925.* New York: Oxford University Press, 1978.

_____. *The Wings of Ethiopia: Studies in African-American Life and Letters.* Ames: Iowa State University Press, 1990.

Mott, A. *Narratives of Colored Americans.* New York: W. Wood, 1877. Reprint, Freeport, N.Y.: Books for Libraries, 1971.

Mudimbe, V. Y. *The Invention of Africa: Gnosis, Philosophy, and the Order of Knowledge.* Bloomington: Indiana University Press, 1988.

Mullin, Gerald W. *Flight and Rebellion: Slave Resistance in Eighteenth-Century Virginia.* New York: Oxford University Press, 1972.

_____. "Gabriel's Insurrection." In *Old Memories, New Moods: Americans from Africa,* edited by Peter I. Rose, 53-73. New York: Atherton Press, 1970.

National Cyclopædia of American Biography. New York: J. T. White, 1893-.

Newton, James E., and Ronald L. Lewis, eds. *The Other Slaves: Mechanics, Artisans and Craftsmen.* Boston: G. K. Hall, 1978.

Nicholson, Hugh G. "Nicholson Family of Virginia and North Carolina." *Tyler's Quarterly Magazine* 17 (1935): 89-101.

Nottingham, Stratton. *Virginia Land Causes: Lancaster County, 1795-1848 and Northampton County, 1731-1868.* Bowie, Md.: Heritage Books, 1991.

Noyes, Russell. *English Romantic Poetry and Prose.* New York: Oxford University Press, 1956.

O'Brien, John. "Factory, Church and Community: Blacks in Antebellum Richmond." *Journal of Southern History* 44, no. 4 (November 1978): 509-36.

_____. "From Bondage to Citizenship: The Richmond Black Community, 1865-67." Ph.D. diss., University of Rochester, 1975.

Oldfield, J. R. *Alexander Crummell (1819-1898) and the Creation of an African-American Church in Liberia.* Lewiston, Canada: E. Mellen Press, 1990.

_____. "The Protestant Episcopal Church, Black Nationalists, and Expansion of the West African Missionary Field, 1851-1871." *Church History* 57, no. 1(1990): 31-45.

Padgett, J. A. "Ministers to Liberia and Their Diplomacy." *Journal of Negro History* 22, no. 1(1937): 50-92.

Palmer, William Pitt, Sherwin McRae, Raleigh Edward Colston, and Henry W. Flournoy. *Calendar of Virginia State Papers and Other Manuscripts ... Preserved in the Capitol at Richmond, 1875-1893.* Richmond: Commonwealth of Virginia, 1875-1893. Reprint, New York: Kraus Reprint, 1968.

Parish, Peter J. *Slavery: History and Historians.* New York: Harper and Row, 1989.

Peterson, M. D., ed. *The Portable Thomas Jefferson.* New York: Penguin, 1986.

Petty, Gerald M. "Virginia 1820 Federal Census: Names Not on the Microfilm Copy." *Virginia Genealogist* 18, no. 20 (April 1974): 136-39.

Pinchbeck, Raymond B. *The Virginia Negro Artisan and Tradesman.* Richmond: William Byrd Press, 1926.

Plumkett, Michael. *Afro-American Sources in Virginia: A Guide to Manuscript.* Charlottesville: University Press of Virginia, 1990.

Pocock, J. G. A. *Virtue, Commerce, and History: Essays on Political Thought and History, Chiefly in the Eighteenth Century.* Cambridge: Cambridge University Press, 1991.

Poe, William A. "Not Christopolis but Christ and Caesar: Baptist leadership in Liberia." *Journal of Church and State* 24, no. 3 (1982): 535-51.

Quarles, Benjamin. "The Revolutionary War as a Black Declaration of Independence." *Slavery and Freedom in the Age of the American Revolution.*, edited by Ira Berlin and Ronald Hoffman, 283-304. Urbana: University of Illinois Press, 1986.

Rabinowitz, Howard N., ed. *Southern Black Leaders of the Reconstruction Era.* Urbana: University of Illinois Press, 1982.

Rachleff, Peter. *Black Labor in the South: Richmond, Virginia, 1865-1890.* Philadelphia: Temple University Press, 1984.

Rawick, George P., ed. *The American Slave: A Composite Autobiography.* 41 vols. Westport, Conn.: Greenwood Press, 1972-79.

_____. *From Sundown to Sunup: The Making of the Black Community.* Westport, Conn.: Greenwood Publishing, 1972.

Redkey, Edwin S. *Black Exodus.* New Haven, Conn.: Yale University Press, 1969.

Reynolds, William Jensen. *Hymns of Our Faith.* Nashville: Broadman Press, 1964.

Richardson, Nathaniel R. *Liberia's Past and Present.* London: Diplomatic Press, 1959.

Rigsby, Gregory U. *Alexander Crummell: Pioneer in Nineteenth-Century Pan-African Thought.* New York: Greenwood Press, 1987.

Robert, Joseph Clarke. *The Tobacco Kingdom: Plantation, Market, and Factory in Virginia and North Carolina, 1800-1860.* Gloucester, Mass.: Peter Smith, 1965.

Rodney, Walter. *How Europe Underdeveloped Africa.* Washington, D.C.: Howard University Press, 1982.

Rogers, Momo K. "Liberian Journalism, 1826-1980: A Descriptive History." Ph.D. diss., Southern Illinois University Carbondale, 1988.

Ross, Dorothy. *The Origins of American Social Science.* New York: Cambridge University Press, 1991.

Russell, John H. *The Free Negro in Virginia, 1619-1865.* Baltimore: Johns Hopkins University Press, 1913.

Sagarin, M. *John Brown Russwurm: The Story of Freedom's Journal and Freedom's Journey.* New York: Lothrop, Lee and Shepard, 1970.

Saha, S. C. "Agriculture in Liberia During the Nineteenth Century: Americo-Liberians' Contribution." *Canadian Journal of African Studies* 12, no. 2 (1988): 225-239.

_____. "Jehudi Ashmun's Agricultural Policy: Organizing the Settlers for Self-Reliance." *International Journal of African Historical Studies* 18, no. 3 (1984): 505-511.

Sawyer, Amos C. *The Emergence of Autocracy in Liberia.* San Francisco: Institute for Contemporary Studies, 1992.

Schreiner-Yantis, Netti, ed. *A Supplement to the 1810 Census of Virginia: Tax Lists of the Counties for Which the Census Is Missing.* Springfield, Va.: Netti Schreiner-Yantis, 1971.

Schwarz, Philip J. "Emancipators, Protectors, and Anomalies: Free Black Slaveowners in Virginia." *Virginia Magazine of History and Biography* 95 (July 1987): 317-38.

_____. *Twice Condemned: Slaves and the Criminal Laws of Virginia, 1705-1865.* Baton Rouge: Louisiana State University Press, 1988.

Schwarzlose, Richard A. *Newspapers: A Reference Guide.* Westport, Conn.: Greenwood Press, 1987.

Scott, Mary Wingfield. *Old Richmond Neighborhoods.* Richmond: William Byrd Press, 1984.

Sheldon, Garrett Ward. *The Political Philosophy of Thomas Jefferson.* Baltimore: Johns Hopkins University Press, 1991.

Sheldon, Marianne B. "Black-White Relations in Richmond, Virginia, 1782-1820." *Journal of Southern History* 45, no. 1 (1979): 27-44.

Sherwood, H. N. "Early Negro Deportation Projects." *Mississippi Valley Historical Review* 2, no. 4 (1916): 484-508.

Shick, Tom W. *Behold the Promised Land: A History of Afro-American Settler Society in Nineteenth-Century Liberia.* Baltimore: Johns Hopkins University Press, 1980.

_____. *Emigrants to Liberia, 1820 to 1843: An Alphabetical Listing.* Newark, Del.: Liberian Studies Association in America, 1971.

_____. "Rhetoric and Reality: Colonization and Afro-American Missionaries in Early Nineteenth-Century Liberia." In *Black Americans and the Missionary Movement in Africa,* edited by Sylvia M. Jacobs, 45-62. Westport, Conn.: Greenwood Press, 1982.

Sibley, J. L. *Education and Missions in Liberia.* New York: American Advisory Committee on Education in Liberia, 1926.

Skinner, Elliot P. *African Americans and U.S. Policy Toward Africa, 1850-1924.* Washington, D.C.: Howard University Press, 1992.

Smith, Edward D. *Climbing Jacob's Ladder: The Rise of Black Churches in Eastern American Cities, 1740-1877.* Washington, D.C.: Smithsonian Institution Press, 1988.

Smith, Raymond T. "Race, Class, and Gender in the Transition to Freedom." In *The Meaning of Freedom: Economics, Politics, and Culture After Slavery*, edited by Frank McGlynn and Seymour Drescher, 257-290. Pittsburgh: University of Pittsburgh, 1992.

Smyke, R. T. "Nathaniel V. Massaquoi: Liberian Educator." Paper presented to the Liberian Studies Conference, Beloit College, Wis., March 29-30, 1985.

Sobel, Mechal. *Trabelin' On: The Slave Journey to an Afro-Baptist Faith.* Princeton, N.J.: Princeton University Press, 1988.

_____. *The World They Made Together: Black and White Values in Eighteenth-Century Virginia.* Princeton, N.J.: Princeton University Press, 1987.

South, Aloha. *Guide to Non-federal Archives and Manuscripts in the United States Relating to Africa.* 2 vols. New York: Hans Zell, 1989.

Sparacio, Ruth, and Sam Sparacio. *Virginia County Court Records: Deed and Will Abstracts of Richmond City, Virginia Hustings Court, 1790-1794.* McLean, Va.: Antient Press, 1993.

Spiller, Brian, ed. *Cowper: Verse and Letters.* Cambridge, Mass.: Harvard University Press, 1968.

Stampp, Kenneth M. "The Tragic Legend of Reconstruction." In *The Old South*, Vol. 1 of *Myth and Southern History*, edited by Patrick Gerster and Nicholas Cords, 155-168. Urbana: University of Illinois Press, 1989.

Staudenraus, J. *The African Colonization Movement, 1816-1865.* New York: Columbia University Press, 1961.

Sterling, Dorothy. *The Making of an Afro-American: Martin Robinson Delany, 1812-1855.* Garden City, N.Y.: Doubleday, 1970.

Stuckey, Sterling. *Slave Culture: Nationalist Theory and the Foundations of Black America.* New York: Oxford University Press, 1987.

Sullivan, Alvin, ed. *British Literary Magazines: The Romantic Age, 1789-1836.* Westport, Conn.: Greenwood Press, 1983.

Swem, E. G. *Virginia Historical Index.* Glouster, Mass.: P. Smith, 1965.

Syfert, D. N. "A History of the Liberian Coasting Trade, 1821-1900." Ph.D. diss., Indiana University, 1977.

_____. "The Liberian Coasting Trade, 1822-1900." *Journal of African History* 18, no. 2 (1977): 217-35.

_____. "The Origins of Privilege." *Liberian Studies Journal* 6, no. 2 (1975): 109-28.

Tate, Thad W. *The Negro in Eighteenth-Century Williamsburg*. Williamsburg: Colonial Williamsburg Foundation, 1985.

Thomas, Emory M. *The Confederate State of Richmond: A Biography of the* Capital. Austin: University of Texas Press, 1971.

Thomas, Percial Moses. "Plantations in Transition: A Study of Four Virginia Plantations, 1860-1870." Ph.D. diss., University of Virginia, 1979.

Thomson, James, ed. *The Seasons and The Castle of Indolence*. Edited by James Sambrook. Oxford: Oxford University Press, 1972.

Tillotson, Geoffrey, Paul Fussell, and Marshall Waingrow. *Eighteenth-Century English Literature*. New York: Harcourt Brace Jovanovich, 1969.

Todd, Loreto. *Pidgins and Creoles*. London: Routledge and Kegan Paul, 1974.

Torrence, Clayton. *Virginia Wills and Administrations, 1632-1800.* Baltimore: Genealogical Publishing, 1965.

Tyler-McGraw, Marie. *At the Falls: Richmond, Virginia, and Its People*. Chapel Hill: North Carolina University Press, 1994.

_____. "'The Prize I Mean Is the Prize of Liberty': A Loudon County Family in Liberia." *Virginia Magazine of History and Biography* 97, no. 3 (1989): 355-74.

_____. "Richmond Free Blacks and African Colonization, 1816-1832." *Journal of American Studies* 21, no. 2 (1987): 207-24.

Tyler-McGraw, Marie, and Gregg D. Kimball. *Bondage and Freedom: Antebellum Black Life in Richmond, Virginia.* Richmond: Valentine Museum, 1988.

Uche, K. O. "Ebony Kinship: Americo-Liberians, Sierra Leone Creoles and the Indigenous African Populations, 1820-1900: A Comparative Analysis." Ph.D. diss., Howard University, 1974.

Ullman, Victor. *Martin R. Delany: The Beginnings of Black Nationalism*. Boston: Beacon Press, 1987.

University of Virginia Library. *Virginia Genealogy: A Guide to Resources in the University of Virginia Library*. Charlottesville: University Press of Virginia, 1983.

U.S. Bureau of Census. *Heads of Families at the First Census of the United States Taken in the Year 1790, Virginia*. Washington, D.C.: Government Printing Office, 1908.

_____. *Negro Population, 1790-1915*. Washington, D.C.: Government Printing Office, 1918.

van der Kraaij, F. P. M. *The Open Door Policy in Liberia: An Economic History of Modern Liberia*. Bremen, West Germany: Ubersee-Museum Bremen, 1983.

Virdin, Donald O. *Virginia Genealogies and Family Histories*. Bowie, Md.: Heritage Books, 1990.

Virginia Genealogical Society Staff. *Richmond City and Henrico County, Virginia: 1850 U. S. Census*. Easley, S.C.: Southern Historical Press, 1981.

Virginia State Library. *Virginia Local History: A Bibliography*. Richmond: Virginia State Library, 1971.

Wade, Richard C. *Slavery in the Cities: The South, 1820-1860*. New York: Oxford University Press, 1964.

Walker, Barbara D., comp. *Index to "Journal of African-American Historical and Genealogical Quarterly."* Bowie, Md.: Heritage Books, 1991.

Walker, James W. S. G. *The Black Loyalists: The Search for a Promised Land in Nova Scotia and Sierra Leone, 1783-1870*. New York: Africana Publishing, 1976.

Wallerstein, Immanuel. *Africa and the Modern World*. Trenton, N.J.: Africa World Press, 1986.

Walsh, Lorena S. "Slave Life, Slave Society, and Tobacco Production in the Tidewater Chesapeake, 1620-1820." In *Cultivation and Culture: Labor and the Shaping of Slave Life in the Americas*, edited by Ira Berlin, and Philip D. Morgan, 170-199. Charlottesville: University Press of Virginia, 1993.

Ward, W. E. F. *The Royal Navy and the Slavers*. New York: Schocken Books, 1970.

Webber, Thomas L. *Deep Like the Rivers: Education in the Slave Quarter Community*. New York: W. W. Norton, 1978.

Weisiger, Benjamin B. *Charles City County, Virginia, Records, 1737-1774*. Richmond: B. B. Weisiger, 1986.

West, Richard. *Back to Africa: A History of Sierra Leone and Liberia*. New York: Harper and Row, 1970.

White, B. Kirke, Jr. ed. *Charles City County Inventory: Circuit Court Clerk*. Richmond: Virginia State Library and Archives, 1976.

White, Blanche Sydnor. *First Baptist Church, Richmond, 1780-1955*. Richmond: Whittey and Shepperson, 1955.

Whitelaw, Ralph T. *Virginia's Eastern Shore: A History of Northampton and Accomack Counties*. Vol. 1. Camden, Maine: Picton Press, 1989.

Williams, Kathleen Booth. *Marriages of Goochland County, Virginia, 1733-1815*. Baltimore: Genealogical Publishing, 1979.

Williams, Walter L. *Black Americans and the Evangelization of Africa, 1877-1900*. Madison: University of Wisconsin Press, 1982.

Williamson, Joel. *New People: Miscegenation and Mulattoes in the United States*. New York: Free Press, 1980.

"Willis vs. Nicholson (Chancery Papers at Williamsburg." Historical and Genealogical Notes. *William and Mary College Quarterly* 1st ser., vol. 6, no. 4, (1898): 258-59.

"Willis vs. Willis (Chancery Papers at Williamsburg." Historical and Genealogical Notes. *William and Mary College Quarterly* 1st ser., vol. 6, no. 4 (1898): 259.

Wills, David W., and Richard Newman. *Black Apostles at Home and Abroad: Afro-Americans and the Christian Mission from the Revolution to Reconstruction*. Boston: G. K. Hall, 1982.

Wilson, Henry S. *The Imperial Experience in Sub-Saharan Africa since 1870*. Minneapolis: University of Minnesota Press, 1977.

_____. *Origins of West African Nationalism*. New York: St. Martin's, 1969.

Wold, J. C. *God's Impatience in Liberia*. Grand Rapids, Mich.: William B. Eerdmans, 1968.

Wood, Emma Jean, Annie Ponder Sarrett, and Kathleen Wood Cook, comp. *Ponder-Teague and Their Connections*. Camden, Ark.: Dan Cook's Printing, 1988.

Wood, Gordon S. *The Creation of the American Republic, 1776-1787*. New York: W. W. Norton, 1972.

Woodson, Carter G. *The Education of the Negro Prior to 1861*. Washington, D.C.: Association for the Study of Negro Life and History, 1919.

_____.,ed. *Free Negro Heads of Families in the United States in 1830, Together with a Brief Treatment of the Free Negro.* Washington, D.C.: Association for the Study of Negro Life and History, 1925.

_____. *The Mind of the Negro as Reflected in Letters Written During the Crisis, 1800-1861.* Washington, D.C.: Associated Publisher, 1926. Reprint, New York: Negro Universities Press, 1969.

Work Projects Administration (WPA), Writers' Program of Virginia. *The Negro in Virginia.* New York: Hastings House, 1940.

_____. *Virginia: A Guide to the Old Dominion.* New York: Oxford University Press, 1956.

Wright, James M. *The Free Negro in Maryland, 1634-1860.* New York: Longman, Green, 1921.

Index

www.ingramcontent.com/pod-product-compliance
Lightning Source LLC
Chambersburg PA
CBHW030248290526
45785CB00001B/7